Don't Throw Away A Fortune!
Invest In
Miller's Price Guides

Please send me the following editions

- ❑ **Miller's Antiques Price Guide 1996** - £21.99
- ❑ **Miller's Classic Motorcycles Price Guide 1996/97** - £12.99
- ❑ **Miller's Collectors Cars Price Guide 1995/96** - £19.99
- ❑ **Miller's Picture Price Guide 1996** - £19.99
- ❑ **Miller's Pine & Country Furniture Buyer's Guide** - £17.99
- ❑ **Miller's Art Nouveau & Art Deco Buyer's Guide** - £17.99

I enclose my remittance for £..................post free (UK only)
or please debit my Access/Barclaycard account number

NAME: *Title   Initial   Surname*

ADDRESS:_____

_____ *Postcode* _____

SIGNATURE:_____

Photocopy this page or write the above details on a separate sheet and send it to Reed Books Services Limited, P.O. Box 5, Rushden, Northants NN10 6PU or telephone the Credit Card Hotline 01933 414000
Lines open from 9:00 to 5:00. Registered office: Michelin House, 81 Fulham Road, London SW3 6RB.
Registered in England number 1974080

745.102/MIL/1996-97
343117-1/34.99

MILLER'S COLLECTABLES PRICE
GUIDE /

DATE DUE

MILLER'S
Collectables
PRICE GUIDE

Consultants
Judith and Martin Miller

General Editor
Madeleine Marsh

1996-97
(Volume VIII)

MILLER'S COLLECTABLES PRICE GUIDE 1996/97

Compiled, edited and designed by
Miller's Publications Ltd
The Cellars, High Street
Tenterden, Kent TN30 6BN
Telephone: 01580 766411

Consultants: Judith & Martin Miller

General Editor: Madeleine Marsh
Editorial & Production Co-ordinator: Sue Boyd
Editorial Assistants: Gillian Judd, Marion Rickman, Jo Wood
Production Assistants: Gillian Charles, Karen Taylor
Design: Jody Taylor, Kari Reeves, Matthew Leppard
Photographic Co-ordinator and Advertising Executive: Elizabeth Smith
Display Advertisements: Liz Warwick, Melinda Williams
Index compiled by: DD Editorial Services, Beccles, Suffolk
Additional photography: Ian Booth, Roy Farthing, Sarah Judd, Robin Saker

First published in Great Britain in 1996
by Miller's
an imprint of Reed Consumer Books Limited
Michelin House, 81 Fulham Road
London SW3 6RB
and Auckland, Melbourne, Singapore and Toronto

A CIP catalogue record for this book is
available from the British Library

ISBN 1-85732-752-7

Bromide output: Perfect Image, Hurst Green, E. Sussex
Illustrations: G. H. Graphics, St. Leonard's-on-Sea, E. Sussex
Colour origination: Scantrans, Singapore
Printed and bound in England by William Clowes Ltd,
Beccles and London

Miller's is a registered trademark of
Reed International Books Ltd

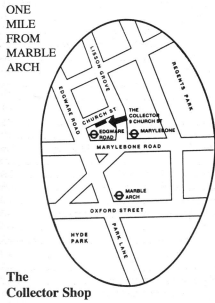

CONTENTS

ACKNOWLEDGEMENTS

We would like to extend our thanks to all the auction houses, dealers and collectors who have assisted us in the production of this book. We would also like to acknowledge with gratitude the great assistance given by our consultants:

JOAN & BOB ANDERSON, Tel: 0181 572 4328 (**Midwinter**)

ANN ATKINS, Gnome Reserve, West Putford, Nr. Bradworthy EX22 7X6 (**Gnomes**)

LINDA BEE, 1–7 Davies Mews, London W1Y 1AR (**Handbags**)

MRS SHIRLEY BURGAN, Victorian & Edwardian Collectables, 120 High Street, Yatton, Avon BS19 4DH (**Sewing**)

ROY BUTLER, Wallis & Wallis, West Street Auction Galleries, Lewes, Sussex BN7 2NJ (**Militaria**)

RAY CLARKE, 62 Murray Road, Horndean, Waterlooville, Hants PO8 9JL (**Goss & Crested**)

MORRIS COOMBS, J & M Collectables, Tel: 01580 891657 (**Postcards & Osbornes**)

JULIETTE EDWARDS, 5 Holly Ridge, Fenns Lane, West End, Surrey GU24 9QE (**Compacts**)

CYNTHIA FENDEL, 5128 Spyglass Drive, Dallas, Texas 75287-7556 USA (**Fans**)

BRIAN HARDEN, Tel/Fax: 01451 810684 (**Pot Lids**)

MO & STEVE HARDING, Dollectable, 53 Lower Bridge, Chester CH1 1RS (**Dolls**)

PETER & ADRIAN HARRINGTON, Chelsea Antiques Market, Kings Road, London SW3 5EL (**Books**)

JANICE HEBERT, Libra Antiques, 81 London Road, Hurst Green, Etchingham, East Sussex TN19 7PN (**Lighting**)

STUART HEGGIE, 14 The Borough, Canterbury, Kent CT1 2DR (**Cameras**)

GORDON HOPWOOD, Tel: 01453 758328 (**Denby**)

JOHN & DAPHNE HISCOTT, J & D Collectables, 53 The Foreland, Canterbury, Kent CT1 3NS (**SylvaC**)

JON LEWIN, Confederate Broadcasting Ltd UK (**Rock & Pop**)

HARRY LYON, New Century Antiques, 69 Kensington Church Street, London W8 4DB (**Rye Potteries & Fifties Textiles**)

DAVID MCKINLEY, Heads n' Tails, Bournes House, 41 Church Street, Wiveliscombe, Taunton, Somerset TA4 2LT (**Taxidermy**)

TIMOTHY MILLETT, A. H. Baldwin & Sons Ltd, 11 Adelphi Terrace, London WC2N 6BJ (**Medals**)

PAUL NACHMAN, Nashers Music Store, 72 Walcot Street, Bath, Avon BA1 5DD (**Records**)

JOHN NEALE, The Old Toy Train Co, 11a Davenport Drive, The Willows, Bromsgrove, Worcs B60 2DW (**Toy Trains**)

PAT OLDMAN, Echoes, 650a Halifax Road, Eastwood, Todmorden, West Yorkshire OL14 6DW (**Costume & Textiles**)

DOUG POULTNEY, 219 Lynmouth Avenue, Morden SM4 4RX (**Comics**)

IAN POUT, Teddy Bears of Witney, 99 High Street, Witney, Oxfordshire OX8 6LY (**Teddy Bears**)

TOM POWER, The Collector, 9 Church Street, London NW8 8EE (**Royal Doulton & Toby Jugs**)

CHRISTOPHER PROUDFOOT, Christie's (South Kensington) Ltd, 85 Old Brompton Road, London SW7 3LD (**Lawn Mowers**)

MICHAEL SINCLAIR, Glitterati, Great Western Antique Centre, Bartlett Street, Bath, Avon BA1 2QZ (**Costume Jewellery**)

PIERRE SPAKE, Dominic Winter Book Auctions, The Old School, Maxwell Street, Swindon, Wiltshire SN1 5DR (**Photographs**)

MAUREEN STANFORD, Childhood Memories, The Farnham Antique Centre, 27 South Street, Farnham, Surrey GU9 7QU (**Dolls**)

CHRISTOPHER SYKES, The Old Parsonage, Woburn, Milton Keynes, Bucks MK17 9QM (**Corkscrews**)

LORRAINE TAYLOR-KENT, 32 West View, Park Road, Barnsley, S. Yorks S70 1QR (**Fans**)

RICHARD VENESS, Elite Designs, Tel: 01424 434856 (**Breweriana**)

TREVOR VENNETT-SMITH, 11 Nottingham Road, Gotham, Nottingham, Notts NG11 0HE (**Ephemera**)

MAJOR R. T. WELSH, 11 Pierrepont Street, Bath, Avon BA1 1LA (**Playing Cards**)

MARK WILKINSON, Christie's (South Kensington) Ltd, 85 Old Brompton Road, London SW7 3LD (**Clarice Cliff**)

TONY WOOLVEN, The British Watch & Clock Collectors Association, 5 Cathedral Lane, Truro, Cornwall TR1 2QS (**Watch & Clocks**)

IAN WRIGHT, Sheffield Railwayana Auctions, 43 Little Norton Lane, Sheffield, Yorkshire S8 8GA (**Railwayana**)

KEY TO ILLUSTRATIONS

Each illustration and descriptive caption is accompanied by a letter code. By referring to the following list of Auctioneers (denoted by *) Clubs (§) and Dealers (•), the source of any item may be immediately determined. Inclusion in this edition in no way constitutes or implies a contract or binding offer on the part of any of our contributors to supply or sell the goods illustrated, or similar articles, at the prices stated. Advertisers in this year's directory are denoted by (†).

If you require a valuation for an item, it is advisable to check whether the dealer or specialist will carry out this service and if there is a charge. Please mention Miller's when making an enquiry. Having found a specialist who will carry out your valuation it is best to send a photograph and description of the item to the specialist together with a stamped addressed envelope for the reply. A valuation by telephone is not possible.

Most dealers are only too happy to help you with your enquiry, however, they are very busy people and consideration of the above points would be welcomed.

AAV * Academy Auctioneers & Valuers, Northcote House, Northcote Avenue, Ealing, London W5 3UR Tel: 0181 579 7466

ACC •† Alberts Cigarette Card Specialists, 113 London Road, Twickenham, Middlesex TW1 1EE Tel: 0181 891 3067

AF • Forsythe, Albert, Mill House, 66 Carsonstown Road, Saintfield, Co Down, Ireland BT24 7EX Tel: 01238 510398

AG * Anderson & Garland (Auctioneers), Marlborough House, Marlborough Crescent, Newcastle-upon-Tyne, Tyne & Wear NE1 4EE Tel: 0191 232 6278

AH * Hartley, Andrew, Victoria Salerooms, Little Lane, Ilkley, Yorkshire LS29 8EA Tel: 01943 816363

AL •† Lingard, Ann, Ropewalk Antiques, Ropewalk, Rye, Sussex TN31 7NA Tel: 01797 223486

ALI • Alien Enterprises, In the Antiques Shop, 30 Henley Street, Stratford upon Avon, Warwickshire CV37 6QW Tel: 01789 292485 (eve 01789 268617)

AMH •† Amherst Antiques, 23 London Road, Riverhead, Sevenoaks, Kent TN13 2BU Tel: 01732 455047

AND • Anderson, Joan & Bob, Calvers Collectables of Ruislip, 156 High Street, Ruislip, Middlesex HA4 8LJ Tel: 0181 561 4517

AnE • Antiques Emporium, The, The Old Chapel, Long Street, Tetbury, Glos GL8 8AA Tel: 01666 505281

ANP • Power, Annette, The Collector, 9 Church Street, Marylebone, London NW8 8EE Tel: 0171 706 4586

ASH •† Ashburton Marbles, Grate Hall, North Street, Ashburton, Devon TQ13 7QD Tel: 01364 653189

B&F • Bears & Friends, 32 Meeting House Lane, The Lanes, Brighton, Sussex BN1 1HB Tel: 01273 202801

BAL •† Baldwin, A. H., & Sons Ltd, Numismatists, 11 Adelphi Terrace, London WC2N 6BJ Tel: 0171 930 6879

BaN • Newman, Barbara Ann, The Weald Antiques Gallery, 106 High Street, Tenterden, Kent TN30 6HT Tel: 01580 762939

Bar • Barge, Chris, Antiques, 5 Southside Place, Inverness, Scotland IV2 3JF Tel: 01463 230128

BAS • Brighton Architectural Salvage, 33 Gloucester Road, Brighton, Sussex BN1 4AQ Tel: 01273 681656

BBA * Bloomsbury Book Auctions, 3/4 Hardwick Street, Off Rosebery Avenue, London, EC1R 4RY Tel: 0171 833 2636

BCA • Beaulieu Cars Automobilia, Beaulieu, Hampshire S042 7YE Tel: 01590 612689

BCO • British Collectables, 1st Floor, 9 Georgian Village, Camden Passage, Islington, London N1 8DU Tel: 0171 359 4560

Bea * Bearnes, Rainbow, Avenue Road, Torquay, Devon TQ2 5TG Tel: 01803 296277

BEN • 20th Century Glass, 291 Westbourne Grove, London, W11 2QB. Tel: 0181 806 7068

Ber • Berry Antiques, Kay Parkin, The Old Butchers Shop, Goudhurst, Kent TN17 1AE Tel: 01580 212115

BEV • Beverley, 30 Church Street, London NW8 8EP Tel: 0171 262 1576

BFB • Books For Cooks, 4 Blenheim Crescent, London W11 1NN Tel: 0171 221 1992/8102

BHa • Harden, Judy & Brian, Antiques Tel: 01451 810684

BHE •† British Heritage Telephones, 11 Rhodes Drive, Unsworth, Bury, Lancashire BL9 8NH Tel: 0161 767 9259

BKK •† Bona Arts Decorative, 19 Princes Mead Shopping Centre, Farnborough, Hampshire GU14 7TJ Tel: 01252 372188

BlA • Brightwell Antiques, Well Cottage Antiques Centre, 20/22 Bell Street, Princes Risborough, Bucks HP27 0AD Tel: 01844 342002

Bon * Bonhams, Montpelier Galleries, Montpelier Street, London SW7 1HH Tel: 0171 584 9161

Bri * Bristol Auction Rooms, St John's Place, Apsley Road, Clifton, Bristol, Avon BS8 2ST Tel: 0117 973 7201

BS • Below Stairs, 103 High Street, Hungerford, Berkshire RG17 0NB Tel: 01488 682317

BTA • Taylor, Brian, Antiques, 24 Molesworth Road, Plymouth, Devon PL1 5LZ Tel: 01752 569061

BTC •† Beatcity Tel: 01634 865428

BWC §† British Watch & Clock Collectors Association, 5 Cathedral Lane, Truro, Cornwall TR1 2QS Tel: 01872 41953

BWe * Biddle and Webb Ltd, Ladywood Middleway, Birmingham, West Midlands B16 0PP Tel: 0121 455 8042

C	*	Christie, Manson & Woods Ltd, 8 King Street, St James's, London SW1Y 6QT Tel: 0171 839 9060
C(S)	*	Christie's Scotland Ltd, 164-166 Bath Street, Glasgow, Scotland G2 4TG Tel: 0141 332 8134
CB	•	Bridge, Christine, Antiques, 78 Castelnau, London SW13 9EX Tel: 0181 741 5501
CBa	•	Barlow, Catherine, 14 Windsor Road, Selston, Nottingham, Notts NG16 6JJ Tel: 01773 860933
CCC	•†	Crested China Co, The, The Station House, Driffield, Yorks YO25 7PY Tel: 01377 257042
CCP	•	Campden Country Pine Antiques, High Street, Chipping Campden, Glos GL55 6HN Tel: 01386 840315
CFA	•	Cambridge Fine Art, Priesthouse, 33 Church Street, Little Shelford, Nr Cambridge, Cambs CB2 5HG Tel: 01223 842866
CMF	•†	Childhood Memories, The Farnham Antique Centre, 27 South Street, Farnham, Surrey GU9 7QU Tel: 01252 724475
CMO	•	Cargin, Brian, & Chris Morley, Ginnell Antiques Gallery, 18-22 Lloyd Street, Gt. Manchester M2 5WA Tel: 0161 833 9037
CNY	*	Christie Manson & Woods International Inc, 502 Park Avenue, (including Christie's East), New York, NY 10022 USA Tel: (212) 546 1000
COB	•†	Cobwebs, 78 Northam Road, Southampton, Hampshire SO2 0PB Tel: 01703 227458
COL	•	Collectables, PO Box 130, Chatham, Kent ME5 0DZ Tel: 01634 828767
CRO	•	Coronets & Crowns, (Robert Taylor) Tel: 01689 875022
CS	•†	Sykes, Christopher, Antiques, The Old Parsonage, Woburn, Milton Keynes, Bucks MK17 9QM Tel: 01525 290259
CSA	•	Church Street Antiques, 15 Church Street, Godalming, Surrey GU7 1EL Tel: 01483 860894
CSK	*†	Christie's South Kensington Ltd, 85 Old Brompton Road, London SW7 3LD Tel: 0171 581 7611
CTO	•	Collector's Corner, (Tudor House) 29-31 Lower Bridge Road, Chester, Cheshire CH1 1RS Tel: 01244 346736/01260 270429
DA	*	Dee, Atkinson & Harrison, The Exchange Saleroom, Driffield, Yorkshire YO25 7LD Tel: 01377 253151
DaD	*	Dockree, David, 224 Moss Lane, Bramhall, Stockport, Cheshire SK7 1BD Tel: 0161 485 1258
DAV	•	Davies Antiques, 40 Kensington Church St, London W8 4BX Tel: 0171 937 9216
DBr	•	Brown, David, 23 Claude Street, Larkhall, Lanarkshire, Scotland ML9 2BU Tel: 01555 880333
DDO	•†	Dowson, Dick, Tel: 01580 714072
DN	*	Dreweatt Neate, Donnington Priory, Donnington, Newbury, Berkshire RG13 2JE Tel: 01635 31234
DOL	•†	Dollectable, 53 Lower Bridge Street, Chester, Cheshire CH1 1RS Tel: 01244 344888/679195
DPO	•	Poultney, Doug Tel: 0181 330 3472
DW	*†	Winter, Dominic, Book Auctions, The Old School, Maxwell Street, Swindon, Wiltshire SN1 5DR Tel: 01793 611340
E	*	Ewbank, Welbeck House, High Street, Guildford, Surrey GU1 3JF Tel: 01483 232134
EaJ	•	Eaton and Jones, 120 High Street, Tenterden, Kent TN30 6HT Tel: 01580 763357
EBB	•	Ella's Button Box, South View, Twyford, Bucks MK18 4EG Tel: 01296 730910
Ech	•†	Echoes, 650a Halifax Road, Eastwood, Todmorden, Yorkshire OL14 6DW Tel: 01706 817505
ED	•	Elite Designs, Tel: 01424 434856
EH	*	Horn, Edgar, Fine Art Auctioneers, 46-50 South Street, Eastbourne, Sussex BN21 4XB Tel: 01323 410419
ELG	•	Lawson, Enid, Gallery, 36a Kensington Church Street, London W8 4DB Tel: 0171 376 0552/0171 937 9559
FAL	•	Falstaff Antiques (Motor Museum), 63-67 High Street, Rolvenden, Kent TN17 4LP Tel: 01580 241234
FOX	•	Foxhole Antiques, High Street, Goudhurst, Kent TN17 1AE Tel: 01580 212025
G&CC	•†	Goss & Crested China Ltd, 62 Murray Road, Horndean, Hampshire PO8 9JL Tel: 01705 597440
GAK	*	Key, G. A., 8 Market Place, Aylsham, Norfolk NR11 6EH Tel: 01263 733195
Gam	*	Clarke & Gammon, The Guildford Auction Rooms, Bedford Road, Guildford, Surrey GU1 4SJ Tel: 01483 66458
GBN	•	Gibbon, Richard (Costume Jewellery), Alfies Antique Market, 13-25 Church Street, London NW8 8DT Tel: 0171 723 0449
GD	•	Gilbert & Dale Antiques, The Old Chapel, Church Street, Ilchester, Nr Yeovil, Somerset BA22 8LA Tel: 01935 840444
GFR	•	Robinson, Geoffrey (Lighting & China), GO75-78, GO91-92 Alfies Antique Market, 13-25 Church Street, London NW8 8DT Tel: 0171 723 0449
GHA	•	Garden House Antiques, 116-118 High Street, Tenterden, Kent TN30 6HT Tel: 01580 763664
GHa	•	Hale, Graham, Great Western Antiques Centre, Bartlett Street, Bath, Avon BA1 2QZ Tel: 01225 446322
GKR	•†	GKR Bonds Ltd, PO Box 1, Kelvedon, Essex CO5 9EH Tel: 01376 571711
GLA	•	Glassform Ltd, 123 Talbot Road, Blackpool, Lancashire FY1 3QY Tel: 01253 695849
GLN	•	Glenville Antiques, 120 High Street, Yatton, Avon BS19 4DH Tel: 01934 832284
GLT	•†	Glitterati, Great Western Antique Centre, Bartlett Street, Bath, Avon BA1 2QZ Tel: 01225 333294
GN	•	Neale Antiques, Gillian , PO Box 247, Aylesbury, Bucks HP20 1JZ Tel: 01296 23754
GNR	•	Gnome Reserve, West Putford, Nr Bradworthy, Devon EX22 7XE Tel: 01409 241435
GR	•	Geoff Read, 176 Brown Edge Road, Buxton, Derbyshire SK17 7AA Tel: 01298 71234
GWo	•	Gnome World, Indian Queens, Nr Saint Columb, Cornwall TR9 6HN Tel: 01726 860812
Har	•	Harbottle, Patricia, Geoffrey Vann Arcade, 107 Portobello Road, London W11 2QB Tel: 0171 731 1972 (Saturdays)

HB	•†	Harrington Bros, The Chelsea Antiques Market, 253 Kings Road, London SW3 5EL Tel: 0171 352 5689/1720
HCC	*	Chapman, H. C., & Son, The Auction Mart, North Street, Scarborough, Yorkshire YO11 1DL Tel: 01723 372424
HCH	*	Hobbs & Chambers, Market Place, Cirencester, Glos GL7 1QQ Tel: 01285 654736
HEA	•	Hearnden, Peter, Corn Exchange Antiques Centre, 64 The Pantiles, Tunbridge Wells, Kent TN2 5TN Tel: 01892 539652
HEG	•†	Heggie, Stuart, 14 The Borough, Northgate, Canterbury, Kent CT1 2DR Tel: 01227 470422
HEM	•	Hemswell Antiques Centre, Caenby Corner Estate, Hemswell Cliff, Gainsborough, Lincolnshire DN21 5TJ Tel: 01427 668389
HER	•	Heritage Antiques, Unit 14, Georgian Village, Camden Passage, London N1 8DU Tel: 0171 226 9822
HEW	•†	Hewitt, Muir, Halifax Antiques Centre, Queens Road Mills, Queen's Road/Gibbet Street, Halifax, Yorkshire HX1 4LR Tel: 01422 347377
HnT	•†	Heads n' Tails, Bourne House, 41 Church Street, Wiveliscombe, Taunton, Somerset TA4 2LT Tel: 01984 623097 Fax: 01984 624445
HOLL	*	Holloways, 49 Parsons Street, Banbury, Oxfordshire OX16 8PF Tel: 01295 253197
HON	•	Honans Antiques, Crowe Street, Gort, County Galway, Ireland Tel: 00 353 91 31407
HSA	•	Samii Antiques, H., S102/3 Alfies Antique Market, 13-25 Church Street, London, NW8 8DT. Tel: 0171 723 5731
HSS/ P(HSS)	*	Spencer, Henry, and Sons (Phillips), 20 The Square, Retford, Notts DN22 6BX Tel: 01777 708633
HUN	•	Huntercombe Manor Barn, Henley-on-Thames, Oxon, Oxfordshire RG9 5RY Tel: 01491 641349
JBL	•	Bland, Judi, Durham House Antique Centre, Sheep Street, Stow-on-the-Wold, Glos GL54 1AA Tel: 01451 870404/01295 811292
JCr	•	Croft, John, Antiques, 3 George Street, Bath, Avon BA1 2EH Tel: 01225 466211
JDC	•	J. & D. Collectables Tel: 01227 452873
JES	•	Jesse, John, 160 Kensington Church Street, London W8 4BN Tel: 0171 229 0312
JFG	•	Jafar Gallery, 24H Grays in the Mews, Davis Mews, London W1Y 1AR Tel: 0171 409 7919/0181 300 2727
JHa	•	Hayhurst, Jeanette, Fine Glass, 32a Kensington Church Street, London W8 4HA Tel: 0171 938 1539
JHo	•	Horne, Jonathan, (Antiques) Ltd, 66C Kensington Church Street, London W8 4BY Tel: 0171 221 5658
JHW	•	Howkins, John, 1 Dereham Road, Norwich, Norfolk NR2 4HX Tel: 01603 627832
JMC	•	J. & M. Collectables Tel: 01580 891657
JO	•†	Oosthuizen, Jacqueline, 23 Cale Street, Chelsea, London SW3 3QR Tel: 0171 352 6071
JON	•	Bird, Jon Tel: 01227 273952
JPr	•	Proops, Joanna, Antiques and Textiles, 3 Saville Row, Bath, Avon BA1 2QP Tel: 01225 310795

JR	•	Rastall, John, Stall GO47/8 Alfies Antique Market, 13-25 Church Street, London NW8 8DT Tel: 0171 723 0449
JTA	•	J. T. Antiques, 16 Christchurch House, Christchurch Road, London SW2 3UA Tel: 0181 671 2354
JUN	•†	Junktion, The Old Railway Station, New Bolingbroke, Boston, Lincolnshire PE22 7LB Tel: 01205 480087/480068
KES	•†	Keystones, PO Box 387, Stafford, Staffordshire ST16 3RX Tel: 01785 256648
KT		Taylor, Karen (Private Collector)
L	*	Lawrence Fine Art Auctioneers, South Street, Crewkerne, Somerset TA18 8AB Tel: 01460 73041
L&E	*	Locke & England, Black Horse Agencies, 18 Guy Street, Leamington Spa, Warwickshire CV32 4RT Tel: 01926 889100
LANG	*	Langlois, Westaway Chambers, Don Street, St Helier, Jersey JE2 4TR Tel: 01534 22441
LAY	*	Lay, David (ASVA), Auction House, Alverton, Penzance, Cornwall TR18 4RE Tel: 01736 61414
LB	•	Lace Basket, 116 High Street, Tenterden, Kent TN30 6HT Tel: 01580 763923/763664
LBe	•	Bee, Linda, Art Deco Stand J20-21 Grays Antique Market, 1-7 Davies Mews, London W1Y 1AR Tel: 0171 629 5921
LBr	•†	Brine, Lynda, Scent Bottles & Smalls, Great Western Antique Centre, Bartlett Street, Bath, Avon BA1 2QZ Tel: 01225 837932/448488 Mobile: 0860 105600
LHB	•	Gallery 'Les Hommes Bleus', Bartlett Street Antique Centre, 5/10 Bartlett Street, Bath, Avon BA1 2QZ Tel: 01225 316606
LIB	•†	Libra Antiques, 81 London Road, Hurst Green, Etchingham, Sussex TN19 7PN Tel: 01580 860569
LT	*	Louis Taylor Auctioneers & Valuers, Britannia House, 10 Town Road, Hanley, Stoke-on-Trent, Staffordshire ST1 2QG. Tel: 01782 214111
MAP	•†	Marine Art Posters, Harbour Way, Merchants Landing, Victoria Dock, Port of Hull, Humberside HU9 1PL Tel: 01482 321173
MAR	*	Marshall, Frank R, & Co, Marshall House, Church Hill, Knutsford, Cheshire WA16 6DH Tel: 01565 653284
MAW	*	Mawer, Thomas, & Son, The Lincoln Saleroom, 63 Monks Road, Lincoln, Lincolnshire LN2 5HP Tel: 01522 524984
MCA	*	Carey, Mervyn, Twysden Cottage, Benenden, Cranbrook, Kent TN17 4LD Tel: 01580 240283
McC	*	McCartneys, Portcullis Salerooms, Ludlow, Shropshire SY8 1PZ Tel: 01584 872636
MCh	•	Chapman, Michael, Priorsleigh, Mill Lane, Cleeve Prior, Worcestershire WR11 5JZ Tel: 01789 773897/Mobile 0831 392542
MGC	•†	Midlands Goss & Commemoratives, The Old Cornmarket Antique Centre, 70 Market Place, Warwick, Warwickshire CV34 4SO Tel: 01926 419119
MIL	•	Milverton Antiques, Fore Street, Milverton, Taunton, Somerset TA4 1JU Tel: 01823 400597
Mit	*	Mitchells, Fairfield House, Station Road, Cockermouth, Cumbria CA13 9PY Tel: 01900 827800

MJB * Bowman, Michael J., 6 Haccombe House, Netherton, Newton Abbot, Devon TQ12 4SJ Tel: 01626 872890

MLa • Langham, Marion Tel: 0171 730 1002

MofC • Millers of Chelsea Antiques Ltd, Netherbrook House, 86 Christchurch Road, Ringwood, Hampshire BH24 1DR Tel: 01425 472062

MR *† Rowe, Martyn, Truro Auction Centre, Calenick Street, Truro, Cornwall TR1 2SG Tel: 01872 260020

MRT • Rees, Mark, Tools Tel: 01225 837031

MRW •† Russ Welch, Malcolm, Worcester Antiques Centre, Reindeer Court, Mealcheapen Street, Worcester, Hereford & Worcs WR1 4DF Tel: 0131 667 1407

MSA • M. S. Antiques, 25a Holland Street, London W8 4JF Tel: 0171 937 0793

MSh • Manfred Schotten, The Crypt Antiques, 109 High Street, Burford, Oxfordshire OX18 4RG Tel: 01993 822302

MSMP• Smith, Mike, Motoring Past, Chiltern House, Ashendon, Aylesbury, Bucks HP18 0HB Tel: 01296 651283

MSW * Swain, Marilyn, Auctions, The Old Barracks, Sandon Road, Grantham, Lincolnshire NG31 9AS Tel: 01476 68861

MUR •† Murray Cards (International) Ltd, 51 Watford Way, Hendon Central, London NW4 3JH Tel: 0181 202 5688

N *† Neales, 192-194 Mansfield Road, Nottingham, Notts NG1 3HU Tel: 0115 962 4141

NAR • Narbeth, Colin, & Son Ltd, 20 Cecil Court, Leicester Square, London WC2N 4HE Tel: 0171 379 6975

NAS • Nashers Music Store, 72 Walcot Street, Bath, Avon BA1 5DD Tel: 01225 332298

NCA •† New Century Antiques, 69 Kensington Church Street, London W8 4DB Tel: 0171 376 2810

ND *† Nock Deighton, Livestock & Auction Centre, Tasley, Bridgnorth, Shropshire WV16 4QR Tel: 01746 762666

NOS • Nostalgia Comics, 14-16 Smallbrook Queensway, City Centre, Birmingham, West Midlands B5 4EN. Tel: 0121 643 0143

NTM † Nostalgia Toy Museum, High Street, Godshill, Isle of Wight PO38 3HZ Tel: 01983 730055/840181

NWE • North Wiltshire Exporters, Farmhill House, Brinkworth, Wiltshire SN15 5AJ Tel: 01666 824133/510876

Oli * Olivers, Olivers Rooms, Burkitts Lane, Sudbury, Suffolk CO10 6HB Tel: 01787 880305

ONS * Onslows, Metrostore, Townmead Road, London SW6 2RZ Tel: 0171 793 0240

OO • Oosthuizen, Pieter, De Verzamelaar, Georgian Village, Camden Passage, London N1 8DU Tel: 0171 359 3322/376 3852

OPH • Old Pine House, 16 Warwick Street, Royal Leamington Spa, Warwickshire CV32 5LL Tel: 01926 470477

ORI •† Oriental Gallery, The Malthouse, Digbeth Street, Stow-on-the-Wold, Glos GL54 1BN Tel: 01451 830944

OTA •† On The Air, 42 Bridge Street Row, Chester, Cheshire CH1 1NN Tel: 01244 348468

P * Phillips, Blenstock House, 101 New Bond Street, London W1Y 0AS Tel: 0171 629 6602

P(B) * Phillips, 1 Old King Street, Bath, Avon BA1 2JT Tel: 01225 310609

P(Ba)* Phillips Bayswater, 10 Salem Road, Bayswater, London W2 4DL Tel: 0171 229 9090

P(HSS)* Phillips (See HSS)

P(S) * Phillips, 49 London Road, Sevenoaks, Kent TN13 1AR Tel: 01732 740310

PBr • Brooks, Pamela Tel: 0116 230 2625

PC Private Collection

PCh * Cheney, Peter, Western Road Auction Rooms, Western Road, Littlehampton, Sussex BN17 5NP Tel: 01903 722264/713418

PEN • Pennard House Antiques, 3-4 Piccadilly, London Road, Bath, Avon BA1 6PL Tel: 01225 313791/ 01749 860260

PIA •† Pianola Shop, The, 134 Islingword Road, Brighton, Sussex BN2 2SH Tel: 01273 608999

PIn • Postcards International, Vintage Picture Postcards, PO Box 2930, New Haven, CT 06515-0030 USA. Tel: 001 203 865 0814

QSA • Quiet Street Antiques, 3 Quiet Street, Bath, Avon BA1 2JG Tel: 01225 315727

RA • Roberts Antiques Tel: 01253 827794

RBA •† Bradbury, Roger, Antiques, Church Street, Coltishall, Norfolk NR12 7DJ Tel: 01603 737444

RBB * Russell, Baldwin & Bright, Fine Art Salerooms, Ryelands Road, Leominster, Hereford HR6 8NZ. Tel: 01568 611166

RHE * Ellis, R. H., & Sons, 44-46 High Street, Worthing, Sussex BN11 1LL Tel: 01903 238999

RIC • Rich Designs, 1 Shakespeare Street, Stratford-upon-Avon, Warwickshire CV37 6RN Tel: 01789 261612

RTw • Twort, Richard Tel: 01934 641900

RUM/• Rum Rumours Decorative Arts, 10 The Mall, Upper Street, Camden Passage, Islington, London N1 0PD Tel: 01582 873561

RWB • Bunn, Roy W, Antiques, 34-36 Church Street, Barnoldswick, Colne, Lancashire BB8 5UT Tel: 01282 813703

RYA • Young, Robert, Antiques, 68 Battersea Bridge Road, London SW11 3AG Tel: 0171 228 7847

S * Sotheby's, 34-35 New Bond Street, London W1A 2AA Tel: 0171 493 8080

S(NY)* Sotheby's, 1334 York Avenue, New York, NY 10021 USA Tel: 001 212 606 7000

S(S) * Sotheby's Sussex, Summers Place, Billingshurst, Sussex RH14 9AB Tel: 01403 783933

SCA • Susie Cooper Ceramics (Art Deco), GO70-4 Alfies Antique Market, 13-25 Church Street, London NW8 8DT Tel: 0171 723 0449

SCR •† Scripophily Shop, Britannia Hotel, Grosvenor Square, London W1A 3AN Tel: 0171 495 0580

SER • Serendipity, 168 High Street, Deal, Kent CT14 6BQ Tel: 01304 369165/366536

SGr • Groombridge, Sarah, Stand 335, Grays Market, 58 Davies Street, London W1Y 1LB Tel: 0171 629 0225

SHA	•	Shambles, 22 North Street, Ashburton, Devon TQ13 7QD Tel: 01364 653848
SHa	•	Shapiro & Co, Stand 380, Grays Antique Market, 58 Davies Street, London W1Y 1LB Tel: 0171 491 2710
ShS	•	Shell Shop, The, 9 The Quay, Brixham, Devon TQ5 8AW Tel: 01803 852039
SIG	•	Sigma Antiques, Water Skellgate, Ripon, Yorkshire HG4 1BH Tel: 01765 603163
SK(B)*		Skinner Inc, 357 Main Street, Bolton, MA 01740 USA Tel: 001 508 779 6241
Sol	•	Solent Railwayana, 31 New Town Road, Warsash, Hampshire SO31 9FY Tel: 01489 578093/584633 (eve)
Som	•	Somervale Antiques, 6 Radstock Road, Midsomer Norton, Bath, Avon BA3 2AJ Tel: 01761 412686
SP	•	Pearson, Sue, 13 Prince Albert Street, Brighton, Sussex BN1 1HE Tel: 01273 329247
SPE	•†	Spectrum, Sylvie, Stand 372, Grays Market, 58 Davies Street, London W1Y 1LB Tel: 0171 629 3501
SRA	*†	Sheffield Railwayana Auctions, 43 Little Norton Lane, Sheffield, Yorkshire S8 8GA Tel: 0114 274 5085 & 0860 921519
STA	•	Stacpoole, Michelina & George, Main Street, Adare, Co Limerick, Ireland Tel: 00 353 6139 6409
STE	•†	Stevenson Brothers, The Workshop, Ashford Road, Bethersden, Ashford, Kent TN26 3AP Tel: 01233 820580/820363
STP	•	Pearce, Stevie, Antique Costume Jewellery, G144 Alfies Antique Market, 13-25 Church Street, London NW8 8DT Tel: 0171 723 1513 /0171 724 9319
SWB	•†	Sweetbriar Gallery, Sweetbriar House, Robin Hood Lane, Helsby, Cheshire WA6 9NH Tel: 01928 723851
SWO	*	Sworder, G. E., & Sons, 15 Northgate End, Bishops Stortford, Hertfordshire CM23 2LF Tel: 01279 651388
TaB	•	Tartan Bow, The Tel: 01379 783057
TAC	•	Tenterden Antiques Centre, 66-66A High Street, Tenterden, Kent TN30 6AU Tel: 01580 765655/765885
TAR	•	Tarrant, Lorraine, Antiques, 7-11 Market Place, Ringwood, Hampshire BH24 1AN Tel: 01425 461123
TBo	•	Tenterden Bookshop, 60 High Street, Tenterden, Kent TN30 6AU Tel: 01580 763005
TBS	•	Travellers Book Shop, The, 25 Cecil Court, London WC2N 4EZ Tel: 0171 836 9132
TED	•†	Teddy Bears of Witney, 99 High Street, Witney, Oxfordshire OX8 6LY Tel: 01993 702616
Tem	•	Great Western Antiques inc Temeraire, The Torre Station, Newton Road, Torquay, Devon TQ5 2DD Tel: 01803 200551
THi	§	Thimble Society of London, The, Stand 134 Grays Antique Market, 58 Davies Street, London W1Y 1LB Tel: 0171 493 0560
TL	•†	Telephone Lines Ltd, 339 High Street, Cheltenham, Glos GL50 3HS Tel: 01242 583699
TMi	•†	Millard, Tim, Antiques, Stand 31-32 Bartlett Street Antique Centre, Bartlett Street, Bath, Avon BA1 2QZ Tel: 01225 469785
TOY	•†	Toystore, The, Unit 32-34 Corn Exchange, Manchester Centre, Gt. Manchester M4 3BW Tel: 0161 839 6882
TP	•†	Collector, The, Tom Power, 9 Church Street, Marylebone, London NW8 8EE Tel: 0171 706 4586
VB	•†	Variety Box, 16 Chapel Place, Tunbridge Wells, Kent TN1 1YQ Tel: 01892 531868/521589
VCL	•	Vintage Cameras Ltd, 254 & 256 Kirkdale, Sydenham, London SE26 4NL Tel: 0181 778 5416/5841
VL		Lewis Valerie, The Rockery, The Moor, Hawkhurst, Kent TN18 4NE (Private Collector)
VS	*†	Vennett-Smith, T., 11 Nottingham Road, Gotham, Nottingham, Notts NG11 0HE Tel: 0115 983 0541
W	*	Walter's, No. 1 Mint Lane, Lincoln, Lincolnshire LN1 1UD Tel: 01522 525454
WAC	•	Worcester Antiques Centre, Reindeer Court, Mealcheapen Street, Worcester, Hereford & Worcs WR1 4DF Tel: 01905 610680
WAG	•	Weald Antiques Gallery, The, 106 High Street, Tenterden, Kent TN30 6HT Tel: 01580 762939
WaH	•	Warehouse, The, 29-30 Queens Gardens, Worthington Street, Dover, Kent CT17 9AH Tel: 01304 242006
WAL	*†	Wallis & Wallis, West Street Auction Galleries, Lewes, Sussex BN7 2NJ Tel: 01273 480208
WAT	•	Waterloo Antiques, 20 The Waterloo, Cirencester, Glos GL7 2PZ Tel: 01285 644887
WCA	•	Wooden Chair Antiques Centre, Waterloo Road, Cranbrook, Kent TN12 0QG Tel: 01580 713671
WeA	•	Wenderton Antiques, 26 Cornwallis Road, London N19 4LT (by appt only)
WEL	•	Wells Reclamation & Co, The Old Cider Farm, Coxley, Nr Wells, Somerset BA5 1RQ Tel: 01749 677087/677484
WIL	*	Wilson, Peter, Victoria Gallery, Market Street, Nantwich, Cheshire CW5 5DG Tel: 01270 623878
WL	*	Wintertons Ltd, Lichfield Auction Centre, Wood End Lane, Fradley, Lichfield, Staffordshire WS13 8NF Tel: 01543 263256
WN	•	What Now, Cavendish Arcade, The Crescent, Buxton, Derbyshire SK17 6BQ Tel: 01298 27178/23417
WP	•†	West Promotions, PO Box 257, Sutton, Surrey SM3 9WW Tel: 0181 641 3224
WRe	•	Walcot Reclamations, 108 Walcot Street, Bath, Avon BA1 5BG Tel: 01225 66291/63245
WTA	•	Witney and Airault, Prinny's Gallery, 3 Meeting House Lane, The Lanes, Brighton, Sussex BN1 1HB Tel: 01273 204554
WW	*	Woolley & Wallis, 51-61 Castle Street, Salisbury, Wiltshire SP1 3SU Tel: 01722 411422
YY	•	Yesteryear Antiques, 24D Magdalen Street, Norwich, Norfolk NR3 1HU Tel: 01603 622908

INTRODUCTION

From the airline fans illustrated at the beginning of the book to the collectables under £5 at the end, *Miller's Collectables Price Guide* is filled with new pictures and collecting areas. The guide captures both the excitement and the remarkable expansion of the collectables market.

Special features this year include a major section on gardening collectables. As gardening grows ever more popular, so old horticultural equipment has been rescued from the garden shed and now appears at the smartest antiques fairs. We take a look at the history of the lawn mower and explore the origins of the garden gnome. Now seen as the ultimate suburban ornament, in the 19th century gnomes graced the most aristocratic country residences and Victorian examples can today be worth hundreds of pounds.

Our appeal in last year's guide for collectables from the fifties inspired a huge response from dealers, private collectors and even designers of the period. Our Fifties section includes a feature on Festival of Britain material whilst in our Ceramics section we cover some of the most innovative post-WWII British potteries, such as Midwinter and Rye. Many collectors will remember these objects from their own childhood, and though at the top of the range prices are expensive, much fifties material is surprisingly affordable and regularly turns up at fêtes and car-boot fairs. As interest in the period increases values are set to rise.

Ceramics are without doubt amongst today's favourite collectables and this is reflected in our expanded coverage this year. Major subjects include Clarice Cliff and Wedgwood and we commemorate the recent deaths of two of the greatest potters of the century: Susie Cooper and Lucie Rie.

Subjects covered in this edition range from playing cards to post boxes, from decorative scent bottles to ceramic lavatory pulls. We also take a close look at sewing antiques. During social events it was commonplace for Victorian ladies to sew as they sat and chatted. Since their needlework tools were on display they were often extremely decorative, and objects such as rare thimbles can be worth hundreds of pounds. At festive occasions today we are more likely to have a glass in our hands than a needle. Drinking has generated its own collectables, as demonstrated in our Breweriana and Corkscrews sections.

Increasingly objects from the recent past are gaining the status of antiques. A recent exhibition in New York, 'Art, Design and Barbie, The Evolution of a Cultural Icon' celebrated the history and social significance of the first teenage fashion doll, and in our Dolls' section we look at some of the Barbies that readers might have at home. Autumn 1995 saw not only the release of a new Beatles single, featuring all four members of the band living and dead, but also the purchase by the National Trust of Paul McCartney's childhood home in Liverpool. Reflecting current interest we have included a varied collection of Beatles' memorabilia in our Rock and Pop section.

Unlike other price guides, Miller's include material from auction houses, dealers and private collectors, covering the whole range of the marketplace, featuring objects that are genuinely affordable, even to those young collectors with only pocket money to spend. We aim to show what people buy on a wide range of budgets. Features planned for future editions of the guide include: seventies and eighties collectables, Royal Winton ceramics and collectable mystery and detective novels. If there are any subjects that you would like to see covered, please let us know.

Last year we asked you to send us your nominations for a collectable of the future. We received a wealth of fascinating suggestions ranging from the toys found inside Kinder Surprise chocolate eggs to mint condition National Lottery scratch cards – should anyone, of course, be brave enough to leave them unused. The winning entry, however, came from David Coverdale of South Shields, Tyne and Wear, who suggested Tetley Tea promotional items, featured in our Collectables of the Future (page 432). Congratulations to him and thank you to everyone who wrote to us. If you can spot what next year's hottest collectable might be, let us know, and the winning entry will win a free copy of *Miller's Collectables Price Guide* until the year 2000.

As ever, happy hunting!

ADVERTISING & PACKAGING
Advertising Fans

Airline fans are new to this guide. First issued in the 1950s, fans were given away free to passengers as, before the general introduction of air conditioning, airline cabins could become unbearably hot. According to American enthusiast Cynthia Fendel, at least 53 commercial airline companies are known to have produced fans, the most prolific being CAAC (Civil Aviation Administration of China), and JAL (Japan Air Lines), both of whom are responsible for some 30 known designs. Fans can often be difficult to date, since many of the companies which produced them no longer exist or have been absorbed by other firms. Research into this field, however, is expanding daily – airline fans are already collected in the USA and are becoming increasingly popular in Britain. Prices, however, have a long way to go before they match the value of turn of the century advertising fans also illustrated.

A double-leaf folding fan, printed with wave pattern blue on blue, showing an Oriental scene on the left, European characters on the right dominated by a Beefeater, the central logo 'BOAC' in white, both sides identical, plain bamboo sticks and guards, c1960s, 8in (20cm) wide.
£10–15 *PC*

A double-leaf folding fan, printed with dragon boats and other Oriental scenes on an off-white background, with 'Cathay Pacific' in green lettering, both sides identical, plain bamboo sticks and guards, c1960–70s, 8in (20cm) wide.
£5–10 *PC*

A white silk leaf fan, printed with a spray of mauve orchids, outlined in back with red glitter centres, printed to the left 'The Royal Orchid Service' and to the right 'Thai International', the 38 bamboo sticks overlapping and pierced, guards lacquered in mauve, with matching double tassel attached to ring in a rivet, 1970s, 8in (20cm) wide, in a cream card box.
£20–30 *PC*

| Cross Reference: |
| Fans |

A chromolithographic fan, advertising the Restaurant du Café de la Paix, signed 'Benjamin Rabier' engraved by Devambez, Paris, with wooden sticks, 1912, 9in (23cm) wide.
£400–500 *CSK*

A chromolithographic fan, advertising the Restaurant Russe dit des Boyards, published by G. Migeon, 18 rue Chapon, Paris, with wooden sticks, c1893, 11in (28cm) wide.
£400–500 *CSK*

r. A double-leaf folding fan, printed with 4 natives and views in panels on a green background with white flower borders, 'Ghana Airways' in yellow top centre, reverse similar with larger lettering replacing panel and a star logo, plain bamboo sticks and guards, c1950s, 8in (20cm) wide.
£20–30 *PC*

Boards & Signs

A French retailer's promotional wall-mounted advertising board, for Georges Kennel, incorporating a thermometer, 20thC.
£80–100 *MCh*

An advertising board, 'Kensitas – That's Good Virginia Tobacco', 1935, 12½ by 9½in (31.5 by 24cm).
£15–20 *MRW*

An advertising card board, 'Peggy Sage Nail Polish', 1950, 10¾ by 8in (27 by 20cm).
£5–7 *MRW*

A Chapman Stock Broker enamelled wall sign, c1880s, 8in (20cm) high.
£200–250 *MCh*

r. A Victorian enamelled tin door sign, 'Avon Brilliant Polish for Boots and Leggings', 11in (28cm) high.
£40–50 *MCh*

A Kodak Film glass sign, lettered in reflecting yellow and silver on a black ground, with circular metal frame and hanging loops, 1920–30s, 14in (36cm) diam.
£175–200 *Bon*

Bottles

A pair of Vittel interlocking mineral water bottles.
£175–200 *Bon*

A Drioli ceramic miniature liqueur bottle, in the shape of a bird, Italian, c1950–70s, 5in (12.5cm) high.
£5–10 *JTA*

A Sloan's Liniment bottle, 1910, 5in (12.5cm) high.
£8–10 *MRW*

Boxes

Nine apothecary bottles, late 19thC.
£15–20 each *WCA*

Bottles containing medicines or potentially dangerous substances were produced in coloured glass so as to provide a warning for the illiterate. They were often ridged or distinctively shaped so that, in poor light, the bottle could be identified by touch.

A Hudson's Concentrated Soap Extract cardboard box, 1930, 6½in (16.5cm) high.
£10–15 *MRW*

A Colman's Starch box, c1900, 18½in (46.5cm) long.
£25–30 *AL*

A Whiteways Cyder Co Ltd box, c1930, 20in (50.5cm) long.
£25–30 *AL*

l. A Boots Magnet Carpet Soap cardboard box, 1930, 3½in (8.5cm) long.
£6–8 *MRW*

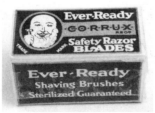

r. An Ever-Ready Corrux Safety Razor Blades cardboard box, with contents, c1940s, 1½in (3.5cm) long.
£10–12 *MRW*

l. A Burma Cheroots PWE Brand cardboard box, 1940, 8in (20cm) wide.
£6–12 *MRW*

Three miniature cigarette packets, c1930s, 1¼in (3cm) high.
£18–20 *MRW*

Ceramics

An Oxo mug, 1920s, 3¾in (9.5cm) high.
£4–5 WAC

A Bovril mug, 1910–20s, 3½in (8.5cm) high.
£4–5 WAC

A selection of 4 Carlton Ware Guinness advertising figures, 1940–50s, 4in (10cm) high, and a Wade figure of the Brew Master, base inscribed, 5½in (14cm) high.
£150–175 WW

Tins

Rare tins are making big money in the current market. Two of the Crawford's biscuit tins shown in this section fetched over £1,000 each at auction. Other recent saleroom results include £2,500 for a tin in the shape of a London bus, again by Crawford's, one of the most celebrated names in this field.

For a tin to fetch a high price, good condition is crucial and form is all-important. Shaped tins, often produced for the Christmas market, tend to be the most desirable, with transport and sporting themes being popular.

A William Crawford & Sons Ltd tinplate biscuit tin, in the shape of an aeroplane, registration 'A-One Crawford's Air Service', 1920–30s.
£1,100–1,300 RHE

A William Crawford & Sons Ltd money box biscuit tin, in the shape of a mushroom, designed by Mabel Lucie Attwell, c1920s, 7½in (18.5cm) high.
£130–150 DA

A Cerebos Table Salt tin, c1920s, 6¾in (17cm) high.
£45–60 MRW

r. An Edgeworth Pipe Tobacco tin, with contents, 1920, 3½in (8.5cm) wide.
£25–30 MRW

A William Crawford's tinplate biscuit tin, in the form of a hurdy-gurdy, made by Barringer Wallis & Manners, c1912, 6½in (16.5cm) high.
£1,400–1,600 LT

A Romac Repair Outfit tin, for mending punctures, c1930s.
£30–40 *MCh*

A Sovereign toffee tin, c1930, 7in (17.5cm) diam.
£10–12 *AL*

The Laurel Ladies Boudoir Safety Razor and tin, 1930, 1¾in (4.5cm) wide.
£8–15 *MRW*

Three throat pastille tins, 1930s–40s, largest 2¼in (5.5cm) wide.
£1–3 each *COL*

l. An Elastoplast tin, 1930–40s, 1¼in (2.5cm) diam.
r. A Zubes throat pastilles tin, 1930–40s, 2½in (6.5cm) diam.
£2–3 each *COL*

A Bow Bells grease tin, with contents, 1920, 6¾in (17cm) high.
£25–35 *MRW*

A Blue Bird toffee tin, c1930s, 9in (22.5cm) diam.
£35–45 *Ber*

Two Oxo tins, c1930s, largest 4in (10cm) square.
£3–5 each *COL*

Two throat pastille tins, 1930s–40s, 2¼in (5.5cm) wide.
£2–4 each *COL*

Two adhesive plaster tins, with
contents, 1930–40s, 1½in
(3.5cm) diam.
£2–4 each *COL*

r. A tin, decorated
with scenes by
Gilbert &
Sullivan, c1920s,
7½in (19cm) wide.
£10–12 *AL*

A hexagonal tin, showing
9 members of Royalty, c1953,
5½in (13.5cm) diam.
£6–7 *AL*

A Cadbury's biscuit tin, c1960,
8½in (21.5cm) wide.
£6–7 *AL*

A Rowntree's Dairy Box tin,
1960, 7½in (18.5cm) wide.
£15–20 *MRW*

Miscellaneous

A Crawford's Biscuits glazed
shop fitting, by Taylor Bros
Ltd, Shopfitters, Sheffield,
with white marble top above
a glazed frieze, the reverse
decorated with Royal coat-of-
arms on a matt, burnished
gilt ground, mahogany
trestle frame with brass
handles, early 20thC,
51½in (130cm) high.
£500–600 *N*

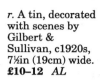

A McVitie & Price
mahogany and glass
display unit, early 20thC.
£350–450 *BWe*

r. A collection of 3 cardboard
Easter eggs, 1930s, largest
7½in (18.5cm) long.
£40–50 *Ber*

A Raleigh Industries
advertising figure, c1925–30,
24in (61.5cm) high.
£75–100 *JUN*

An Asmidar Headache Powder
packet, with contents, 1920,
2in (5cm) wide.
£45–50 *MRW*

AERONAUTICA

Rarity is all-important in the aeronautica market, and for the more unusual items prices can fly sky high. Material connected with airships is hugely sought after and a humble 1920s cup and saucer, sold by Christie's South Kensington, fetched a four-figure sum thanks to the famous 'LZ' Zeppelin logo on the front and the inscription 'Graf Zeppelin' on the underside of the saucer.

Built in 1928, the Graf Zeppelin inaugurated transatlantic flight services and made a total of 144 ocean crossings. It was decommissioned in 1937, the same year that its sister airship, the giant Hindenburg, tragically exploded, thus bringing interest in building rigid airships to an abrupt and painful end. Memorabilia associated with both these celebrated airships commands a particularly high premium in salerooms.

The following section also includes items relating to the French aviator, Louis Blériot, who made the first cross-channel aeroplane flight in 1909, winning everlasting fame and a prize of £1,000 from the *Daily Mail*. At the other end of the aviation time scale we illustrate a small selection of space memorabilia which, as international space programmes are running down, continues to appear on the market.

Airships

r. A frosted glass model of an airship, moulded with a gondola, fins and labelled 'MU-UN', 1920–30, 9½in (24cm) long.
£350–400 *CSK*

Cross Reference:
Advertising & Packaging
Ephemera

l. A *Daily Mirror* 'Zepp Raid' pictorial newspaper vendor's stand poster, WWI, 24¾ by 17¾in (63 by 45cm).
£350–400 *ONS*

A coffee cup and saucer, with gilt and blue banding, by Heinrich & Co Bavaria, with Zeppelin logo, the saucer inscribed 'Graf Zeppelin', 1928, saucer 4¼in (10.5cm) diam.
£1,700–2,000 *CSK*

Blériot

l. Two gelatin-silver prints, one depicting Blériot and his wife, autographed and inscribed in ink 'Presented to Sir Walter Windham Mons: & Madame Blériot, Sep 15th 1909', 8 by 6in (20 by 15cm), the other of S. F. Cody, inscribed and similarly dated, 8 by 6in (20 by 15cm), and another print, possibly of Capt. W. G. Windham.
£200–250 *CSK*

An Aéroplanes Blériot poster, published by Louis Galice Paris, early 20thC, 30¼ by 39½in (76.5 by 100cm).
£350–400 *ONS*

A silver metal and gilt spoon, commemorating Louis Blériot's cross-channel flight, engraved 'Entente Cordiale', and 'Louis Blériot 1909', 4¼in (10.5cm) long, in lined leather case.
£80–100 *CSK*

Two gelatin-silver prints, one of an Auzani engine and unusual propeller, 10 by 12in (25 by 30.5cm), the other depicting a group of aeronauts at the House of Commons, Sep 15th 1909, and another print, probably taken at Doncaster, 1909.
£100–140 *CSK*

MAKE THE MOST OF MILLER'S

Condition is absolutely vital when assessing the value of any item. Damaged pieces appreciate much less than perfect examples. However, a rare, desirable piece may command a high price even when damaged.

A dinner menu, from The Hotel Cecil, in honour of the first cross-channel flight, signed 'L. Blériot', September 15 1909.
£350–400 *CSK*

Books, Brochures & Magazines

Hermann Hoernes, *Buch des Fluges,* Volumes 1–3, Wien, 1911 (Volume 3, 1912), original gilt pictorial cloth boards, numerous colour plates, diagrams, photographs, sepia and black and white, some colour, German text, the details of flight to date, aircraft, ballooning, Zeppelin and technical information.
£400–450 *CSK*

r. A brochure entitled *At the time of Building the World's Largest Land based Civil Aircraft,* the Bristol Brabazon, with gilt embossed cover, colour frontispiece by Terence Cuneo, colour interior, original slip case, 1950.
£125–150 *CSK*

A catalogue entitled *The Birthplace of Aerial Power,* for the Grahame-White Company Ltd, including plates of wartime factory views, aircraft and trophies, 1919.
£70–90 *ONS*

Six copies of *L'Illustration* magazine, Numéro de l'Aéronautique, 1924, 1930, 1932, 1934, 1936 and 1938, by Geo. Ham. and A. Brenet.
£200–250 *CSK*

Flying Helmets

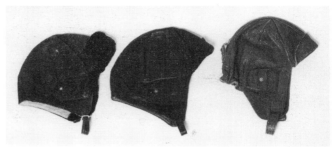

A selection of flying helmets, c1930s.
£60–100 *Ech*

A leather flying helmet, c1930s.
£60–100 *Ech*

r. An uncovered
model Sopwith Pup,
⅛in:1ft scale, with
braced wooden
airframe 42in
(106.5cm) wingspan.
£800–900 *CSK*

Model Aeroplanes

A model of a Boeing B-52C Stratofortress,
31in (78.5cm) long, and a Northrop F-15
Reporter Serial 9549, 11in (28cm) long.
£60–80 *CSK*

r. A flying scale model
of a Mitsubishi A6M2
Zero, .1/7 scale, Serial
V-117, with fabric-
covered wooden
airframe, some damage,
63in (160cm) wingspan.
£400–450 *CSK*

A radio-controlled flying model helicopter,
Lark 25, with glazed cabin, landing skids,
single cylinder glow plug engine, gear and
belt drive to main and tail rotors, finished
in red, blue and white, 42in (106.5cm)
rotor diam, with Futaba transmitter.
£500–600 *CSK*

A flying scale model of a
Focke-Wulf FW56 'Stosser',
Serial D-IAQA, with fabric-
covered wooden airframe,
finished in silver, 105in
(266.5cm) wingspan.
£850–1,000 *CSK*

r. A flying scale model
of an RAF SE5,
.1/5 scale, with fabric-
covered wooden
airframe, 80in
(203cm) wingspan.
£450–550 *CSK*

Paintings, Posters & Photographs

J. Pritchard, *First Solo, Tiger Moth with Apprehensive Student,* oil on canvas, signed, 23¾ by 29⅜in (60.5 by 75.5cm).
£600–700 *CSK*

A lithograph colour poster, Shipyards of the Future, c1920, 30 by 20in (76 by 50.5cm).
£300–350 *CSK*

D. J. Sawyer, *Miles Satyr G-ABVG,* gouache, signed and dated 1933, 10¼ by 15¼in (26 by 38cm), together with a photograph and 2 postcards of Mrs. Bruce standing by the aircraft, one signed.
£60–80 *ONS*

Space

Two ESRO 1 & 2 satellite demonstration models of the first and second satellites, produced as part of the programme of the European Space Research Organisation, 1960s.
£100–150 *CSK*

A poster, by Whitlock, for Empire Air Day, Saturday May 20th, 1939, 15 by 10in (38 by 25cm), together with an official programme for the event and a pictorial circular window label, 5½in (14cm) diam.
£70–100 *ONS*

Miscellaneous

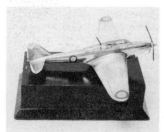

A silver plate on brass desk mascot, depicting a Fairey aeroplane, built to scale, WWII, 7in (17.5cm) long.
£200–300 *TAR*

Eight Aircraft Manufacturing Co Ltd silver gelatin prints, taken by the Company and F. N. Birkett of Shepherd's Bush, 1918–19, 8¾ by 11in (22 by 28cm).
£60–80 *ONS*

A model of a Spitfire, on a Bakelite ashtray, WWII, 5in (12.5cm) diam.
£140–180 *MCh*

An RAF sector clock, with fusee movement by T. W. Elliott Ltd, No. 5548, white enamelled dial with Roman numerals, with brown, blue and orange triangles and RAF wings, 1938, dial 13½in (34.5cm) diam.
£650–750 *CSK*

ART DECO

The term Art Deco derives from the 1925 Paris 'Exposition Internationale des Arts Décoratifs et Industriels Modernes', the first major international exhibition of Decorative Arts to be held after WWI. Leading designers, including René Lalique (glass), Paul Poiret (fashion) and Clarice Cliff (ceramics), exhibited their wares. The Art Deco style – streamlined, geometric and modernistic – dominated design in the 1920s and '30s from the finest hand-crafted works of art to the cheapest, mass-produced tableware.

The Ceramics section also features Art Deco pottery and porcelain, and other Art Deco objects are included throughout the guide. For their location, please consult the index.

A ceramic powder bowl, c1930, 5in (12.5cm) high.
£25–30 *PC*

A Sadler racing car teapot, with silver lustre decoration on a yellow ground, 8in (20.5cm) long.
£130–150 *LANG*

l. A Katshütte ceramic figure, c1935, 10½in (26.5cm) high.
£150–175 *CSA*

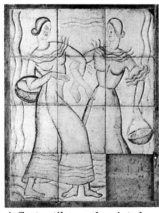

A Carter tile panel, painted with 2 women arm-in-arm, carrying baskets, painted in shades of blue, yellow and green on a cream ground, one tile missing, one chipped, impressed factory marks, 24in (61cm) high.
£200–250 *CSK*

l. A string of glass and ceramic flapper beads, 1920s, 33in (84cm) long.
£45–75 *Ech*

A string of pink and black glass flapper beads, 1920s, 34in (86.5cm) long.
£35–55 *Ech*

An ivory tulle cocktail dress, embroidered with arches in opalescent sequins, with a band of rosettes at the hip, mid-1920s.
£300–350 *CSK*

A blue tinted glass model of a fish, by Guy Underwood, on a green painted metal wave scroll base, registration number, signature and dated '1931' on base, 7¼in (18.5cm) high.
£140–180 *DN*

An opalescent glass vase, 'Beliers', by René Lalique, with beast-shaped handles, on a circular foot, etched mark, c1925, 7½in (19cm) high.
£800–900 *DN*

A WMF decorative pewter plaque, 1920s, 10 by 13in (25 by 33cm).
£250–300 *HEM*

A gilt spelter figure, 'The Hoop Dancer', on marble base, 15in (38cm) high.
£500–550 *WTA*

An HMV chromium plated electric heater, designed by Christian Barman, consisting of 4 graduated rounded layers, maker's label on reverse, 8¼in (21cm) high.
£450–550 *P*

A brass table lamp, with a green glass shade, 1920s, 18in (45.5cm) high.
£125–135 *LIB*

A brass mascot, of a swallow, c1930.
£120–160 *MCh*

A bronzed half-kneeling nude female figure table lamp, her arms outstretched to a frosted glass globular shade, on a rectangular base with leaf motif corners, 7½in (19cm) high.
£375–475 *MCA*

A work basket on a stand, c1920, 28in (71cm) high.
£75–85 *MofC*

ART NOUVEAU

An oak cigar box, decorated with pewter strapwork of organic form and green cabochon stones, early 20thC, 5½in (14cm) high.
£110–150 *WIL*

A Liberty Tudric pewter jug, of slightly tapering form, the lower body cast with leaping fish, stamped 'Tudric 0174', c1903, 7½in (19cm) high.
£225–275 *MSW*

A Royal Dux allegorical figure vase, 'Historia', drilled for electricity, 14in (35.5cm) high.
£375–450 *AAV*

A coloured lithograph poster, 'Cycles Perfecta', by Achille Butteri, printed by Kossuth, Paris, backed on linen, framed, damaged, 63 by 47in (160 by 119.5cm).
£625–725 *CSK*

A pair of cast bronze candlesticks, by Henn Sorensen, Paris, c1900, 12in (30.5cm) high.
£2,000–2,750 *SHa*

An Austrian enamelled on silver cigarette case, by Georg Adam Scheld, marked 'G.A.S.', c1900, 3in (7.5cm) long.
£650–700 *JES*

Miller's is a price GUIDE not a price LIST

An Art Nouveau metal belt, c1900, 28in (71cm) long.
£50–75 *Ech*

An Art Nouveau metal belt, c1900, 25in (63.5cm) long.
£45–75 *Ech*

ARTISTS' EASELS

An artist's oak drawing table, with adjustable tilt and height mechanism, 71in (180.5cm) high unextended.
£275–350 *CSK*

An artist's oak studio easel, with adjustable winding mechanism on an H-frame, 64½in (164cm) high unextended.
£475–575 *CSK*

A late Victorian artist's tubular brass easel, with adjustable picture rest, 60in (152.4cm) high.
£500–600 *HCC*

An artist's oak studio easel, with adjustable winding mechanism on an H-frame, labelled 'Lefranc/Paris', 65in (165cm) high unextended.
£350–450 *CSK*

MAKE THE MOST OF MILLER'S

Price ranges in this book reflect what you should expect to *pay* for a similar example. When selling, however, you should expect to receive a lower figure. This will fluctuate according to a dealer's stock and saleability at a particular time. It is always advisable, when selling a collectable, to approach a reputable dealer or an auction house which has specialist sales.

An easel, c1880, 74in (188cm) high.
£50–60 *AL*

l. An artist's oak studio easel, with adjustable winding mechanism on an H-frame, 92¾in (235.5cm) high unextended.
£500–600 *CSK*

An easel, c1920, 49in (124.5cm) high.
£30–35 *AL*

A blackboard easel, c1920, 69in (175.5cm) high.
£65–75 *AL*

AUTOMOBILIA

A selection of items commemorating Sir Malcolm Campbell's world land speed record in 'Bluebird', c1930.
Top. **£200–250**
Bottom. **£100–150** *MCh*

l. A wooden advertising panel, from the Piccadilly, London, showrooms of Lovegroves, London Motoring Suppliers, c1903, 24in (61cm) square.
£350–450 *MCh*

A pair of Marchal headlights, chrome plated with aluminium rims, reflector and bull's-eyes, 10in (25.5cm) diam.
£500–600 *CSK*

An Austin Motor Co crimson leather scripted factory photograph frame, and a cased silver lapel pin, mid-1920s, 12in (30.5cm) high.
£200–250 *MCh*

r. A wooden and aluminium scratch-built model of a 1907 Rolls-Royce Silver Ghost, built during WWII by a prisoner of war, 14in (35.5cm) long.
£300–400 *MCh*

An original black and white photograph of Lord Harmsworth and passengers on board his entry for the Automobile Club 1000 Miles Trial, 1900, 8¾ by 10¼in (22 by 26cm), framed.
£90–110 *ONS*

Top. An 18ct gold plated limited edition Jaguar key chain, c1980.
£20–30
Bottom. A nickel silver Michelin 'Bibendum' key chain, c1920.
£40–60 *MCh*

A calendar showcard for Automobiles, Richard Raoul, 1933, 8 by 19½in (21 by 49cm).
£200–250 *ONS*

A selection of Mercedes-Benz publicity booklets, including Hans Bretz, *Mannschaft und Meisterschaft, Eine Bilanz der Grand-Prix-Formel, 1934–37,* published by Daimler-Benz, 1938, German text, and *Mercedes-Benz Presse Information*, c1955, with 3 factory brochures and a letter from Mercedes-Benz, 1937.
£190–240 *CSK*

An enamel lapel badge, inscribed 'HRG', late 1940s, 1in (2.5cm) wide.
£50–60 *MSMP*

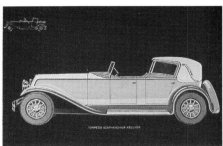

A Renault Cars thirty-page brochure, including illustrations of the Reinastella Eight Cylinder, Vivastella Six Cylinder and Monastella Six Cylinder, with colour coachwork studies, published by Draeger, Paris, 1920–30s.
£90–110 *CSK*

Frederick Gordon Crosby, French Grand Prix Montlhéry, July 1925, Benoist in the winning Delage at 69.7mph, watercolour and charcoal heightened with white, signed and inscribed 'Paris', dated '27.7.25', 14½in (37cm) square, framed.
£1,700–2,200 *ONS*

r. L'Illustration magazine, Automobile et Tourisme issue, colour cover artwork by Geo. Ham., 3rd October 1936, and another, 5th October 1935.
£45–60 *CSK*

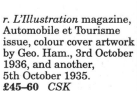

A Rothmans Formula 5000
European Championship
programme, 1974.
50p–£2 *PC*

A replica motorcycle helmet, cork and leather construction by
Cromwell, finished in white and gold with red lining and Isle of Man
flag, autographed by Mike Hailwood, size 7⅛in.
£225–250 *CSK*

Badges

An Edwardian
RAC Full Member's
double-sided car
badge, 6½in (16.5cm)
high, mounted
on a plinth.
£100–150 *MCh*

An Edwardian RAC Full
Member's car badge, 6½in
(16.5cm) high.
£140–160 *MCh*

r. A leather rimmed steering
wheel, by Momo, from the
winning car driven by Ronnie
Peterson in the 1973 French
Grand Prix, the plaque
engraved by W. R. Bullen Ltd,
jewellers, Norwich, 11in
(28cm) diam.
£1,000–1,250 *CSK*

r. An RAC Associate
Member's car badge,
late 1920s.
£60–80 *MCh*

l. A Motor Racing
Register enamel badge,
No. 276, in 3 colours,
4½in (11.5cm) high, on
a wooden base, and a
copy of *The Motor
Racing Register,
1961–62,* members'
booklet, first edition.
£260–300 *S*

An AA display badge, 1920s,
14in (35.5cm) high.
£150–200 *MCh*

Ceramics

A biscuit porcelain cruet, inscribed
'A Present From Blackpool',
c1914, 4in (10cm) wide.
£100–140 *MCh*

A selection of Morris Bullnose commemorative
items, including a glass, spirit bottle and a one
pint teacup with saucer, 1950s, bottle 4in
(10cm) high.
£60–70 *MCh*

Mascots

A frosted glass erotic car
mascot, after a design
believed to be by Red
Ashay, repair to right
foot, 8½in (21.5cm) high.
£600–650 *S*

A German porcelain model of a car,
with flowers on the front, c1903, 3in
(7.5cm) long.
£140–170 *MCh*

A Wedgwood Rolls-Royce
limited edition plate, 1986.
£60–80 *MCh*

A mascot of a hornet, by Asprey &
Co, set with garnet eyes, 1920s,
7in (17.5cm) wingspan.
£350–450 *MCh*

An alsatian dog mascot,
by E. Illinisky, cast by
Lumière et Cie, signed,
1920s, 6¼in (16cm) high,
mounted on a turned
wooden base.
£1,200–1,500 *S*

A German relaxed dog
mascot, on a pillar
radiator cap mount,
c1914, 6in (15cm) high.
£220–260 *MCh*

l. A mascot of a British bulldog,
1920s, 5in (12.5cm) high.
£200–260 *MCh*

A Riley chromium plated mascot, of a ski-ing lady, stamped with registered No. '759377', mounted on a wood display base, c1920, 5in (12.5cm) high.
£500–600 CSK

A brass mascot of a swift, from a Swift two-seater car, c1922, 3in (7.5cm) high.
£140–180 MCh

A bronze mascot of a pagan goat, 1920s, 3½in (9cm) high.
£220–280 MCh

r. A mascot of a running fox, by A. E. L., 1920s, 4in (10cm) high.
£120–180 MCh

An American chrome plated greyhound mascot, for a Lincoln car, c1929, 8in (20cm) high.
£300–400 MCh

A polished brass mascot of King George V, rubbed and worn, c1910, 4¼in (11cm) high.
£95–120 S

A French mascot of a cockerel, from a Gallier Oil Company delivery lorry, 1926, 4in (10cm) high.
£220–260 MCh

l. A mascot of a bald eagle, c1930, 5in (12.5cm) high.
£120–150 *TAR*

r. A mascot of a prancing horse, 1950s.
£160–180 *MCh*

A mascot, depicting a caricature of a Morris Motors' foreman, c1920.
£200–300 *MCh*

l. A Rolls-Royce Spirit of Ecstasy mascot, for the Silver Shadow and Corniche, c1970.
£250–300 *MCh*

A brass mascot of Mercury, c1910, 6in (15cm) high.
£140–185 *MCh*

A bronze display model of the the Rolls-Royce Spirit of Ecstasy, the base signed 'Charles Sykes No. 28', mounted on a circular marble base, 21in (53.5cm) high.
£3,200–3,500 *CSK*

A Straker-Squire nickel plated mascot, 1921, unmarked, 5¼in (13.5cm) high, on a turned wooden base.
£150–175 *S*

An enamelled mascot, of Hermione the witch and the wheel of fortune, with a revolving roulette wheel, c1921, 5½in (14cm) high.
£300–400 *MCh*

Mascots

- Mascots appear in motoring accessory catalogues from c1905
- Many different varieties of mascots were produced between the two World Wars
- Mascots fall into two main categories:
  - Official mascots, approved by vehicle manufacturers and designed for a specific type of car, eg the Rolls-Royce 'Spirit of Ecstasy', created by Charles Sykes
  - Decorative mascots such as animals, comic characters and sporting themes, produced as accessories for any vehicle
- The rising value of mascots has led to the appearance of many reproductions on the market
- Beware of mascots that have been replated and look 'as good as new'
- Buy from a reputable auction house or dealer

Posters

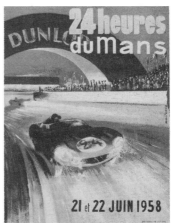

After Geo. Ham., a poster for the 2e Grand Prix de Paris, 24 April 1949, at Linas-Montlhéry, 23½ by 15¾in (60 by 40cm).
£350–380 *ONS*

Geo. Ham., a lithograph for Yacco, Rallye Monte Carlo, 1959, in colours, backed on linen, printed by Bouchet Lakara, Paris, slight damage, 31 by 23in (79 by 59cm).
£250–300 *CSK*

After Beligond, a poster on linen for the 24 heures du Mans race, June 1958, 15½ by 11½in (39 by 29cm).
£150–200 *ONS*

Tankards & Trophies

Miller's is a price GUIDE not a price LIST

l. Two Jack Lemon Burton trophies, Midland Automobile Club Autumn Open Hillclimb Shelsley Walsh team event winners, Bugatti Owners' Club 1932, and fast time Racing Cars Class 3 1932, each with wooden bases with Midland Automobile Club enamel badges.
£170–220 *ONS*

An EPNS motorcycle tankard, awarded to J. L. Goddard in the 10 lap Handicap at Brooklands, 1934, 6in (15cm) high.
£140–180 *MCh*

A BARC Brooklands Junior Car Club clubhouse silver plated half pint beer tankard, early 1930s.
£100–150 *MCh*

BELLS

A goat's bell, with a leather and brass collar, c1930, bell 3½in (9cm) wide.
£18–20 *TaB*

r. A French metal bell, early 19thC, 13½in (34.5cm) high.
£15–20 *AnE*

BICYCLES

A Vandre gentleman's solid tyred safety bicycle, French, c1884–88.
£850–1,150 *MCh*

A Matchless penny-farthing bicycle, c1884, leading wheel 60in (152cm) diam.
£2,250–2,850 *MCh*

A reproduction Ordinary bicycle, with metal spoked rubber tyred wheel, turned wooden handlebars, seat, lamp and bell, leading wheel 47in (119cm) diam.
£550–650 *CSK*

A Dursley & Pederson duplex cross-framed gentleman's safety bicycle, with strung suspended saddle and original maker's badge, three-speed open cog gearing, front and back braking, unrestored, c1900.
£1,700–2,000 *HOLL*

A Victorian child's solid tyred tricycle, German, 1880s.
£500–700 *MCh*

A Sunbeam gentleman's bicycle, with three-speed gearing and ornate Brooks saddle, original condition, c1920.
£210–250 *MR*

An Antelope lady's bicycle, unrestored, c1926.
£160–180 *MR*

A general purpose delivery bicycle, with small front wheel and tubular front carrier and stand, 1940s.
£150–160 *MR*

A Sunbeam gentleman's bicycle, with three-speed high and low gearing, original condition, c1924.
£210–250 *MR*

A Vindec gentleman's bicycle, by Brown Bros Ltd, 1940s.
£50–60 *S*

A butcher's delivery bicycle, with basket, mid-20thC.
£60–70 *S*

A Halford's gentleman's bicycle, with rod-operated brakes, 1950s.
£15–20 *S*

A Power Pak 50cc assisted bicycle, 1962.
£200–250 *S*

This is an example of the ubiquitous Power Pak 50cc two-stroke engine attached to a Rudge Whitworth gentleman's bicycle.

A Lotus Sport monocoque bicycle, designed by Mike Borrows, with carbon fibre frame and Turbolite saddle, 27in (68.5cm) frame, with Lotus Sport quilted custom cover, cycle stand, a copy of *QED The Bike* script and *Freewheel Cycling Directory*, 1993.
£2,400–2,800 *S*

Lamps

A Lucas King of the Road penny-farthing lamp, c1890, 9in (23cm) high.
£475–500 *FAL*

A Lucas nickelled bicycle candle headlamp, with box of Price's cycle candles, 1890s.
£300–400 *MCh*

A Miller 'Edlite' oil bicycle headlamp, English, c1910.
£200–300 *MCh*

A Lucas Colonia bicycle lamp, c1910, 7in (17.5cm) high.
£55–65 *FAL*

A Lucas King of the Road acetylene bicycle lamp, c1910, 7in (17.5cm) high.
£65–75 *FAL*

A Victorian 'The Dot' bicycle oil headlamp, c1898.
£220–260 *MCh*

l. A French acetylene cycle headlamp, nickel finish on brass, early 20thC.
£120–160 *MCh*

A Lucas 'Microphote' oil bicycle headlamp.
£200–300 *MCh*

A Powell & Hanmer Demon bicycle lamp, 1920s, 4½in (11.5cm) high.
£15–20 *FAL*

A nickelled brass acetylene bicycle headlamp, c1910.
£100–140 *MCh*

r. A Lucas Aceta bicycle lamp, 1920s, 6in (15cm) high.
£30–40 *FAL*

A Lucas 'Planet' oil bicycle rear lamp, with original box, unused, c1928.
£130–160 *MCh*

A Powell & Hanmer Colonial bicycle lamp, c1922, 4½in (11.5cm) high.
£20–25 *FAL*

A Miller bicycle lamp, 1920s, 6in (15cm) high.
£20–28 *FAL*

BIRD CAGES

A French bird cage, c1900, 21in (53cm) wide.
£40–65 *FOX*

A Welsh primitive linnet trap, with original painted surface and wirework, c1840, 9¼in (23.5cm) high.
£200–300 *RYA*

A Spanish bird cage, c1950, 10in (25.5cm) high.
£30–40 *TaB*

BOOK ILLUSTRATIONS

Barbara Constance Freeman, 'The Letter', signed 'B.C. Freeman', pen and black ink and watercolour, heightened with touches of white heightening, 12 by 9in (30.5 by 23cm).
£200–250 *CSK*

Gerald Edward Moira, 'Blow, Blow, thou Winter Wind . . .', signed 'G. E. Moira', inscribed as title and further extensively inscribed, pen and black ink, 11½ by 8in (29 by 20in).
£225–275 *CSK*

John Austen, An illustration to Gustave Flaubert's *Madame Bovary*, 'The Vicomte was far away', signed and dated, John. Austen. 28', pencil, pen and grey ink and grey wash, unframed, 7 by 4½in (17.5 by 11.5cm).
£200–250 *CSK*

l. William Heath Robinson, 'The Storks; The Marsh King's Daughter', 2 illustrations for Hans Andersen's *Fairy Tales*, signed with monograms, pen and ink on paper, 1913, 14½ by 10½in (36.5 by 26.5cm).
£300–350 *BBA*

Edward Ardizzone, *Hugh the Drover; or, Love in the Stocks*, signed 'Diz' and inscribed as title, pen and black ink, 7½ by 13in (19 by 33cm).
£325–400 *CSK*

Alan Elsden Odle, An illustration to John Austen's *The ABC of Pen and Ink Rendering*, pencil, pen and black ink and brush, unframed, 11 by 8in (28 by 20cm).
£350–400 *CSK*

BOOKMARKS

A silver bookmark, Birmingham, c1900, 3½in (9cm) long.
£55–65 *GLN*

A silver bookmark, Birmingham 1901, 2½in (6.5cm) long.
£40–50 *GLN*

A sterling silver bookmark, c1900, 2½in (6.5cm) long.
£30–40 *GLN*

BOOKS

This year we have decided to concentrate on travel books, a field that continues to grow in popularity. As antiquarian book dealer Peter Harrington explains, collectors often tend to buy along nationalistic lines: the English want books about English voyages, Middle Eastern collectors buy accounts of the Orient and Americans lead the demand for works exploring the United States.

According to the Travel Bookshop in London, popular subjects at the moment include Africa, India, the Middle East, Asia and Russia, with European countries lagging somewhat behind these more exotic locations. With travel books, as with books in general, good condition is crucial to value and desirability.

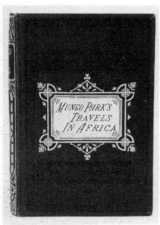

Mungo Park, *The Life and Travels of Mungo Park,* with illustrations, Edinburgh, 1872, good condition, small 8vo.
£8–10 *HB*

Richard F. Burton, *Vikram and the Vampire, or Tales of Hindu Devilry,* illustrated by Ernest Crisel, first edition, 1870, 7½ by 5¼in (19 by 13cm).
£150–200 *HB*

Paul B. Du Chaillu, *Land of the Midnight Sun,* with map and 235 illustrations, in 2 volumes, published by Harper & Brothers, New York, 1881, clean copies internally, inner hinges split, worn at extremities, 8vo.
£40–50 *HB*

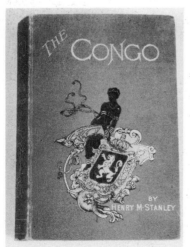

Henry M. Stanley, *The Congo,* published by Harpers, New York, 1885, 7½ by 5in (19 by 12.5cm).
£200–240 *TBS*

> **Miller's is a price GUIDE not a price LIST**

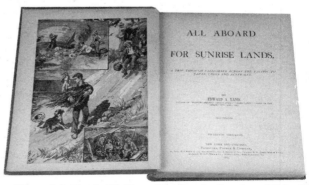

Edward A. Rand, *All Aboard for Sunrise Lands,* published by Fairbanks, Palmer & Company, New York and Chicago, 1883, 9 by 7¼in (23 by 18.5cm).
£35–45 *TBS*

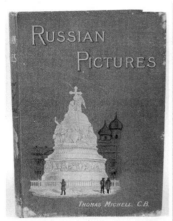

Thomas Michell, *Russian Pictures,* published by Religious Tract Society, 1889, 11 by 8in (28 by 20cm).
£20–30 *HB*

Lady Brassey, *In the Trades, The Tropics, & The Roaring Forties,* published by Henry Holt, New York, 1885, 8 by 5½in (20 x 14cm).
£40–50 *HB*

r. Voyages and Travels, published by E. W. Walker, 1887, 12½ by 9½in (31.5 by 24cm).
£10–20 *HB*

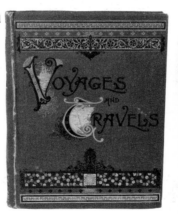

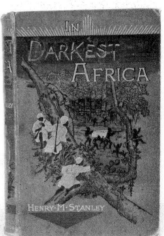

George Smith, *Assyrian Discoveries,* published by Sampson Low & Co, 1883, 8 by 5½in (20 by 14cm).
£70–80 *HB*

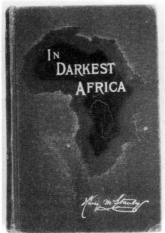

r. Henry M. Stanley, *In Darkest Africa,* published by Scribners, 1890, 7½ by 5in (19 by 12.5cm).
£145–165 *TBS*

Henry M. Stanley, *In Darkest Africa,* with 150 woodcut illustrations and maps, first edition, London, 1890, good condition, 8vo.
£90–120 *HB*

Murray's Hand-Book, New Zealand, first edition, published by Mercantile Library, 1893, 6¾ by 4¾in (17 by 12cm).
£10–15 *HB*

A. Henry Savage Landor, *The Forbidden Land,* first edition, published by William Heinemann, London, 1899, 9 by 6in (23 by 15cm).
£35–45 *HB*

l. Frank Fox, *Australia,* painted by Percy F. S. Spence, published by A. & C. Black, 1910, 9 by 6¾in (23 by 17cm), with loose jacket.
£125–150 *TBS*

Indian Pictures, c1870, 11 by 8in (28 by 20cm).
£20–30 *HB*

Cross Reference: Aeronautica

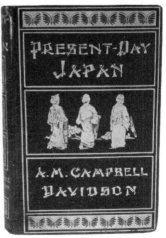

Martin Conway, *The Alps,* painted by A. D. McCormick, first edition, published by A. & C. Black, London 1904, 9 by 6½in (23 by 16.5cm).
£30–40 *HB*

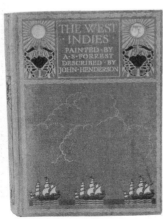

l. John Henderson, *The West Indies,* illustrated by A. S. Forrest, first edition, published by A. & C. Black, 1905, 9 by 6½in (23 by 16.5cm).
£40–50 *HB*

Augusta M. Campbell Davidson, *Present-Day Japan,* published by J. B. Lippincott Company, Philadelphia, T. Fisher Unwin, London, 1904, 8 by 5½in (20 by 14cm).
£35–45 *HB*

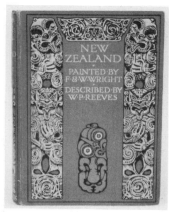

W. P. Reeves, *New Zealand,*
illustrated by F. & W. Wright,
first edition, with map,
published by A. & C. Black,
1908, 9½ by 7in (24 by 17.5cm).
£50–60 *HB*

Eileen Bigland, *Into China,*
published by Macmillan, 1940,
9½ by 6½in (24 by 16.5cm).
£35–40 *TBS*

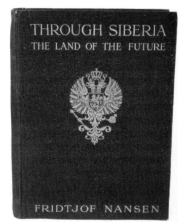

Fridtjof Nansen, *Through Siberia,
The Land of the Future,* first
English edition, published by
W. Heinemann, 1914, 10 by 7½in
(25.5 by 19cm).
£75–90 *HB*

l. Revd Samuel G. Green,
French Pictures, published by
Religious Tract Society, c1870,
8 by 5½in (20 by 14cm).
£10–15 *HB*

Jane Morris, *Venice,* published by
Faber & Faber, 1960, 7½ by 5in
(19 by 12.5cm).
£8–10 *TBS*

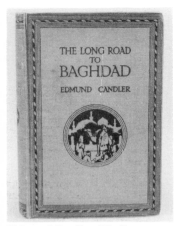

Edmund Candler, *The Long Road to Baghdad,* published by Cassell & Co, 1919, 9½ by 6in (24 by 15cm).
£30–40 *HB*

Julian Street, *Mysterious Japan,* published by Doubleday, Page & Co, New York, 1925, 7½ by 5in (19 by 12.5cm).
£45–50 *TBS*

Bernard Newman, *Tito's Yugoslavia,* published by Robert Hale, London, 1952, 8¾ by 5½in (22 by 14cm).
£10–15 *TBS*

l. H. V. Morton, *A Traveller in Rome,* first published 1957 by Methuen, 7½ by 5in (19 by 12.5cm).
£10–12 *TBS*

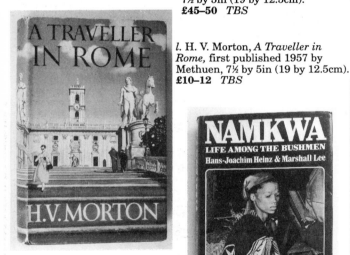

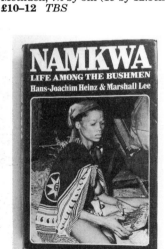

Hans-Joachim Heinz and Marshall Lee, *Namkwa, Life Among the Bushmen,* published by Jonathan Cape, 1978, 7½ by 5in (19 by 12.5cm).
£8–10 *TBS*

l. Ernle Bradford, *The Wind off the Island,* published by Hutchinson, 1960, 8¾ by 5¾in (22 by 14.5cm).
£10–15 *TBS*

Revd Samuel Manning, *Italian Pictures,* published by Religious Tract Society, c1870, 11 by 8in (28 by 20cm).
£20–30 *HB*

BOXES

A Victorian tooled leather letter holder, 10in (25cm) wide.
£100–120 *WCA*

A Swiss singing bird box, the tortoiseshell case with engraved gilt metal oval cover, 4in (10cm) wide, in box, with key.
£1,200–1,500 *DN*

A rosewood tea caddy, of sarcophagus form, inlaid with panels of mother-of-pearl, scrolls and foliage and with brass lines, the interior fitted with 2 compartments, on compressed bun feet, 19thC, 9½in (24cm) wide.
£80–100 *GAK*

A Regency mahogany tea caddy, with 2 interior lidded compartments and glass mixing bowl, 11in (28cm) wide.
£150–200 *TMi*

l. A burr walnut tea caddy, the domed lid applied with central gilt metal cruciform motif and ivorine panels, similar escutcheon, with 2 interior compartments, 19thC, 9in (23cm) wide.
£110–140 *GAK*

A rosewood writing slope, with brass banding, early 19thC, 13½in (34.5cm) wide.
£200–250 *TMi*

l. An Anglo-Indian tortoiseshell and bone jewellery box, with mounted pierced, engraved and painted plaques, interior mirror, lift-out fitted tray and blue plush lining, on claw feet, 13¼in (33.5cm) wide.
£620–650 *Bri*

BREWERIANA

According to breweriana specialist Richard Veness, most enthusiasts begin with an appreciation of beer itself and much as the informed drinker wants real ale, so the breweriana collector wants material from rare and interesting breweries. Popular sources include the now extinct small breweries, taken over by major firms such as Watney's and Whitbread's in the early 1960s and, more recently, the many smaller micro-breweries that have opened up over the last 15 years or so, only to close again almost immediately, leaving desirable memorabilia behind them.

Objects collected include pub jugs, Wade examples being particularly desirable, pump clips as well as beer labels are extremely popular in the current market. The latter are prized both for the rarity of the beer or brewery and the aesthetic qualities of the colour printing. Most of the best quality beer labels came direct from the bottling plants in sheets and were never applied to the bottles in the first place.

Advertising Figures

A Heineken Beer advertising figure, 1960s, 9in (23cm) high.
£50–60 *DBr*

A set of 3 Worthington E advertising figures, 1960s, 9in (23cm) high.
£350–400 *DBr*

Ashtrays

A Guinness matchbox holder and ashtray, by Minton, 1940s–50s, ashtray 5in (12.5cm) diam.
£38–45 *ED*

A Lamb's Navy Rum ceramic ashtray, by Royal Norfolk, 1960s, 5in (12.5cm) diam.
£10–12 *COL*

Beer Bottle Labels

A Meux's Brewery Co Limited London, Country Brown Ale label, 1940s, 4½in by 2½in (11.5 by 6.5cm).
£5–6 *ED*

> **Cross Reference**
> Advertising & Packaging
> Drinking

l. A Bass ceramic ashtray, by T. G. Green, 1940s, 7in (17.5cm) wide.
£10–12 *ED*

The Obsessional Collector

Local government official, Keith Osborne's collection of beer labels, numbering some 30,000 examples and worth a reputed £50,000, earned him a place in the Guinness Book of Records and the reputation of being the leading 'labologist' in Britain. It also brought his downfall. In 1994, Osborne was sentenced to 18 months in prison (reduced to 6 months on appeal) for stealing 28 beer labels, dating between 1884–1925, from the Public Record office at Kew.

A Cheltenham & Hereford Breweries Ltd Cheltenham Ale label, 1950s, 2¾ by 2in (7 by 5cm).
£7–8 *ED*

A Clubs Aylesford Brewery Club Brown label, 1930s, 4 by 3in (10 by 7.5cm).
£12–15 *ED*

A Benskin's Brewery Jubilee Beer label, 1948, 3 by 2in (7.5 by 5cm).
£7–8 *ED*

A Gardener's Ash Brewery Extra Stout label, 1940s, 4 by 2½in (10 by 6.5cm).
£8–10 *ED*

A Fred[k]. Smith's Aston, Birmingham Brewery Strong Ale label, 1940s, 3 by 1¾in (7.5 by 4.5cm).
£5–6 *ED*

A Guinness Dublin & London Brewery Extra Stout label, 1930s, 4 by 2½in (10 by 6.5cm).
£8–10 *ED*

A Tennants, Sheffield, Lion Pale Ale label, 1950s, 2¾ by 1¾in (7 by 4.5cm).
£3–4 *ED*

A Charrington & Co Ltd London Brewery Oatmeal Stout label, 1940s, 4½ by 2½in (11.5 by 6.5cm).
£8–10 *ED*

A Chas. Hammerton & Co Ltd London Brewery Essex Brown Ale label, 1940s, 4 by 2½in (10 by 6.5cm).
£8–10 *ED*

An H. E. Thornley Leamington Brewery Dreadnought Strong Ale label, 1950s, 3 by 2in (7.5 by 5cm).
£6–7 *ED*

A James Hole Newark-on-Trent Brewery Light Bitter Ale label, 1950s, 3½ by 2½in (9 by 6.5cm).
£4–5 *ED*

A John Joule & Sons' Limited Brewery Stone Ale label, 1940s, 3½ by 1¾in (9 by 4.5cm).
£6–7 *ED*

A Mowbray's Grantham Brewery Brown Ale label, 1950s, 3 by 2½in (7.5 by 6.5cm).
£7–8 *ED*

A Mappin's Brewery Ltd, Rotherham, India Pale Ale label, 1950s, 4 by 2in (10 by 5cm).
£4–5 *ED*

Label Removal

The bottle should be soaked in lukewarm water overnight. The label should detach itself and be left floating on the surface of the water.

A Matthews & Co, Gillingham, Dorset Brewery, Pale Ale label, 1950s, 4 by 2½in (10 by 6.5cm).
£6–7 *ED*

l. A Mappin's Brewery Ltd Rotherham, Chantry Ale label, 1950s, 4 by 2in (10 by 5cm).
£4–5 *ED*

A Wards Ltd Foxearth Brewery Imperial Ale label, 1940s, 2½ by 1½in (6.5 by 4cm).
£5–6 *ED*

Beer Mats

A Watney Mann World Cup Ale mat, 1966, 5¼in (13.5cm) high.
£2–3 *PC*

A Walkers Summit Stout mat, 1960s, 3½in (9cm) square.
25–50p *PC*

An England's Glory matches beer mat, 1960s, 3½in (9cm) square.
40–50p *PC*

Pub Jugs

l. A glass water jug, advertising John Jameson Whiskey, 1950s, 4in (10cm) high.
£50–60 *COL*

r. A Woodbine beer mat, 1960, 3¼in (9cm) diam.
40–50p *PC*

A Dartmouth Pottery water jug, advertising Plymouth Gin, 1950s, 11in (28cm) high.
£25–30 *ED*

A Martell Cognac pottery water jug and ashtray, by Seton Pottery, Cornwall, as a limited edition for the Grand National 1994, jug 10in (25.5cm) high, ashtray 6in (15cm) wide.
£30–35 *ED*

A Wade water jug, advertising VAT 69 Scotch Whisky, 1960s, 6in (15cm) high.
£18–20 *COL*

A Wade water jug, advertising Teacher's Whisky, 1960s, 4½in (11.5cm) high.
£20–25 *COL*

A Wade water jug, advertising Johnnie Walker Whisky, 1960s, 6½in (16.5cm) high.
£18–20 *COL*

Pump Clips

An Adnams, Southwold, Bitter enamel on metal pump clip, 1980s, 4½in (11.5cm) high.
£8–10 *ED*

The Old Forge Brewery, Hastings, Brothers Best plastic pump clip, 1990s, 4½ by 3in (11.5 by 7.5cm).
£4–5 *ED*

A Flowers (Whitbread), London, Original Bitter enamel on brass pump clip, 1980s, 3½in (9cm) diam.
£8–10 *ED*

A Greene King, Bury St Edmunds, IPA Bitter china pump clip, 1980s, 5in (12.5cm) high.
£8–10 *ED*

A Walker, Warrington, Best Bitter enamel on brass pump clip, 1980s, 5in (12.5cm) high.
£8–10 *ED*

A King & Barnes, Horsham, Sussex Mild plastic pump clip, 1980s, 4½in (11.5cm) diam.
£4–5 *ED*

r. A Titanic Brewery Valiant Stout plastic pump clip, 1990s, 2½ by 4in (6.5 by 10cm).
£4–5 *ED*

BUTTONS

Buttons are known to have been used from the 6th Century AD, but the most commonly found examples date from the 19th and 20th centuries. According to Mrs Meredith, proprietor of Britain's only button museum, buttons are often extremely hard to date. 'If a particular line sold well it could go on being produced for ages and ages,' she explains. 'Similarly designs would go in and out of fashion and two buttons that appear identical might have been produced at different periods by different techniques.'

Buttons have been made from every conceivable substance from the finest jewels in the 16th century to the cheapest modern-day plastics. In the 19th century, Britain (notably Birmingham), was the main centre for the mass production of buttons both of metal and shell (known as pearl or mother-of-pearl).

As Mrs Meredith notes, until the 20th century, buttons were not generally washable and were removed when clothes were cleaned, hence the reason why they came with detachable clips. 'Some could be extremely fine and people would buy a boxed set of buttons in the same way that they might a gift of jewellery,' she explains.

There are collectors of every type of button. One of the best and cheapest sources of finding old examples is in the family button boxes that often turn up at charity shops or car-boot sales. These can contain buttons preserved by several generations.

A French black glass button, with fly design, c1900, ½in (12.7mm) diam.
£15–18 *MRW*

A button, with lithograph of a sportsman, c1900, ½in (12.7mm) diam.
£18–20 *MRW*

r. Two reverse painted buttons, mounted in brass with borders of colour set brilliants, c1790, largest ¾in (19mm) diam.
£50–60 each *EBB*

l. A glass embossed button, 1890, 1½in (38mm) diam.
£20–25 *MRW*

l. Four Victorian stamped brass studs, decorated with sporting images and galante figures in high relief, 1½in (38mm) diam.
£8–12 each *EBB*

A Japanese Meiji button, c1890, 1¾in (45mm) diam.
£60–80 *MRW*

A French repoussé button, c1900, 1½in (38mm) diam.
£15–25 *MRW*

A picture button, c1970, ¾in (19mm) diam.
£10–12 *MRW*

A set of 6 late Victorian cut steel buttons, 1½in (38mm) diam.
£18–25 *MRW*

A selection of shell buttons, 19thC, largest 1½in (38mm) diam.
£3–5 each *EBB*

Six buttons, each with a lithograph of a lady's head, c1900, ½in (12.7mm) diam.
£15–18 each *MRW*

A selection of glass boot buttons, c1900, ¼in (6.3mm) diam.
£6–20 each *MRW*

r. A boxed set of 6 Edwardian enamel and mother-of-pearl inlay buttons, with rings, ½in (12.7mm) diam.
£20–30 *Ech*

BUTTONHOOKS

A silver buttonhook, Birmingham 1908, 8¾in (22cm) long.
£20–25 *WN*

Two mid-Victorian mother-of-pearl buttonhooks, with silver blades, 1¼ and 2¼in (3 and 5.5cm) long.
£18–25 each *MRW*

CAMERAS

An Asahi Pentax S1a camera, f2.2
Auto-Takumar lens, c1959, 5½in
(14cm) wide.
£50–70 *VCL*

A Canon F-1 camera,
No. 107866, with Canon
Booster-T finder, 250 film
chamber, motor drive unit,
battery case and handgrip.
£750–850 *CSK*

An Agfa camera, 127 film,
c1936, 2½in (6.5cm) wide.
£20–30 *VCL*

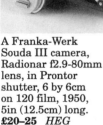

A Coronet Vogue brown
Bakelite camera, c1937,
4in (10cm) wide.
£50–60 *VCL*

A Contax I camera, f1.5 Sonnar lens,
c1936, 5½in (14cm) wide.
£150–300 *VCL*

A Franka-Werk
Souda III camera,
Radionar f2.9-80mm
lens, in Prontor
shutter, 6 by 6cm
on 120 film, 1950,
5in (12.5cm) long.
£20–25 *HEG*

An Ensign Midget camera,
c1936, 3½in (9cm) wide.
£30–40 *VCL*

l. A Franke & Heidecke
Rolleiflex camera, f2.8
No. 2418692 with light
meter, Heidosmat f2.8
80mm viewing lens No.
869026, Carl Zeiss Planar
f2.8 80mm, taking lens
No. 3405066 in a Synchro-
Compur shutter, in maker's
leather ever-ready case.
£720–800 *CSK*

A Horizont Panoramic 35mm camera, Russian, c1969, 5½in (14cm) wide.
£100–200 *VCL*

A Houghton Ticka camera, with polished metal body, lens cap attached to body by chain, viewfinder, time and instantaneous shutter, with instruction booklet, in maker's box.
£200–250 *P*

A Franke & Heidecke Baby Rolleiflex camera, 4 by 4cm on 127 film, c1938, 2½in (6.5cm) wide.
£100–200 *VCL*

An Ilford Advocate 35mm camera, cast metal with ivory enamelled finish, 1953, 5½in (14cm) wide, with leather case.
£50–75 *HEG*

A Houghton Carbine camera, 6 by 9cm, c1930, 3in (7.5cm) wide.
£10–20 *VCL*

A Kodak vest pocket camera, 127 film, c1920, 2½in (6.5cm) wide.
£15–30 *VCL*

> **Miller's is a price GUIDE not a price LIST**

An Ilford Craftsman Reflex camera, c1950, 3in (7.5cm) wide.
£20–30 *VCL*

A Kodak Jiffy vest pocket camera, black Bakelite, 127 film, c1940, 6in (15cm) long.
£25–35 *HEG*

An Eastman Kodak Bantam Special folding camera, f2 Kodak Anastigmat Ektar lens and Compur Rapid, 1 sec-1/500 sec shutter, c1938, in an Art Deco metal case.
£200–250 *DN*

A Kodak Duo 620 camera, with folding finder and Compur shutter, c1938, 5in (12.5cm) wide.
£30–40 *HEG*

A Kodak Hawkeye Ace Deluxe box camera, 127 roll film, 1938, 3½in (9cm) long.
£10–15 *HEG*

A Kodak Retinette IIB camera, c1960, 5in (12.5cm) wide.
£50–60 *VCL*

The Kombi combined camera and viewer, c1892, 1½in (3.5cm) wide.
£100–200 *VCL*

A Leica M2 camera, serial No. 989739, Summicron 5cm 1.2 chrome lens and meter M.R., with instructions, guide and case.
£650–750 *WIL*

A Russian Leica II copy camera, gold with all Leitz markings, f3.5 Elmar lens, post-WWII, 5in (12.5cm) wide.
£500–1,000 *VCL*

l. A Lancaster Le Merveilleux wood and brass quarter-plate camera, c1886, 5½in (14cm) wide.
£100–200 *VCL*

A Ciné Kodak Eight 20 camera, c1940, 6in (15cm) long, with box.
£20–30 *HEG*

The Ciné Eight 20 was the first 8mm spool-load movie camera.

An Optomax 110 telephoto
camera and binoculars, c1970,
4in (10cm) wide.
£40–50 *VCL*

A Newman & Guardia Baby
Sibyl camera, 4 by 6cm plate,
c1920, 2½in (6.5cm) wide.
£200–300 *VCL*

A Prince Flex miniature TLR
worm camera, 1950s, 3in
(7.5cm) long.
£5–8 *HEG*

A Minolta 35 Super Rokkor camera,
f2.8, c1948, 5½in (14cm) wide.
£200–300 *VCL*

A Meagher tailboard camera,
mahogany and brass, 5 by 4in
plate, brass barrel lens with
Waterhouse stops, c1890, 7in
(18cm) long, together with tripod,
dark slides, plates and leather box.
£200–250 *HEG*

A Pilot Reflex
camera, 4 by 4cm on
127 film, c1936, 3in
(7.5cm) wide.
£100–200 *VCL*

A Shew eclipse camera, with dark slide,
c1890, 7in (18cm) long.
£100–150 *HEG*

A Praktica Super TL camera,
f1.8 Pancolor, c1970, 6in
(15cm) wide.
£25–40 *VCL*

A Russian Sputnik Bakelite
stereoscopic camera, 120 film,
c1970, 6in (15cm) wide.
£75–150 *VCL*

A Selfix 620 folding roll film
camera, with Epsilon shutter,
1950s, 5in (12.5cm) long.
£20–30 *HEG*

A Voigtländer Avus plate camera, with roll film back, 9 by 12cm, Skopar f4.5-135mm, Compur shutter, 1920s, 5in (12.5cm) long.
£45–65 *HEG*

A Wonderflex Special Comet TLR styled mouse camera, 1950s, 4in (10cm) long.
£5–10 *HEG*

A Voigtländer Vito B camera, c1950, 4½in (11.5cm) wide.
£40–50 *VCL*

A Zeiss Nettar 515 camera, c1940, 5in (12.5cm) long.
£15–25 *HEG*

A Stereo-Mikroma 16mm camera, bound with green leather, c1961, 5½in (14cm) wide.
£100–200 *VCL*

A Russian Zenith-80 camera, copy of Hasselblad, c1974, 4in (10cm) wide.
£100–150 *VCL*

A Russian Zorki-4K 35mm camera, with coupled rangefinder f2 lens, c1975, 5½in (14cm) wide.
£20–30 *VCL*

A Zeiss Ikon camera, 6 by 9cm, c1960, 3½in (9cm) wide.
£30–40 *VCL*

l. A Zenith photo-sniper, with 300mm lens and rifle butt, Russian, c1970, 5in (12.5cm) wide.
£75–150 *VCL*

A Zeiss Nettar 510/2 camera, 120 film, c1939, 3in (7.5cm) wide.
£20–30 *VCL*

CANDLE SNUFFERS

l. A metal candle snuffer and tray, 19thC, 7in (18cm) wide.
£40–50 *WCA*

r. A Royal Crown Derby candle snuffer, standing on match holder, Sarah Gamp, c1870, 3in (7.5cm) high.
£225–250 *MLa*

Worcester was the first company to produce this figure which they called 'Granny Snow'. Royal Crown Derby copied the model, adding a base for matches and a match striker, changing the name to 'Sarah Gamp'.

A pair of Minton candle snuffers with tray, c1880, 3¼in (8cm) high.
£100–130 *MLa*

CANDLESTICKS

A pair of brass candlesticks, each with knopped stem and stepped circular foot, c1760, 10in (25.5cm) high.
£200–240 *WIL*

A blue enamel chamberstick, c1930s, 6in (15cm) diam.
£5–6 *TaB*

A Stuart's enamelled glass candlestick, c1930s, 3¼in (8cm) high.
£15–25 *JHa*

A pair of French bronze bedroom candlesticks, in high rococo style, each with a putto holding up the candleholder, 19thC.
£250–300 *WW*

A silver plated on copper five-light candelabrum, together with a pair of matching three-light candelabra, 19thC.
£375–450 *Mit*

CERAMICS

The ceramics section is organized alphabetically by object, period and factory, for example Animals, Art Deco, Belleek. Each year we reflect current trends in the market. For example, the bicentenary of the death of Josiah Wedgwood in 1795 has brought a vast array of ceramics into auction houses and antique shops, as illustrated in our Wedgwood feature. Clarice Cliff continues to weave her colourful magic. Sales and shows of her work are invariably packed with eager collectors, and this year we are delighted to include a survey of her distinctive ceramics. Clarice Cliff's great rival, Susie Cooper, died in 1995 at the age of 93, and we offer our own small tribute to this major designer by illustrating a selection of her pieces. In the opinion of many, her work was sadly underrated during her lifetime and interest in her ceramics, from all periods, looks set to increase. Another major ceramic artist who died in 1995 was Lucie Rie, one of the most outstanding artist-potters of the 20th century, whose work is shown in our Contemporary Ceramics section.

Animals – 19th Century

r. A pearlware dove tureen and cover, naturalistically modelled nesting, enriched in colours, predominantly blue and brown, some damage, c1800, 7in (17.5cm) long.
£525–625 *CSK*

l. A creamware figure of a seated lion, splashed in brown, on oval base, c1800, 7½in (19cm) high.
£375–450 *DN*

A pair of pearlware figures of recumbent deer, each decorated in orange, on oval mound base, antlers damaged, one head glued, c1820, 5½in (14cm) high.
£250–300 *DN*

A pair of figures of lions, each standing on a stepped base with rope-twist borders and covered overall with a crackled glaze, some cracks and chips, 19thC, 9in (23cm) long.
£550–650 *DN*

A creamware bear-baiting jug and cover, c1800, 8in (20cm) high.
£550–650   *JBL*

This type of jug was made as a protest against the baiting of bears by dogs.

A George Jones Aesthetic period majolica teapot, in the form of a fish, complete with flat fish-shaped stand, late 19thC.
£340–400   *L&E*

A Sarreguemines figure of a seagull, No. 3527, c1900, 10½in (26.5cm) high.
£150–175   *PC*

l. A Sarreguemines penguin jug, No. 3567, c1900, 7in (18cm) high.
£75–90   *PC*

Animals – 20th Century

A Bernard Moore flambé standing tortoise, with head raised, jewel eyes, painted mark to base, early 20thC, 4½in (11.5cm) long.
£200–250   *WIL*

A Royal Dux figure of a donkey, 1960s, 5½in (14cm) high.
£120–130   *YY*

A Sung flambé figure of a bear, signed 'Noke' and monogram 'FA', c1920, 4in (10cm) high.
£750–850   *LT*

Six Beswick figures of A. A. Milne characters, including Winnie the Pooh, Eeyore, Piglet, Rabbit, Owl, Kanga, designed 1968, withdrawn in 1990.
£190–240   *WIL*

r. A Hornsea Pottery jar, in the form of an owl, with removable head, c1970, 4½in (11.5cm) high.
£12–15   *HEW*

Art Deco

A set of 3 Adams jugs, with Cries of London scenes different on each side, c1920s, tallest 6¾in (17cm) high.
£150–200 *WN*

Cross Reference:
Carlton
Clarice Cliff
Susie Cooper

A Barton Pottery vase, c1920, 6in (15cm) high.
£20–25 *AnE*

A Thomas Forrest footed vase, decorated in Syrian pattern, 1930s, 7½in (19cm) high.
£80–100 *BKK*

An Edna Best bowl, made for Lawleys, 1930s, 10in (25.5cm) diam.
£100–125 *WTA*

r. A Barker Bros trio, by John Guildford, hand painted with Arabesque pattern, 1930s, plate 7in (18cm) diam.
£60–75 *WN*

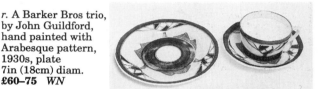

r. A Falcon ware jug, 1930s, 6in (15cm) high.
£18–20 *COL*

A Crown Ducal Orange Tree pattern tea set, c1928, teapot 6in (15cm) high.
£100–120 *BKK*

A Bretby figure group, inscribed 'Three little maids from school are we, Turn us round and you will see, Back views may deceptive be, Grand-mammas all three are We', 1920s, 9in (23cm) high.
£165–200 *SIG*

A Goldscheider figure of a lady with a parasol, c1930, 13in (33cm) high.
£650–700 *WTA*

A Gray's pottery jug, with lustre finish, 1920–30s, 4½in (11.5cm) high.
£40–50 *YY*

A Coronaware Lagoon pattern plate, by S. Hancock & Son, c1930s, 10in (25cm) diam.
£25–30 *HEM*

A Coronaware dragon bowl, by S. Hancock & Son, Stoke-on-Trent, 1920–30s, 8½in (21.5cm) diam.
£50–60 *HEM*

A French figure group of Harlequin and ladies, by L. Leyritz, from the commedia dell'arte, c1930, 10¾in (27cm) high.
£700–750 *JES*

A Maling ware bowl, 1920–30s, 3½in (9cm) diam.
£60–70 *WN*

A Kensington coffee pot, with raised sunflower decoration, c1934, 8in (20cm) high.
£25–30 *BKK*

A Rosenthal Art Deco figure,
11in (28cm) high.
£450–550 *LT*

A Radford ware plate,
painted mark, 1920–30,
10in (25.5cm) wide.
£20–25 *WN*

A Tamsware hand painted bowl,
c1932, 7¼in 18.5cm) diam.
£35–40 *BKK*

A Tuscan Decoro vase, by
R. H. & S. L. Plant, c1935,
5¾in (14.5cm) high.
£35–40 *BKK*

An Arthur Wood hand painted
wall vase, c1935, 8½in
(21.5cm) high.
£40–45 *BKK*

A pair of Wilkinson lustre spill
vases, decorated in Paris Garden
pattern, c1929, 9in (23cm) high.
£150–200 *WTA*

Art Nouveau

A pair of Royal Bonn vases,
c1900, 8in (20cm) high.
£100–110 *COL*

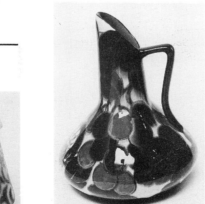

An Elton Ware jug,
c1880–1920, signed 'Elton',
5½in (14cm) high.
£50–55 *HEM*

A Royal Dux porcelain
figural vase, depicting a
semi-clad maiden by a
stream and leaning against
a rock, wearing a pink
dress and green shoes,
12½in (31.5cm) high.
£550–650 *AH*

Belleek

A Belleek pierced basket, with central twig-shaped loop handle, the rim boldly encrusted with flowers and leaves, impressed mark 'Belleek' on a ribbon, c1870, 10¾in (27.5cm) wide.
£650–750 *DN*

A Belleek pierced basket, with twig-shaped handles, the rim encrusted with sprays of lily of the valley, impressed 'Belleek Co Fermanah' on a ribbon, c1870, 11½in (29cm) diam.
£1,400–1,600 *DN*

Blue & White

A Victorian Middlesbro' Pottery meat dish, with blue and white decoration depicting a river scene within a floral border, 17¾in (45cm) wide.
£120–150 *Gam*

Belleek

- The Belleek porcelain factory was founded at Belleek, County Fermanah, Northern Ireland in 1857.
- Wares were produced in high quality feldspar porcelain, similar to parian, but with a lustrous, iridescent glaze.
- The factory specialised in intricately modelled openwork baskets, applied with finely executed flowerheads.
- Pieces were often impressed with a single pad on the underside, inscribed 'Belleek'. From 1863 to c1880, wares also carried a printed black mark of a seated Irish wolfhound, harp and a round tower. After 1880 'County Fermanah' and several pad marks were added. The more pad marks there are, the later the piece.

r. A Belleek cake plate, with applied twig handles, the centre with a weave pattern, bordered by fine threads of swirling lattice work, glazed throughout with a pearl lustre, firing crack to base, impressed marks to base, 19thC, 9½in (24cm) diam.
£275–300 *WIL*

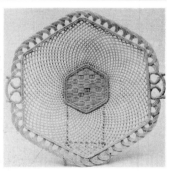

A Rogers earthenware serving plate, printed in underglaze blue, depicting a man and a boy driving a water buffalo before temple ruins, with floral border, cracked, impressed mark, early 19thC, 17in (43cm) wide.
£250–300 *WIL*

A pearlware blue and white two-handled reticulated basket and stand, printed with cattle watering before ruins within floral borders, early 19thC, stand 11in (28cm) wide.
£420–480 *WIL*

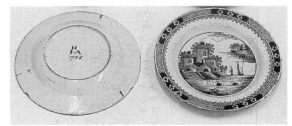

A pair of documentary Liverpool blue and white delft marriage plates, decorated with 2 swans on a river in front of a castle, bearing the initials 'HIA 1765' on the reverse, mid-18thC, 9in (23cm) diam.
£650–750 *Mit*

A double-leaf folding fan, advertising BOAC, printed with 6 people in national costume, signed 'Adelman', 1950s, 7½in (19cm) wide.
£10–15 *PC*

A double-leaf folding fan, advertising Japan Airlines, with blossom spray and black calligraphy, 1950s, 7½in (19cm) wide.
£10–15 *PC*

A double-leaf folding fan, advertising Cathay Pacific Airways, printed with modern Oriental scenes, 1950s, 8in (20cm) wide.
£10–15 *PC*

A double-leaf folding fan, advertising Philippine Airlines, printed with a map of the world, 1950s, 8in (20cm) wide.
£10–15 *PC*

l. A Willow pattern dish, advertising Schweppes Lemon Squash, early 20thC, 4¼in (11cm) diam.
£12–15 *TaB*

A Stephenson's Floor Polish display box, c1925, 12½in (32cm) long.
£20–25 *JUN*

A Lux box and contents, c1930, 4¾in (12cm) high.
£18–22 *MRW*

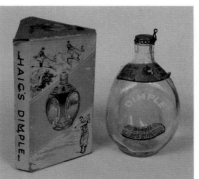

A Haig's Dimple whisky bottle and original box, 1930, 8in (20cm) high.
£14–16 *AL*

Two advertising boards, for P.K. Chewing Gum and Sharps Toffees, 1945, 13½in (34.5cm) long.
£8–15 each *MRW*

An Oakey's Knife Polish box, c1900, 11in (28cm) long.
£18–20 *AL*

A Royal Ediswan Pearl Lamp box, with bulb inside, c1920, 6¼in (16cm) high.
£15–20 *MRW*

A Double-N Liquid Grate Polish tin, c1910, 5in (12.5cm) high.
£15–20 *MRW*

A Camphorated Oil bottle, c1910, 5¾in (14.5cm) high.
£5–6 *MRW*

A Cowan's Bonzo toffee tin, c1930, 6in (15cm) high.
£50–70 *MRW*

A Patchquick French Chalk tin, with contents, c1930, 2in (5cm) high.
£12–20 *MRW*

A Huntley & Palmers biscuit tin, shaped as a bookcase, c1915, 6¼in (16cm) square.
£80–100 *WN*

A Fox's Glacier Mints tin, c1930, 10in (25.5cm) high.
£10–15 *AL*

A sweet tin, 1930s, 6¼in (16cm) high.
£10–12 *AnE*

A Crawford's biscuit tin, 1940s, 7½in (19cm) wide.
£40–50 *WN*

An amber and plastic
cigarette holder, c1920,
case 6in (15cm) long.
£15–25 *WCA*

A beaded 'flapper'
dress decoration,
1920s, 26in (66cm)
long. **£25–35** *Ech*

A gilt spelter lamp, of a
female nude with globe,
23in (58.5cm) high.
£600–650 *WTA*

A chalk figure of a girl in a metal
hoop, registered No. 804866,
c1935, 12in (30.5cm) high.
£75–85 *BKK*

A Calendox Bakelite calendar,
1930s, 4½in (11.5cm) high.
£25–30 *HEM*

Two rows of 'flapper'
beads, with tassel ends,
1920s, 24in (61cm) long.
£35–65 each *Ech*

A Czechoslovakian ceramic galleon
flower holder, c1925, 9in (23cm) wide.
£50–60 *BKK*

A Davidson's glass lamp,
c1935, 15in (38cm) high.
£80–90 *BKK*

Two enamelled book match covers,
c1930, 2½in (6.5cm) high.
£15–25 each *PC*

A Bagley pressed glass vase,
c1920, 7½in (19cm) high.
£60–70 *GLN*

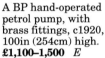

A Power glass
petrol pump
globe, 1950s,
22in (56cm) wide.
£300–350 *BS*

A Shellmex petrol pump globe,
c1950, 18in (45.5cm) wide.
£250–275 *BS*

A BP hand-operated
petrol pump, with
brass fittings, c1920,
100in (254cm) high.
£1,100–1,500 *E*

A Chinese glazed porcelain
cycling plate, late 19thC,
9in (23cm) diam.
£80–140 *MCh*

An aluminium AA Box logo sign,
c1940, 13in (33cm) wide.
£80–90 *BS*

A mug, with 22ct gold band,
inscribed with 'The Motorist's
Prayer', 1960s, 5½in (14cm) high.
£8–10 *COL*

Two gouache paintings, by
Roy Nockolds, one of Bob
Dicker, the other of a
Duesenberg on the track at
Brooklands, early 20thC,
11½ by 17½in (29 by 44.5cm).
£900–1,100 each *E*

A delivery bicycle, with lever back brake,
steering bar and leather saddle.
£225–275 *MAW*

An Elswick Hopper gentleman's bicycle, with
Sturmey-Archer gears and mileometer, 1950s.
£25–35 *S*

A Victorian silver bookmark, with agate handle, 4½in (11.5cm) long.
£25–35 *GLN*

Arabella Boxer and Tessa Traeger, *Vogue Food Diary*, published by Condé Nast, c1977, 9 by 7½in (23 by 19cm).
£1–2 *BFB*

A. F. Calvert, *Southern Spain*, illustrated by Trevor Haddon, first edition, published by A. & C. Black, London, 1908, 9 by 6½in (23 by 16.5cm).
£130–150 *HB*

M. A. Fairclough, *The Ideal Cookery Book*, published by Blackfriars Publishing Co, c1910, 10 by 7½in (25 by 19cm).
£25–35 *HB*

George Perrot & Charles Chipiez, *History of Art in Chaldæa and Assyria*, published by Chapman & Hall, London, 1884, 10½ by 7in (26.5 by 18cm).
£75–90 *HB*

r. A pair of Kathausen book ends, 20thC, 5in (12.5cm) high.
£50–60 *HEM*

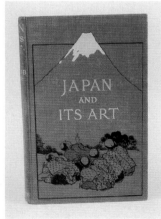

Marcus B. Huish, *Japan and Its Art*, third edition, published by B. T. Batsford, London, 1912, 8¾ by 6¾in (22 by 17cm).
£30–40 *HB*

Nico & Beatrix Jungman, *Holland*, published by A. & C. Black, London, first edition, 1904, 9 by 6½in (23 by 16.5cm).
£30–40 *HB*

Henri-Paul Pellaprat, *Modern French Culinary Art*, published by Virtue, c1967, 10½ by 7½in (26.5 by 19cm).
£45–50 *BFB*

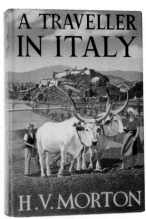

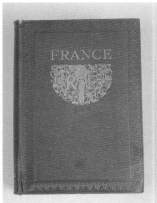

H. V. Morton, *A Traveller In Italy*, published by Methuen, London, 1964, 8½ by 5½in (21.5 by 14cm).
£10–15 *TBS*

Gordon Hone, *France*, published by A. & C. Black, London, 1914, 9 by 6½in (23 by 16.5cm).
£10–15 *TBS*

Robert William Rogers, *A History of Ancient Persia*, first edition, with 70 illustrations and maps, published by Charles Scribners, New York, 1929.
£30–40 *HB*

H. V. Morton, *In Search of England*, published by Penguin, London, 1960.
£2–3 *TBS*

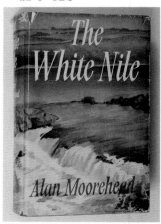

Ian Fleming Introduces Jamaica, edited by Morris Cargill, 1965, published by André Deutsch Ltd, London, 7½ by 5in (19 by 12.5cm).
£10–12 *TBS*

Alan Moorehead, *The White Nile*, published by Hamish Hamilton, dedicated to Freya Stark, 1960, 8½ by 5¾in (21.5 by 17cm).
£10–12 *TBS*

A William IV rosewood workbox, with brass inlay and fitted interior, on bun feet, c1830, 12in (30.5cm) long.
£350–400 *TMi*

An early Victorian walnut vanity box, with brass and ivory banding, 9½in (24cm) long.
£200–240 *TMi*

A mid-Victorian rosewood sarcophagus-shaped tea caddy, with mixing bowl, 12in (30.5cm) long.
£200–300 *MRW*

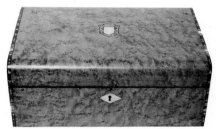

A mid-Victorian bird's-eye maple lady's writing slope, with ebony and mother-of-pearl banding, 13in (33cm) long.
£200–250 *TMi*

An Art Deco oak and satinwood jewel box, 12in (30.5cm) long.
£80–120 *CCP*

A painted box, early 19thC, 8½in (21.5cm) long.
£60–80 *TMi*

A Victorian walnut letter box, with domed top, brass banding and key, c1870, 8in (20cm) long.
£100–150 *TMi*

A German satinwood lover's box, with brass banding, glass and paste stones, late 19thC, 12in (30.5cm) long.
£150–200 *TMi*

A Wade ashtray, advertising Trophy Best Bitter, c1965, 4in (10cm) wide.
£5–6 *COL*

An advertising bar item, for Younger Beers, 1960s, 9in (23cm) high.
£18–22 *COL*

A plastic advertising item, for Bulmer's Woodpecker Cider, 1960s, 8in (20cm) high.
£12–15 *COL*

An enamel on brass beer pump clip, for Theakston Best Bitter, 1980s, 5in (12.5cm) high.
£8–10 *ED*

Two advertising water jugs, Whyte & Mackays by Wade, 1990s, 10in (25cm) high, and Haig by Seton Pottery, 1990s, 9in (23cm) high.
£8–10 each *ED*

A Beswick water jug, advertising Worthingtons, 1950s, 9in (23cm) high.
£90–110 *ED*

A Wade jug, advertising Johnnie Walker Whisky, 1960s, 5½in (14cm) high.
£15–18 *COL*

A light, advertising Amstel Beer, 1990s, 5½in (14cm) high.
£5–6 *COL*

l. A Wade water jug, advertising Grant's Scotch Whisky, 1960s, 6½in (16.5cm) high.
£20–25 *COL*

A Wade water jug, advertising Carling Black Label, 1960s, 6½in (16.5cm) high.
£15–18 *COL*

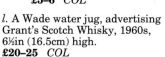

A Wade water jug, advertising Gordon's
Gin, 1960s, 5½in (14cm) high.
£15–18 *COL*

Three plastic and cork whisky bottle pourers,
advertising Jamie Stuart, Tullamore Dew and
Crawford's whiskies, 1960–80s.
£4–12 each *COL*

A Courage Best Bitter
E.I.P.A. plastic beer pump
clip, 1950s, 3in (7.5cm) high.
£8–10 *ED*

A Batemans Draught Mild
plastic beer pump clip, 1980s,
5in (12.5cm) square.
£4–5 *ED*

A metal powder compact,
advertising Skol Lager, 1970s,
2½in (6.5cm) diam.
£6–8 *COL*

A Watneys plastic beer pump
clip, 1960s, 2½in (6.5cm) wide.
£6–8 *ED*

A Morland enamel on brass
beer pump clip, c1990,
4in (10cm) wide.
£8–10 *ED*

A Tetley enamel on brass
beer pump clip, c1990,
4½in (11.5cm) high.
£8–10 *ED*

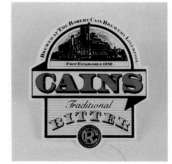

A Cains plastic beer pump clip,
c1994, 5in (12.5cm) high.
£4–5 *ED*

An Amey's Brewery Home Brewed Ale label, 1940s, 3 by 2in (7.5 by 5cm).
£10–12 *ED*

A Kenward & Court Ltd Treble Brown beer label, 1950s, 3¾ by 2in (9.5 by 5cm).
£8–10 *ED*

A Reffell's Nut Brown Ale label, 1950s, 4 by 2⅛in (10 by 6.5cm).
£7–8 *ED*

A Ruddle's 'Old Bob' Ale label, 1940s, 4 by 2½in (10 by 6.5cm).
£7–8 *ED*

A Timothy Chudley Bitter screw-on beer pump label, 1990s, 5in (12.5cm) high.
£3–4 *PC*

A Courage OK Family Ale bottle label, 1940s, 4 by 2⅛in (10 by 6.5cm).
£12–15 *ED*

Two City Brewery, Exeter, Oatmeal Stout and Double Brown Ale bottle labels, 1950s, 3½ by 2in (9 by 5cm).
£4–5 each *ED*

A Pompey Royal screw-on beer pump label, 1990s, 5in (12.5cm) high.
£3–4 *PC*

A Morland Old Masters screw-on beer pump label, 1990s, 5in (12.5cm) high.
£3–4 *PC*

A Charrington's Golden Dinner Ale label, 1940s, 4½ by 2in (11.5 by 5cm).
£8–10 *ED*

A John Smith's Yorkshire Bitter clip-on beer pump badge, 1990s, 5in (12.5cm) high.
£3–4 *PC*

A Whitbread & Co pump cover, 1990s, 5in (12.5cm) high.
£4–5 *PC*

A set of 6 Japanese Satsuma buttons, c1900, 1¼in (35mm) diam. **£100–150** *MRW*

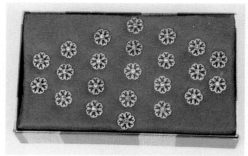

A set of stamped metal buttons, decorated with cut steel and painted, c1890, ¾in (20mm) diam. **£3–4 each** *EBB*

Five lithographed hunting scene buttons, 1930, each ½in (15mm) diam.
£50–75 *MRW*

A Ruskin button, c1930, 1½in (40mm) diam. **£8–15** *MRW*

l. A silver-backed enamel button, 20thC, 1in (25mm) diam. **£12–15** *r.* An enamel button, 19thC, 1½in (40mm) diam. **£25–30** *EBB*

A Thornton-Pickard Triple Victo half-plate camera, with Busch Rapid Aplanet No. 2 lens, early 20thC.
£175–200 *Gam*

A Coronet Midget camera, c1930, 1½in (40mm) high, with original box.
£90–100 *HEG*

A Coronet Midget camera, c1930, 1½in (40mm) high, with case. **£30–40** *JHW*

A Houghton's brass and teak tropical carbine camera, 1930s, 8in (20cm) long, with canvas case.
£85–100 *HEG*

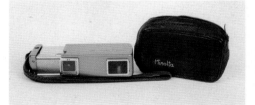

A Minolta 16 Mark II camera, 1960–66, 3¼in (8.5cm) long, with green leather zip case.
£45–50 *HEG*

A pair of decorative vases, 1930s,
12in (30.5cm) high.
£40–50 *WCA*

A Burleigh Foliate bowl, Florentine
pattern 4752, designed by Charlotte
Rhead, c1930, 13in (33cm) diam.
£265–300 *PC*

A Fielding's Crown Devon vase,
1930s, 5½in (14cm) high.
£25–35 *YY*

A Burleigh Double Diamond
vase, c1930, 7¼in (18.5cm) high.
£800–850 *BKK*

A Burslem Paysanne
two-handled vase, 1930s,
8in (20cm) high.
£20–25 *HEM*

A Burleigh Avon bowl, designed
by Charlotte Rhead, pattern 4000,
c1927, 10in (25.5cm) diam.
£250–300 *PC*

A Lincrusta pattern vase, by
Thomas Forester Son & Co,
c1930, 8in (20cm) high.
£50–60 *BKK*

A jug, designed by John
Guildford, c1930, 4½in
(11.5cm) high.
£100–120 *BKK*

A Coronaware cake plate, by S. Hancock & Sons, c1930, 8½in (21.5cm) diam.
£35–40 *BKK*

An Ivory ware 15-piece coffee service, by S. Hancock & Sons, c1930, coffee pot 7½in (19cm) high.
£280–300 *BKK*

A Wadeheath cruet set, 1930s, tallest 4½in (11.5cm) high.
£25–35 *BKK*

A cone-shaped sugar sifter, unmarked, c1935, 5½in (14cm) high.
£100–120 *BKK*

A Maling vase, decorated in Daisy pattern, 1920s, 9½in (24cm) high.
£200–225 *WN*

l. A Tams Ware hand painted vase, c1931, 6in (15cm) high.
£35–40 *BKK*

An Arthur Woods Dick Whittington jug, 1930s, 7in (18cm) high.
£70–80 *WTA*

A John Maddock & Sons Royal Ivory Sunset ware vase, c1930, 6½in (16.5cm) high.
£30–35 *WN*

A Tuscan Decoro vase, c1932, 7in (18cm) high.
£40–45 *BKK*

A Carlton Ware bowl, decorated with
an enamelled heron, original label, on
a conical foot, c1935, 9in (23cm) diam.
£250–300 *CSA*

A Victorian Baron Art Pottery
vase, 8½in (21.5cm) high.
£100–115 *AnE*

A Beswick prancing horse,
1945–70s, 10¼in (26cm) high.
£50–60 *YY*

A Carlton Ware tea caddy,
1930s, 5¼in (14cm) high.
£180–200 *YY*

A pair of Carlton Ware
vases, with mark, c1920,
10in (25.5cm) high.
£150–160 *YY*

A Carlton Ware vase, decorated
with acorns and leaves, 1930s,
8in (20cm) high.
£50–60 *TAR*

A Carlton Ware Rouge Royale bowl,
with 3 feet, c1930, 10in (25.5cm) diam.
£135–160 *YY*

A blue and white Crown Derby trio, c1928,
plate 7in (18cm) diam.
£30–40 *YY*

A Clarice Cliff candlestick,
Shape 331, Mondrian pattern,
c1928, 2in (5cm) high.
£200–250 *RIC*

A Clarice Cliff egg cup stand,
Geometric pattern, 1930s,
6in (15cm) diam.
£150–200 *RIC*

A Clarice Cliff Athens shape
jug, Crocus pattern, c1930,
7in (18cm) high.
£200–220 *BKK*

A Clarice Cliff Fantasque
clog, decorated with Blue
Eyed Marigold pattern,
1930s, 5¼in (13.5cm) wide.
£150–200 *YY*

A Clarice Cliff bowl, Shape
475, Idyll pattern, 1930s,
12½in (32cm) wide.
£450–500 *RIC*

A Clarice Cliffe Biarritz plate,
decorated with Alton pattern,
1930s, 9in (23cm) diam.
£275–300 *WTA*

A Clarice Cliff plate, decorated
with Blue Chintz pattern, 1930s,
6in (15cm) diam. **£150–200** *PC*

A Clarice Cliff jam pot and cover,
Windbells pattern, 1930s, 4in
(10cm) diam. **£250–300** *RIC*

A Clarice Cliff lemonade set tray, decorated
with Crocus pattern, 1930s, 12½in (32cm) long.
£180–200 *BKK*

A Clarice Cliff tray, decorated with Original
Geometric pattern, 1920s, 12¾in (32.5cm) long.
£350–450 *RIC*

A Clarice Cliff plate, Blue Autumn pattern, 1930s, 6in (15cm) diam. **£250–300** *PC*

A Clarice Cliff Bizarre plate, Orange Roof Cottage pattern, 1930s, 9in (23cm) diam. **£500–550** *WTA*

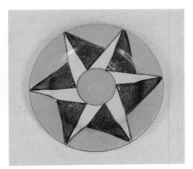

A Clarice Cliff plate, Geometric pattern, c1928, 6in (15cm) diam. **£100–150** *PC*

A Clarice Cliff bowl, Trees and House pattern, c1930, 10in (25.5cm) diam. **£750–800** *BKK*

A Clarice Cliff Original Bizarre plate, c1928, 10in (25.5cm) diam. **£380–400** *BKK*

A Clarice Cliff plate, Buttercup pattern, 1930s, 6in (15cm) diam. **£100–150** *PC*

A Clarice Cliff plate, Fragrance pattern, 1930s, 6in (15cm) diam. **£100–150** *PC*

A Clarice Cliff vase, Shape 370, Patina Coastal pattern, c1934, 6¼in (16cm) high. **£900–1,000** *BKK*

A Clarice Cliff plate, Tralee pattern, 1930s, 6in (15cm) diam. **£150–200** *PC*

l. A Clarice Cliff plate, Summerhouse pattern, 1930s, 6in (15cm) diam. **£200–250** *PC*

r. A Clarice Cliff Biarritz plate, Cabbage Flower pattern, c1934, 10½in (26.5cm) wide. **£250–300** *RIC*

Brannam

A Brannam blue and green bulbous vase, with 3 swirling strap handles, incised fish head decoration, monogrammed 'J D' for James Dewdney, 12¾in (34.5cm) high.
£140–180 *DA*

A Brannam ewer, in the shape of a grebe, after a design by F. Carruthers Gould, with incised decoration on a blue and green ground, 11½in (29cm) high.
£160–200 *DN*

A Brannam wall plaque, decorated with fish and seaweed on a pale blue ground, incised marks for 1903 and decorator's monogram for Thomas Liverton, 13¼in (33.5cm) diam.
£275–325 *DN*

A Brannam candlestick, with detachable sconce, in the form of a stork standing beside bamboo and picked out in colours, on a blue ground, incised marks for 1899, 10¼in (26cm) high.
£130–160 *DN*

A Brannam green glazed character jug, modelled from a cartoon of President Kruger, after designs by F. Carruthers Gould, in the form of an elderly man smoking a pipe, the handle modelled as a boar's head, minor chips, incised marks for 1900, 6¼in (16cm) high.
£225–250 *DN*

A Brannam two-tier bowl, with 3 dolphin supports, incised with fish and seaweed and picked out in colours, incised marks for 1901 and decorator's monogram for Arthur Barkin, 8¼in (21cm) high.
£200–250 *DN*

r. A Brannam chamber candlestick, in the form of a grotesque mask, with a blue ground, some restoration, incised marks for 1898 and decorator's monogram for Beachamp Wimple, 5in (12.5cm) long.
£120–140 *DN*

Burleigh

A Burleigh lustre jug, c1938,
7¼in (18.5cm) high.
£35–40 *CSA*

Carlton Ware

A Burleigh Ware
toilet set, comprising:
2 chamber pots,
jug, basin, soap
dish and liner,
c1932, basin 15¾in
(40cm) diam.
£250–300 *BKK*

A Carlton Ware eight-piece
breakfast set, decorated in
Buttercup design, 1930s, largest
plate 9½in (24cm) diam.
£450–500 *WN*

A Carlton Ware chocolate
cup and cover, c1930, 5in
(12.5cm) high.
£60–75 *WN*

A Carlton Ware chamber
stick, marked, 1930s, 5½in
(14cm) diam.
£140–160 *YY*

l. A Carlton Ware
mushroom vase and flower
holder, both signed, c1934,
12in (30.5cm) diam.
£100–120 *BKK*

A Carlton Ware Rouge Royale
dish, signed, stamped mark,
c1930, 8½in (21.5cm) wide.
£50–60 *WN*

MAKE THE MOST OF MILLER'S

Condition is absolutely vital when
assessing the value of any item.
Damaged pieces appreciate much less
than perfect examples. However, a
rare, desirable piece may command a
high price even when damaged.

r. Three pieces of Carlton
Ware Rouge Royale, 1930s,
jug 6in (15cm) high.
£40–45 *COL*

Clarice Cliff

Clarice Cliff is probably the most collectable name in Art Deco ceramics. She dominated the British pottery scene in the late 1920s and '30s, and it is to this period that the following examples belong.

Christie's, South Kensington, now hold two sales a year devoted to her ceramics, bringing in an annual total of some half a million pounds, with each auction attracting up to one thousand registered bidders. 'Her works are hugely in demand,' says Christie's expert Mark Wilkinson. 'They offer a wide selection of colourful and inventive designs and a good range of prices. You can begin collecting for under £100, although, at the top end of the market, prices will run into thousands of pounds.'

Currently sought after are the small items such as sugar sifters, salt and peppers and preserve pots. 'People have come to recognize

that these are just as well designed and painted as the larger pieces,' explains Wilkinson. 'You can build up a good collection of them without running out of space.' Some enthusiasts will concentrate on a specific object, collecting the various different patterns.

The following section includes a fine display of tea plates, illustrating the remarkable variety of designs available. The increasing popularity of Clarice Cliff's ceramics has inspired not only honest reproductions, such as the Wedgwood copies illustrated in this section, but also contemporary fakes. According to dealers in the field, these can fall into two categories: ceramics created from scratch as fakes and genuine Clarice Cliff dinner plates from the 1930s, which have been subsequently overpainted with a more interesting and consequently more valuable pattern.

A Clarice Cliff clog, decorated in blue Taormina pattern, 5¼in (13.5cm) long.
£150–250 *RIC*

A Clarice Cliff match holder, 3in (7.5cm) high.
£100–200 *RIC*

r. A pair of Clarice Cliff Bizarre wall plaques, each moulded in relief with garlands of flowers, decorated in shades of yellow, orange, blue and green on a silver lustre ground, some damage, printed factory marks, 16½in (42cm) high.
£230–280 *CSK*

A Clarice Cliff napkin ring, in the form of an elephant, 3in (7.5cm) wide.
£150–250 *RIC*

A Clarice Cliff Toby jug, 2¼in (5.5cm) high.
£150–250 *RIC*

> **FURTHER READING**
> *The Rich Designs of Clarice Cliff*
> Rich Designs Publishing
> November 1995

A Clarice Cliff Conical bowl, decorated in Ravel pattern, 6in (15cm) diam.
£50–80 *RIC*

A Clarice Cliff cruet set, decorated in Delecia Citrus pattern, mustard pot 2½in (6.5cm) high.
£200–250 *RIC*

A Clarice Cliff Newport Pottery jug and matching bowl, painted in relief with a budgerigar perched on a branch, jug 8½in (21.5cm) high.
£220–250 *Gam*

l. A Clarice Cliff Bizarre biscuit barrel, decorated with Delecia pattern in coloured enamels, with silver plated cover and swing handle, on 3 tapering section feet, printed marks in black, 6¾in (17cm) high.
£250–300 *DN*

l. A Clarice Cliff Bizarre sugar caster, decorated in My Garden pattern, the flowerhead moulded base picked out in colours on a mottled ground, printed and painted marks in black, 5¾in (14.5cm) high.
£180–220 *DN*

A Clarice Cliff Bizarre Double Conical bowl, decorated in Inspiration Persian pattern in shades of yellow, blue and purple on a turquoise ground, on stepped foot, restored chip to rim, printed factory marks, 7in (18cm) high.
£475–575 *CSK*

Issued in June 1929, Shape 380 was called a 'Conical Double Deck' in factory literature, and this evocative name describes this one-piece vessel which has two wells for water.

A Clarice Cliff part dinner service, comprising: 66 pieces, with hand painted floral decoration and gilt edging on a cream ground, pattern No. 6836, printed marks to base.
£550–650 *WIL*

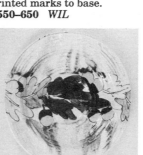

A Clarice Cliff Lynton saucer, decorated in Acorns pattern, 4½in (11.5cm) diam.
£50–60 *BKK*

A Clarice Cliff plate, decorated in Secrets pattern, 9in (23cm) diam.
£70–80 *YY*

A Clarice Cliff Bizarre plate, designed by Dame Laura Knight, the well printed and painted with 3 sea lions balancing balls, the rim with an audience, 9in (23cm) diam.
£475–525 *Bri*

Candlesticks

A pair of Clarice Cliff Bizarre candlesticks, decorated in Alpine pattern, 8in (20.5cm) high.
£1,000–1,300 WTA

Preserve Pots

A Clarice Cliff Bizarre Conical preserve pot, decorated in Windbells pattern, rubber stamp mark, 4in (10cm) high.
£250–300 GAK

A Clarice Cliff Bizarre jam pot and cover, decorated in House and Bridge pattern, 4in (10cm) high.
£200–250 WTA

A Clarice Cliff candlestick, decorated in Delecia Citrus pattern, 3½in (9cm) diam.
£80–150 RIC

A Clarice Cliff honey pot and cover, with bee knop, decorated in Crocus pattern, green printed mark, 3¾in (9.5cm) high.
£220–250 DN

A Clarice Cliff Bizarre candlestick, decorated in Geometric pattern, the base with hand painted 'Bizarre' mark, 1928, 4½in (11.5cm) diam.
£150–250 RIC

l. A Clarice Cliff jam pot and cover, decorated in Viscaria pattern, 4in (10cm) diam.
£100–200 RIC

Tea Plates

A Clarice Cliff tea plate,
decorated in blue Luxor
pattern, 6in (15cm) diam.
£250–350 *PC*

A Clarice Cliff tea plate,
decorated in Brown Lily
pattern, 6in (15cm) diam.
£100–200 *PC*

A Clarice Cliff tea plate,
decorated in Farmhouse pattern,
6in (15cm) diam.
£200–300 *PC*

A Clarice Cliff tea plate,
decorated in Goldstone
pattern, 6in (15cm) diam.
£80–150 *PC*

Two Clarice Cliff tea plates, decorated in Cowslip
pattern, one yellow, the other green 6in (15cm) diam.
£100–200 each *PC*

A Clarice Cliff tea plate,
decorated in Trees and House
pattern, 6in (15cm) diam.
£100–200 *RIC*

A Clarice Cliff tea plate,
decorated in Solitude pattern,
6in (15cm) diam.
£200–300 *PC*

A Clarice Cliff tea plate,
decorated in House and Bridge
pattern, 6in (15cm) diam.
£200–300 *PC*

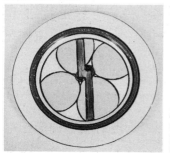

r. A Clarice Cliff tea plate,
decorated in black and red
Umbrellas pattern, 6in
(15cm) diam.
£100–200 *PC*

l. A Clarice Cliff tea plate,
decorated in Picasso Flower
pattern, 6in (15cm) diam.
£100–200 *PC*

Teapots and Tea Services

A Clarice Cliff Bonjour teapot, from Artist's in Industry Series, 5½in (14cm) high.
£200–300 *RIC*

A set of 6 Clarice Cliff Conical cups and saucers and sugar bowl, decorated in Forest Glen pattern, some damage.
£550–650 *AAV*

A Clarice Cliff Newport Pottery tête à tête.
£325–425 *W*

Vases

r. A Clarice Cliff three-footed vase, decorated in My Garden pattern, c1937, 9in (23cm) high.
£80–100 *BKK*

l. A Clarice Cliff vase, Shape 265, decorated in Crocus pattern, c1931, 6in (15cm) high.
£250–280 *BKK*

A Clarice Cliff vase, decorated in Limberlost pattern, 6in (15cm) high.
£350–450 *RIC*

A Clarice Cliff Fantasque vase, Isis shape, boldly decorated with a stylised flowerhead band within yellow and orange borders, restored, printed mark in black, 9¾in (24.5cm) high.
£350–400 *DN*

Wedgwood Copies of Clarice Cliff – Produced c1993

These Wedgwood copies of Clarice Cliff ceramics have increased in value in their own right.

Two Wedgwood copies of Clarice Cliff Age of Jazz dancing figures, from a limited edition of 150, c1993, 8in (20.5cm) high.
£300–350 each *PC*

These figures cost £175 each when made c1993.

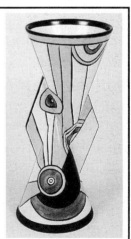

A Wedgwood copy of a Clarice Cliff Yo Yo vase, limited edition of 250, c1993, 9in (23cm) high.
£360–380 *PC*

This vase cost £225 when made c1993.

Contemporary

Contemporary ceramics represent one of Britain's most significant contributions to 20th century art and the international modern movement. Major potters, such as Bernard Leach, Hans Coper and Lucie Rie, command high prices and in particular values of Lucie Rie's wares have risen since her death in 1995.

Young British potters are continuing to produce fine work at prices that can seem very affordable compared to contemporary painting and sculpture. It is likely that many of the pots being produced today will become the collectables of the future.

A black and white porcelain footed bowl, by Suzanne Bergne, c1990, 15½in (40cm) high.
£300–350 *ELG*

A St Ives footed porcelain bowl, by Shoji Hamada, in glazed pale celadon, the interior with stylised chrysanthemums, impressed 'Shoji' and 'St Ives' seal, c1922, 8¼in (21cm) high.
£3,200–3,500 *Bon*

A stoneware covered jar, by Michael Cardew, decorated in olive-brown, incised 'Flour' on both jar and cover, impressed 'MC' and 'Wenford Bridge' seals, c1970, 7½in (19cm) high.
£250–300 *Bon*

A green and gold porcelain teapot, by Bridget Drakeford, 1990s, 9in (23cm) high including handle.
£75–85 *ELG*

A raku bowl, by Ljerka Njers, slab built with painted foliate decoration in green and yellow, the exterior and overted rim with impressed floral decoration, 13¾in (35cm) wide.
£200–240 *Bon*

l. A stoneware vase, by William Staite Murray, decorated in beige with brown painting of fishes and underwater foliage, impressed 'M' in an oblong, 11¼in (28.5cm) high.
£430–500 *Bon*

A white composite vessel form, by Hans Coper, the interior dark brown, impressed 'HC' seal, c1968, 10in (25.5cm) high.
£10,000–11,000 *Bon*

l. A black stoneware pot, by Janet Leach, with 2 lugs on the shoulders, white rim, the matt body decorated with 2 shiny brown overlapping stripes, impressed 'JL' and 'St Ives' seals, 5½in (14cm) high.
£275–300 *Bon*

A rounded earthenware vase, by Magdalene Odundo, with unglazed burnished surface, reduced black in the firing, inscribed 'Odundo 10/82', 10in (25.5cm) high.
£1,000–1,200 *Bon*

A cylindrical-shaped vase, by George Wilson, 1990s, 9½in (24cm) high.
£300–350 *ELG*

A stoneware vase, by Dame Lucie Rie, covered in a grey and blue spiralling pitted glaze, some shading of brown around top of drum base, impressed 'LR' seal, c1972, 8in (20.5cm) high.
£3,200–3,600 *Bon*

An earthenware vessel, by James Tower, with deep brown and white radiating abstract design, incised 'James Tower '83', 20½in (52cm) high.
£5,500–6,000 *Bon*

A porcelain bowl, by Dame Lucie Rie, very thinly thrown, the interior bronze with sgraffito radiating lines, the exterior white with inlaid purple radiating lines, a bronze foot and bronze band at rim, impressed 'LR' seal, c1975, 9¾in (24.5cm) diam.
£9,500–10,500 *Bon*

A bronze stoneware container and lid, by Dame Lucie Rie, with bands of terracotta and diagonal sgraffito, impressed 'LR' seal, c1965, 4in (10cm) high.
£1,400–1,600 *Bon*

A carved and burnished pumpkin-shaped vessel, by Antonia Salmon, 1990s, 14in (35.5cm) diam.
£400–500 *ELG*

A stoneware bronze vessel, by Jan Van Der Vaart, the undulating rim forms 4 petal-like sections, the rounded body with a dividing central band to the base, 14in (35.5cm) high.
£275–325 *Bon*

Susie Cooper

A Susie Cooper Modernist pattern coffee cup and saucer, c1932, cup 2in (5cm) high.
£85–125 *SCA*

A Susie Cooper toast rack, with sgraffito decoration, the space at either end for jam and butter, 1930s, 6in (15cm) long.
£35–45 *SCA*

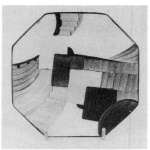

A Susie Cooper Cubist pattern sandwich plate, c1929, 5in (12.5cm) wide.
£90–100 *SCA*

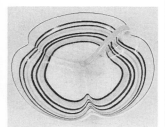

A Susie Cooper hors d'oeuvres dish, with hand painted banded decoration, 1930s, 9in (23cm) diam.
£50–85 *SCA*

A Susie Cooper green vase, incised with squirrels at play, 1930s, 12in (30.5cm) high.
£120–180 *SCA*

This pattern of vase is also available in blue which is rarer than the green version.

l. A Susie Cooper hors d'oeuvres dish, 1930s, 10½in (26.5cm) diam.
£80–110 *SCA*

Miller's is a price GUIDE not a price LIST

A Susie Cooper punch bowl and 7 beakers, painted with a band of stylised leaves in shades of green and grey, crack to rim of bowl, printed factory marks, 1930s, bowl 11in (28cm) diam, and 8 similar coasters.
£600–800 *CSK*

A Susie Cooper breakfast service, each piece brightly painted with sprays of flowers and leaves, comprising 16 pieces, printed marks in brown and pattern No. 'E/284', 1930s.
£800–1,000 *DN*

A Susie Cooper Falcon ware 'tea for two' service, with sgraffito decoration, c1939, teapot 5½in (14cm) high.
£150–350 *SCA*

It is rare to find a complete set.

Cottages
Lilliput Lane

A Lilliput Lane ceramic model, Seven Dwarfs' Cottage, No. 470 of limited edition, produced for Disney, USA, 1986, 4½in (11.5cm) high.
£850–1,000 *ANP*

A Lilliput Lane ceramic model, Settler's Surprise, 1991, 3¾in (9.5cm) wide.
£60–80 *ANP*

This model is only available in New Zealand.

A Lilliput Lane ceramic model, Wishing Well, 2¼in (5.5cm) high.
£100–140 *ANP*

Two Lilliput Lane cottages, South Bend exclusives, limited editions of 350, 1990–92.
l. Rowan Lodge, 3½in (9cm) high.
£275–350
r. Game Keeper's Lodge, 4in (10cm) high.
£175–225 *ANP*

A Lilliput Lane ceramic model, Bridge House, flat back, second version, 1982–84, 4in (10cm) high.
£300–350 *ANP*

A Lilliput Lane ceramic model, Craigievar Castle, Scottish collection, 1989–91, 7in (18cm) high.
£140–175 *ANP*

Two Lilliput Lane cottages, the backs showing Car Collectors Club Members' exclusive.
l. Forget-Me-Not Cottage, 1992–93, 3¼in (8.5cm) high.
£120–190
r. Heavenlea Cottage, 1993–94, 4in (10cm) high.
£80–120 *ANP*

Heavenlea Cottage is a model of Forget-Me-Not Cottage having been restored and modernised.

A Lilliput Lane ceramic model, Holly Cottage, second version, 1983–88, 3½in (9cm) high.
£60–80 *ANP*

Two Lilliput Lane ceramic models,
April Cottage, 1982–89.
l. First version, 1¾in (4.5cm) high.
£50–65
r. Second version, 2¼in (5.5cm) high.
£300–400 *ANP*

r. A Lilliput
Lane ceramic
model, Tintagel,
1984–88, 3in
(7.5cm) high.
£150–200 *ANP*

A Lilliput Lane ceramic model, The Red Lion, showing front and
back, 1983–87, 5½in (14cm) high.
£200–275 *ANP*

A Lilliput Lane ceramic model,
Rose Cottage, Skirsgill, Second
version, 3in (7.5cm) high.
£150–200 *ANP*

*This model was only available
to collectors visiting Lilliput
Lane in Penrith, and only one
was allowed per visitor.*

David Winter

Two David Winter models, Oast Houses,
4½in (11.5cm) high.
l. First version, 1981–85. **£150–175**
r. Second version, 1985–93.
£30–35 *ANP*

A David Winter model,
Castle Cottage of Warwick,
event exclusive, 1993, 9in
(23cm) high.
£180–220 *ANP*

A David Winter model,
Christmas cottage,
produced annually, 1994,
7½in (19cm) high.
£100–120 *ANP*

l. A David Winter
model, Falstaff's
Manor, produced
1990–91, 7in
(18cm) high.
£200–300 *ANP*

r. A David
Winter cottage,
the Crown Inn,
Chiddingfold,
1980–82, 3in
(7.5cm) wide.
£275–350 *ANP*

A David Winter cottage, House On Top, 1982–88, 6½in (16.5cm) high. **£175–250** *ANP*

A David Winter cottage, Queen Elizabeth Slept Here, Guild piece No. 2, 1987–89, 7½in (19cm) wide. **£250–350** *ANP*

r. A David Winter cottage, Arches Three, only available on US tour of April/May 1993, 7½in (19cm) wide. **£180–220** *ANP*

A David Winter cottage, Little Mill, Third version, 1980–83, 5½in (14cm) wide. **£600–800** *ANP*

A David Winter model, Cotton Mill, 1983–89, 9in (23cm) high. **£275–350** *ANP*

A David Winter model, Fairy Tale Castle, 1982–89, 10in (25.5cm) high. **£175–225** *ANP*

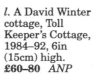

l. A David Winter cottage, Toll Keeper's Cottage, 1984–92, 6in (15cm) high. **£60–80** *ANP*

A David Winter model, Triple Oast, first version, 1981–85, 5½in (14cm) high.
£175–225 *ANP*

A David Winter model, 1983, The Bakery, 4in (10cm).
£25–30 *ANP*

A David Winter cottage, Audrey's Tea Room, 1991–92, 4in (10cm) high.
£100–140 *ANP*

The mould for this model has been destroyed.

r. A David Winter cottage, Wine Merchants, 1980–83, 4in (10cm) high.
£275–350 *ANP*

> **Miller's is a price GUIDE not a price LIST**

Crown Devon

l. A Fielding's Crown Devon jug, c1930, 5½in (14cm) high.
£40–50 *WN*

A Crown Devon ovoid vase, decorated in cloisonné style with flowering prunus, enamelled in bright orange, purple and yellow against a sea-blue mottled ground, gilt printed marks to base, numbered '2073', c1930, 9in (23cm) high.
£120–150 *WIL*

r. A Crown Devon figure of a girl, 1930s, 10in (25.5cm) high.
£150–175 *WTA*

Two Crown Devon plates, 1930s, largest 10in (25.5cm) diam.
£15–25 each *HEM*

Denby

Collectors familiar with Denby's bottles and kitchenware may be surprised by the wide variety of decorative ceramics produced by this versatile stoneware factory since its foundation in 1809. With Denby, as in many other fields, it is not only 19th and early 20th century material that is now collectable. 'Look out for 1950s and even '60s and '70s Denby', advises collector Gordon Hopwood. Denby's most important post-war designer was Glyn Colledge, whose work is becoming increasingly sought after. The following section illustrates Colledge's ceramic designs from the 1950s, as well as examples of work produced after his retirement in 1983.

A Denby matt glazed pastel ware vase, c1935, 5in (12.5cm) high.
£30–40 *PC*

A Denby grey vase, with handle, sgraffito decoration in cobalt blue, mid-1930s, 7in (17.5cm) high.
£55–65 *KES*

A Denby two-handled decorative pot and lid, with running glazes, c1925, 5½in (14cm) high.
£45–50 *PC*

A Denby tube-lined jug, c1925, 6in (15cm) high.
£65–70 *PC*

A Denby matt glazed vase, by Alice Teichner, c1937, 8in (20cm) high.
£50–55 *PC*

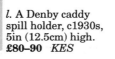

l. A Denby caddy spill holder, c1930s, 5in (12.5cm) high.
£80–90 *KES*

A Denby matt glazed bowl, by Alice Teichner, c1937, 11½in (29cm) diam.
£45–50 *PC*

A Denby Cheviot dish, c1955, 8in (20cm) high.
£25–30 *PC*

A Denby Tigo ware plate, c1955, 10¼in (26cm) diam.
£60–65 *PC*

A Denby two-handled bowl, designed by Glyn Colledge, c1950, 8in (20cm) diam.
£40–50 *PC*

A Denby 'cloisonné' plate, c1955, 6½in (16.5cm) diam.
£10–12 *PC*

A Denby table lamp, designed by Glyn Colledge, c1955, 7¼in (18.5cm) high.
£45–50 *PC*

A Denby jug, designed by Glyn Colledge, c1950, 4½in (11cm) high.
£35–40 *PC*

Two Denby tankards, designed by Glyn Colledge, c1950, 5¾in (14.5cm) high.
£30–35 each *PC*

A Denby bowl, designed by Glyn Colledge, c1950, 8¾in (22cm) diam.
£55–60 *PC*

A Denby tankard, designed by Glyn Colledge, c1950, 5¾in (14.5cm) high.
£30–35 *PC*

A Denby jug, designed by Glyn Colledge, c1950, 5in (12.5cm) high.
£35–40 *PC*

Four Denby tankards, designed by Glyn Colledge, c1950, 5in (12.5cm) high.
£30–35 each *PC*

A Denby hand painted bowl,
designed by Glyn Colledge,
c1990, 10¾in (27cm) diam.
£90–100 *PC*

FURTHER READING
G. & A. Key
*Denby Stonewares –
A Collector's Guide*
Keystones, PO Box 387,
Stafford ST16 3FG

Dutch Pottery

An Arnhem pottery clog,
decorated in Linear design,
c1920, 6in (15cm) long.
£75–85 *OO*

A Gouda pottery humidor,
decorated in Rhodian
design, c1918, 8½in
(21.5cm) high.
£120–160 *OO*

*Sponge was kept in the lid
to keep the tobacco moist.*

A Denby jug, designed by
Glyn Colledge, c1950, 7in
(18cm) high.
£45–50 *PC*

A Denby hand painted bowl,
designed by Glyn Colledge,
c1990, 4½in (11.5cm) diam.
£45–50 *PC*

r. A Denby hand painted bowl,
designed by Glyn Colledge,
c1990, 6½in (16.5cm) diam.
£50–55 *PC*

A Gouda pottery candlestick,
Zenith factory, designed by
W. Stourman, c1931, 5in
(12.5cm) high.
£90–120 *OO*

A Denby Arabesque pattern trio,
c1960, plate 6¼in (16cm) diam.
£12–16 *PC*

A Denby hand painted bowl,
designed by Glyn Colledge,
c1990, 7¼in (18.5cm) diam.
£60–70 *PC*

A Chris Lanooij vase, with
usual signature, c1913, 6½in
(16.5cm) high.
£100–160 *OO*

Doulton

A Royal Doulton flambé vase, decorated with a country landscape, c1930s, 11in (30cm) high.
£100–150 *YY*

A Doulton Lambeth stoneware compressed baluster-shaped vase, decorated by Arthur B. Barlow, with a band of scrolling leaves within stiff leaf bands, impressed mark, incised signature and dated '1872', 9½in (24cm) high.
£350–400 *DN*

A Royal Doulton pottery loving cup, with 2 crossover handles, commemorating the Coronation of Elizabeth II, designed by Milner Grey for Courage & Co Ltd, 1953, 5½in (14cm) high.
£75–95 *Gam*

> **Cross Reference**
> Toby & Character Jugs

r. A Royal Doulton 18-piece dessert service, decorated with sprays of flowers and leaves, within blue and gilt leaf borders, some damage, printed marks in puce, registration No. 72067, c1910.
£550–600 *DN*

Children's Ware

A Royal Doulton child's mug, decorated in Sorrento pattern, c1895, 4in (10cm) high.
£175–200 *AMH*

A Royal Doulton Nursery Rhyme Series Ware plate, decorated by Savage Cooper, c1903–39, 7in (18cm) diam.
£35–45 *HER*

A Doulton five-piece nursery breakfast set, each piece printed in colours with nursery rhyme characters, with 3 silver spoons and a knife, printed factory marks, 'H & H Birmingham 1932', in silk-lined presentation case.
£400–450 *CSK*

Figures

l. A Royal Doulton bone china figure, entitled 'Lady Charmian', HN 1949, 1940–75, 8in (20cm) high.
£120–140 *Gam*

A Royal Doulton figure of Henry Lytton as Jack Point, designed by C. J. Noke, small chip to headdress, printed mark in green, painted title and 'HN610', c1900, 6¾in (17cm) high.
£240–280 *DN*

Jack Point, the tragic clown in Gilbert and Sullivan's, Yeoman of the Guard, *was a favourite role for Sir Henry Lytton.*

r. A Royal Doulton pilot figure, of a young girl selling balloons, decorated in coloured enamels, unmarked, c1970, 8⅝in (22cm) high.
£180–220 *DN*

Goss & Crested China

With the expansion of the railways in the second half of the 19th century, ordinary working people could enjoy day trips to the seaside. W. H. Goss was the first ceramics factory to exploit the potential of this new British tourist industry. In the 1870–80s the firm began to market their souvenir wares across the country. White porcelain miniatures were modelled on museum antiquities, celebrated buildings and local monuments and decorated with the coats-of-arms of British towns. The porcelain was high quality, prices were affordable and Goss souvenirs were an instant success with the holidaying public. Many other ceramics factories, such as Carlton, Shelley and Arcadian, jumped on the bandwagon, supplying a wide range of extremely successful ceramic collectables.

The fashion for collecting Goss and crested china was at its height from the 1890s–1920s, the period to which most of the following examples belong. Production tailed off during the Depression and ceased altogether with the outbreak of WWII.

Today W. H. Goss pieces still command the highest prices, with cottages tending to be the most expensive items. Popular crested china themes include military subjects, appealing to both crested china and militaria collectors, comic novelty items and animals. As well as concentrating on individual models, enthusiasts also collect the crests of specific towns.

Goss

A Goss bowl, with Welsh decorations, c1900, 2½in (6.5cm) diam.
£70–90 *MGC*

A Goss jug, bearing the Llangollen crest, c1881–1934, 3¼in (8cm) high.
£10–15 *MGC*

A Goss crested jug, commemorating the Coronation of Edward VII, 1902, 3¼in (8.5cm) high.
£80–90 *MGC*

A Goss Worcester jug, c1910–30, 2½in (6.5cm) high.
£8–10 *G&CC*

A Goss urn, bearing the Seaford crest, c1900–30, 2in (5cm) high.
£18–25 *MGC*

A Goss Bagware jug, bearing the Pembroke crest, c1800–1900, 3in (7.5cm) high.
£30–40 *MGC*

l. A Goss model of Queen Victoria's first shoe, c1880–1930, 4in (10cm) long.
£35–45 *MGC*

A Goss model of Venus emerging
from 2 shells, c1858–87, 7in
(17.5cm) high.
£400–450 *G&CC*

A selection of Goss flower girls,
1930s, smallest 5½in (14cm) high.
£240–300 each *G&CC*

A Goss witches' cauldron,
inscribed 'Double, double
toyle and trouble, Fyer
burne and caldrone bubble',
c1900, 1¾in (4.5cm) high.
£20–30 *MGC*

A Goss dish, commemorating
the Empire Exhibition 1938,
7in (17.5cm) wide.
£40–45 *MGC*

l. A Goss
Peace plate,
1919, 8in
(20cm) diam.
£250–300
G&CC

A Goss pine
cone, bearing
the Bournemouth
crest, c1900, 3½in
(8.5cm) high.
£20–25 *MGC*

A Goss parian bust of
Lady Godiva, c1880,
4¼in (11cm) high.
£100–120 *MLa*

Crested China

A dromedary, bearing the City of London crest, unnamed, c1900–20, 2¼in (5.5cm) high.
£25–30 *MGC*

An elephant, bearing Durban crest, unnamed, c1900–20, 2½in (6.5cm) high.
£30–35 *MGC*

An Arcadian Scottie dog, c1910–20, 2½in (6.5cm) long.
£12–15 *G&CC*

A collection of crested china cats, c1900–20.
£15–75 each *CCC*

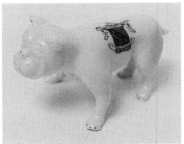

An Alexandra crested china bulldog, c1910–20, 3in (7.5cm) high.
£15–25 *MGC*

A comic crested china cat, c1910–20, 4in (10cm) high.
£15–25 *MGC*

l. An Arcadian Gretna Green blacksmith's shop, c1900–20, 3½in (9cm) high.
£40–50 *MGC*

A Carlton Scottish bagpiper, c1914–18, 5¾in (14.5cm) high.
£300–350 *MGC*

A crested china figure, with pint of beer, bearing Bury St Edmunds crest, c1910–20, 5in (12.5cm) high.
£30–35 *BCO*

A Willow Art Boer War crested Memorial, with Ashington & Hirst crest, c1910–20, 5½in (14cm) high.
£80–90 *BCO*

A Swan crested china model of the Lucitania, c1910–20, 7½in (19cm) long.
£90–100 *MGC*

An Arcadian bust of John Bull, c1910–20, 2¾in (7cm) high.
£15–20 *MGC*

A Captain Scott crested china Boscombe memorial, c1910–20, 6in (15cm) high.
£30–35 *BCO*

A Whitby Captain Cook crested china monument, c1910–20, 5¼in (13cm) high.
£40–50 *BCO*

An Arcadian parian bust of George V, c1910–20, 5½in (14cm) high.
£50–60 *MGC*

A crested china charabanc, unnamed, c1910–20, 5in (12.5cm) high.
£40–50 *MGC*

Honiton

A Honiton jug, 1930s,
2¾in (7cm) high.
£8–10 *YY*

A Honiton jug, 1930s,
4¾in (12cm) high.
£15–20 *YY*

A jug, impressed 'Honiton
England', c1950, 4½in
(11.5cm) high.
£10–12 *WN*

Meissen

A Meissen figure of the Dame of
the Order of Mops, after the
model by J. J. Kändler, decorated
in coloured enamels, on canted
tapering marbled base, 2 small
chips, blue mark and incised
number '549', 19thC, 11¼in
(28.5cm) high.
£800–900 *DN*

A Meissen pot-pourri vase,
modelled as an urn, on a
branch-moulded support
applied with flowers and
foliage, with a seated lady, a
cat on her lap being menaced
by a pug dog, enriched in
colours and gilt, damaged and
restored, cover lacking, blue
crossed swords mark, c1745,
7¼in (18.5cm) high.
£620–680 *CSK*

A Meissen dish, the centre
painted with a military
encampment inscribed
'Das Feldlager', by P. H.
Wouwermann, with pink
painted and gilt scroll border,
underglaze blue crossed swords
mark and impressed '113',
19thC, 7½in (19cm) diam.
£240–280 *AG*

A Meissen model of a donkey,
No. R215, after a model by Erich
Oehme, c1943, 5in (12.5cm) long.
£40–60 *DAV*

A set of 10 large and 6 small Meissen blue and white
plates, c1935, 7 and 8¾in (18 and 22cm) diam.
£575–650 *SIG*

Midwinter

Midwinter, founded in 1910, was one of the most innovative British ceramic factories of the 1950s. Inspired by contemporary designs from the USA, Roy Midwinter (1923–90), launched the 'Stylecraft' range in 1953, introducing new shapes and modernist patterns to the British market. The firm's resident designer, Jessie Tait (b1928), produced tableware with distinctive abstract decoration and Roy Midwinter also commissioned designs from figures such as Sir Terence Conran, Sir Hugh Casson and the bird painter, Sir Peter Scott. Roy Midwinter's wife, Eve, also designed for the firm. Particularly helpful for today's collectors is that the name of the factory, the artist and the individual pattern, are often inscribed on the underside of each piece.

For the moment, Midwinter pottery is often very reasonably priced and is still readily available, sometimes for a few pounds at car-boot sales. As interest in 1950s collectables increases, however, prices are set to rise.

A Midwinter Stylecraft soup bowl and saucer, Riviera design by Sir Hugh Casson, c1954, saucer 6½in (16.5cm) diam.
£5–7 *PC*

l. A Midwinter Fashion tureen, Chequers design by Sir Terence Conran, 1957.
£20–22 *AND*

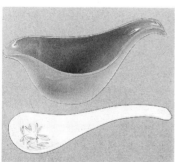

A Midwinter Cassandra pattern gravy boat and ladle, 1950s, 8½in (21.5cm) long.
£18–22 *JR*

A Midwinter Fashion plate, Melody design by Sir Terence Conran, 1958, 6in (15cm) diam.
£7–8 *AND*

A Midwinter Stylecraft coffee cup and saucer, Riviera design by Sir Hugh Casson, c1954.
£10–12 *AND*

A Midwinter Fine one pint jug, Diagonal design by Nigel Wilde, c1964, 7¼in (18.5cm) high.
£8–10 *AND*

A Midwinter Fashion 37-piece dinner service, Riverside design by John Russell, c1962.
£125–150 *AND*

Jessie Tait

A Midwinter Stylecraft platter, Ming Tree design by Jessie Tait, c1953, 13½in (34.5cm) wide.
£25–28 *AND*

A Midwinter Stylecraft plate, Red Domino design by Jessie Tait, c1953, 8½in (21.5cm) diam.
£7–9 *AND*

This pattern was also produced in blue and called Blue Domino.

r. A Midwinter side plate, Zambesi pattern by Jessie Tait, 1950s, 6½in (16.5cm) diam.
£5–7 *JR*

A Midwinter Stylecraft coffee cup and saucer, Spruce design by Jessie Tait, c1953.
£8–9 *AND*

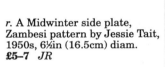

A Midwinter Fashion cruet and gravy boat, Cherokee design by Jessie Tait, c1957, cruet base 6in (15cm) wide. **£18–20** gravy boat 8½in (21.5cm) long. **£6–8** *AND*

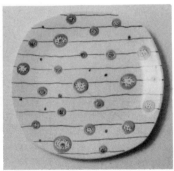

A Midwinter Fashion plate, Festival design by Jessie Tait, c1955, 8¾in (22cm) diam.
£15–16 *AND*

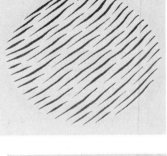

A Midwinter Fashion plate and milk jug, Zambesi design by Jessie Tait, c1956, plate 6in diam. **£6–8** milk jug 4½in (11.5cm) high.
£12–15 *AND*

The Zambesi pattern by Jessie Tait was widely copied by other potteries.

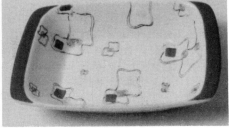

A Midwinter Fashion dish, Cuban Fantasy design by Jessie Tait, c1957, 6½in (16.5cm) long.
£12–14 *AND*

A Midwinter Fine milk jug and sugar bowl, Graphic design by Jessie Tait, c1964, bowl 3¾in (9.5cm) diam.
£8–10 *AND*

Eve Midwinter

A Midwinter Style tureen, pattern design by Eve Midwinter, c1983, 11½in (29cm) wide.
£14–16 *AND*

A Midwinter Style platter, pattern design by Eve Midwinter, c1983, 12in (30.5cm) wide.
£10–12 *AND*

A Midwinter Style beverage dispenser, pattern design by Eve Midwinter, c1983, 9in (23cm) high.
£18–20 *AND*

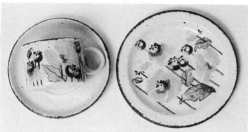

A Midwinter Stonehenge plate and cup and saucer, Autumn design by Eve Midwinter, c1974, plate 7in (18cm) diam.
£10–12 each *AND*

Animals

r. A Midwinter deer's head wall plaque, c1950, 6¼in (16cm) high.
£18–21 *AND*

A Midwinter model of Peggy the Calf, c1930, 5in (12.5cm) high.
£45–50 *AND*

A Midwinter blackbird pie funnel, c1950, 4½in (11.5cm) high.
£10–12 *AND*

A Midwinter model of a fawn, c1950, 2½in (6.5cm) high.
£18–21 *AND*

A Midwinter model of a swan, c1950, 2½in (6.5cm) high.
£22–25 *AND*

r. A Midwinter model of Larry the Lamb, c1930, 3½in (9cm) high.
£18–20 *AND*

Minton

A Minton blue barrel-shaped garden seat, 19thC, 17in (43cm) high.
£250–300 *SIG*

A pair of Minton Secessionist vases, with double-loop handles, each decorated in silver lustre with stylised flowers and leaves, on a green ground, restored, impressed marks and No. '594', early 20thC, 15¾in (40cm) high.
£85–120 *DN*

A Minton two-handled vase and cover, the green ground moulded with peach and gilt scrollwork, painted panels to both sides, the cover with rococo-scrolled knop, damaged, 19thC, 14in (36cm) high.
£300–350 *HSS*

A Minton game pie dish and cover, modelled as a wicker basket with oak branch handles and feet, the cover moulded with game including a mallard and a hare, enriched in coloured glazes, damaged and repaired, impressed marks and date code for 1861, 13½in (34.5cm) wide.
£500–600 *CSK*

l. A Minton majolica spirally moulded jardinière, with putti handles, moulded laurel garlands issuing from lions' masks, within oak leaf borders, on a blue ground, impressed marks, c1865, 10½in (27cm) high.
£750–850 *DN*

A Minton jardinière and stand, with patera and ribbon-tied laurel garlands picked out in blue, on a purple ground, damaged, impressed mark and numerals, late 19thC, 40in (101.5cm) high.
£175–225 *DN*

A Minton vase, modelled as a fish upheld by a hand issuing from lilies, on a shaped base, enriched in green and gilt, shape No. 1321, slight wear, impressed marks, date code for 1868, 8½in (21.5cm) high.
£210–250 *CSK*

A Minton parian ware figure of Cupid, modelled ice-skating, his wings slightly spread, with glass stand, minor chips and firing cracks, c1860, 12in (30.5cm) high.
£425–475 *CSK*

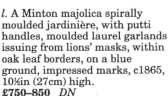

Moorcroft

A Moorcroft vase, tube-lined with pansies beneath a rich flambé glaze, impressed and painted marks, c1919–45, 13in (33cm) high.
£750–850 *S(S)*

A William Moorcroft Florian Ware Poppy design vase, the flowers in shades of yellow and blue, c1902, 8½in (21.5cm) high.
£1,100–1,300 *RUM*

A William Moorcroft Commonwealth commemorative beaker, c1935, 8½in (21.5cm) high.
£700–900 *RUM*

A William Moorcroft Brown Cornflower design vase, c1912, 13in (33cm) high.
£2,200–2,500 *RUM*

l. A Moorcroft Leaf and Berry design vase, c1946, 4in (10cm) high.
£120–150 *HEA*

A William Moorcroft Persian design vase, c1916, 10in (25.5cm) high.
£2,000–2,400 *RUM*

A Moorcroft Claremont design vase, with a smokey blue ground, chipped, printed mark of Liberty and Co, green signature beneath, early 20thC, 7½in (19cm) high.
£550–650 *WL*

A William Moorcroft Florian Ware Cornflower design cachepot, c1902, 4½in (11.5cm) high.
£500–600 *RUM*

r. A Walter Moorcroft Arum Lily design cachepot, c1959, 4½in (11.5cm) high.
£250–350 *RUM*

A Walter Moorcroft Caribbean design covered mug, decorated with flying fish, c1960, 5in (13cm) high.
£400–450 *RUM*

A Moorcroft Hibiscus design vase, 1960s, 7½in (19cm) high.
£120–140 *HEA*

A Moorcroft Coral Hibiscus design box and cover, 1970s, 5in (12.5cm) wide.
£40–50 *HEA*

A Moorcroft Columbine design vase, c1980, 8in (20cm) high.
£140–170 *HEA*

A Moorcroft Clematis design vase, 1960s, 5in (13cm) high.
£100–130 *HEA*

A Moorcroft Anemone design vase, 1970s, 5½in (14cm) high.
£50–60 *HEA*

A Moorcroft Coral Hibiscus design vase, 1970s, 7in (18cm) high.
£60–70 *HEA*

A Moorcroft Anemone design jardinière, c1980, 7in (18cm) high.
£150–200 *HEA*

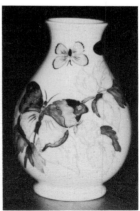

A Walter Moorcroft Butterfly design limited edition vase, c1984, 7in (18cm) high.
£150–175 *RUM*

Myott

The firm of Myott & Son was founded in Stoke-on-Trent in 1898. The Company moved to Cobridge, Staffordshire, in 1902 and to Hanley in 1947. The following ceramics date from the 1930s, when the firm was known for its confident Art Deco style, epitomised by Myott's distinctive vases, with their bold geometric shapes and colourful, freely-painted decoration. The factory suffered from a fire in 1947 and though it re-opened three days later all the early pattern records were lost.

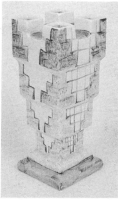

A Myott Castle vase, painted in green, pink, blue and mauve, c1930, 8½in (21.5cm) high.
£140–160 *BKK*

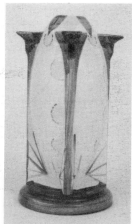

A Myott Torpedo shape vase, c1930, 8½in (21.5cm) high.
£220–250 *BKK*

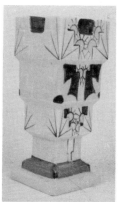

r. A Myott cup and saucer, c1935, cup 2in (5cm) high.
£25–30 *BKK*

A Myott Pyramid vase, painted green, brown and yellow, with orange flowers, c1931, 8¾in (22cm) high.
£100–125 *BKK*

A Myott Castle vase, painted in brown, orange and black, c1930, 8½in (21.5cm) high.
£120–150 *BKK*

r. A Myott Pyramid vase, decorated in orange, brown and green, 1931–36, 9in (23cm) high.
£65–75 *BEV*

A Myott jug, painted in green and brown, 1931–36, 8in (20.5cm) high.
£45–55 *BEV*

A Myott jug, decorated in brown, green, blue and orange, c1930, 7½in (19cm) high.
£40–50 *BKK*

r. A pair of Myott jugs, painted in yellow, green and black with pink flowers, c1932, 9in (23cm) high.
£180–200 *BKK*

Pictorial Pot Lids

'Shrimping, Pegwell Bay', No. 33, 1850, 3½in (9cm) diam.
£100–120 *BHa*

'The Residence of Anne Hathaway', No. 228, 1860, 4in (10cm) diam.
£55–65 *BHa*

'The Old Watermill', No. 318, 1860, 2¾in (7cm) diam.
£90–110 *BHa*

'Harbour of Hong Kong', No. 221, 1860, 4¼in (11cm) diam.
£80–90 *BHa*

'On Guard', No. 340, 1860, 4¼in (11cm) diam.
£60–70 *BHa*

'The Shrimpers', No. 63, 1850, 4in (10cm) diam.
£40–45 *AnE*

r. 'The Allied Generals, F. M. Lord Raglan, Gen. Canrobert', No. 168, 1854, 4¼in (10.5cm) diam.
£130–145 *BHa*

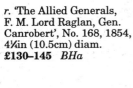

'May Day Dancers at the Swan Inn', No. 233, 1860, 4in (10cm) diam.
£75–85 *BHa*

'The Late Prince Consort', No. 153, 1862, 4in (10cm) diam.
£35–40 *AnE*

l. 'The Donkey's Foal', No. 386, 1865, 3½in (9cm) wide.
£95–110 *BHa*

'Sandringham The Seat of HRH The Prince of Wales', No. 181, 1862, 4¼in (11cm) diam.
£90–110 *BHa*

'Holborn Viaduct', No. 202, 1870, 4in (10cm) diam.
£90–100 *BHa*

Pictorial Pot Lids

- The lids were for pots which contained edible or cosmetic products that were oily, greasy, powdery or paste.
- Premium lids are undamaged and show sharp, unblemished pictures, good colours and few abrasions.
- Pot lids date from the first known engraving. Some were made for over thirty years and the plates had to be reconditioned, giving rise to interesting variations.

'Peace', No. 219, 1860, 4in (10cm) diam.
£35–40 *AnE*

'The Rivals', No. 322, 1860, 4in (10cm) diam.
£85–95 *BHa*

'Victor Emmanuel and Garibaldi', No. 211, 1861, 4in (10cm) diam.
£80–90 *BHa*

'Seven Ages of Man', No. 230, 1860, 4in (10cm) diam.
£40–45 *AnE*

'Hide and Seek', No. 255, 1860, 4in (10cm) diam.
£60–70 *BHa*

'Belle Vue Tavern', No. 28, 1860, 4¼in (10.5cm) diam.
£60–70 *AnE*

l. 'The Village Wedding', No. 240, third edition, 1857, 4in (10cm) diam.
£50–60 *BHa*

Miller's is a price GUIDE not a price LIST

Quimper

A Quimper vase, with painted flags, marked 'Henriot Quimper', c1920, 4¼in (10.5cm) high.
£70–80 *MofC*

r. A pair of Quimper plates, with yellow rims, c1920, 9½in (24cm) diam.
£70–80 each *MofC*

Charlotte Rhead

A Bursley footed 'Kew' bowl, designed by Charlotte Rhead, printed and painted, pattern No. 876, c1926, 10in (25.5cm) diam.
£100–200 *PC*

A Crown Ducal dish, designed by Charlotte Rhead, with pink flowers on a mottled brown ground, shape No. 9, 1940s, 7in (18cm) wide.
£35–40 *PC*

A Crown Ducal vase, designed by Charlotte Rhead, coloured green, pink, blue and yellow, Persian Rose pattern No. 4040/A, shape No. 212, c1935, 7in (18cm) high.
£200–250 *PC*

Shape and colour are all important in assessing Charlotte Rhead's work. Bright colours and a strong Art Deco form make this vase particularly collectable – patterns incorporating pink, blue and violet are keenly sought after. Crown Ducal wares decorated in mottled brown are less desirable.

A Crown Ducal vase, designed by Charlotte Rhead, pattern No. 4926, shape No. 175, c1937, 6in (15cm) high.
£140–165 *PC*

l. A cream ground and bordered charger, decorated with leaves in autumnal colours, signed 'Charlotte Rhead', 1930s, 13in (33cm) diam.
£125–150 *PCh*

Frederick Rhead

A 'Korea' bowl, designed by Frederick Rhead, c1900, 9in (22.5cm) diam.
£35–50 *HEM*

Royal Winton

A Royal Winton celery dish, 1930s, 13in (33cm) long.
£25–30 *COL*

A Royal Winton Chintz ware bowl, decorated in Marguerite pattern, 1930s, 8in (20.5cm) diam.
£60–70 *Ber*

A Grimwades Royal Winton jug, 1930s, 8in (20cm) high.
£25–30 *COL*

Two Royal Winton plates, decorated with ducks, 1930s, 8½in (21.5cm) diam.
£30–35 each *HEM*

A Royal Winton Chintz ware sandwich set, decorated in Marguerite pattern, 1930s, plate 5½in (14cm) diam.
£140–160 *MLa*

Rye

In 1947, the Cole brothers, Wally and John, purchased Rye Pottery, which had been closed down during the war. Sculptors and potters in the 1930s, the Coles made stoneware studio pottery: expensive, one-off pieces. 'Why don't you produce something good that I could use rather than putting in a show case?' complained Victoria & Albert ceramics curator and client W. B. Honey. Rye gave the brothers this opportunity, as Wally Cole, now 82, recalls. 'We set out to make decent ware that could be used on the table and that Stoke-on-Trent wasn't able to produce. Inspired by English delft, Lambeth and Liverpool, we settled on traditional tin-glazed earthenware, every piece hand-painted.' Affordable to a middle-class market, this domestic ware was well crafted and decorated, the brothers experimenting with both abstract surface designs and texture, bringing craft and artistry to everyday pottery. Rye ceramics were shown at the Festival of Britain and sold around the world (Heal's was a major stockist in London).

A Rye Pottery cup and saucer, c1950, cup 3in (7.5cm) high.
£30–35 NCA

A Rye Pottery candy striped tankard, 1950s, 4in (10cm) high.
£18–22 JR

A Rye Pottery black candy-striped cruet set, 1950s, 3in (7.5cm) high.
£18–22 JR

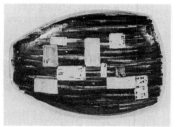

A Rye Pottery avocado dish, 1950s, 5¾in (14.5cm) wide.
£25–30 NCA

A Rye Pottery dish, decorated with a green and white pattern, c1950, 9in (23cm) wide.
£60–65 NCA

A Rye Pottery dish, decorated with a yellow, white and green pattern, c1950, 9in (23cm) wide.
£70–75 NCA

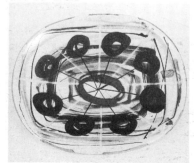

A Rye Pottery dish, c1950, 8½in (21.5cm) wide.
£70–80 NCA

A Rye Pottery vase, c1950s, 4½in (11.5cm) high.
£35–40 NCA

A Rye Pottery cruet, 1950s, 6½in (16.5cm) high.
£20–25 each NCA

Shelley

r. A Shelley advertising figure, chipped, 1930s, 12in (30.5cm) high.
£800–1,000 *McC*

l. A Shelley porcelain 16-piece coffee service, of octagonal form, printed in yellow and black enamel, depicting a gate below tall trees, the sun in the background, 1930s.
£275–325 *Bea*

l. A Shelley child's chamber pot, decorated with children and pixies, beneath a blue line rim, after designs by Mabel Lucie Attwell, printed marks, 1930s, 7in (18cm) diam.
£200–225 *DN*

Staffordshire
Animals

A Staffordshire porcellaneous spill vase, in the form of a lone horn cow, c1840, 6in (15cm) high.
£650–750 *MSA*

A Staffordshire figure of a peacock, c1830, 4in (10cm) high.
£500–550 *RWB*

Staffordshire

- Staffordshire figures became popular during the first years of Queen Victoria's reign and by the mid-19thC were being mass-produced.
- Most pieces are unmarked.
- Intended for mantelpiece display, they generally have an undecorated flattened back, and are often referred to as 'flatbacks'.
- The most collectable themes include Royalty, military figures (particularly Crimean War), animals, theatrical and sporting subjects.
- Many of the 19thC moulds are still being used. Victorian originals should have crisp moulding, good decoration and well-executed facial details.
- Prices depend on subject matter, rarity and condition.

A pair of Staffordshire figures of Dalmatians, c1850, 5½in (14cm) high.
£500–550 *RWB*

A pair of Staffordshire figures of cats, one with a kitten, c1835, 2¾in (7cm) high.
£400–500 *JO*

A pair of Staffordshire figures of spaniels, with flower baskets in their mouths, decorated with brown marks and gilt chains, c1860, 7½in (19cm) high.
£750–850 *RWB*

A Staffordshire porcelain figure of a hound, decorated in brown and wearing a gilt collar, standing on a gilt decorated mound base, c1830–40, 5in (12.5cm) high.
£125–150 *DN*

A Staffordshire tobacco jar, in the form of a bulldog, late 19thC, 6¼in (16cm) high.
£100–125 *JO*

A pair of Staffordshire figures of bearded collies, c1860, 6¼in (16cm) high.
£600–800 *JO*

l. A pair of Staffordshire pottery figures of greyhounds, one with a hare in its mouth, the other with a hare at its feet, each standing on an oval base, 19thC, 10in (25.5cm) high.
£350–400 *DN*

A Staffordshire group of a recumbent Newfoundland bitch with puppies, c1850, 9½in (24cm) long.
£600–650 *RWB*

A pair of Staffordshire figures of spaniels, one chipped, 19thC.
£270–300 *LT*

Figures

Three Staffordshire figures of Wesley, c1860, tallest 7¼in (18.5cm) high.
£100–250 each *JO*

A Staffordshire group entitled 'Highland Jessye', c1857, 14in (35.5cm) high.
£450–500 *RWB*

A Staffordshire figure of Charity Girl, by Kent and Parr, c1880, 7in (18cm) high.
£75–85 *SER*

r. A Staffordshire porcelain group, depicting a shepherd, his dog and sheep on a grass knoll, by Lloyd of Shelton, c1850, 5½in (14cm) high.
£200–300 *CB*

A Staffordshire figure of John Liston as Ali Baba, c1820, 6¾in (17cm) high, (E439).
£80–100 *SER*

A Staffordshire figure of Red Riding Hood and the wolf, c1860, 9½in (24cm) high.
£120–150 *SER*

l. A Staffordshire figure of a female musician on a couch, c1860, 8¾in (22cm) high.
£55–65 *SER*

A trio of Staffordshire religious portrait figures, c1851, largest 9½in (24cm) high.
£1,200–1,350 *RWB*

A Staffordshire figure of a female gardener, c1850, 8in (20.5cm) high.
£150–185 *SER*

A Staffordshire figure, The Soldier's Dream, from a poem by Thomas Campbell, c1854, 10¼in (26cm) high, (C275).
£70–80 *SER*

A Staffordshire figure of a bearded gentleman, with plumed top hat, standing by a plinth, mid-19thC, 11in (28cm) high.
£160–200 *GAK*

A Staffordshire quill holder, depicting a girl with a goat, c1840, 5in (12.5cm) high.
£100–125 *SER*

r. A Staffordshire figure, entitled 'Garibaldi', standing with his horse on a rocky base, by William Kent of Burslem, c1920, 13in (33cm) high.
£450–550 *JBL*

Staffordshire Figures

The letters and figures in brackets at the end of some captions (ie H429) refer to the cataloguing system used by P. D. Gordon Pugh, in *Staffordshire Portrait Figures*, published by Antique Collectors' Club Ltd, 1970

r. A Staffordshire figure of Wellington on horseback, c1845, 4in (10cm) high.
£75–85 *SER*

l. A Staffordshire figure of a gardener with flowers, restored, c1850, 7in (18cm) high.
£150–185 *SER*

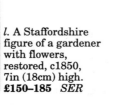

A Staffordshire figure of Milton, c1850, 7½in (19cm) high, (H429).
£75–85 *SER*

Pastille Burners

r. A Staffordshire porcellaneous pastille burner, modelled as an octagonal cottage with umbrella roof, by Samuel Alcock, c1835, 5½in (14cm) high.
£270–300 RWB

l. A Staffordshire porcellaneous pastille burner, modelled as a house, c1835, 4½in (11.5cm) high.
£225–250 RWB

SylvaC

A SylvaC model of a pixie and mushroom, with green and fawn glaze, c1930, 5in (13cm) high.
£20–25 COL

A SylvaC model of a dog, with a bow, red glaze, No. 1119, c1930, 3½in (9cm) high.
£50–60 PC

Spill Vases

A Staffordshire spill vase, modelled as a stag and hound, c1860, 7½in (19cm) high.
£90–100 RWB

A Staffordshire spill vase, modelled as the fortune teller, c1870, 11½in (30cm) high.
£160–180 RWB

r. A SylvaC chutney pot, with glossy glaze, No. 4753, c1980, 5in (12.5cm) diam.
£20–25 JDC

l. A SylvaC model of a poodle, brown glaze, No. 170, c1960, 5in (13cm) high.
£20–25 HEM

Toby Jugs

Toby jugs were first produced by the Staffordshire potteries in the second half of the 18th century. The name comes from a poem published in 1761 about one 'Toby Philpot'. The traditional design: a squat old man, jug of ale in hand and wearing a three-cornered hat, The Toper, derives from an engraving illustrating the verse, sold by London print dealer Carrington Bowles to the Staffordshire potter Ralph Wood.

Ralph Wood was the first, and perhaps the most celebrated, producer of Toby jugs. At first only the familiar figure of The Toper was represented but other characters such as The Squire, The Sailor and The Snuff Taker were soon being modelled. Eighteenth century Toby jugs are rare and extremely sought after. The most commonly found examples date from the 19th century onwards. The Victorian period saw the introduction of Toby jugs modelled on specific individuals, literary characters, military, naval and political heroes. Character jugs remain popular in the 20th century with Royal Doulton being one of the major producers in the field.

A Ralph Wood style Toby jug, with black hat, green jacket, brown leggings and black boots, late 18thC, 10in (25.5cm) high.
£525–600 *Mit*

A Ralph Wood style Toby jug, with brown hat, green jacket and blue leggings, on brown base, late 18thC, 9½in (24cm) high.
£375–425 *Mit*

A Staffordshire pearlware Toby jug, decorated in underglaze colours and sponged base, c1800, 10in (25.5cm) high.
£500–550 *RWB*

A character jug, depicting a sailor seated on a money chest, with black hat and scarf, blue jacket with yellow buttons, blue striped trousers and black shoes with cream buckles, paintwork scuffed, c1800, 10in (25.5cm) high.
£300–350 *GAK*

A Staffordshire Toby jug, with sponged and underglaze decoration, c1790, 10½in (26.5cm) high.
£550–600 *RWB*

A Ralph Wood Toby jug, with black hat, green jacket, brown leggings and boots, supporting a pipe with his right hand, late 18thC, 9½in (24cm) high.
£1,700–2,000 *Mit*

A Toby Willow cruet set, comprising: salt, mustard, pepper and vinegar, the figures with underglaze blue coats, yellow trousers and red vests, c1900, 6in (15cm) high.
£650–750 *JBL*

Beswick

A Beswick character jug, Old Bill, impressed mark, 4¾in (12cm) high.
£120–150 *DN*

A Beswick colour trial Toby jug, Martha Gunn, printed and impressed marks, 3½in (9cm) high.
£100–120 *DN*

Continental

A pair of Continental majolica character jugs, in the form of Industry and Liberty, decorated in coloured enamels, impressed marks, early 20thC, 10¼in (26cm) high.
£275–325 *DN*

r. A Sarreguemines advertising jug, No. 3181, overprinted in Australia, c1902, 8in (20cm) high.
£350–400 *PC*

l. An Onnaing jug, No. 784, shaped as a lady wearing a bonnet, with red interior, inscribed 'La Jupe-Culotte', c1904, 12in (30.5cm) high.
£200–250 *PC*

An Onnaing jug, No. 741, depicting a politician, with red interior, c1904, 11in (28cm) high.
£300–400 *PC*

Kevin Francis

A Kevin Francis character jug, Josiah Wedgwood, designed by D. Tootle, printed mark in black, No. 19 from an edition of 350, 8¾in (22cm) high.
£125–150 *DN*

A Kevin Francis character jug, Charlotte Rhead, designed by D. Tootle, No. 126 from an edition of 350, printed mark in black, 9in (23cm) high.
£140–160 *DN*

Kevin Francis

Kevin Francis has produced a series of character jugs commemorating the great potters of the past. Whilst Josiah Wedgwood was in no position to comment on his representation, Susie Cooper certainly was when interviewed two years ago. She was indignant that she should have been portrayed sitting on a teapot and dismissed both the concept and the jug as 'horrible and quite ridiculous'.

r. A Kevin Francis character jug, Susie Cooper, designed by D. Tootle, No. 148 from an edition of 350, printed mark in black, 9in (23cm) high.
£100–120 *DN*

Royal Doulton

A Royal Doulton character jug, 'arriet, designed by H. Fenton, printed mark in green, 6¼in (16cm) high.
£100–120 *DN*

A Royal Doulton character jug, Jarge, 6½in (16.5cm) high.
£125–150 *DA*

A Royal Doulton character jug, John Barleycorn, designed by C. J. Noke, D5327, printed mark in green, 7in (18cm) high.
£65–85 *DN*

Five Royal Doulton character jugs, Louis Armstrong, Groucho Marx, W. C. Fields, Jimmy Durante and Mae West, D6707, 6710, 6674, 6708 and 6688, printed marks in green, 7½in (19cm) high.
£270–320 *DN*

A Royal Doulton Toby jug, blue version Winston Churchill, printed mark in green, 9¼in (23.5cm) high.
£130–160 *DN*

A Royal Doulton character jug, 'ard of 'earing, designed by D. Biggs, D6594, printed mark in green, 2½in (6.5cm) high.
£400–450 *DN*

A Royal Doulton colour trial character jug, Don Quixote, designed by G. Blower, D6460, printed mark in green, 4in (10cm) high.
£150–175 *DN*

A Royal Doulton character jug, Bahamas Policeman, designed by W. K. Harper, D6912, printed mark in gilt, 7¼in (18.5cm) high.
£90–110 *DN*

A series of 6 Royal Doulton character jugs, The Wild West collection, designed by S. J. Taylor, comprising: Annie Oakley, Geronimo, Buffalo Bill, Wyatt Earp, Doc Holliday and Wild Bill Hickok, D6731–33, 6711, 6735 and 6736, 6in (15cm) high.
£200–240 *DN*

A Royal Doulton character jug,
The Fortune Teller, first version,
designed by G. Sharpe, D6497,
printed mark in green, 6½in
(16.5cm) high.
£180–210 *DN*

Seven Royal Doulton character jugs, Henry VIII and his
wives, 6642–6646, 6653 and 6664, Henry VIII designed
by E. Griffiths, printed marks in green, 6¾in (17cm) high.
£200–250 *DN*

A Royal Doulton
character jug, Captain
Hook, designed by
M. Henk and D. Biggs,
D6601, printed mark in
green, 4in (10cm) high.
£160–180 *DN*

A Royal Doulton character
jug, Santa Claus, with 'sack
of toys' handle, D6690,
printed mark in green,
7in (18cm) high.
£60–75 *DN*

A Royal Doulton character jug,
Old King Cole, with yellow
crown, registered No. 832354,
5½in (14cm) high.
£850–1,000 *AG*

Wilkinson

A Wilkinson character
jug, depicting George V
in naval uniform,
designed by F. Carruthers
Gould, facsimile
signature to base, from
an edition of 1,000,
c1919, 11in (28cm) high.
£900–1,200 *JBL*

A Wilkinson character
jug, depicting Lord
Kitchener in naval
uniform, designed by
F. Carruthers Gould,
holding a jug inscribed
'Bitter for the Kaiser',
facsimile signature to
base, from an edition
of 250, c1919, 10in
(25.5cm) high.
£400–500 *JBL*

A Wilkinson character
jug, Marshal Foch,
designed by
F. Carruthers Gould,
with a glass and a
bottle of frothing
champagne, inscribed
'Au Diable le Kaiser',
black printed marks,
'FCG' monogram on
side of base, c1914,
12¼in (31cm) high.
£875–1,000 *C*

A Royal Doulton
character jug, Ronald
Reagan, designed by
E. Griffiths, D6718,
printed mark in gilt
and numbered '428',
from an edition of
5,000, with certificate,
7¾in (19.5cm) high.
£160–180 *DN*

Victorian & Edwardian

A set of 4 German porcelain figures of putti, depicting the elements, decorated in coloured enamels, damaged, pseudo crossed swords mark in blue, late 19thC, 9in (23cm) high.
£475–575 *DN*

A set of 5 Victorian pottery jugs, with blue transfer design, 2½ to 6in (6.5 to 15cm) high.
£50–60 *TAC*

A Brownhills Pottery blue and white jasper ware biscuit barrel, c1892, 6in (15cm) high.
£100–120 *GLN*

A William Brownfields white porcelain basket, decorated with acorns, c1870, 8in (20cm) long.
£100–125 *GLN*

A white porcelain vase, decorated with flowers and foliage, impressed 'Moore', c1870, 9½in (24cm) wide.
£350–375 *GLN*

l. A Continental porcelain box and hinged cover, moulded in relief with panels of classical figures, picked out in coloured enamels, within gilt scroll cartouches, damaged, pseudo Naples marks, late 19thC, 10½in (26.5cm) wide.
£425–525 *DN*

A late Victorian pottery cache-pot, with floral decoration on a cream and brown ground, beneath a pierced brass rim, on raised base, 14¾in (37.5cm) diam.
£120–150 *Gam*

A Bloor Derby figure of a kneeling child, entitled 'Night', 19thC, 3½in (9cm) high.
£250–300 *RA*

A Measham ware kettle, with stand, 1893, 11in (28cm) high.
£140–160 *JBL*

Cheese Dishes

A cheese dish and cover, moulded and painted with flowers and foliage, within gilt borders, on cream ground, late 19thC, 9½in (24cm) diam.
£110–150 *GAK*

A smear glazed stoneware Stilton cheese dish and cover, with blue ground, late 19thC, 11in (28cm) diam.
£90–110 *PCh*

A majolica cheese dome, decorated in brown, pink and green, c1880, 15in (38cm) high.
£400–450 *JBL*

Lustreware

Lustreware is pottery with a shiny, iridescent surface produced by using metallic oxides. Silver gives golden tones and copper a rich ruby-red. The technique, popular in the Middle Ages and early Renaissance, was revived by potters in the 19th century.

r. A copper lustre jug, with scalloped rim, decorated with cupid riding on a lion, late 19thC, 4½in (11.5cm) high.
£65–75 *GLN*

A copper lustre jug, the body hand painted with trailing yellow berries and blue and white flowerheads, mid-19thC, 5½in (14cm) high.
£100–125 *DA*

A Pilkington Royal Lancastrian vase, decorated in lustre by William S. Mycock, with birds, scrolling flowers and leaves, on a mottled blue ground, impressed marks and painted monogram, late 19thC, 5¾in (14.5cm) high.
£375–425 *DN*

Use the Index!

Because certain items might fit easily into any number of categories, the quickest and surest method of locating any entry is by reference to the index at the back of the book.

This index has been fully cross-referenced for absolute simplicity.

A Sunderland type pink splash lustre jug, printed in black with 3 boxers and verse, c1900, 6in (15cm) high.
£60–80 *WIL*

Mugs

An earthenware mug, with grey floral transfer print, c1860, 3in (7.5cm) high.
£25–35 *GLN*

An earthenware cider mug, with colour transfer decoration, c1860, 5in (12.5cm) high.
£100–135 *GLN*

A Mochaware mug, with strap handle, decorated in black between a black and pale blue border, late 19thC, 5in (12.5cm) high.
£125–145 *DA*

A two-handled painted mug, inscribed 'Alfred Harris, The Caves, Banwell, 1890', 5in (12.5cm) high.
£85–95 *GLN*

An early Victorian earthenware frog mug, painted in blue, purple, green and black with a continuous floral design, possibly Scottish, 3½in (9cm) high.
£110–130 *WIL*

A pottery frog mug, painted with roses in relief, small chip, c1850, 4in (10cm) high.
£90–115 *GLN*

l. A Victorian two-handled pottery cider mug, with colour transfer decoration, c1850, 5in (12.5cm) high.
£65–75 *GLN*

Plates & Dishes

A Samuel Alcock dessert service, each piece decorated in coloured enamels with flowers and leaves within green and gilt leaf scroll-decorated borders, comprising: a pair of oval two-handled dishes, 3 low round stands and 12 plates, pattern number '3/4749' in red, c1845.
£400–500 *DN*

A William Brownfield porcelain dessert service, each piece decorated in coloured enamels with a brightly coloured bird on a branch, within brown and gilt borders, on a puce ground, comprising: 12 plates, 2 tall and 4 low round stands, impressed marks for 1879 and pattern number '1353'.
£850–1,000 *DN*

A Copeland saucer dish, painted with a central sprig of mistletoe, the rim and well with a continuous band of holly, green printed mark, impressed crown, printed registration mark, 'No. 8275', late 19thC, 16¼in (41.5cm) diam.
£200–250 *L*

A porcelain plate, painted in the centre with a titled scene within a fluted pink ground, turquoise and gilt border, firing faults, slight wear, inscribed in iron red to reverse, impressed '8', c1885, 9½in (24cm) diam.
£170–200 *CSK*

A bread dish, with central printed Pratt style view of a lake in front of a mountain, painted in turquoise and orange, decorated with ears of corn and motto 'Give us this day our daily bread', 13in (33cm) wide.
£80–100 *WIL*

> **Miller's is a price GUIDE not a price LIST**

A Taylor, Tunnicliffe & Co pickle dish, with raised gold and silver decoration, c1880, 6¼in (16cm) wide.
£60–70 *GLN*

Wade

A Wade musical jug, decorated with and inscribed 'Snow White & The Seven Dwarfs', damaged, c1938, 7½in (19cm) high.
£200–250 *WTA*

A Wade fairy, made for Pex, painted in bright polychrome enamels, c1940, 2½in (6.5cm) high.
£90–120 *WIL*

Two Wade Nursery Favourites characters, No. 5 Humpty Dumpty and No. 6 Willie Winkie, from a set of 20, 1970s, 2½in (6.5cm) high, boxed.
£10–15 each *CBa*

Four Wade Disney characters, from a set of 12, re-made 1981–87, 1½in (4cm) high, boxed.
£10–12 each *CBa*

Wedgwood

Josiah Wedgwood (1730–95) was one of the most celebrated and influential ceramic designers of all times. The bicentenary of his death in 1995 inspired both exhibitions and specialist auctions of Wedgwood ware, bringing a host of ceramics on to the market. Over the past 30 years, much 18th century material has been exported to the United States and in recent times collectors have been concentrating on later items, particularly 20th century Wedgwood and works by designers such as Daisy Makeig-Jones, creator of Fairyland lustre, Keith Murray, Eric Ravilious and John Skeaping are all featured in this year's guide.

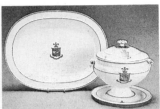

A Wedgwood pearlware 12-piece part dinner service, each piece printed in black with a crest and armorial, inscribed with the motto 'Fide sed Cui Fede' picked out in green within green line borders, damage, impressed marks, c1815.
£325–400 *DN*

A Wedgwood caneware jug, c1790, 2½in (6.5cm) high.
£70–85 *GLN*

A Wedgwood & Bentley black basalt intaglio seal of Hercules and the Nemean lion, mounted on a silver ring, impressed with 'Wedgwood & Bentley' and '9', c1780, ¾in (2cm) high.
£100–150 *Bon*

A Wedgwood creamware basket, Staffordshire or Yorkshire, with entwined rope handles, the flared sides cut with diamonds and hearts, unmarked, c1780, 11in (28cm) diam.
£200–250 *Bon*

A Wedgwood sucrier, enamelled with flowers, impressed, c1810, 3in (7.5cm) high.
£85–95 *GLN*

A Wedgwood creamware twin-handled tureen, cover and stand, the cover with flower finial, painted in sepia tones with a coat-of-arms within borders of stylised garlands and husks, brown-line rims, some damage, impressed upper case marks, c1775, 16in (40.5cm) wide.
£375–450 *CSK*

r. A Wedgwood black teapot, lid repaired, 1817, 4½in (11.5cm) high.
£85–95 *GLN*

A Wedgwood 10-piece dessert service, printed and painted with insects and botanical subjects on a cream ground, pierced Greek key border, some restoration, impressed marks, 19thC.
£500–600 *WL*

A Wedgwood majolica game pie dish and cover, with bird knop and griffin handles, moulded with game, flowers and leaves picked out in bright colours, on a brown ground, registration mark, impressed marks for 1870, 9¾in (25cm) wide.
£400–500 *DN*

A Wedgwood blue jasper jug, fitted with a hinged pewter cover, impressed marks, 19thC, 8¼in (21cm) high.
£70–100 *Bon*

A Wedgwood black basalt cream jug, c1850, 2½in (6.5cm) high.
£60–70 *GLN*

l. A Wedgwood black basalt bust, modelled as an allegorical classical lady, wearing a crown, impressed 'WEDGWOOD', 19thC, 2¾in (7cm) high, mounted on an agate ashtray.
£100–150 *Bon*

A Wedgwood black basalt Portland vase, the dipped ground bearing a frieze of Thetis awaiting Peleus, 19thC, 9½in (24cm) high.
£900–1,000 *Bon*

r. A Wedgwood 'Simple Yet Perfect' teapot and cover, printed with the Peony design, impressed and printed 'SYP' marks, late 19thC, 7¾in (19.5cm) high.
£200–300 *Bon*

A pair of Wedgwood 'Victoria Ware' vases, each brown body applied with green ground medallions representing the seasons, with white festoons and laurel frames under upright gilt loop handles, damage and repairs, replacement wooden covers, late 19thC, 8½in (21.5cm) high.
£250–350 *Bon*

A set of 3 Wedgwood green jasper ground plaques, comprising a pair of square panels applied with pairs of putti by a tree and another with a central panel framing an oval medallion within bay leaves and ribbons, impressed 'WEDGWOOD' marks, 19thC, 7½in (19cm) square.
£400–500 *Bon*

A pair of Wedgwood green jasper bottles, each decorated with 4 Muses, cracked, printed retailer's mark 'Humphrey Taylor' and impressed 'WEDGWOOD', c1900, 9in (23cm) high.
£75–120 *Bon*

A Wedgwood dark blue jasper salad bowl and servers, the sides decorated with numerous classical figures against a dipped ground, the servers with acanthus borders, EPNS rim and mounts, 20thC, 9½in (24cm) diam.
£100–200 *Bon*

A Wedgwood tri-colour engine-turned bowl, decorated with cane florettes under a ribbon meander, impressed upper case marks, '77', printed gilt 'Museum Series' mark, 'No.¹⁷%‰', c1977, 8in (20cm) diam, in presentation box with certificate.
£200–300 *Bon*

A Wedgwood black basalt model of an elephant, with glass eyes and painted tusks, impressed marks, c1930, 5¾in (14.5cm) high.
£200–225 *Bon*

Commemorative

A Wedgwood mug, the design sponsored by The Shakespeare Anniversary Council – Stratford 1564–1964, c1964, 4¾in (12cm) high.
£20–25 *BCO*

A Wedgwood plate, in commemoration of President Kennedy, 1960s, 4½in (11.5cm) diam.
£25–50 *CRO*

John F. Kennedy was President of the United States from 1961–63.

A Wedgwood creamware bowl, the interior printed with a chain of 13 founding states, the exterior with scenes and vignettes of American founders, inscribed 'The American Bicentennial 1776–1976', scratch in glaze, printed 'Wedgwood Collectors Society' mark, 12¼in (31cm) diam.
£100–150 *Bon*

Wedgwood Artists

l. A Wedgwood creamware plate, designed by Elaine Thérèse Lessore, decorated with a figure before a dressing table mirror, artist's signature in lustre, impressed 'WEDGWOOD' and date code, c1920, 9¼in (23.5cm).
£150–200 *Bon*

Elaine Thérèse Lessore (1883–1944), daughter of Jules Lessore and married to painter Walter Sickert, decorated ceramics for Wedgwood in the 1920s and '30s.

A Wedgwood lustre Boston cup, designed by Daisy Makeig-Jones, the interior with an open-outline butterfly on a mottled pink and orange ground, the exterior with butterflies on a mother-on-pearl ground, gilt printed Portland vase mark, gilt painted '24832F', 5in (12.5cm) diam.
£100–125 *Bon*

l. A Wedgwood Queensware 16-piece coffee set, designed by Sir Charles Holmes, each piece printed in black with the silhouettes of birds against a fish scale ground with pink banding, printed 'Seabirds, Wedgwood, Etruria, England', puce painted 'AE 8723 P', c1930, coffee pot 7in (18cm) high.
£200–250 *Bon*

Sir Charles Holmes (1868–1936), art critic, collector and Director of the National Gallery, was employed as an art consultant by Wedgwood 1930–34.

A Wedgwood black basalt ware coffee set, designed by Keith Murray, one of 2 experimental sets, comprising: a coffee pot and lid, jug and sugar basin with lid, each piece signed, c1936, coffee pot 7¾in (20cm) high.
£1,300–1,500 *BKK*

Born in 1892, the architect Keith Murray was one of the most influential designers of pottery and glass during the 1930s. First employed by Wedgwood in 1933, he used their famous black basalt ware and traditional techniques to create ceramics that were crisp in outline, architectural in decoration and modernist in style.

A Wedgwood lustre box and cover, designed by Daisy Makeig-Jones, the cover with an open outline butterfly coloured in blue, yellow and green on a mother-of-pearl ground, the inside of the box and cover with a solid butterfly against a mottled orange ground, gilt printed Portland vase mark, black painted '24832', c1915, 4in (10cm) square.
£200–225 *Bon*

Daisy Makeig-Jones (1881–1945) was the creator of Fairyland lustre, launched in 1915, and inspired by turn of the century children's illustrators such as Rackham and Dulac. Popular in its own day, Makeig's iridescent fanciful lustreware is currently commanding good prices in the market place.

A Wedgwood Queensware Windsor grey cup and saucer, with Balloon design by Eric Ravilious, from the Travel series, c1936, 2½in (6.5cm) high.
£40–50 *YY*

A Wedgwood Queensware Windsor grey plate, with Train design by Eric Ravilious, from the Travel series, c1936, 10in (25.5cm) diam.
£70–80 *YY*

l. A Wedgwood Queensware Windsor grey soup bowl and saucer, with Balloon design by Eric Ravilious, from the Travel series, saucer 6½in (16.5cm) diam.
£70–80 *YY*

A Wedgwood Queensware Windsor grey side plate, with Sailboat design by Eric Ravilious, from the Travel series, c1936, 7in (18cm) diam.
£40–50 *YY*

Eric Ravilious (1903–1942), artist and book illustrator, was commissioned by Wedgwood to create several designs for tablewares during the 1930s, the last being created in 1940. His designs were re-used by the company in the 1950s.

A Wedgwood earthenware figure of a kangaroo, after a model by John Skeaping, with a white glaze, impressed 'J. Skeaping, Wedgwood', 8¾in (22cm) high.
£400–500 *Bon*

John Rattenbury Skeaping (1901–80), sculptor and first husband of sculptress Barbara Hepworth, was commissioned by Wedgwood in 1926 to create a series of animal figures. The 14 models produced were extremely popular and remained in production until the 1950s.

A Wedgwood Queensware Windsor grey dessert bowl and soup dish, Travel design by Eric Ravilious, the dessert bowl printed in black with a biplane, the clouds heightened in turquoise, c1954, 8¼in (21cm) diam, and a soup dish, printed in black with the Train pattern.
£110–120 *Bon*

A pair of Wedgwood mugs, designed by Eric Ravilious, commemorating the Coronation of HM Queen Elizabeth II in 1953, printed in black and washed in yellow and pink, crack to one base, black printed marks, 1953, 4in (10cm) high.
£140–150 *C*

r. A Wedgwood earthenware figure of a duiker, after a model by John Skeaping, with a matt white glaze, impressed 'J. Skeaping, Wedgwood', printed 'Wedgwood Etruria England', 8¼in (21cm) high.
£100–150 *Bon*

MAKE THE MOST OF MILLER'S

Price ranges in this book reflect what you should expect to *pay* for a similar example. When selling, however, you should expect to receive a lower figure. This will fluctuate according to a dealer's stock and saleability at a particular time. It is always advisable, when selling a collectable, to approach a reputable dealer or an auction house which has specialist sales.

A Wedgwood earthernware figure of a tiger and buck, after a model by John Skeaping, the tiger with a dead buck in its jaws, unmarked, 13in (33cm) wide.
£150–200 *Bon*

r. A Wedgwood earthenware figure of a deer, after a model by John Skeaping, covered in a grey-blue glaze, 7in (18cm) wide.
£150–200 *Bon*

A Wedgwood earthenware bowl, designed by Norman Wilson, the fluted bowl tapering to a short circular foot, under a matt moonstone glaze, printed circular mark, impressed 'Wedgwood', 10¾in (27.5cm) high.
£125–150 *Bon*

Norman Wilson (1902–85), born into a family of Staffordshire potters, was employed by Wedgwood from 1927 until 1963, when he retired from his position as Joint Managing Director.

A Wedgwood earthenware vase, designed by Norman Wilson, of tapering cylindrical form, intaglio fluted, under a matt moonstone glaze, printed circular mark, 7¼in (18.5cm) high.
£125–150 *Bon*

Three earthenware moon flasks, designed by Norman Wilson, 2 moulded in low relief with circular foliate panels to both sides, the third with a band of moulded points to edge, all under matt white glaze, converted to lamp bases, printed circular marks, impressed 'Wedgwood' and initials 'NW', 8¾in (22cm) high.
£200–225 *Bon*

Wemyss

In 1883 the Wemyss factory, Fife, Scotland, employed the Bohemian artist Karel Nekola. His exuberant works, simple in form and brightly decorated with flowers, were extremely popular and retailed by the firm until the closure of the Fife pottery in 1930.

r. A Wemyss cylindrical pot, decorated with coloured fruit, 3½in (9cm) high.
£60–80 *GAK*

l. A Wemyss box and cover, with honeycomb design, 7½in (19cm) square.
£450–550 *W*

A Wemyss cylindrical pot, with hand painted pink roses, 3½in (9cm) high.
£40–60 *DA*

A Wemyss 12-piece toilet service, decorated with cabbage roses, retailed by Thomas Goode, damaged.
£600–700 *WL*

Worcester

A Worcester bowl, the exterior printed in black with the Red Ox pattern, picked out in coloured enamels, chips to rim, c1758, 5in (12.5cm) diam.
£140–200 *DN*

A Worcester double-lipped sauceboat, with 2 C-scroll handles, the interior painted in blue with landscape design, the exterior painted in blue with Chinese landscapes, birds and flowers, within leaf-moulded roundels, decorator's mark, c1775, 7½in (18.5cm) long.
£600–800 *DN*

A Worcester straight-sided mug, with spreading foot and loop handle, decorated in coloured enamels with Chinese figures, chips to foot rim, c1754, 4½in (11.5cm) high.
£375–475 *DN*

A Royal Worcester ewer, the handle formed as a lizard, the body decorated with gilt studs and gilt on a blush ivory ground with stylised foliage, crack to handle, printed mark and date cipher for 1889, 7in (18cm) high.
£70–100 *GAK*

A Worcester First Period blue and white teapot, with matched lid, 18thC, 4½in (11.5cm) high.
£150–200 *Mit*

A Royal Worcester pepper pot, modelled as Bonzo, c1930, 3¼in (8.5cm) high.
£500–600 *MLa*

A Royal Worcester globular pot pourri and cover, hand painted with bluebells and other flowers on an ivory coloured background, with gilt highlights, restored, 1889, 5½in (14cm) high.
£95–110 *QSA*

Worcester

- Worcester is the longest lived British porcelain factory and has undergone many changes of name and management.
- Founded is 1751, the first era of the factory's history is known as the 'Dr Wall period', after founding member John Wall. Production included domestic table ware and vases. Ceramics were often decorated with chinoiserie motifs and in 1757 transfer printing was introduced.
- Thomas Flight purchased the Worcester factory in 1783. The 'Flight period' lasted until 1793, when Flight was joined in partnership by Martin Barr. The factory was known as 'Flight & Barr' from 1793–1807, as 'Barr, Flight & Barr' from 1807–13 and 'Flight, Barr & Barr' from 1813–40.
- In 1852, W. H. Kerr joined the firm which was renamed 'Kerr and Binns' and in 1862 the company became known as the 'Royal Worcester Porcelain Company', the title it retains to the present day.

Figures

A Royal Worcester porcelain figure of the cherub Bacchus, painted in gold, green, pink and purple, c1862–65, 3in (7.5cm) high.
£225–265 *QSA*

Two Royal Worcester blush porcelain figures, 19thC:
l. a lady holding a bird's nest, wearing a hat and floral dress, on a rustic base, 9½in (24cm) high.
r. a man sharpening a scythe, wearing a hat, open-necked shirt and breeches, on a rustic base, 8½in (21.5cm) high.
£700–800 *AH*

A pair of Royal Worcester bone china figures, depicting a boy and a girl playing, each decorated in pink, blue, cream, green and brown on glazed parian ground, models A 2/101 and 102, 1865, 12½in (32cm) high.
£1,200–1,350 *QSA*

A Royal Worcester porcelain figure, by James Hadley, modelled as a boy wearing a hat, sitting on a tree stump in front of a pool, 1895, 4in (10cm) high.
£700–750 *QSA*

l. A Royal Worcester Yankee figure from the Countries of the World series, by James Hadley, wearing a stetson, boots and decorated in blush ivory colours, 1892, 7in (18cm) high.
£450–475 *QSA*

A Royal Worcester group of a young boy and girl, modelled in Kate Greenaway style, by James Hadley, picked out in gilt, on an oval mound base, one hat with rim chip, printed mark in puce for 1884, applied registration mark for 1882, 8in (20cm) high.
£500–600 *DN*

l. A Royal Worcester figure, entitled 'Sea Breeze', by Freda Doughty, modelled as a girl on tip toe, with a seagull by her feet on the rocks, 1936, 8½in (21.5cm) high.
£350–380 *QSA*

l. A Royal Worcester figure from the London Cries series, after a model by James Hadley, entitled 'Water', modelled as a bearded man carrying a pitcher, on a circular base moulded to simulate cobbles, damaged, shape No. 1002, printed and impressed marks, late 19thC, 7in (18cm) high.
£300–350 *CSK*

A Royal Worcester figure, entitled 'Michael', by Freda Doughty, modelled as a crawling baby, 1950, 2½in (6.5cm) high.
£125–145 *QSA*

A Royal Worcester figure, entitled 'Tommy', modelled by Freda Doughty, numbered '2913', printed marks to base, 1939, 4in (10cm) high.
£90–110 *WIL*

A Royal Worcester figure, from the Children of the Nations series, entitled 'Egypt', by Freda Doughty, modelled as a boy, wearing a fez and djellaba, 1940, 3in (7.5cm) high.
£200–225 *QSA*

A Royal Worcester figure, entitled 'Tuesday's Child is full of Grace', by Freda Doughty, modelled as a boy skating, c1960, 8½in (21.5cm) high.
£150–165 *QSA*

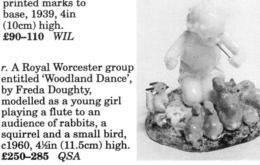

r. A Royal Worcester group entitled 'Woodland Dance', by Freda Doughty, modelled as a young girl playing a flute to an audience of rabbits, a squirrel and a small bird, c1960, 4½in (11.5cm) high.
£250–285 *QSA*

A Royal Worcester figure, entitled 'Wednesday's Child is full of Woe', by Freda Doughty, modelled as a girl losing her shoe, c1970, 7in (18cm) high.
£100–135 *QSA*

A Royal Worcester figure, entitled 'Thursday's Child has Far to Go', by Freda Doughty, modelled as a boy walking with a stick, c1970, 6½in (16.5cm) high.
£130–160 *QSA*

A Royal Worcester figure, entitled 'Sunday's Child is Fair and Wise, Good and Gay', modelled by Freda Doughty, c1980, 7in (18cm) high.
£100–115 *QSA*

A Royal Worcester figure, entitled 'Masquerade Boy', by Freda Doughty, modelled as a boy dressed in a Georgian costume, c1970, 7in (18cm) high.
£140–160 *QSA*

Plates & Dishes

A Worcester saucer dish, by Robert Hancock, printed in black with a portrait of the King of Prussia, the border with military trophies and a figure emblematic of Fame, within a black line rim, chips to rim, printed signature 'RH, Worcester' and an anchor, c1757, 7in (18cm) diam.
£150–200 *DN*

A Worcester lobed dish, decorated in the atelier of James Giles, with a central grisaille urn, garlanded in coloured enamels with flowers and leaves, within a gilt anthemion roundel, the blue ground decorated in gilt with a vine scroll band, blue crescent mark, c1770, 7¾in (20cm) square.
£450–550 *DN*

A Worcester kidney-shaped dish, decorated in the atelier of James Giles, in coloured enamels with a bold spray of flowers and fruits, scattered flowers and cherries, within a gilt line rim, damaged, c1770, 10¼in (26cm) wide.
£140–170 *DN*

A Worcester fluted dish, painted in blue with the K'ang Hsi Lotus pattern, chips to rim, pseudo Chinese emblem mark, c1770, 9¾in (25cm) wide.
£230–260 *DN*

A Worcester cabbage leaf-shaped dish, printed in blue with the Wispy Chrysanthemum Spray pattern, chips to rim, hatched crescent mark, c1770, 10in (25.5cm) wide.
£220–250 *DN*

A Worcester junket dish, decorated in coloured enamels with 3 butterflies, within an underglazed blue flower and scroll band, the border with sprays of flowers and leaves within radiating blue and gilt flower panelled bands, blue seal mark, c1770, 10¼in (26cm) diam.
£1,400–1,600 *DN*

> **Miller's is a price GUIDE not a price LIST**

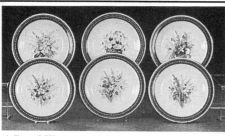

A Royal Worcester 16-piece part dessert service, each piece painted with a central spray of flowers within a turquoise and gilt jewelled border, some damaged, impressed and printed factory marks, c1875.
£600–700 *S(S)*

r. A Chamberlain's Worcester dish, with gadrooned rim, decorated in coloured enamels, with a named view of Hampton Court, Hereford, within a gilt stiff leaf roundel, on a puce ground, c1830, 9in (23cm) square.
£225–300 *DN*

Vases

A pair of Royal Worcester cabinet vases and lids, each hand painted with birds in oval panels, probably by John Hopewell, edged with moulded gilt laurels, highlighted with gilt, on a puce background, raised on socle bases, unsigned, marked, 1863, 10½in (26.5cm) high.
£1,200–1,450 *QSA*

A Royal Worcester vase, hand painted with chrysanthemums on a blush ivory ground, with 2 ornate gilt handles, on a moulded circular base, 1890, 10in (25.5cm) high.
£450–485 *QSA*

A Royal Worcester porcelain vase, with flared rim, pierced grotesque handles and applied masks, painted with clematis on an ivory coloured ground with buff and gilt banding, 19thC, 13¼in (33.5cm) high.
£750–850 *AH*

r. A Royal Worcester vase, hand painted with roses on a shaded ground, with gilded highlights, 1924, 4¼in (11cm) high.
£200–220 *QSA*

r. A Royal Worcester moulded vase, hand painted with roses on a shaded ground, with gilt highlights, 1910, 6in (15cm) high.
£100–125 *QSA*

l. A Royal Worcester vase, with twin handles, hand painted with flowers on a blush ivory ground, raised on a moulded gilded base with spreading foot, 1913, 6½in (16.5cm) high.
£350–400 *QSA*

A Royal Worcester vase, in the form of a lady's high-heeled and laced shoe, decorated in coloured enamels with flowers and leaves, within gilt borders, on a cream ground, printed marks in green, late 19thC, 4¾in (12cm) high.
£225–275 *DN*

A pair of Royal Worcester vases, each hand painted with roses on a shaded ground, highlighted with gilt, on pedestal bases, 1909, 6in (15cm) high.
£350–375 *QSA*

CLOCKS

A French striking and repeating carriage clock, by Alfred Drocourt, with 8-day movement, striking hours and half-hours on a gong, original Breguet moon hands, Corniche case, signed on backplate, 1870–75, 5in (12.5cm) high.
£850–900 *QSA*

Cross Reference:
Watches

A French brass striking carriage clock, the movement with bimetallic balance to lever platform, striking on a bell, the white enamel Roman dial with blued moon hands and subsidiary alarm ring, signed 'Moser à Paris', late 19thC, 5½in (14cm) high.
£400–500 *CSK*

A French striking carriage clock, with silvered dial, ornate hands and ormolu centrepiece, 8-day movement, original lever escapement, striking hours on a gong, engraved 'Presented to Lady Day, May 19th 1900 by her Servants at 50 Rutland Gate, London', in a decorative Corinthian column case, 1895–1900, 8in (20cm) high.
£800–825 *QSA*

A gilt-metal striking table clock, the Continental associated going barrel movement with strike on bell, foliate cast bezel to the white enamel Roman and Arabic dial, blued hands, the arch with enamel plaque signed 'Pinchbeck' with floral bouquet above and flanked by amorini, on foliate feet, late 19thC, 11in (28cm) high.
£375–425 *CSK*

A French brass carriage clock, with white enamelled dial inscribed 'J. C. Vickery, To Their Majesties, 177 to 183 Regent Street, W.', black Roman numerals, 8-day movement by Duverdrey & Bloquel, on a plinth base, bracket feet, early 20thC, 4¾in (12cm) high, with original leather carrying case.
£140–180 *Gam*

An enamel and gilt-faced clock, c1880, 5in (12.5cm) high.
£100–125 *Ber*

A mahogany wall clock, the white painted Roman dial signed 'Camerer Cuss & Co, 56 New Oxford St, London', black painted hands, the single chain fusee movement with anchor escapement, late 19thC, 15in (38cm) diam.
£400–450 *CSK*

A Black Forest wall clock, with painted dial, black Roman numerals, two-train weight driven movement striking on a coiled gong, in an octagonal inlaid rosewood case with emblems commemorating peace in the Crimea, 1854, 12½in (32cm) high.
£160–220 *Gam*

An Edwardian Georgian style bracket clock, with silvered dial, black Roman numerals, 8-day movement by Gustav Becker, chiming and striking on a straight gong, in a red walnut case with arched top on a plinth base, spherical feet, 15½in (39.5cm) high.
£225–325 *Gam*

A French wall clock, with white enamel Roman dial signed 'Veizt Jeune a Nerac' within repoussé bezel, the movement with inverted verge escapement with folding pendulum, vertical rack strike and alarm on bell, late 19thC, 15in (38cm) high.
£175–225 *CSK*

A Paris porcelain cased mantel clock and stand, the shell and scroll-moulded case decorated in coloured enamels with flowers and leaves, on a turquoise ground, within gilt borders, blue mark, probably for Michel-Isaac Aaron, the 8-day two-train movement with gilt suspension and outside count wheel strike with repeat on a bell, mid-19thC, 14in (35.5cm) high.
£275–375 *DN*

A Black Forest cuckoo clock, the twin-barrel movement with anchor escapement, with Roman dial and pierced bone hands, the automaton cuckoo appearing beneath the foliate carved gabled roof, late 19thC, 14½in (37cm) high.
£250–300 *CSK*

A time recording clock, with white circular dial inscribed 'The Gledhill-Brook Time Recorders Ltd, Patent, Huddersfield, Halifax, London, Birmingham', black Roman numerals, fusee movement with pendulum and handle below, No. 73152, on a plinth base, 41¾in (106cm) high.
£120–160 *Gam*

r. A Lalique arched moulded glass Moineaux pattern clock case, with etched surface, the silver dial with central stylised petals, chipped, lacks movement and hands, engraved signature 'R. Lalique, France', face signed 'Ato. Made in France', 6¼in (16cm) high.
£900–1,300 *LAY*

COMMEMORATIVE WARE
Boer War
(1899–1902)

A commemorative medal, inscribed 'To the memory of those who gave their lives for Queen and Country' and 'South African Campaign 1899–1900'.
£80–90 *OO*

A commemorative medal, inscribed 'Lent to British Govt for use in Transvaal War by Pres. of Atlantic Transport Coy' and 'S. S. Maine Bernard N. Baker Esq 1899'.
£40–50 *OO*

r. A Copeland Spode teapot, commemorating the Boer War and the merger of England, Scotland and Wales, c1900, 7in (18cm) high.
£350–450 *OO*

A silver metal plaque, inscribed 'A Gentleman in Kharki 1899–1900' and 'Transvaal War', 2¼ x 1½in (5.5 x 4cm).
£50–65 *OO*

| Cross Reference: |
| Toby Jugs |
| Wedgwood |

l. A bronze plaque, inscribed 'President Krüger' and 'Eendragt Maakt Magt' ('Unity Is Strength'), 2 by 1½in (5 by 4cm).
£80–90 *OO*

Winston Churchill
(1874–1965)

A Sutherland mug, inscribed 'Winston Churchill', c1940, 3in (7.5cm) high.
£75–125 *CRO*

A match slide, inscribed 'The Prime Minister' and 'Mr Winston Churchill', 1941, 2in (5cm) high.
£10–25 *CRO*

A commemorative 22ct gold medal, the obverse with head and shoulders portrait of Churchill with books and paint brushes behind, inscribed 'Winston Churchill 1874–1965', the reverse with a soldier on a battlefield shaking his fist at passing German fighter planes, inscribed 'Very Well, Alone', 1½in (4cm) diam, 48g, in red morocco presentation case.
£300–350 *CSK*

Military & Naval

An engraving, entitled 'Nelson', published by Smeeton, 17 St Martin's Lane, London, c1800, 4½ by 3in (11.5 by 7.5cm).
£50–100 *CRO*

A Doulton & Watts Lambeth salt glazed stoneware jug, depicting Lord Nelson, chips to base, c1830, 7¾in (19.5cm) high.
£340–400 *WL*

A Collingwood mug, inscribed 'To commemorate "Peace" 1919', 3in (7.5cm) high.
£30–35 *MGC*

A blue and white mug, by J. & S. Chown, Cornwall, inscribed '50th Anniversary of D-Day', 3¼in (8.5cm) high.
£8–10 *BCO*

A Grimwades 'Old Bill' plate, inscribed 'At present we are Staying at a Farm', 1914–18, 7½in (19cm) diam.
£80–100 *MGC*

A blue and white mug, commemorating the relief of Mafeking, inscribed, c1850, 3¼in (8.5cm) high.
£65–75 *JHW*

An ivory coloured cotton handkerchief, entitled 'Woman's Rights and What Came of it, "1981"', printed in black illustrating women and inscribed 'Army, Navy, Law, Politics, Science', and 'Men at Hard Work, Nothing To Do, Perfect Bliss, Frozen Out M.D.s', Reg'd No. '364805', c1880, 22 by 24in (60 by 61cm).
£250–300 *CSK*

Political

A beaker, inscribed 'V J Day 15th Aug 1945 B. Copland', 4in (10cm) high.
£15–18 *BCO*

A cup and saucer, commemorating the abolition of British slavery, c1830, saucer 6in (15cm) diam.
£150–170 *BCO*

A Susie Cooper 'tea for two', for Gray's Pottery, c1930, saucers 6in (15cm) diam.
£320–380 *SCA*

A porcelain bowl, by Dame Lucie Rie, impressed 'LR' seal, c1981, 8in (20cm) diam.
£4,000–4,500 *Bon*

A Susie Cooper hand painted cruet set, 1930s, tray 5in (12.5cm) wide.
£85–125 *SCA*

A Susie Cooper Paris shape jug, Moon and Mountain pattern, 1928, 4¾in (12cm) high.
£120–200 *SCA*

A vase and lidded pot, by Emily Myers, c1990, vase 9in (23cm) high.
£40–60 each *ELG*

A Susie Cooper plate, 1930s, 7in (18cm) diam.
£8–9 *WN*

A Susie Cooper lustre decorated serving plate, 1930s, 11½in (29cm) diam.
£500–600 *SCA*

A Winchcombe plate, by Michael Cardew, impressed, c1938, 9in (23cm) diam. **£200–250** *Bon*

A Susie Cooper Studio ware Kestrel shape jug, 1930s, 6½in (16.5cm) high. **£85–95** *SCA*

A stoneware spout pot, by Elizabeth Fritsch, c1976, 7¼in (18cm) high. **£1,500–1,800** *Bon*

A Denby Regent pastel vase, decorated with antelopes, c1930, 7in (18cm) high.
£65–85 *KES*

A Denby Cascade vase, c1970, 8in (20cm) high.
£25–30 *PC*

A Denby tube-lined tobacco jar, with ceramic closure, c1925, 7in (18cm) diam.
£75–85 *KES*

A Denby Orient ware jug, with decorative glazes, c1930, 7¼in (18.5cm) high.
£30–40 *PC*

A Denby salt glazed 'Ally Sloper' jug, c1900, 7in (18cm) high.
£75–85 *KES*

A Denby nursery rhyme mug, by Glyn Colledge, c1950, 4in (10cm) high.
£35–40 *PC*

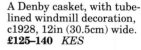

A Denby casket, with tube-lined windmill decoration, c1928, 12in (30.5cm) wide.
£125–140 *KES*

A hand painted bowl, designed by Glyn Colledge, c1990, 6½in (16.5cm) diam.
£50–55 *PC*

A Denby Falstaff dinner plate, c1970, 10in (25cm) diam.
£10–12 *PC*

A Denby bowl, by Glyn Colledge, c1950, 7⅜in (18cm) diam. **£40–45** *PC*

A Royal Doulton Art Nouveau jardinière, c1905, 6½in (16.5cm) high.
£140–180 *YY*

A Royal Doulton Art Nouveau jardinière, c1905, 7½in (19cm) high.
£140–160 *YY*

A Royal Doulton vase, designed by Mark Marshall, c1910, 12in (30.5cm) high.
£350–400 *YY*

l. A French pottery platter, 20thC, 13¾in (35cm) diam.
£100–115 *AnE*

A Royal Doulton Sung vase, designed by C. Noke, c1920, 7in (18cm) high.
£140–160 *YY*

A Gouda Pottery candlestick, c1925, 8¼in (21cm) high.
£120–150 *OO*

A Royal Doulton Nursery Rhyme series mug, plate and spoon set, c1916–40, plate 5in (12.5cm) diam.
£100–130 *HER*

A Gouda Pottery Regina bowl, Avia design, c1920, 10in (25cm) diam.
£180–220 *OO*

A pottery loudspeaker cover, by Royal Doulton for Artandia Ltd, c1930, 14½in (37cm) high.
£250–285 *SIG*

An Arnhem vase, Lindus design, c1925, 10¾in (27.5cm) high.
£150–200 *OO*

A Goss aeroplane, bearing the crest of Ramsgate, c1915, 5½in (14cm) long.
£20–25 *MGC*

A Carlton Humpty Dumpty inkwell, bearing crest of Christchurch, c1915, 4in (10cm) high.
£150–185 *BCO*

An Arcadian bottle and figure, bearing crest of Folkestone, 1920s, 3in (7.5cm) high.
£40–50 *BCO*

A Carlton British Pavilion, British Empire Exhibition 1924, 3½in (9cm) wide.
£100–130 *MGC*

A Goss oven, c1920, 3in (7.5cm) wide.
£320–350 *MGC*

A Goss brooch, first period, 1858–87, 1¾in (45mm) high.
£50–70 *MGC*

A Carlton Mother Shipton, c1920, 4in (10cm) high.
£50–60 *MGC*

A Willow Art ceramic memorial, c1920, 5¼in (13.5cm) high.
£40–50 *BCO*

A globe, unmarked, c1910, 3½in (9cm) high.
£40–50 *MGC*

A Carlton Jackie Coogan inkwell, c1910, 3in (7.5cm) high.
£50–70 *MGC*

A Midwinter Handicrafts bowl, Woodland scene, possibly by Jessie Tait, c1950, 9in (23cm) diam. **£40–60** *AND*

A Midwinter Stonehenge plate, Strawberry design by Eve Midwinter, c1974, 10½in (26.5cm) diam. **£14–16** *AND*

A Midwinter Fashion plate, Fishing boat pattern designed by Cobelle, c1960, 9½in (24cm) diam. **£8–10** *AND*

A Midwinter bowl, with floral pattern by Nancy Great-Rex, 1930s, 9in (23cm) diam. **£40–60** *AND*

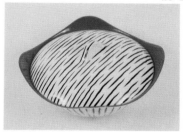

A Midwinter tureen and cover, Zambesi pattern designed by Jessie Tait, 1950s, 9in (23cm) diam. **£30–40** *JR*

A Midwinter Fashion bowl, Bella Vista pattern, c1960, 8¼in (21cm) wide. **£20–25** *AND*

A Midwinter Fashion tureen, Homespun pattern designed by Jessie Tait, c1960, 10in (25cm) wide. **£18–20** *AND*

A Midwinter jug, Hollywood pattern designed by Jessie Tait, 1950s, 5½in (14cm) high. **£30–35** *JR*

A Midwinter Stylecraft dish, designed by Sir Peter Scott, c1955, 4in (10cm) diam. **£6–8** *AND*

A Midwinter Stylecraft trio, designer unknown, 1950s, plate 6½in (16.5cm) diam. **£14–18** *JR*

A Midwinter Stylecraft cruet, Red Domino pattern, c1953, 6in (15cm) long. **£20–25** *AND*

A geometric fan vase,
by Myott & Son, c1931,
8½in (21.5cm) high.
£200–220 *BKK*

A William Moorcroft Wisteria
pot pourri and cover, c1912,
5in (12.5cm) high.
£700–750 *Rum*

A posy bowl, by Myott & Son,
c1932, 5in (12.5cm) diam.
£40–50 *BKK*

A diamond-shaped posy bowl
and insert, by Myott & Son,
c1931, 10½in (26.5cm) wide.
£80–100 *BKK*

A bow tie vase, by
Myott & Son, 1931–36,
8in (20cm) high.
£120–135 *BEV*

A Moorcroft Clematis pattern
vase, 1960s, 9in (23cm) high.
£180–240 *HEA*

A Noritake bowl, featuring a cottage
on a hillside, and sheaves of corn in
a field, c1950, 5in (12.5cm) wide.
£10–15 *YY*

A Moorcroft vase,
decorated with an orchid
1950s, 10in (25cm) high.
£450–550 *HEA*

A jug, by Myott & Son,
1931–36, 8in (20cm) high.
£60–70 *BEV*

A Noritake teapot, c1950, 4in (10cm) high.
£20–25 *YY*

A Crown Ducal coffee set, designed by Charlotte Rhead, Aztec Pattern, No. 2800, c1932.
£400–500 *PC*

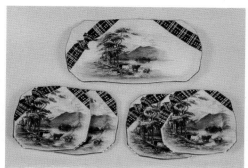

A Grimwades Royal Winton sandwich set, c1930.
£20–25 *COL*

A Shelley footed fruit bowl, c1932, 10in (25cm) diam.
£80–100 *BKK*

A Rye Pottery striped vase, c1950, 7½in (19cm) wide.
£60–75 *NCA*

A Rye Pottery vase, c1950, 7¼in (18.5cm) high.
£55–60 *NCA*

A Savoie teapot, c1890, 4in (10cm) high.
£35–40 *MofC*

A Burleigh Avon bowl, by Charlotte Rhead, c1927, 10in (25cm) diam.
£200–250 *PC*

A Shelley butter dish, c1932, 5in (12.5cm) square.
£30–40 *YY*

Two Savoie jugs, with marbled decoration, c1890, largest 6½in (16.5cm) high.
£30–60 each *MofC*

A pair of Shelley vases, 1920s, 5in (12.5cm) high.
£30–35 *COL*

A pair of Staffordshire spill vases, depicting red deer, c1860, 11½in (29cm) high.
£400–450 *JO*

A Staffordshire spill vase, depicting an English sheepdog, c1860, 10½in (26.5cm) high.
£1,000–1,400 *JO*

A Staffordshire group, of Napoleon and Albert, c1858, 14in (35.5cm) high.
£650–700 *MSA*

A pair of Staffordshire figures of spaniels, with separate front legs, c1850, 10½in (26.5cm) high.
£340–380 *RWB*

A Staffordshire spill vase, depicting a dog, goose and duck, c1860, 7½in (19cm) high.
£130–150 *JO*

A Staffordshire group, 'John Anderson My Jo', c1850, 10¼in (26cm) high.
£400–450 *RWB*

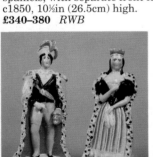

A pair of Staffordshire figures of Hamlet and Lady Macbeth, c1850, 8½in (21.5cm)
£600–700 *JO*

A Staffordshire spill vase, c1860, 8½in (21.5cm) high.
£70–80 *RWB*

A Staffordshire figure of Jenny Lind, c1847, 10in (25cm) high.
£630–700 *RWB*

A Staffordshire spill vase, c1860, 9in (23cm) high.
£90–100 *RWB*

Royalty
Great Britain

Date Chart

Monarch	Reigned	Married
George III	1760–1820	Sophia Charlotte of Mecklenburg-Strelitz
George IV	1820–30	Caroline of Brunswick Wölfenbuttel
William IV	1830–37	Adelaide of Saxe-Meiningen
Victoria	1837–1901	Prince Francis Albert, Duke of Saxony, Prince of Saxe-Coburg & Gotha
Edward VII	1901–10	Alexandra of Denmark
George V	1910–36	Mary Teck
Edward VIII	1936–abdicated	Mrs Ernest Simpson
George VI	1936–1952	Lady Elizabeth Bowes-Lyon
Elizabeth II	1952–	HRH Prince Philip, Duke of Edinburgh

A Green-Bag jug, with pink lustre overglaze, with a picture and inscription 'God Save Queen Caroline!' on one side, 'Long Live Caroline!' and a verse on the other side, 5½in (14cm) high.
£450–550 *CRO*

r. A jug, commemorating the coronation of George III and Queen Charlotte, c1780, 5in (12.5cm) high.
£1,200–1,350 *JHo*

A plate, commemorating the coronation of William IV, inscribed, 1831, 7in (18cm) diam.
£300–400 *MGC*

l. A jug, transfer-printed in black, commemorating the coronation of William IV and Queen Adelaide, 1831, 5in (12.5cm) high.
£300–400 *CRO*

r. A Swansea transferware mug, commemorating Queen Victoria's coronation, c1837, 2¼in (5.5cm) high.
£600–700 *BCO*

A pottery punchbowl, commemorating the coronation of William IV, printed with a central crown within inscription 'William The Fourth For Ever' within a vine pattern border and shaped rim, moulded to the exterior with stylised scrolls, damaged, printed mark to base, c1830, 9¾in (25cm) diam.
£200–300 *CSK*

Edward VII's nappy pin, ½in (1.25cm) long.
£20–30 *MRW*

A jug, by J. & M. P. Bell & Co Ltd, Glasgow Pottery, to commemorate the wedding of The Prince of Wales and Princess Alexandra, 1863, 8in (20cm) high.
£125–175 *CRO*

A mug, commemorating Queen Victoria's Jubilee, given by the Mayor of Gravesend, 1887, 3½in (9cm) high.
£50–95 *CRO*

An octagonal plate, by Wallis Gimson & Co, commemorating Queen Victoria's Jubilee, 1887, 9½in (24cm) wide.
£80–100 *MGC*

A Doulton plate, depicting Queen Alexandra, inscribed 'Britons All', 1902, 9in (23cm) diam.
£65–100 *CRO*

r. A Royal Doulton teapot, commemorating the coronation of King George and Queen Mary, 1911, 4in (10cm) high.
£100–190 *CRO*

A Jackfield teapot, commemorating Queen Victoria's Jubilee, 1887, 6½in (16.5cm) high.
£120–140 *MGC*

A German plate, commemorating Queen Victoria's Jubilee, 1887, 7in (18cm) diam.
£60–100 *CRO*

A plate, depicting Queen Victoria and 4 Boer War generals, c1900, 7½in (19cm) diam.
£60–80 *MGC*

A Foley mug, commemorating the wedding of King George V and Queen Mary, 1893, 3in (7.5cm) high.
£75–150 *CRO*

A Crown Derby loving cup, commemorating Her Majesty Queen Elizabeth The Queen Mother's 85th birthday, 1985, from a limited edition of 500, 3in (7.5cm) high.
£95–175 *CRO*

A Spode mug, commemorating Her Majesty Queen Elizabeth The Queen Mother's 80th birthday, 1980, 3½in (9cm) high.
£50–100 *CRO*

A mug, commemorating the coronation of King George V and Queen Mary, presented to the Mayor of Rochester, June 22nd, 1911, 3in (7.5cm) high.
£30–35 *COL*

l. A plate, by David Sharp Ceramics, Rye, Sussex, inscribed 'Her Majesty Queen Elizabeth The Queen Mother, Lord Warden of the Cinque Ports, 1st August 1979', 10½in (26.5cm) diam.
£40–80 *CRO*

l. A Bell china cup, saucer and plate, commemorating King Edward VIII's coronation, c1936, plate 5in (12.5cm) wide.
£60–125 *CRO*

A souvenir paper napkin, commemorating the Great National Day of Prayer and Thanksgiving Services, Sunday January 6th 1918, 13in (33cm) square.
£8–10 *COL*

A mug, commemorating Her Majesty Queen Elizabeth The Queen Mother's 94th birthday, 1994, 3½in (9cm) high.
£20–30 *CRO*

A Coverswall mug, commemorating Her Majesty Queen Elizabeth The Queen Mother's 80th birthday, 1980, 3½in (9cm) high.
£40–75 *CRO*

A collection of 24 figures, by Graham Farish, depicting the coronation of Queen Elizabeth II, including the Queen, Duke of Edinburgh, Archbishop of Canterbury, various members of the Royal family, Lords, dignitaries and attendants at Westminster Abbey, 1953.
£550–650 *P(Ba)*

A mug, by J. & S. of Hayle Cornwall, commissioned by J. G. & I. S. Cooper, Dundonald, Belfast, to commemorate the Prince of Wales' visit to Ulster, 1994, No. 49 of a limited edition of 75, 3½in (9cm) high.
£30–40 *BCO*

A Coronet Pottery mug, commemorating Queen Elizabeth II's visit to Russia, 1994, 3¼in (8.5cm) high.
£25–35 *BCO*

A Coverswall beaker, commemorating the marriage of the Princess Royal to Timothy Lawrence, 1992, from a limited edition of 1,000, 4½in (11.5cm) high.
£75–150 *CRO*

Items commemorating the Princess Royal's second marriage are rare.

l. A mug, commemorating the 30th birthdays of Prince Edward, Lady Helen Taylor, James Ogilvy, and Lady Sarah Armstrong-Jones, from a limited edition of 30, 1994, 3½in (9cm) high.
£30–40 *CRO*

A mug, commemorating the wedding of Lady Sarah Armstrong-Jones, from a limited edition of 180, 1994, 3½in (9cm) high.
£25–35 *CRO*

Monaco

l. An ashtray depicting Prince Rainier and Princess Grace of Monaco, produced for Prince Rainier's silver jubilee, 1974, 5½in (14cm) wide.
£15–35 *CRO*

A vase, decorated with a picture of Princess Grace of Monaco, 1982, 4in (10cm) high.
£50–75 *CRO*

CORKSCREWS

An all-steel open frame corkscrew, with butterfly nut handle, c1790, 6in (15cm) long.
£400–475 *Har*

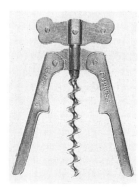

An all-steel corkscrew, the Bonsa, c1880, 4¼in (11cm) long.
£200–230 *CS*

l. A German corkscrew, named 'Express' on one side and 'Smart' on the other, c1900.
£80–95 *CS*

l. An Antiquary corkscrew, by J. & W. Hardie, c1900, 6¼in (16cm) long.
£25–30 *Bar*

A bone-handled corkscrew, 19thC, 5½in (14cm) long.
£45–55 *Bar*

l. An all-steel combination 8-tool folding bow corkscrew, with facet-cut handle, 19thC, 4in (10cm) long.
£75–85 *CS*

A silver-handled corkscrew, with onion-shaped finials, Birmingham hallmark, 1902, 5½in (14cm) long.
£200–265 *Har*

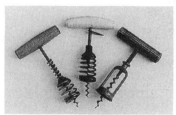

A rosewood-handled corkscrew, with brush and carrying ring, hour glass steel shaft with petal-shaped Henshall style button, 1840, 6½in (16.5cm) long.
£65–75 *Har*

A London Rack corkscrew, with open barrel and side-wind handle, c1870, 7in (18cm) long.
£40–60 *CS*

A double-lever corkscrew, with bladed worm, marked 'Magic Lever Cork Drawer' and 'Pat Appd For', c1880, 5¾in (14.5cm) long.
£20–25 *CS*

Two Thomason type bone-handled corkscrews, the barrels embossed with autumnal fruits, 19thC, 7in (18cm) long.
£320–340 each *CS*

Points to Check when Assessing Antique Corkscrews

Important factors when assessing an antique corkscrew include age, condition, shape, material and marks.

- Condition affects value; check that mechanisms are working and that handles are not too damaged (bone handles are particularly prone to breakage). Many corkscrews are also missing their brushes used to sweep dust off the bottle top before opening
- Elaborate mechanical corkscrews tend to be worth more than simple T-bar shapes
- Ivory and silver examples often command the highest prices
- Check for a maker's name, a registration or patent number which can sometimes be traced back to reveal the maker and the date of production
- An original box can increase value. Interesting corkscrews are being produced today – for example designer Philip Stark has recently created a new model – and should these become collectable in the future, preserving their packaging will add to their appeal

A French all-steel corkscrew, with maker's name 'Perille', c1900, 6¼in (16cm) long.
£10–12 *CS*

l. A Thomason Variant corkscrew, c1820, 7in (18cm) long.
£240–300 *CS*

Five simple type metal corkscrews, 19thC, 4in (10cm) long.
£15–25 each *Bar*

An open steel-framed corkscrew, with turned walnut handle, marked 'G. Twigg's Patent', c1870, 7¼in (18.5cm) long.
£180–200 *CS*

A Wolverson's design corkscrew, registered 1873, marked 'The Tangent Lever', c1880, 8in (20cm) long.
£75–85 *Har*

A selection of brass figure corkscrews, 20thC, largest 6½in (16.5cm) long.
£5–12 each *CS*

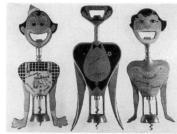

A souvenir brass key corkscrew, with antiqued finish, c1930, 5in (12.5cm) long.
£8–10 *CS*

l. A Weir's compound lever corkscrew, patent No. 12, c1890, 12½in (32cm) extended.
£80–90 *Har*

Three Italian corkscrews, decorated as a clown, barman and barmaid, c1950, 9½in (24cm) long.
£30–45 each *CS*

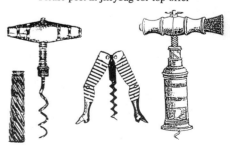

Six German 'ladies' legs' pocket corkscrews, in green and white, pink and white, blue and white and flesh-coloured combinations, c1890, 2½in (6.5cm) long.
£100–120 each *CS*

COSMETIC ACCESSORIES

The following section includes a display of compacts, already widely collected in the USA and becoming increasingly popular in Britain. 'There can be few articles which evoke the glamour of the "roaring twenties" and "decadent thirties" as effectively as the powder compact,' enthuses compact historian Juliette Edwards. Compacts first came into general use after WWI when, as women gained greater independence, the wearing of cosmetics gradually became acceptable.

Compacts reflected Art Deco style with geometric designs and such popular motifs as animals and the ubiquitous crinoline lady. Innovative shapes were created, such as 1940s compact bracelets and pocket vanity cases, whose various compartments held powder, lipstick and cigarettes, the latter another symbol of female emancipation.

During WWII, with the restrictions on production and materials, compacts tended to be utilitarian in style. The late 1940s and '50s saw many exciting designs, and the growing use of plastic, the material from which most compacts are produced today.

Prices for collectable compacts depend on age, rarity and condition. A compact with all its original elements – the outer box, the soft bag designed to protect its surface, the powder puff and powder sifter – will command a premium price.

A Victorian coromandel wood and brass-bound lady's dressing case, with fitted interior, glass boxes and bottles, implements engraved 'Joseph Rodgers & Sons', 2 semi-secret spring loaded drawers, one velvet lined for jewellery, all within a pigskin travelling case, 1862.
£1,300–1,600 *MAR*

A French brass-bound rosewood lady's jewellery box, with original contents, hidden mirror, 15 bottles and jars with hallmarked silver lids, tray of tools, drawer for jewellery and secret compartments, 1830, 15in (38cm) long.
£2,500–2,850 *QSA*

A Regency rosewood and brass-bound vanity box, containing 6 glass plated bottles and 2 glass scent flasks and stoppers, early 19thC, 12½in (32cm) long.
£225–275 *GAK*

Two silver-backed clothes brushes, with Chester hallmarks for 1888 and 1906, 6½in (16.5cm) long.
£18–25 each *WN*

A silver brush and comb set, with Birmingham hallmark for 1915.
£60–100 *Ech*

l. A silver shoe horn, c1900, 6½in (16.5cm) long.
£15–18 *WN*

A tortoiseshell comb,
19thC, 8½in (21.5cm) high.
£15–25 *Ech*

Compacts

A compact, decorated with a
spider and web pattern, by
Schuco, c1928, 2in (5cm) diam.
£65–75 *LBe*

Miller's is a price GUIDE
not a price LIST

A Bakelite and enamel
compact, shaped as a
bangle, 1940s, 3in
(7.5cm) diam.
£200–225 *LBe*

r. A selection of
ceramic powder
bowls, 1930–50,
largest 6in
(15cm) high.
£10–25 each *PC*

A compact, in the form of a
cat's face, by Schuco, c1928,
2¼in (5.5cm) diam.
£65–75 *LBe*

An American gilt and
enamel compact, by Elgin,
1940s, 4in (10cm) diam.
£55–60 *LBe*

A gilt globe-shaped compact,
by Pygmalion, 1940s, 2in
(5cm) diam.
£65–75 *LBe*

A compact, in the form of
a telephone dial, 1940s,
3½in (9cm) diam.
£65–70 *LBe*

A gilt compact and lipstick
case, by Richard Hudnut,
c1950, 3¼in (8.5cm) long.
£20–30 *LBe*

A compact, shaped as a
suitcase, by Kigu, 1950s, 3in (7.5cm) long.
£35–40 *LBe*

COSTUME & TEXTILES

Antique costume is an area of collecting that is often surprisingly unappreciated. Whilst people buy antiques to decorate their homes, how many dress in antique clothing? According to costume and textiles dealer Pat Oldman, the majority of her clients are specialist collectors, some who wear the garments, others simply enjoy owning them. Victorian costume is difficult to put to practical use as sizes tend to be tiny. 'A lot of costume is bought to put on dummies,' explains Pat, adding that amongst the most collectable items of this pre-1900 period are garments produced from coloured material, as opposed to the far more commonplace black.

Clothes from the 1920s, flapper dresses, etc, are both desirable and wearable, although in this, as in every other period, condition is all-important. 'Certain fabrics just cannot take the strain,' advises Pat. 'Some 1920s silks were very unstable and will perish at the least stress. Beaded dresses, however, might look fragile, but those beaded on cotton voile are quite resilient and although some beads will come off, these can be replaced.'

Whilst the best Victorian and 1920s pieces will always be in demand, to some extent the market for antique clothes is driven by contemporary fashion: currently popular with a younger clientele are clothes from the 1960s and 70s, reflecting 1990s styles and the modern music scene.

One of the joys of wearing antique fashions is that you can choose a period to suit your personality and physique; 1930s shapes for the long and lean, 1950s style for the more curvaceous figure. Much can still be found in charity shops and flea markets, prices can be very reasonable, and one can almost guarantee that no one else will be wearing the same dress.

A pair of rose pink harem trousers, the bodice of silk, legs overlaid with chiffon and the cuffs of silver lamé lace, alterations, unlabelled, possibly Paul Poiret, c1910.
£300–350 *CSK*

A pierrot ivory silk satin costume, trimmed with black pompoms, comprising a jacket, collar, trousers, and pair of ruffle-trimmed shoes, c1880.
£70–90 *CSK*

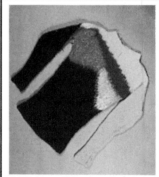

A Vivienne Westwood mohair jumper, knitted in red, blue, pink and black blocks, unlabelled, 1970s.
£150–200 *CSK*

l. A straw bustle, labelled 'The Mikado Bustle', patented 1886, 16in (40.5cm) wide.
£40–80 *Ech*

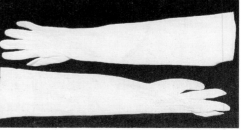

A pair of Edwardian hand-stitched white linen gloves, 21½in (54.5cm) long.
£5–15 *Ech*

Beadwork

A Victorian miser's beaded purse, 6½in (16.5cm) long.
£15–30 *Ech*

A Victorian beaded bag, 10in (25.5cm) long.
£55–75 *Ech*

A Victorian beaded drawstring pouch bag, 8in (20cm) long.
£35–55 *Ech*

An Edwardian beaded evening purse, 7in (18cm) long.
£50–100 *Ech*

A cut-steel beaded bag, c1900, 12in (30.5cm) long.
£100–150 *Ech*

A beaded evening purse, c1930, 6¼in (16cm) wide.
£50–80 *Ech*

A beaded purse, c1920, 4in (10cm) diam.
£18–25 *MRW*

l. A black and white beaded purse, c1930, 7in (18cm) wide.
£15–20 *Ech*

Cross Reference:
Handbags

l. A beaded evening purse, c1920, 6in (15cm) long.
£30–50 *Ech*

A black beaded belt, 1920s, 80in (203cm) long.
£75–100 *Ech*

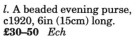

Children's Wear

A lawn white work bib, c1920, 8in (20cm) wide.
£10–20 *LB*

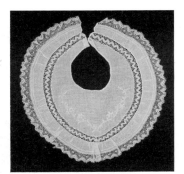

A Victorian bib, with Valencia lace and separate cotton backing, 8in (20cm) wide.
£30–40 *LB*

A Victorian child's christening cape.
£100–150 *LB*

An Edwardian child's cream dress.
£30–50 *Ech*

A Victorian cotton christening gown.
£125–175 *Ech*

A Victorian cotton voile christening gown.
£50–80 *Ech*

An Edwardian child's pinafore.
£10–20 *Ech*

A Victorian child's red woollen dress.
£40–60 *Ech*

A child's sky-blue taffeta silk dress, with short puffed sleeves, two-tier skirt with gathered hem, high neckline with pinked frill, tape and hook fastening to back, lined with figured cotton, altered, c1860.
£100–140 *P*

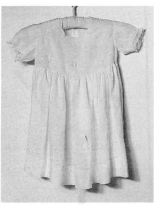

A child's hand-stitched linen dress, c1920.
£25–35 *Ech*

A child's crocheted silk dress, c1920.
£10–20 *Ech*

A child's cotton voile dress, c1920.
£25–40 *Ech*

A child's lawn dress, with cotton smocking, 1930s.
£30–40 *LB*

Coats & Jackets

r. A Chinese black satin front-fastening coat, with 8 phoenix roundels over a sea border, self-facings with butterfly designs, sleeves with blue silk bands, worked in couched gold metal embroidery, late 19thC.
£375–450 *P*

A raspberry pink satin opera wrap, fastening with passementerie buttons, probably French, unlabelled, c1910.
£175–225 *CSK*

An Edwardian cream silk carrying cape.
£30–80 *Ech*

l. A bead on net bolero, with a beaded fringe, c1910.
£100–125 *Ech*

An ivory silk damask evening coat, with deep cape collar, trimmed with lace, lined with fleecy lambskin, c1915.
£250–300 *CSK*

r. A black silk velvet opera cloak, with a deep fur collar and a chiffon velvet panel woven with a Liberty design, lined in gold, labelled 'Liberty, London', 1920s.
£500–600 *CSK*

r. An electric blue velvet opera cape, trimmed with clear beads and rhinestones, with deep ruched velvet collar, c1920.
£525–625 *CSK*

l. A blue plush velvet coat, with wrap-over front and high collar, lined with white fur, labelled 'Mantles, Dickens & Jones Ltd, London W', 1920s.
£140–180 *CSK*

A fuchsia pink satin opera coat, woven with dove grey velvet arabesques, with fur trimmed cuffs, 1920s.
£375–425 *CSK*

A black beaded jacket, on voile, c1928.
£150–200 *Ech*

A purple silk beaded opera coat, c1920.
£250–300 *Ech*

An orange plush maxi coat, with deep stand collar, labelled 'Biba', 1970s.
£200–250 *CSK*

An Italian lady's chain mail bolero jacket, with three-quarter length sleeves, the hems trimmed with deep chain fringes, c1967.
£50–70 *CSK*

A taupe chiffon velvet evening jacket, woven with Japanese style motifs and trimmed with silk fringes, 1920s.
£285–300 *CSK*

Dresses & Blouses

An Edwardian cotton voile blouse.
£35–40 *Ech*

A black silk chiffon evening gown, embroidered with jet beads, with an ivory chemical lace underdress, c1910.
£175–225 *CSK*

An ivory chiffon cocktail dress, embroidered with a simulated belt of silvered glass beads, imitation pearls and bugle beads, the skirt with a tiered scalloped hem, labelled 'Paquin, rue de la Paix 3, Paris, London', c1920.
£575–600 *CSK*

A black lace dress, woven with silver lamé flowers, in the manner of Raoul Dufy wood block prints, unlabelled, c1920.
£650–750 *CSK*

A cotton voile blouse, c1918.
£30–35 *Ech*

l. An Edwardian cream silk tea dress.
£125–175 *Ech*

A lemon cotton voile beaded dress, c1922.
£400–450 *Ech*

An aquamarine silk blouse, with white tie, 1920s.
£25–35 *Ech*

A black chiffon cocktail dress, looped with clear bugle beading, c1924.
£350–400 *CSK*

A black silk fringed dress, embroidered with flowers, c1925.
£125–150 *Ech*

A lamé floral evening dress, c1930.
£75–150 *Ech*

An emerald chiffon blouse, the three-quarter length sleeves with deep frilled cuffs, labelled 'BIBA', 1970s.
£70–90 *CSK*

l. A linen blouse, with embroidered motifs, 1930s.
£15–30 *Ech*

r. A white silk blouse, embroidered with flower motifs, c1930.
£10–20 *Ech*

A rayon crêpe floral evening dress, 1930s.
£50–80 *Ech*

A blue and white chiffon dress and bolero, c1930.
£75–125 *Ech*

A multi-coloured pattern rayon crêpe dress, 1940s.
£20–50 *Ech*

A raspberry pink satin sleeveless ball gown, labelled 'Jeanne Lanvin' and 'Castillo', c1960.
£150–200 *CSK*

Hats & Hatpins

An Edwardian embroidered velvet smoking cap.
£30–45 *Ech*

Three velvet caps, c1890.
£35–55 each *Ech*

A straw cloche hat, c1920.
£50–75 *Ech*

A brown felt cloche hat, c1925.
£40–60 *Ech*

A straw boater, c1930.
£20–30 *Ech*

A brown silk hat, c1925.
£60–80 *Ech*

A pair of paste hatpins, c1900,
1½in (4cm) diam.
£35–55 *Ech*

l. A hatpin holder, c1900.
£15–30 *Ech*

An amethyst hatpin, c1900,
2in (5cm) diam.
£30–50 *Ech*

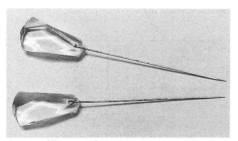

A pair of Perspex hatpins, c1930,
6in (15cm) long.
£20–30 *Ech*

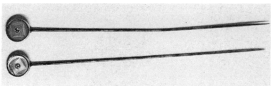

A pair of mother-of-pearl hatpins, 1920s,
½in (1.5cm) diam.
£20–30 *Ech*

Lace

A Brussels needle lace border, worked with an undulating ribbon, the handmade ground with flowers and butterflies, c1730, 62in (157.5cm) long.
£225–275 *CSK*

An Italian needle lace border, worked with carnations, 17thC.
£300–350 *CSK*

A pair of Point de Saxe drawn threadwork lappets, worked with scalloped edges, mid-18thC, 21in (53.5cm) long.
£475–575 *CSK*

A handkerchief, edged in Bedfordshire lace, c1920, 8in (20cm) square.
£12–14 *LB*

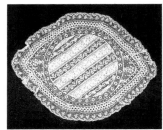

A Normandy lace mat, c1900, 8in (20cm) wide.
£6–8 *LB*

A Victorian linen camisole, with Irish crochet work and lace, c1890.
£30–50 *LB*

l. A Maltese cream silk lace collar, c1910.
£30–40 *Ech*

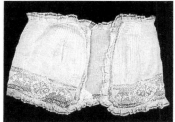

An Edwardian Irish crochet collar, c1910.
£35–40 *LB*

A length of Maltese lace, 19thC, 70in (178cm) long.
£50–60 *LB*

A length of Honiton lace, 19thC, 40in (101.5cm) long.
£50–60 *LB*

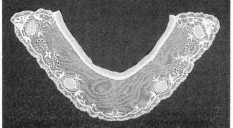

A lawn and whitework collar, c1920.
£20–25 *LB*

A silk handkerchief, edged in Maltese lace, c1920, 12in (30.5cm) square.
£15–20 *LB*

A lawn handkerchief, edged in Bedfordshire lace, c1900, 12in (30.5cm) square.
£20–28 *LB*

A white chemical lace collar, c1910.
£25–35 *Ech*

A Brussels applied needle lace stole, worked with formal floral pattern, late 19thC, 23 by 108in (58.5 by 274.5cm).
£250–300 *CSK*

An Irish cream crochet collar, 1920s.
£30–40 *Ech*

A late Victorian cream tape lace cape.
£45–55 *Ech*

A Brussels lace collar, c1890.
£40–50 *LB*

A baby's machine lace over lawn christening gown, with slip, 1930, 23in (58.5cm) long.
£40–50 *LB*

Menswear

A Victorian silk
brocade waistcoat.
£60–100 *Ech*

A brown leather
jacket, 1940s.
£30–60 *Ech*

A pair of leather
jodhpurs, 1951.
£30–60 *Ech*

Shawls

An ivory wool kirking shawl,
with blue and pink floral cones
on green leaf bases, 1830s,
144 by 72in (366 by 183cm).
£160–210 *CSK*

A reversible woollen Paisley
pattern shawl, c1865, 70in
(178cm) square.
£200–250 *Ech*

A mid-Victorian indigo wool
Paisley pattern shawl, with
a broad band of mosaic
boteh, leaves and flowers in
pale yellow, scarlet, green
and blue, on a plain field,
63in (160cm) square.
£175–225 *DN*

A Paisley shawl, woven in
red, orange, green and
ivory, the mihrabs and
anthemion leaves outlined
in black, 136 by 64in
(345.5 by 162.5cm).
£325–400 *Bon*

A woollen crocheted
shawl, with silk
fringe, c1925.
£100–150 *Ech*

A black cut velvet on
chiffon shawl, with
fringe, c1925.
£150–250 *Ech*

A multi-coloured
lamé shawl, 1920s.
£150–250 *Ech*

Shoes

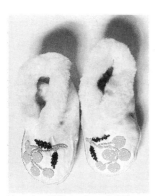

A pair of Victorian child's beaded slippers.
£20–30 *Ech*

A pair of landworker's leather boots, with wooden and iron soles, c1910.
£30–35 *TaB*

A pair of brocade and kid shoes, 1930s.
£50–80 *Ech*

A pair of brown crocodile skin lace-up shoes, 1920s.
£80–100 *Ech*

Shoe Museums

The Shoe Museum,
C. & J. Clark Ltd,
40 High Street,
Street,
Somerset BS16 0YA
Tel: 01458 443131

Northampton Central
Museum & Art Gallery,
Guildhall Road,
Northampton NN1 1DP
Tel: 01604 39415

This museum boasts a shoe and boot collection of international importance.

A pair of Edwardian black lace-up boots.
£40–60 *Ech*

A pair of child's black leather boots, 1930s.
£20–30 *Ech*

A pair of child's brown leather shoes, 1940s.
£20–25 *Ech*

A pair of green leather shoes, unworn, 1940s.
£20–30 *Ech*

l. A pair of cream and brown leather shoes, unworn, 1940s.
£30–50 *Ech*

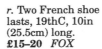

r. Two French shoe lasts, 19thC, 10in (25.5cm) long.
£15–20 *FOX*

Underwear & Nightwear

A Victorian cotton
long-sleeved
nightdress, trimmed
with broderie anglaise.
£35–55 *Ech*

A Victorian
hand embroidered
linen shift.
£30–45 *Ech*

A Victorian cotton
long-sleeved
nightdress, trimmed
with broderie anglaise.
£35–65 *Ech*

An Edwardian
cotton petticoat,
trimmed with
broderie anglaise.
£50–75 *Ech*

An Edwardian cotton camisole.
£20–30 *Ech*

An Edwardian
cotton camisole.
£20–30 *Ech*

An Edwardian cotton
petticoat, trimmed
with lace.
£30–50 *Ech*

A silk garter, with badge
inscribed 'Happy Returns
Bee Lillie', 1930s.
£10–15 *Ech*

An Edwardian
cotton camisole.
£20–30 *Ech*

A pair of Edwardian
cotton combinations.
£35–55 *Ech*

Textiles

An Edwardian cushion cover, gauze with tapestry, 19in (48.5cm) square.
£40–60 *Ech*

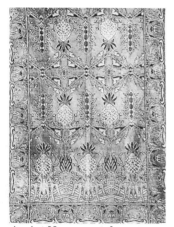

An Art Nouveau style green plush wall hanging, woven in dark blue, brown and cream with stylised pineapple plants arranged in a lattice with other floral and leafy stems, within a similar border, c1900, 113 by 60in (287 by 152.5cm).
£350–400 *CSK*

A pair of printed filet curtains, with intricate design of medieval figures and suits of armour among scrolling strapwork and armorial motifs, within scalloped edge border, late 19thC, 132 by 54in (335.5 by 137cm).
£275–350 *CSK*

An Edwardian embroidered black velvet tea cosy.
£25–35 *Ech*

r. An Edwardian embroidered fire screen, with brass frame, 33 by 24½in (84 by 62cm).
£180–220 *ASH*

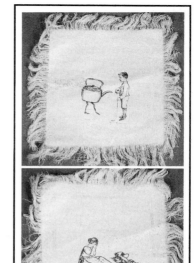

A set of 5 Edwardian silk mats, with pencil drawings, 7in (18cm) square.
£40–60 *LB*

l. A corner panel of a linen cover, the border with elaborate drawn threadwork and shadow stitched flowers, c1735, 24 by 19in (61 by 48.5cm).
£575–675 *CSK*

An Edwardian black silk mantel runner, 78 by 11in (198 by 28cm).
£15–30 *Ech*

A cover, composed of filet squares worked with animals and figures, within a cutwork border, the components late 16thC, 41in (104cm) square.
£1,400–1,600 *CSK*

An Edwardian hand embroidered linen tray cloth, 31 by 22in (79 by 56cm).
£15–25 *Ech*

A feathered star pattern quilt, of plain and printed cottons on a cream ground, quilted with hanging diamonds to follow pattern and feathers, late 19thC, 80in (203cm) square.
£400–450 *CSK*

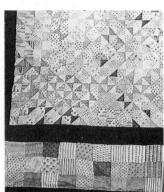

A patchwork coverlet, of small print light-coloured cottons, the field of pinwheels within a red frame and border of squares and an outer frame of red, 19thC, 84 by 90in (213.5 by 228.5cm).
£210–260 *CSK*

A patchwork quilt, of large diamonds of mainly blue and white printed cottons, with pink gingham diamonds on 2 borders, all within a frame of brown and cream cotton printed with a lattice of small red flowers, quilted to follow design, 19thC, 92 by 100in (234 by 254cm).
£350–400 *CSK*

An Edwardian linen tablecloth, with crocheted border, 48in (122cm) square.
£35–65 *Ech*

An early Victorian unfinished quilt, of plain and printed cotton, with hexagonal, diamond, heart, leaf and flowerhead appliqué patches and a central hexagon on an ivory ground.
£200–300 *Bon*

A log cabin quilt, c1880, 90in (228.5cm) square.
£200–300 *Ech*

An Edwardian linen supper cloth, with crocheted edge, 30in (76cm) square.
£25–30 *Ech*

Samplers & Embroidered Pictures

The majority of samplers featured in this section date from the 19th century, and from the information contained on them they can be dated with absolute precision. Price depends on the decorative quality of the image, the colours of the silks and the fineness of the stitching. Condition is crucial since, like other textiles, samplers and embroidered pictures are prone to fading and general deterioration.

A needlework sampler, comprising 12 bands of decorative knotwork in silks in a variety of stitches, by Elizabeth Heathe, aged 8, 1700, 35 by 10in (90 by 25cm), 19thC framing and glazing.
£1,700–1,800 *WL*

A sampler, worked in dark green silks on a coarse ground with alphabet and numerals, by Sarah Ann Wood, 1777, 9 by 7in (23 by 18cm), framed and glazed.
£150–200 *CSK*

r. A needlework sampler, worked on linen, by Jane Foster, aged 9, 1806, 12in (30.5cm) square, in a mahogany frame.
£250–300 *Mit*

A needlework sampler, worked with flowers, butterflies, alphabet, numerals and verse, by Hannah Backhouse, 1785, 17 by 16in (43 by 40.5cm), in Hogarth frame.
£1,600–1,800 *Mit*

A sampler, worked on linen, by Ann Orton, 19thC, 16½ by 12in (42 by 30.5cm), in oak frame.
£325–375 *Mit*

A needlework sampler, decorated with Adam and Eve in the Garden of Eden, by Ann Bowden, aged 12, 1811, 15¾ by 12in (40 by 30.5cm), in maple frame.
£2,000–2,200 *AG*

A sampler, depicting Peterborough Cathedral, worked in coloured wools in cross stitch, within a floral border, 1834, 16½ by 19½in (42 by 49.5cm), framed and glazed.
£250–300 *CSK*

A sampler, by Annie Parker, worked with her hair, aged 34, 1820, 14in (35.5cm) square.
£1,500–1,800 *RA*

A sampler, worked in silk cross stitch on canvas, depicting a house with a green front door, flanked by 2 trees, alphabets above, by Jane Richardson, aged 13, 1855, 12¼ by 11in (31 by 28cm).
£225–275 *P*

A sampler, worked on linen, by Eliza Pain Burdge, 1834, 14 by 13in (35.5 by 33cm), in stained wooden frame.
£425–500 *Mit*

An embroidered woolwork picture, with silk highlights of a parrot perched in a basket filled with roses, tulips and other flowers, mid-19thC, 25½ by 20in (65 by 51cm), framed and glazed.
£250–300 *CSK*

An Italian silkwood panel, with sprays of pink roses in a stylised urn, by Costanza Palandri, dated 1819, 19 by 15½in (48.5 by 39.5cm).
£200–250 *Bon*

A crewel embroidered panel, with a central cartouche depicting a shepherdess greeting a man at a fountain with a young girl pouring water, with a hunting scene below, the corners having detailed figurative scenes, with a camel and leopard at either end, early 18thC, 21 by 34½in (53.5 by 87.5cm), framed and glazed.
£400–500 *CSK*

A pair of painted silk pictures, in shades of grey, one with a man seated under a tree with his gun and dog by the side of a river, with walled city on the far bank, the other of similar composition with a shepherdess and her flock, c1800, 8½ by 11in (21.5 by 28cm), framed and glazed.
£400–500 *CSK*

A coloured silk embroidered picture, with couched gilt threads and spangles, depicting the death of Absalom, 19thC, 16½ by 13in (42 by 33cm), framed and glazed.
£225–275 *CSK*

DOLLS
Barbie

Barbie, still the favourite of little girls across the world, was the first teenage fashion doll. Launched by the American company Mattel in 1959, the first Barbie model had holes in the feet for a stand, whilst the second had a stand which fitted under the arms and no holes in the feet. Early Barbies had pale colouring and a slightly Oriental appearance, but by the late 1960s warmer flesh tones were introduced and the doll came to epitomise the American ideal of healthy good looks.

Barbie's success was largely due to the range and quality of her wardrobe. Dolls dating from the early 1960s, known as the couture period, wore clothes inspired by the great Paris fashion houses such as Dior and Givenchy. Barbie's hair changed accordingly; 1961 for example, saw the introduction of a bouffant bubble cut and titian red hair.

It is only recently that Barbie, Ken and their attendant friends have become collectable. As doll dealer Maureen Stanford explains, 'Barbies were produced in their millions. Specialist collectors want mint, first edition Barbies in their original boxes, particularly rare examples such as the black Barbie.' Clothes, which were labelled with the characters' names, are very important, as is the condition of the dolls; pen marks, for example, soak into the plastic and cannot be removed without leaving a stain.

r. A Barbie doll, in good condition, 11½in (29cm), 1990s, and Starlight bed.
£5–8 *PC*

l. A talking Ken doll, wearing Arabian Nights outfit, 1972, 12in (30.5cm) high.
£25–28 *CMF*

A black ballerina Barbie doll, mint condition, unused, 1988, 11½in (29cm) high.
£30–35 *CMF*

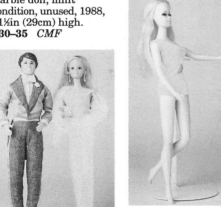

A Barbie and Ken Superstar set, with twist-and-turn bodies and bendable legs, 1970, 12in (30.5cm) high.
£45–50 *CMF*

Stacey, a friend of Barbie, with twist-and-turn body and bendable legs, 1960s, 11½in (29cm) high.
£35–40 *CMF*

This doll is rare.

Bisque

Six all-bisque dolls' house dolls, with movable arms and legs, 4in (10cm) high.
£100–130 *P(B)*

A pair of bisque dolls' house dolls, one marked '627(12.1/2)', 4¾in (12cm) high.
£15–18 *P(B)*

A bisque china-headed doll, with closing blue paperweight glass eyes, open mouth, pierced ears, blonde wig, jointed composition body, impressed 'K.R.'(?) and '11', 22¾in (58cm) high.
£450–550 *Bea*

r. A bisque-headed doll, with googly eyes, some damage, c1920, 5in (12.5cm) high.
£150–200 *BaN*

A Belton type bisque-headed doll, with flattened-dome head, fixed blue glass eyes, open/closed mouth, pierced ears, blonde real hair wig, jointed wood and composition body with straight wrists, dressed in blue, lace-panelled dress, some damage, c1880, 14in (35.5cm) high.
£600–700 *S*

A bisque-headed doll, with sleeping brown eyes, painted and real lashes, open mouth with 4 teeth, pierced ears, blonde mohair wig, composition ball-jointed body with inoperative crying mechanism, wearing a pale blue candy-striped silk and lace dress, woven straw hat, black leather buckled and buttoned shoes, marked 'DEP 8', impressed '8', 20in (51cm) high.
£450–550 *DN*

German

A German all bisque Kewpie doll, in original romper suit, 6in (15cm) high.
£150–200 *DOL*

A bisque shoulder-headed doll, probably by Kling, with fixed spiral blue glass eyes, closed mouth, blonde wig, cloth body with kid lower arms, in original costume, 16¼in (41cm) high.
£750–850 *S(S)*

A bisque-headed doll, by Simon & Halbig, mould No. 939, with brown paperweight eyes, c1890, 22in (56cm) high.
£1,200–1,500 *DOL*

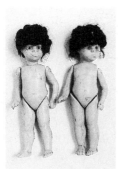

Two bisque Mulatto dolls, c1900, 3½in (9cm) high.
£200–300 *DOL*

l. A bisque socket-head Chinese doll, with fixed brown glass eyes, painted eyebrows and eyelashes, open mouth with 2 upper teeth, a black plaited mohair wig, on a wood and composition ball-jointed body, neck stamped '6/0', 10in (25.5cm) high.
£325–400 *HSS*

r. An Armand Marseille bisque-headed doll, with sleeping brown eyes, open mouth with 4 teeth, brown mohair wig, on jointed composition body, small chip to eye socket, marked 'A13M', 30½in (77.5cm) high.
£400–450 *DN*

A bisque-headed doll, by Kämmer & Reinhardt and Simon & Halbig, with original clothes, c1900, 14in (35.5cm) high.
£450–550 *DOL*

A bisque-headed character doll, by Kestner, mould No. 241, original wig and some original clothes, c1920, 26in (66cm) high.
£1,300–1,500 *DOL*

An Armand Marseille bisque-headed doll, with blue weighted eyes and open mouth, on a jointed composition body, No. 390/3, c1905, 19¾in (50cm) high.
£100–150 *P(B)*

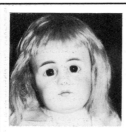
Miller's is a price GUIDE not a price LIST

An Armand Marseille 390 bisque-headed doll, with brown sleeping eyes, on a composition body, 1910, 18in (45.5cm) high.
£250–300 *BaN*

A Schoenau & Hoffmeister bisque socket-head doll, with closing blue glass eyes, real hair upper lashes, painted eyebrows and eyelashes, open mouth with 4 teeth, shoulder length blonde mohair wig, on a wood and composition ball-jointed body, wearing a broderie anglaise and pin-tucked dress and undergarments, some damage, head stamped 'SH', centred by a star stamped 'PB' over '1909 7½ Germany', 25in (63.5cm) high.
£325–400 *HSS*

China & Porcelain

A German porcelain pincushion doll, c1920, 8in (20cm) high.
£40–50 *BaN*

Fabric

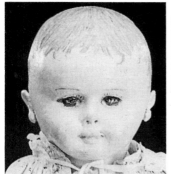

A German china shoulder-headed doll, with blue painted eyes, closed mouth, moulded brown hair, cloth body and wooden arms, in original costume, c1860, 13in (33cm) high, together with a quantity of dolls clothes.
£425–500 *S(S)*

l. An American cloth doll, by Martha Chase, the stockinette head painted with oils, with blue eyes, closed mouth, thickly painted blonde hair and jointed body, wearing a muslin dress and crochet bonnet, some damage, c1920, 20in (51cm) high.
£240–300 *S(S)*

Composition

A composition doll, with fixed brown eyes, flaxen wig, body and limbs, in original pink costume and shoes, c1905, 21¾in (55cm) high.
£220–260 *WL*

A stockinette rag doll, dressed in an Eastern costume, 13¾in (35cm) high.
£20–25 *P(B)*

A Nora Wellings felt doll, with painted face, wearing original clothes, c1928, 18in (45.5cm) high.
£250–300 *BaN*

Oriental

A Chinese family of Door of Hope Mission wooden dolls, from Ning-Po, with fully carved jointed bodies, c1901.
£500–600 *Bon*

Dolls

- Classified by the medium from which the head is made: bisque, celluloid, wax, etc
- Many are marked. On bisque dolls the mark is often on the back of the head, underneath the wig
- Some are marked on the shoulder, whilst many French and German dolls have maker's stamps or sticky labels attached to the body
- Some cloth dolls, like teddy bears, are marked on the sole of the foot
- Wood, papier mâché, wax, parian and china dolls are rarely marked

Two Oriental Gofun socket-headed dolls, dressed in Chinese costume, one with shoe missing, 1910, husband 14¼in (36cm) high.
£80–100 *P(B)*

Wax

A wax-over-composition shoulder-headed doll, with black glass eyes, calico stuffed body and wooden lower limbs, crack to face, 15¾in (40cm) high.
£45–55 *P(B)*

l. A Montanari-type poured wax shoulder-headed doll, with fixed blue glass eyes, closed mouth, inserted blonde mohair wig, cloth body with poured wax lower limbs, in original costume, some damage, c1870, 14½in (37cm) high.
£500–600 *S*

Wooden

l. A Grödnertal wooden doll, the wooden head covered in gesso, with painted features, peg-jointed limbs and spade hands, wearing a contemporary cotton dress and undergarments, early 19thC, 19½in (49.5cm) high.
£450–550 *HSS*

A carved wooden doll, with turned head and painted features, on a jointed body, dressed in a later crinoline dress, 19thC, 21in (53cm) high.
£150–200 *P(B)*

A Grödnertal wooden doll, with painted carved features, pierced ears with earrings, jointed body, in original costume, mid-19thC, 10in (25.5cm) high.
£675–800 *S(S)*

Dolls' Accessories

r. A mahogany half-tester doll's bed, complete with later mattress and hangings, late 19thC, 20in (51cm) high, together with a composition doll.
£350–450 *S*

l. A Victorian cast iron doll's smoothing iron and trivet, 2in (5cm) long.
£10–15 each *MRW*

Dolls' Clothes

A mid-18thC style doll's cotton voile dress, with antique Maltese lace trimmings, 1990s, 17in (43cm) high.
£140–180 *JPr*

A 19thC style doll's dress, made from the fabric of a wedding gown and old lace, 1990s, 14in (35.5cm) high.
£240–300 *JPr*

A doll's silk dress, c1800, 15in (38cm) high.
£220–240 *JPr*

> **Miller's is a price GUIDE not a price LIST**

A late 19thC style doll's cotton dress and bonnet, with lace trimmings, 1990s, 15in (38cm) high.
£120–160 *JPr*

A 19thC style doll's moiré silk and old lace dress, 1990s, 18in (45.5cm) high.
£140–180 *JPr*

A 19thC style doll's dress, handmade from antique fabrics, 1990s, 18in (45.5cm) high.
£180–220 *JPr*

Dolls' Houses

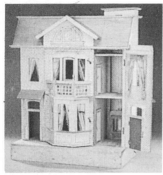

A wooden three-storey dolls' house, painted to simulate a brick façade, the hinged front opening in 2 sections to reveal a string-wound lift operating between each floor, original wallpapers and flooring, mounted on grey painted base with side steps, some damage, pencil No. '4687', c1900, 24¾in (63cm) high, possibly German.
£1,100–1,400 *S(S)*

A Victorian dolls' three-storey town house, painted to simulate a brick façade, lift-off pitched roof with central chimneys, the hinged front opening to 6 rooms, each with fireplace, some damage, 60¼in (153cm) high, together with a quantity of dolls' house furniture.
£700–900 *S(S)*

A two-storey dolls' house, covered with paper to simulate a brick façade, opening at front, 1906, 26in (66cm) high.
£600–650 *WAG*

l. A Victorian wooden dolls' house, with simulated tiled roof over front bay and tiled portico, opening to reveal internal turned wood stairwell, fireplaces and 6 panel interior doors, wired for electricity, 31in (79cm) high.
£175–250 *EH*

A Lines Brothers three-storey dolls' house, c1920, 30in (76cm) high.
£450–500 *DOL*

Furniture

A selection of mid-Victorian cast iron dolls' house fireside tools.
£15–40 each *MRW*

A dolls' house washing machine, 1940, 3in (7.5cm) high.
£10–15 *MRW*

A Victorian cast iron dolls' house step ladder, 2¾in (7cm) high.
£20–40 *MRW*

A pair of Victorian tinplate dolls' house trays.
£10–15 *MRW*

DRINKING

A Norwegian ale jug, with original spout and shaped handle, worn painted surface, c1790, 8in (20cm) high.
£250–300 *RYA*

A Scandinavian beech bowl, with 2 horses' head lifts, the inscribed rim with polychrome decoration, and flowerhead inside, 19thC, 11in (28cm) wide.
£700–800 *WW*

A silver-mounted cork stopper, the cast silver shell with shaped nameplate engraved 'CLARET', London 1820.
£100–150 *CS*

A silver punch or toddy ladle, with fruitwood handle and shaped silver bowl, hallmarked for 1774.
£100–150 *CS*

A silver-mounted cork stopper, with handle of fruiting vines, Birmingham 1848.
£50–70 *CS*

A mahogany, brass and silver plated port or claret decanting cradle, or tilter, c1870.
£100–250 *CS*

A silver-plated cocktail shaker, formed as a bell, by Asprey, c1930, 12in (30.5cm) high.
£200–250 *WTA*

Two silver-plated wine tasters, or tastevins, one with an advertisement for Calvet of Beaune.
£25–45 *CS*

A bottle opener, advertising 'Bouvet Brut', 1970s.
£3–4 *COL*

Bottles

A green glass dumpy bottle, with a long neck, c1750, 9in (23cm) high.
£225–260 *Har*

A green cylinder-shaped bottle, with seal, dated '1791', 7½in (19cm) high.
£350–400 *Har*

A black glass flagon, with handle, 1810, 11½in (30cm) high.
£525–565 *Har*

l. A hand painted and gilt decorated port bottle, c1870, 13in (33cm) high.
£70–80
r. A hand painted and gilt decorated brandy bottle, c1870, 12¼in (31cm) high.
£65–75 *RYA*

l. A black glass bottle, with seal, inscribed 'Thomas Gerrard, Gibbs Town', c1860, 11½in (30cm) high.
£75–85 *Har*

l. A green cylinder-shaped bottle, painted with a stag and bunch of grapes, inscribed 'P. MINT', c1870, 12½in (32cm) high.
£100–145 *Har*

r. A bottle of Château Montrose, Bordeaux bottled, Cruse Frères, 'St. Estèphe, 2ème Cru Classé', soiled and torn label, ullage low to bottom level, 1870.
£475–550 *S*

Ceramics

A salt glazed whisky flagon, with treacle glaze, 18thC, 13in (33cm) high.
£100–120 *BS*

A two-tone glazed beer flagon, with slab seal incised 'Halls Oxford Brewery Swan Brewery Oxford', mid-19thC, 11in (28cm) high.
£40–45 *BS*

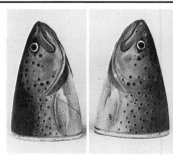

A pair of Derby stirrup cups, each in the form of a trout, coloured pink, grey and brown, with gilt and white bands, inscribed 'The Anglers Delight', one cracked, 19thC, 5in (13cm) high.
£750–850 *P(S)*

A grey glazed spirit jar, with slab seal, incised 'Ekin Spirit Merchant Cambridge', mid-19thC, 16in (40.5cm) high.
£70–80 *BS*

A two-tone glazed bellied flagon, incised 'Welch, Bear Hotel Hungerford', late 19thC, 15in (38cm) high.
£40–45 *BS*

A set of 4 stone bottles, incised 'Gin', 'Brandy', 'Irish Whiskey' and 'Scotch Whisky', with registered date of 1877, 7in (18cm) high.
£175–200 *BS*

Five stoneware bottles, inscribed by various wine merchants, c1900, 7in (18cm) high.
£10–15 each *BS*

A salt glazed stone jar, incised with maker's name and retailer, 19thC, 15in (38cm) high.
£50–60 *BS*

A two-tone glazed wine and spirit bellied jar, with incised details of retailer, late 19thC, 16in (40.5cm) high.
£45–50 *BS*

l. A brown glazed flagon, with beaded decoration, c1900, 10in (25.5cm) high.
£30–35 *BS*

A Portuguese wine jug, c1960, 8in (20cm) high.
£20–25 *COL*

A shop's ginger beer flagon, with hole for a tap, transfer printed 'Thomas Weaver, Reading', c1910, 13in (33cm) high.
£25–30 *BS*

A shop's ginger beer flagon, with hole for a tap, printed 'S. R. Elms & Co, 110 & 112, High St, Dover', c1910, 19in (48.5cm) high.
£55–65 *BS*

A two-tone glazed straight-sided beer flagon, incised 'South Berks Brewery Limited, Hungerford', c1920, 11in (28cm) high.
£30–35 *BS*

A spirit flagon, by Taylor, Tunnicliffe & Co, with silver mount and cork, Birmingham 1903, 7in (18cm) high.
£150–175 *GLN*

l. A French china peach brandy bottle, with handle, labelled 'Dolfi', c1950, 10in (25.5cm) high.
£6–7 *ED*

A quart measure or mug, with a grey glaze and printed crown, 19thC, 6in (15cm) high.
£60–65 *BS*

A Mochaware ale measure/mug, with applied one pint stamp, late 19thC, 5in (12.5cm) high.
£70–75 *BS*

A Mochaware ale measuring jug, with Customs & Excise quart stamp, late 19thC, 6in (15cm) high.
£100–130 *BS*

A saki cup, with magnifying lens in base, c1910, 1¾in (4.5cm) high.
£45–55 *PC*

When this cup is filled with clear liquid a female nude is revealed!

ENTERTAINMENT
Film & TV Memorabilia

A Hawkeye basket outdoor 'refrigerator', used by Clark Gable, with removable hinged top, the interior lined with stainless steel, stencilled on the cover with initials 'C.G.', c1950, 15 by 19in (38 by 48cm).
£800–1,000 *CNY*

A gelatin silver print of Laurence Olivier as Henry V, 1945, 9½ by 7½in (24 by 19cm).
£35–50 *Bon*

A collection of 230 black and white photographs used in Charles Castle's biography, *Joan Crawford The Raging Star*, a copy of *The Films of Joan Crawford* by Lawrence J. Quirk, 9 front-of-house cards/song sheets, and a *Screen Star* library book, many stills reprinted and prepared for publication.
£250–350 *Bon*

A leather bound doctor's case, adapted by Stanley Hall as a make-up box, the drawered compartments contain his famous combs and scissors, brushes, pom-sticks, spirit gums and eyeliners used to make up famous film stars, and a collection of make-up.
£400–500 *Bon*

A pair of black leather boots, by Icarus of Spain, with 3½in (9cm) stack heels, worn by Karen Lynn Gorney in the film *Saturday Night Fever*, 1977.
£3,250–3,500 *CNY*

A customised Schick injector razor, the Bakelite handle engraved 'Boris S. Karloff', original hard case, 1941.
£425–525 *CNY*

A collection of items regarding the Hollywood Writers' Mobilization, including a signed letter from the blacklisted writer, Howard Koch, an affidavit of Sam Jaffe, dated '1959', with a handwritten note clipped to it, and 2 black and white photographs of anti-Communist picketers, 8 by 10in (20 by 25cm).
£100–120 *CNY*

A pair of dance shoes, worn by Karen Lynn Gorney in the film *Saturday Night Fever*, and a photograph of the actress rehearsing with John Travolta, 1977, 8 by 10in (20 by 25.5cm).
£2,500–2,700 *CNY*

Six flapper costumes used in the film *The Best Things in Life are Free*, including 3 hats, and a continuity photograph from the studio, 1957.
£150–250 *CNY*

A pair of black patent leather gloves, worn by Michele Pfeiffer as Catwoman in *Batman Returns*, mounted in a yellow and black lucite display case, 15in (38cm) long, and a photograph, 1992.
£3,300–3,700 *CNY*

A pair of custom-designed Martian shoes, worn by Andy Warhol at a dinner dance during the Seattle Art Museum's Warhol Portrait Show at the Modern Art Pavilion.
£1,000–1,200 *CNY*

The artist wore the specially designed shoes and signed them in black felt pen. The metal ridged clog-style shoes feature rubber and stud soles with brown leather straps, and were constructed so that they could be worn comfortably over a pair of normal shoes.

A Cyberman costume, with Cyber head, from the 25th Anniversary series of *Dr Who, Silver Nemesis*.
£700–800 *Bon*

A pair of red boots, worn by Jason in the children's television programme, *The Mighty Morphin Power Rangers*, with stainless steel tips, black embossed rubber trim and 4 white clasp closures along the front, and a *Power Rangers* logo card.
£650–750 *CNY*

These boots demonstrate how quickly objects can become collectable. It was only in 1994 that Power Rangers shot to international TV stardom (see Miller's Collectables Price Guide 1995/96, 'Collectables of the Future'). According to the story line, Jason has now been despatched to a World Peace Conference, in other words dropped from the TV series, hence perhaps the reason why his boots came up for auction. Only time will tell whether interest in Power Rangers toys and memorabilia will survive the current craze.

Eight pottery figures, depicting characters from *Snow White and the Seven Dwarfs*, hand painted in bright colours, each dwarf carrying a different gardening tool, 1937, Snow White 10½in (27cm) high.
£450–600 *Bon*

Three Wade porcelain 'Blow Up' Walt Disney characters from *Lady and the Tramp*, 1955, largest 6in (15cm) high.
£120–160 each *MRW*

Animation Cels

A production cell, from Walt Disney's *Canine Patrol*, depicting a tired turtle, mounted.
£150–200 *Bon*

© *The Walt Disney Company*

An animation cel, from Walt Disney Studios' *Bambi*, gouache on full celluloid applied to a key production background, c1980, 8½ by 11½in (21.5 by 29cm).
£300–350 *CSK*

© *The Walt Disney Company*

An animation cel, depicting Hanna-Barbera Studios' *The Jetsons*, gouache on full celluloid applied to a printed background, signed, c1970, 9 by 11½in (23 by 29cm).
£300–350 *CSK*

A television advertising cel, depicting Mickey Mouse, from an unknown Walt Disney Studios' production, gouache on full celluloid applied to a colour xerox background, c1980, 8½ by 11½in (21.5 by 29cm).
£300–370 *CSK*

© *The Walt Disney Company*

An animation cel, from Walt Disney's *Winnie The Pooh*, depicting Piglet's kite landing on Eeyore's head, gouache on full celluloid applied to a key watercolour background, c1980, 8½ by 11½in (21.5 by 29cm).
£300–350 *CSK*

© *The Walt Disney Company*

An animation cel, depicting Hanna-Barbera Studios' *The Flintstones*, gouache on full celluloid applied to a printed background, signed, c1980, 9 by 11¾in (23 by 29.5cm).
£175–225 *CSK*

An animation cel, depicting Hanna-Barbera Studios' *America's Cup*, with Fred Flintstone, Scooby-Doo, Yogi Bear and friends, gouache on full celluloid applied to a printed background, No. '136/400', signed, 1992, 14¾ by 18¾in (37.5 by 47.5cm).
£400–500 *CSK*

EPHEMERA
Autographs

An autograph album, page with sketches in pencil and signed by L. Alma-Tadema, dated '4 December 1879', spine damaged, some pages loose, good condition.
£110–150 *VS*

A signed colour photograph of Pamela Anderson, in a white bikini, excellent condition, 10 by 8in (25.5 by 20cm).
£50–60 *VS*

A signed colour photograph of Muhammad Ali, excellent condition, 10 by 8in (25.5 by 20cm).
£80–90 *VS*

A legal judgement document, between the 'Andrews Sisters Eight To The Bar Ranch, Inc.', and Arthur R. Krausse & Co, signed in blue and black ink on the last page by the Andrews Sisters, 1955.
£400–450 *CNY*

Two signed and dedicated photographs of Ingrid Bergman, from *A Month in the Country* and as Natalia Petrovna, one slightly damp stained, 10 by 8in (25 by 20cm).
£125–175 *Bon*

A signed and dedicated postcard photograph of Enrico Caruso, 10½ by 8½in (26.5 by 21.5cm).
£450–550 *S*

l. A hardback edition of *Highgrove: Portrait of an Estate*, signed by HRH Prince Charles, and dated '1994', with a covering letter from his assistant private secretary, excellent condition.
£650–750 *VS*

A first day cover, signed by 4 British Prime Ministers, postmarked '8 June, 1977', very good condition.
£60–70 *VS*

A colour reproduction of a painting by Marc Chagall, signed by the artist, overmounted in light blue, very good condition, 8 by 6in (20 by 15cm).
£80–100 *VS*

A colour window card from the 1951 film *Payment On Demand*, signed by Bette Davis, matted with engraved name plate, 10 by 13in (25.5 by 33cm).
£300–350 *CNY*

A black and white photograph of James Stewart and Marlene Dietrich in *Destry Rides Again*, 1940, signed in blue and black ink by both, 10 by 8in (25.5 by 20cm).
£600–650 *CNY*

l. A signed colour photograph of Danny de Vito, as the Penguin, excellent condition, 10 by 8in (25.5 by 20cm).
£30–40 *VS*

l. A signed and inscribed photograph of Bing Crosby, good condition, 10 by 8in (25.5 by 20cm).
£50–60 *VS*

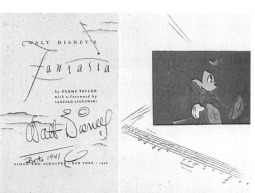

An American large hardback edition of *Fantasia*, signed by Walt Disney to title page, colour illustrations, 1941, good condition.
£1,200–1,400 *VS*

An autograph book, including signatures of Clark Gable, Gregory Peck, Lex Barker, Stewart Granger, Glynis Johns and Miriam Karlin.
£220-250 *Bon*

Three black and white photographs of Melanie, Prissy and Ashley from *Gone with the Wind*, 1939, signed by Olivia de Havilland, Butterfly McQueen and Leslie Howard, 10 by 8in (25.5 by 20cm).
£325–400 *CNY*

A signed black and white photograph, and a letter from Errol Flynn, written from the Hotel Cecil in Delhi while he was shooting *Kim*, letter dated '11 Dec'.
£800–1,000 *Bon*

A signed colour photograph of Tom Hanks, from *Philadelphia*, 10 by 8in (25.5 by 20cm).
£55–65 *VS*

A signed colour laminated magazine photograph of Audrey Hepburn in *My Fair Lady*, very good condition, 11½ by 8½in (29 by 21.5cm).
£100–120 *VS*

A typed letter to Stanley Hall from Greta Garbo, signed in black ink 'G. G.', dated 'June 2, 1972', with the envelope.
£400–500 *Bon*

A signed colour photograph of Jack Nicholson as the Joker, excellent condition, 10 by 8in (25.5 by 20cm).
£50–60 *VS*

r A signed postcard of Vivien Leigh, as Scarlett O'Hara from *Gone with the Wind*, good condition.
£700–800 *VS*

l. A signed postcard of Laurel and Hardy, on their last tour of the UK.
£240–280 *Bon*

A signed and dedicated photograph of Elizabeth Taylor, from *The VIPs*, 10 by 8in (25.5 by 20cm).
£140–180 *Bon*

A collection of photographs, posters and playbills signed by Joan Sutherland.
£375–475 *S*

A signed magazine photograph of John Wayne, probably as Davy Crockett, very good condition, 10 by 8in (25.5 by 20cm).
£275–350 *VS*

A signed photograph of Paul Robeson and Elisabeth Welch, from *A Song of Freedom*, 8 by 10in (20 by 25cm), and another, dated '1950'.
£225–300 *Bon*

r. A signature by G. Bernard Shaw, laid down to an album page.
£60–70 *VS*

A signed sepia photograph of David Niven, very good condition, 7 by 5in (18 by 12.5cm).
£80–100 *VS*

A signature by Pablo Picasso, laid down to card, good condition, 4½ by 4in (11.5 by 10cm).
£300–350 *VS*

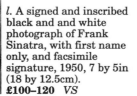

l. A signed and inscribed black and and white photograph of Frank Sinatra, with first name only, and facsimile signature, 1950, 7 by 5in (18 by 12.5cm).
£100–120 *VS*

Cigarette Cards

W. A & A. C.
Churchman, Treasure
Trove, set of 12 large
cards, 1937.
£10–15 *MUR*

W. D. & H. O. Wills, Old
Pottery & Porcelain, set
of 30, 1934.
£25–35 *MUR*

Ardath Tobacco Co Ltd, Figures of Speech,
set of 50, 1936.
£40–80 *ACC*

W. & F. Faulkner Ltd, Nautical
Terms, set of 12, c1899.
£210–420 *ACC*

Ardath Tobacco Co Ltd, Your
Birthday Tells Your Fortune,
set of 50, 1937.
£30–50 *ACC*

Scottish CWS,
Famous Pictures,
set of 25, 1927.
£30–50 *MUR*

Animals & Birds

Gallaher Ltd, British Birds,
series of 48, 1937.
£11–22 *ACC*

Ardath Tobacco Co. Ltd, Champion
Dogs, set of 25, 1934.
£20–25 *MUR*

Senior Service, Dogs,
set of 48, 1939.
£15–25 *ACC*

Ardath Tobacco Co. Ltd, Dog Studies, set of 25, 1938.
£55–65 *MUR*

Beauties

American Tobacco Co, Flower Beauties, 4 from set of 25, 1900.
£6–8 *WAL*

Taddy & Co, Dogs, Nos. 1, 11, 15 and 50, 1900.
£22–26 *WAL*

l. Richmond Cavendish & Co Ltd, Beauties, with playing card inset, one card from set of 52, 1897.
£45–90 *ACC*

Murray, Sons & Co Ltd, Types of Dogs, set of 20, c1924.
£100–200 *ACC*

Gallaher Ltd, Wild Animals, series of 48, 1937.
£11–18 *ACC*

Salmon & Gluckstein Ltd, Star Girls, one card from set of 25, 1899.
£85–100 *WAL*

Mexe, hand coloured picture of a ballet dancer, c1920.
£25–40 *ACC*

This Greek card was issued in Athens, and has never been catalogued.

Entertainment

Gallaher Ltd, Shots from
Famous Films, set of 48, 1935.
£28–56 *ACC*

Godfrey Phillips Ltd, Cinema
Stars, set of 25, circular, 1924.
£35–40 *VS*

l. Carreras Ltd,
Film Stars, set
of 54, 1937.
£36–70 *ACC*

Salmon & Gluckstein
Ltd, Music Hall
Celebrities, No. 29 from
set of 30, 1902.
£20–22 *WAL*

Historical

Stephen Mitchell & Son, Wonderful Century,
set of 50, 1937.
£30–50 *ACC*

Stephen Mitchell & Son, Famous Scots,
set of 50, 1933.
£32–64 *ACC*

Ogden's, Leaders of Men, set of 50, 1924.
£80–160 *ACC*

John Player & Sons, Napoleon, set of 25, c1915.
£24–54 *ACC*

Military

Stephen Mitchell, British Warships, Second Series, set of 25, 1915.
£150–300 *ACC*

John Player & Sons, History of Naval Dress, set of 25 large cards, 1929.
£30–40 *MUR*

Lambert & Butler, Famous British Airmen and Airwomen, set of 25, 1935.
£28–48 *ACC*

John Player & Sons, RAF Badges, set of 50, 1937.
£28–56 *ACC*

W. A. & A. C. Churchman, Air Raid Precautions, set of 48, 1938.
£12–22 *ACC*

Natural History

John Player & Sons, Struggle for Existence, set of 25, 1923.
£5–25 *ACC*

W. D. & H. O. Wills, Rose, series of 40, 1936.
£45–90 *ACC*

Sporting

Franklyn, Davey & Co, Hunting, set of 25, 1925.
£24–48 *ACC*

l. Ogden's Cigarettes, Greyhound Racing, second series, set of 25, 1928.
£75–175 *ACC*

Royalty

Adkin & Sons, A Royal Favourite, Queen Victoria, Empress of Germany, Queen of Greece, Czarina of Russia, 4 cards from set of 12, 1900.
£6–8 *WAL*

Gallaher Ltd, Racing Scenes, set of 48, 1938.
£28–56 *ACC*

John Player & Sons, Hints on Association Football, set of 50, 1934.
£24–48 *ACC*

W. D. & H. O. Wills, The King's Art Treasures, set of 40, 1938.
£10–20 *ACC*

Topographical

Lambert & Butler, The Thames from Lechlade, set of 50, 1907.
£225–450 *ACC*

African Tobacco Manufacturers, Cape Town, Houses of Parliament, various issues, 1923.
£1–4 each *ACC*

Comics

American comics tend to be the most valuable. Collectors are prepared to spend vast amounts in order to obtain rare issues, particularly those comics marking the first appearance of superheroes such as Batman, Superman and Spiderman. The *Batman* comics sold recently at auction in New York represent the ultimate in comic desirability as reflected in their distinctly superheroic price ranges. Whilst few people are likely to have a first edition American *Batman* comic lurking in the loft, rare British comics can also make good, though scarcely comparable, prices.

According to comic dealer, Doug Poultney, whilst younger enthusiasts are concentrating on American comic books, many British comic collectors tend to be in their mid-fifties. 'They want to buy the comics they read as children,' he explains. 'Comics from the 1940s are the best sellers, in particular the big four: *Wizard*, *Hotspur*, *Rover* and *Adventure*.' For all collectors, however, whether their passion is British or American comics, *Batman* or *Beano*, the ultimate is to obtain a first issue.

Two copies of *The Champion*, dated 'December 27, 1952', and 'April 4, 1953'. **£1.50–3.50 each** *DPO*

Detective Comics No. 27, D. C. Publications, dated 'May 1939'. **£46,000–50,000** *S(NY)*

This comic book features the first appearance of Batman drawn by Bob Kane. This dynamic hero has lived on to be one of the most popular characters in comic history. Less than 100 copies are known to exist. This book, along with Action Comics No. 1, continues to be the most sought after 'origin' issue of the Golden Age. This copy has an OWL paper of 7.5, with very bright colours to the front cover.

Comic Cuts and Chips, overseas edition, Harmsworth/ Amalgamated Press, dated 'January 7th, 1939'. **£2–10** *DPO*

The Boys' Friend, Amalgamated Press, dated 'Oct 2nd, 1920'. **£2–5** *DPO*

l. Batman No. 1, D. C. Comics, Spring 1940, featuring the first appearance of the Joker and the Catwoman. **£15,500–16,000** *S(NY)*

The Hotspur, dated
'Sept 25th, 1937'.
£2–8 *DPO*

The Penny Wonder,
Amalgamated Press, dated
'September 28th, 1912'.
£2–3 *DPO*

The Magnet,
Amalgamated Press,
dated 'July 10th, 1937'.
£2–4 *DPO*

Two copies of *Chicks' Own*, Amalgamated
Press, dated 'January 13th, 1923' and
'January 6th, 1949'.
£2–10 each *DPO*

Wow, No. 55, two-colour,
16 pages, 1946.
£8–10 *NOS*

*RoboCop versus
Terminator*, Dark House
Comics, Platinum
Edition, late 1980s.
£30–35 *NOS*

l. Three copies of *The
Rover*, dated 'March 8th,
1947', 'June 3rd, 1939',
and June 7th, 1947'.
£2–8 each *DPO*

Three copies of *The Union Jack*, one dated
'May 14th, 1932'.
£2–3 each *DPO*

The Union Jack *was published by Sampson Low
1880–82, Brooks 1882–83, Harmsworth 1884–1903,
and Amalgamated Press 1903–33.*

Two copies of *The Wizard*, dated 'July 1st, 1939',
and 'November 25th, 1939'.
£2–8 each *DPO*

Postcards

The first British postcards were introduced on the 1st October 1870. The postage rate then was a halfpenny (half that of a letter). By the turn of the century the fashion for decorative postcards took off, and collecting became one of the most popular hobbies of the pre-WWI period. Amongst the most common themes were topographical cards which included both photographic images and views depicted by artists. Artist's signatures are often found on the painted scenes and collectable names include Alfred R. Quinton (1853–1934), who worked for J. Salmon Ltd of Sevenoaks. Photographs showing some form of activity, including people and vehicles tend to be the most desirable today.

Another popular area was comic postcards, a field in which the British excelled and which were produced by a wide range of artists including Louis Wain (1860–1939), Mabel Lucie Attwell (1879–1964) and Donald McGill (1875–1962).

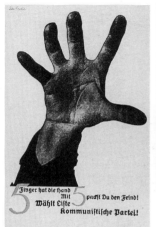

A Russian postcard, by John Heartfield, for distribution in Communist Germany, 1932.
£350–400 *PIn*

A postcard, by Clarence Coles Phillips, of the silent movie star Blanche Sweet, c1912.
£50–60 *PIn*

A German postcard, designed by Ludwig Hirschfeld-Mack, advertising the Bauhaus Art Exposition in Weimar, 1923.
£1,200–1,400 *PIn*

l. A postcard, entitled 'We ARE Enjoying Ourselves', 1920s.
50p–£2 *PC*

Three alcohol related postcards, c1910.
£1–3 each *JMC*

Alcohol related cards have always been popular and appear in many publishers' series.

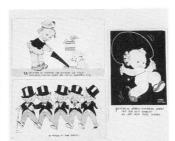

A selection of 3 postcards, from Valentine's Attwell Series, by Mabel Lucie Attwell, 1930s.
£3–5 each *JMC*

Four postcards, from Valentine's Attwell Series, by Mabel Lucie Attwell, 1930s.
£3–5 each *JMC*

Children were one of the most popular themes and Mabel Lucie Attwell (1879–1964) was perhaps the most celebrated artist in this genre.

A set of 3 postcards, from the Bamforth song series, entitled 'Down Home In Tennessee', c1914.
£3–4 *JMC*

A set of 3 postcards, from the Bamforth song card series, c1914.
£3–4 *JMC*

This type of postcard was popular with the forces and their sweethearts during WWI and cards were usually issued in sets of 3 or 4. Each card was numbered, eg 4924/1, 4924/2, 4924/3, as in the 'There's a Long, Long Trail' set. Numbers range from 4500–5129 and cover a wide range of song titles. Colours of some sets can vary.

Three postcards, by Philip Boileau, from the Glamour series, c1910.
£5–6 each *JMC*

Four postcards, published by Davidson Brothers, from Tom Browne originals, c1905.
£3–4 each *JMC*

Tom Browne cards were usually issued in sets of 6 and covered various themes.

Three postcards, by Philip Boileau, from the Glamour series, c1910.
£5–6 each *JMC*

Glamour cards in one form or another are to be found in almost every original album, and were collected mainly in France or by British troops in WWI. This selection of cards by Philip Boileau were printed in America and published by Reinthal & Newman, New York.

Three postcards, from the Write-aways series, published by W. & A. K. Johnston Ltd, c1905.
£1–3 each *JMC*

A set of 6 embossed greetings postcards, one entitled 'Bonne année', good condition, early 1900s.
£60–70 *VS*

Four postcards, by Lawson Wood, from the Gran'pop series, published by Valentine & Sons Ltd, c1935.
£3–6 each *JMC*

Three postcards, in the Celesque series, illustrated by David Wilson, published by Photochrom Co. Ltd, c1907.
£1–3 each *JMC*

A set of 6 postcards, by Louis Wain, one entitled 'White Persian', in good condition, c1900.
£110–140 *VS*

Four postcards in the Write-aways series, published by E. Wrench Ltd, c1905.
£3–5 each *JMC*

Write-aways were intended to encourage people to complete a message.

Names

Twelve postcards, depicting names, c1907.
25p–£2 each *JMC*

*Postcards depicting ladies' and gentlemens'
names were very popular between 1905 and 1910
and apart from the Flower series often showed a
selection of Edwardian actors and actresses.
Prices average from 25p to £2, depending on
rarity of name and actor/actress content.*

Topographical

l. A photographic
postcard, showing
an internal scene at
Chatham Dockyard,
Kent, c1920.
£13–15 *JMC*

l. A photographic
postcard, depicting
a street scene
in Staplehurst,
Kent, c1920.
£15–20 *JMC*

r. A photographic
postcard, depicting
Eastbourne Station,
Sussex, c1905.
£13–15 *JMC*

r. A photographic
postcard, depicting
Hastings Station,
Sussex, c1905.
£20–25 *JMC*

r. A photographic
postcard depicting
Robertsbridge Station,
Sussex, c1905.
£20–22 *JMC*

Two postcards, by A. R. Quinton, from
the Salmon Watercolour Series, c1915.
£1–6 each *JMC*

*No. 1551 of High Street Gate, Salisbury,
with original on left and the figure
removed version on right.*

Four postcards, by A. R. Quinton, from the
Salmon Watercolour Series, c1911.
£1–6 each *JMC*

Transport

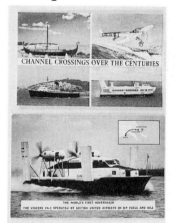

Two photographic postcards,
depicting Channel crossings
over the centuries, 1960s.
£1–7 each *JMC*

Four postcards, depicting Hovercrafts at various
ports, 1960s.
£1–2 each *JMC*

A sectional postcard, of *The Princess Anne*, Hoverspeed
SRN Super 4, 1960s.
£1–2 *JMC*
A photographic postcard, of Seaspeed Hovercraft *Princess
Anne*, card No. ET6173, 1960s.
50p–£1 *JMC*

Posters

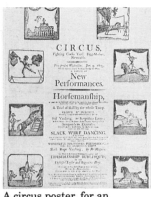

A circus poster, for an appearance in Newcastle, illustrated with 8 woodcuts, 1805, 19 by 15¼in (48.5 by 39cm).
£300–400 *S*

This poster features members of the Ducrow family and other performers.

A Ph. de Noran and Datura coloured lithographic advertising poster, published by Affiches Marci, Brussels, c1900, 39½ by 25½in (100 by 65cm).
£80–100 *DW*

A Cognac Quevedo coloured lithographic advertising poster, Paris, c1900, 30 by 23½in (76 by 60cm).
£110–130 *DW*

l. A Radiophone Viel coloured lithograph poster, printed by Agènce Havas, Rennes, backed on linen good condition, c1935, 46½ by 30in (118 by 76cm).
£125–150 *CSK*

A L'Engrais Vital coloured lithographic advertising poster, French, c1910, 26¼ by 19¾in (67 by 50cm).
£40–60 *DW*

l. Two Careless Talk series posters, by Fougasse, 1940, 40¼ by 25¼in (102 by 64cm).
£450–550 each *ONS*

Fougasse was the pseudonym of British cartoonist Cyril Kenneth Bird. As the artist explained, 'fougasse' was the name given by sappers to a landmine that was notably unpredictable. These particular posters were the first off the press and were issued by The Ministry of Information on 6th February 1940. They were received enthusiastically by the press and general public.

A coloured concert poster, for an appearance by Carmen Miranda at The London Palladium, 1950s, 29½ by 19½in (75 by 49.5cm) framed.
£325–375 *CNY*

A coloured concert poster, for an appearance by Lena Horne at The London Palladium, 1950s, 29½ by 19½in (75 by 49.5cm) framed.
£250–300 *CNY*

A coloured concert poster, for an appearance by Maurice Chevalier at the London Hippodrome, c1950, 29½ by 19½in (75 by 49.5cm) framed.
£180–200 *CNY*

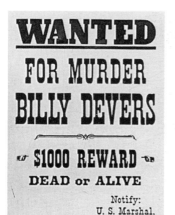

An original poster for *Gunsmoke*, used in the television western series, 1955–75, 12 by 9in (30.5 by 23cm).
£140–160 *CNY*

A film poster, *Forbidden Planet,* Loew's Inc, half sheet, style B, linen-backed, very good condition, 1956, 22 by 28in (56 by 71cm).
£1,200–1,400 *S(NY)*

Borrowing its original inspiration from Shakespeare's The Tempest, Forbidden Planet *went on to become one of the most popular successful science fiction films of the 1950s.*

A film poster, *The Day of the Triffids,* Security, British quad, linen-backed, in mint condition, 1963, 30 by 40in (76 by 101.5cm).
£325–375 *S(NY)*

r. A film poster, *Godzilla,* Jewell Enterprises, linen-backed, very good condition, Italian, 1956, 76 by 53in (193 by 134.5cm).
£800–900 *S(NY)*

l. A film poster, *The Mysterians,* RKO Teleradio Pictures, six sheet, linen-backed, very good condition, 1958, 81in (206cm) square.
£325–375 *S(NY)*

A film poster, *It Came From Outer Space*, Universal Pictures, one sheet linen-backed, very good condition, 1953, 41 by 27in (104 by 68.5cm).
£425–500 *S(NY)*

A film poster, *The Last Will of Dr. Mabuse*, Goodwill Pictures, one sheet, linen-backed, good condition, 1940s re-issue, 41 by 27in (104 by 68.5cm).
£175–225 *CNY*

A film poster, *Meet John Doe*, Warner Bros, one sheet, good condition, linen-backed, 1943, 42 by 27in (106.5 by 68.5cm).
£250–300 *CNY*

Travel

l. An American Line coloured lithographic poster, printed by The Liverpool Printing and Stationary Co Ltd, some damage, c1905, 39 by 25in (99 by 63.5cm).
£375–425 *CSK*

A Talyllyn Railway coloured lithographic poster, by Terence Cuneo, printed by Waterlow & Sons Ltd, London, creased, some damage, c1960, 41 by 25in (104 by 63.5cm).
£225–275 *CSK*

A British European Airways coloured lithographic poster, by John Bainbridge, linen-backed, excellent condition, 1949, 39 by 25in (99 by 63.5cm).
£300–350 *CSK*

l. A Pan American coloured lithographic poster, by Edward McKnight Kauffer, linen-backed, creased, some damage, c1950, 42 by 28in (106.5 by 71cm).
£100–150 *CSK*

r. A KLM Douglas DC-3 coloured lithographic poster, by Jean Walther, linen-backed, in excellent condition, c1950, 23½ by 30in (60 by 76cm).
£230–260 *CSK*

Valentines & Greetings Cards

A valentine card, watermarked 'J. Whatman', with cameo embossed and pierced paperlace cover, hand painted silk centre, mirror and message 'A Sweet Reflection', c1859, 10 by 8in (25 by 20cm), together with 2 other hand painted cards.
£120–150 *CSK*

An early Victorian paper lace Christmas card, together with box, 4½ by 6¼in (11.5 by 16cm).
£50–70 *MRW*

An early Victorian valentine card, 3½ by 2¾in (9 by 7cm).
£50–60 *MRW*

A paper lace valentine card, with matching envelope, inscribed 'Constant Love', 1855 postmark, 5¼ by 7¼in (13.5 by 18.5cm).
£40–60 *MRW*

A mid-Victorian padded greetings card, 4¼ by 2½in (11 by 6.5cm).
£30–40 *MRW*

An early Victorian paper lace greetings card, 5½ by 3½in (14 by 9cm).
£40–50 *MRW*

A late Victorian Christmas card, inscribed both sides, 2½ by 4in (6.5 by 10cm).
£8–10 *MRW*

An early Victorian paper cut-out greetings card, 5½ by 3½in (14 by 9cm).
£50–60 *MRW*

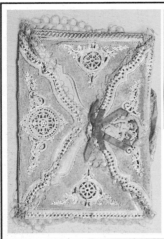

An early Victorian valentine card, with silk envelope, inscribed, slight damage, 3 by 4in (7.5 by 10cm).
£50–70 *MRW*

An early Victorian cut-out valentine card, bearing a poem entitled 'Love's Thoughts', 5½in (14cm) high.
£30–50 *MRW*

A valentine card, by J. King, with a scene of cupids rowing a gondola, embossed and outlined in blue, with inscribed message, registry mark, light green tissue backing, 5 by 7in (12.5 by 18cm), together with 2 other cards.
£80–100 *CSK*

Six hand coloured valentine lithographs, double sheets, all with elaborate gilt scroll design borders and decoration, medallion centres and verses, c1865, 10 by 8in (25 by 20cm), together with another embossed card.
£120–150 *CSK*

A set of 5 gold powder frame valentine lithographs, with hand coloured medallion centres and verses, c1840, 10 by 8in (25 by 20cm).
£220–300 *CSK*

An early Victorian Christmas cut-out card, 3 by 4in (7.5 by 10cm) wide.
£20–30 *MRW*

MAKE THE MOST OF MILLER'S

Condition is absolutely vital when assessing the value of any item. Damaged pieces appreciate much less than perfect examples. However, a rare, desirable piece may command a high price even when damaged.

A book of greetings cards samples, dated 1936, 13½ by 10½in (34.5 by 26.5cm).
£80–120 *MRW*

FAIRGROUND & AMUSEMENT ARCADE COLLECTABLES

r. A painted wood fairground fare sign, 1950s, 16 by 11½in (40.5 by 29cm).
£25–35 *JUN*

An Edwardian hand-turned carousel, with 12 carved horses, a boat and motor car.
£9,000–10,000 *JUN*

An American carved wooden carousel horse, c1920, 72in (183cm) long.
£1,800–2,000 *JUN*

A painted cased wall-mounted ball bearing amusement game, 'All Win Deluxe', c1910.
£250–350 *MAW*

An Aristocrat Arcadian Fiesta one-arm bandit, the chrome-plated front inset with pictorial Perspex panels, triple drums, electrical fittings to back, 1950s.
£140–220 *MAW*

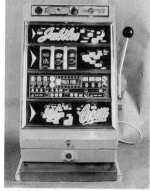

An Arcadian Aristocrat Hot Wheels one-arm bandit, the chrome-plated front panel inset with decorative Perspex panel, triple drums, and side pull handle, electrical fittings for backlight display, 1950s.
£110–160 *MAW*

An Aristocrat Sheerline one-arm bandit, by Ainsworth Consolidated Industries PTY Ltd, the cast-iron frame with chrome-plated front and single glass display window revealing 3 drums, 1950s.
£140–220 *MAW*

A Jubilee Crown one-arm bandit, the chrome-plated front frame inset with 4 pictorial Perspex panels, triple drum, electrical fittings for backlight display, 1950s.
£100–150 *MAW*

FANS

A printed leaf fan, with hand coloured etching, entitled 'The birth of Esau and Jacob, Gen. 25', inscribed No. '206', with ivory sticks pique in silver, the guardsticks cloute in tortoiseshell and mother-of-pearl, repaired, c1740, 10in (25cm) wide.
£340–380 *CSK*

A blue silk leaf parasol cockade fan, with turned ivory handle, repaired, c1859, 6in (15cm) diam.
£325–375 *CSK*

A French green feather fan, 1920s, 11in (28cm) wide.
£60–80 *Ech*

Miller's is a price GUIDE not a price LIST

r. A Dutch painted leaf fan, the scene entitled 'The Judgement of Paris', the reserve and verso painted with flowers, carved, pierced and gilt ivory sticks, c1775, 11in (28cm) wide.
£375–450 *CSK*

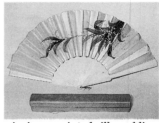

An Art Nouveau silk leaf fan, painted with a lady with white poppies against a starlit sky, horn sticks, the upper guardstick applied with a carved girl's head amongst stars of mother-of-pearl and bone, damaged, signed 'Duvelleroy' on verso, c1900, 11in (28cm) wide.
£400–500 *CSK*

Cross Reference:
Advertising & Packaging

A black painted silk fan, c1905, 14in (35.5cm) wide.
£30–50 *Ech*

A Brussels lace fan, c1900, 11in (28cm) wide.
£50–100 *Ech*

An ivory painted silk wedding fan, c1900, 13in (33cm) wide.
£75–100 *Ech*

A Mauchline ware fan, each section showing a different view, c1860, 12in (30.5cm) wide.
£180–200 *WAG*

A painted leaf fan, with wooden guard sticks, c1900, 11in (28cm) wide.
£50–100 *Ech*

A black ostrich feather fan, 1920s, 16in (40.5cm) wide.
£75–100 *Ech*

A SylvaC Scottie dog, No. 773504, c1930–40, 7½in (19cm) high.
£65–75 *HEM*

A Nelson Toby jug, decorated in underglaze and overglaze in the colours of a Naval uniform, c1900, 11in (28cm) high.
£100–150 *JBL*

A Toby jug, 'The Small American Sailor', possibly Walton, c1820, 10in (25cm) high.
£750–850 *JBL*

A SylvaC vase, with a swan, 1970s, 4½in (11.5cm) high.
£6–7 *HEM*

A Goebel Toby jug, 1960s, 5in (12.5cm) high.
£20–30 *YY*

A Continental Toby jug, c1910, 6¼in (16cm) high.
£15–20 *WN*

A Wilkinson Toby jug, modelled as Sir John French, c1915, 10in (25cm) high. **£300–400** *JBL*

A set of 4 Royal Doulton character jugs, depicting The Beatles, designed by S. J. Taylor, marked, 5¼in (13.5cm) high.
£200–250 *DN*

A Royal Doulton character jug, 'Ugly Duchess', by M. Henk, 7in (18cm) high.
£275–325 *DN*

A Wedgwood teapot, enamelled
with flowers, impressed mark,
1810, 6in (15cm) high.
£85–95 *GLN*

A Wedgwood plate, decorated
with Blue Bamboo pattern,
c1805, 18½in (47cm) wide.
£350–500 *GN*

A Wedgwood earthenware
figure of a kangaroo, after John
Skeaping, designed 1926, 8in
(20cm) high. **£500–600** *Bon*

A pair of Wedgwood vases,
impressed mark, c1890, 7½in
(19cm) high. **£300–350** *SIG*

A Wedgwood turquoise
majolica figure of a girl with a
basket, c1880, 7in (18cm) high.
£200–235 *GLN*

A Wedgwood rosso antico
style pastille burner, 19thC,
5in (12.5cm) high.
£80–100 *Bon*

A Wedgwood soup plate, designed
by Eric Ravilious, c1936, 10in
(25cm) diam. **£70–80** *YY*

A Wedgwood rabbit menu
holder, 1930s, 2¾in (7cm)
high. **£100–150** *Bon*

A Wedgwood lustre bowl, decorated
with a nightingale, 1920s, 5½in
(14cm) diam. **£150–200** *HEM*

A Wedgwood jasper biscuit barrel,
with silver plated cover, 19thC,
7in (18cm) high. **£125–140** *GLN*

A Worcester Marchioness of Huntley pattern plate, c1770, 6in (15cm) diam.
£450–500 *DN*

A Royal Worcester vase, hand painted by R. Austin, 1913, 9½in (24cm) high. **£250–285** *QSA*

A Royal Worcester ashtray, hand modelled by Doris Lindner, c1930, 4in (10cm) diam. **£100–125** *MLa*

A Royal Worcester hand painted vase, c1924, 5½in (14cm) high.
£150–200 *QSA*

A Royal Worcester vase and cover, decorated in Art Deco style, c1919, 8½in (21.5cm) high. **£200–250** *QSA*

A Royal Worcester figure, 'Friday's Child', c1970, 7in (18cm) high.
£150–175 *QSA*

A Hadley's Royal Worcester figure, marked, c1890, 10¾in (27.5cm) high. **£450–485** *QSA*

A Royal Worcester figure, 'Rose', by Anne Acheson, c1939, 3½in (9cm) high. **£200–265** *QSA*

A Royal Worcester figure, 'June', 1936, 6in (15cm) high.
£150–180 *QSA*

A Doulton Silicon ware jug, commemorating the death of Disraeli, 1881, 4in (10cm) high. **£120–160** *MGC*

A plate, inscribed 'The Allies, Honour, Defence, Peace', 1914, 9in (23cm) diam. **£75–125** *CRO*

A copper plaque, depicting Queen Victoria bestowing a knighthood on Lord Roberts, 1900, 17 by 12in (43 by 30.5cm). **£150–200** *OO*

A Paragon Edward VIII coronation mug, 1937, 3¾in (9.5cm) high.. **£45–50** *COL*

A Rington's Silver Jubilee teapot, 1935, 7½in (19cm) wide. **£50–70** *MGC*

A Spode chalice, commemorating York Minster, 1472–1972, 12½in (31.5cm) high. **£120–150** *Gam*

A King Edward VIII commemorative loving cup, unmarked, 1937, 6¼in (15.5cm) high. **£130–160** *MGC*

An Edward VIII coronation mug, 1937, 3½in (9cm) high. **£50–80** *CRO*

A set of 6 Wedgwood tri-colour jasper-mounted silver teaspoons, for the Silver Jubilee, 1977. **£400–475** *Bon*

A 'Battle of Britain' tankard, by Gordon Danes, c1990, 5in (12.5cm) high. **£25–35** *BCO*

An Arthur Wood Queen Elizabeth II coronation tankard, 1953, 4½in (11.5cm) high. **£40–60** *MGC*

A Victorian silk
and cut steel purse,
10in (25.5cm) long.
£50–80 *Ech*

A Victorian tapestry cushion,
17in (43cm) square.
£20–35 *Ech*

A silk needlework cushion, c1910,
30in (76cm) wide.
£75–85 *Ber*

A beaded handbag, 1920s,
8in (20cm) long.
£40–60 *Ech*

A reversible wool shawl, c1865,
60in (152.5cm) square.
£300–350 *Ech*

A French damask cushion cover,
late 19thC, 17in (43cm) wide.
£100–120 *JPr*

A selection of velvet fruit, made
from old fabric and stuffed with
sawdust, 20thC. **£22–28 each** *Ber*

An embroidered picture, signed
'E. Dixon Box', c1950,
10½in (26.5cm) high.
£15–25 *PC*

A sampler by Ann Chattaway,
1863, 19¼in (49cm) high.
£800–1,000 *MRW*

A Berlin woolwork sampler,
1853, 11 by 14in (28 by 35.5cm).
£90–110 *JPr*

A sampler, with the Lord's
Prayer, 1768, 13in (33cm) high.
£1,100–1,400 *S(S)*

A Gebrüder Heubach glass-eyed character doll, with extra clothing, c1910, box 11½in (29cm) long. **£400–500** *DOL*

A black papier mâché doll, with mechanical mouth and squeaker, c1890, 12in (30.5cm) high. **£150–175** *DOL*

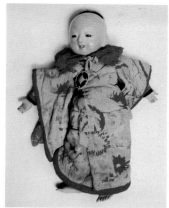

An Oriental boy doll, wearing original robes, c1910, 24in (61cm) high, with box and toys. **£700–800** *DOL*

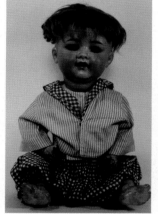

A Kämmer & Reinhardt/Simon & Halbig bisque character doll, No. 126, 1920s, 14in (35.5cm) high. **£350–450** *BaN*

A Heubach 'piano baby', c1903, 11in (28cm) long. **£350–400** *DOL*

An Armand Marseille bisque-headed doll, No. 390 2/0, 1925, 14¼in (36cm) high. **£50–60** *P(B)*

A wax-over-composition shoulder-headed doll, 1890s, 21¾in (55cm) high. **£20–25** *P(B)*

A Kestner bisque shoulder-headed doll, No. 148, kid body, 1890s, 18in (45.5cm) high. **£400–500** *BaN*

A German bisque-headed doll, No. 6, with jointed composition body, c1920, 17in (43cm) high. **£70–80** *P(B)*

An Armand Marseille bisque-headed doll, No. 390 2, on a stand, 1910, 19¾in (50cm) high. **£100–150** *P(B)*

A boxed set of dressed celluloid dolls, by Sydney Buckle, 1925.
£150–200 *DOL*

A Pedigree 'Flirty-Eye' walking doll, 1950s, 21in (53.5cm) high.
£75–85 *CMF*

A Rosebud black doll, 1950s, 14in (35.5cm) high.
£35–45 *CMF*

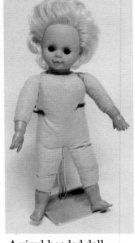

A vinyl-headed doll, with blonde synthetic hair, stuffed body and vinyl lower limbs, 1970s, 16½in (42cm) high.
£30–50 *P(B)*

An Austrian celluloid souvenir doll, 1940s, 5in (12.5cm) high.
£8–10 *CMF*

A Chad Valley felt and velvet doll, original button, 1930s, 15in (38cm) high.
£140–150 *CMF*

A Steiff felt character doll, with large wooden shoes, c1911, 12½in (32cm) high.
£60–80 *P(B)*

A black composition 'Topsy' doll, 1930s, 10in (25.5cm) high.
£120–130 *CMF*

A Simon & Halbig Santa doll, mould No. 1249, c1900, 24in (61cm) high.
£1,000–1,200 *DOL*

A doll's velvet winter outfit, with ermine handbag, 1990s, 17in (43cm) high.
£180–220 *JPr*

A Madame Alexander Cinderella doll, in mint condition, c1929, 15in (38cm) high, with box.
£150–200 *DOL*

A Disney dolls' house bedroom set, painted plywood with Mickey Mouse and Donald Duck transfers, 1930s. **£140–180** *P(B)*

An Action Man Russian soldier, 1960s, 11½in (29cm) high. **£65–85** *TOY*

A Sindy doll, c1968, by Pedigree, 11in (28cm) high. **£20–25** *CMF*

Barbie's dog, by Mattel, 1963, 5½in (14cm) long. **£15–20** *CMF*

A Sindy record player, by Pedigree, 1960s, 7½in (19cm) wide. **£14–16** *CMF*

An Action Man storm trooper, 1970s, 11½in (29cm) high. **£50–65** *TOY*

A Sindy doll, c1965, by Pedigree, 11in (28cm) high. **£25–30** *CMF*

A Barbie Hollywood Hair doll, by Mattel, 12in (30.5cm) high, 1990s. **£5–8** *PC*

A painted wooden dolls' house, c1920, 17½in (44.5cm) long. **£70–80** *Ber*

A dolls' house, with simulated brick and tile exterior, c1930s, 22in (56cm) high. **£150–165** *Ber*

The Bionic Woman doll, by Kenner, 1970s, boxed, 14 by 10in (35.5 by 25.5cm). **£35–45** *TOY*

John Player & Sons, Sea Fishes, set of 50 cigarette cards, 1935.
£12–24 *ACC*

P. Lorillard Co, Circus Scenes, set of 25 cigarette cards, c1886.
£55–110 each *ACC*

Godfrey Phillips Ltd, Characters Come to Life, set of 36 cigarette cards, 1938.
£18–36 *ACC*

John Player & Sons, Wild Birds, set of 50 cigarette cards, 1932.
£16–32 *ACC*

Wm Clarke & Son, Tobacco Leaf Girls, set of 20 cigarette cards, c1898.
£375–750 each *ACC*

W. D. & H. O. Wills Ltd, Dogs 1st Series, set of 25 cigarette cards, 1914.
£75–150 *ACC*

John Player & Sons, Flags of the League of Nations, set of 50 cigarette cards, 1928.
£14–28 *ACC*

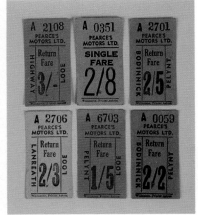

John Player & Sons, Gilbert & Sullivan 2nd Series, set of 50 cigarette cards, 1925.
£48–96 *ACC*

A selection of bus tickets, issued by Pearce's Motors Ltd, for various Cornish routes, 1940s.
25–50p each *JMC*

John Player & Sons, Poultry, set of 50 cigarette cards, 1931.
£58–116 *ACC*

J. Wix & Sons Ltd, 'Henry' cigarette cards, c1936, 4in (10cm) square.
50p–£1 each *JMC*

A selection of Whitbread Inn Signs trade cards, c1974, 3 by 2in (7.5 by 5cm). **£1–2 each** *JMC*

Adventure comic, No. 1156, 1946.
£2–8 *DPO*

A selection of South African confectionery trade cards, depicting1950s Film Stars.
£2–3 each *ACC*

Ten Brooke Bond 'Chimp Stickers', issued 1986.
25–50p each *JMC*

The Wizard comic, No. 1074, April 14th, 1945.
£4–5 *NOS*

A set of Bassetts Sweets trade cards, *Dandy* and *Beano* comic collection, c1990.
£5–6 *ACC*

Knockout comic, No. 885, February 11th, 1956.
£4–5 *NOS*

An album of Stollwerck's Chocolate trade cards, Animals of the World, 1902.
£130–160 *MRW*

Mickey Mouse Magazine, Vol. 3, issues 5–10, March 1938.
£850–950 *S(NY)*

Sunbeam comic, No. 280, New Series, June 13th, 1931.
£2–5 *DPO*

An early Victorian cut-out Christmas card, 3¼ by 4¼in (8.5 by 11cm).
£20–30 *MRW*

An advertising postcard for Cherry Smash soda, c1910.
£350–400 *PIn*

An early Victorian embossed greetings card, 5¾ by 4in (14.5 by 10cm).
£40–50 *MRW*

Two A. R. Quinton postcards depicting Cranbrook, Kent, 1930s. **£5–6 each** *JMC*

Two alcohol related postcards, by Tuck, and Hutson Bros, c1920. **£1–3 each** *JMC*

The Majestic private greetings cards sample book, 1912, 10 by 12in (25.5 by 30.5cm).
£120–150 *MRW*

A Santa 'hold-to-light' die-cut Christmas card, printed in Germany, c1908.
£150–200 *PIn*

Four postcards by Tom Browne, published by Davidson Brothers, 1905–10.
£3–4 each *JMC*

Four 'Bonzo' postcards, published by Valentine, 1930s.
£4–5 each *JMC*

Three comic postcards, by Tuck, and Brown & Rawcliffe, 1904–10.
£2–4 each *JMC*

A Festival of Britain South Bank Exhibition Guide, 96 pages, 1951.
£8–10 *PC*

A Festival of Britain Pleasure Gardens Guide, 52 pages, 1951.
£8–10 *PC*

Two Festival of Britain five shillings crowns, in original lid-type boxes, 1951.
£7–8 each *PC*

A Denby Cheviot dish, c1955, 8¼in (21cm) long.
£20–25 *PC*

A set of 34 Festival of Britain souvenir postcards, showing sights of London, 1951.
£5–6 *PC*

l. A Worcester ware tin cocktail tray, 1950s, 7½in (19cm) wide.
£4–6 *PC*

A plastic fox, c1950, 8in (20cm) long.
£8–10 *BEV*

A transistor radio, 1950s, 10in (25.5cm) wide.
£18–20 *PC*

A Poole Pottery vase, c1950, 10in (25.5cm) high.
£85–95 *HEM*

A Broadhurst hand painted plate, designed by Kathie Winkle, 1950s, 6½in (16.5cm) diam.
£1–2 *PC*

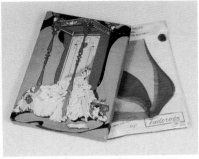

A pair of Tudorose stockings, c1950, in original box, 9¼ by 7in (23.5 by 18cm).
£8–10 *LBe*

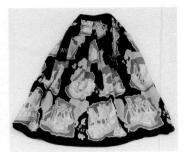

A cotton skirt, with pattern of continents and galleons, 1950s.
£20–30 *PC*

A pair of curtains, 1950s, each 60in (152.5cm) wide.
£14–18 *PC*

A length of cotton fabric, Sunlover design, c1950, 120 by 50in (305 by 127cm).
£65–75 *NCA*

A home-made cotton dress, with floral pattern, 1950s.
£10–15 *PC*

A length of Moygashel fabric, by Peter Perritt, 1960s, 120 by 50in (305 by 127cm).
£85–100 *NCA*

Four PVC cushions and a handbag, by Peter Max, c1967.
Cushions £275–300
Handbag £35–50 *Bon*

A length of satinised cotton, Galleria design by Barbara Brown, for Heal's, c1960, 120 by 50in (305 by 127cm). **£100–130** *NCA*

A length of cotton fabric, design attributed to Marion Mahler, early 1950s, 120 by 50in (305 by 127cm). **£180–200** *NCA*

Two plastic egg cruets, 1960s, 2⅝in (6.5cm) high.
£5–6 *HEM*

FIFTIES & SIXTIES

In Spring 1947, Parisien designer Christian Dior launched his New Look collection. In startling contrast to utilitarian wartime fashions, Dior's clothes were feminine and extravagant: jackets padded over the hips, tiny waists and most shocking of all, swirling skirts using yards of precious and, as far as the general public was concerned, rationed material. The 'New Look' not only provided a pattern for fifties fashion but became a symbol of the new spirit in design that distinguished the following decade.

Characteristic features of fifties style include organic and asymmetric shapes, the use of new, often synthetic materials and bold patterning inspired by abstract art, scientific symbols and everyday life. A lightness of touch runs throughout many creations of this period, a sense of optimism epitomised in the UK by the Festival of Britain in 1951. With its central exhibition on London's South Bank and related events around the country, the Festival was designed as a massive showcase for British arts, crafts and industry. As the catalogue explained, it celebrated 'the arts of peace' offering what Festival Director, Gerald Barry, described as 'a tonic to the nation'.

The following section opens with a collection of Festival of Britain memorabilia, followed by a range of fifties and sixties collectables. Many objects remain comparatively low in price and are readily available from car-boot sales and flea markets. Dealers and auction houses, however, are paying increasing attention to the decorative arts of the period and as the 50th anniversary of the Festival of Britain approaches, interest in fifties material will increase and values are set to rise.

Festival of Britain

The *News Chronicle – Festival of Britain Souvenir in Pictures,* 34 pages, 1951.
£8–10 *PC*

The Illustrated London News No. 5849, 'Exhibition Number', 95 pages, 25th May, 1951.
£10–12 *PC*

The Illustrated London News No. 5847, 'The Exhibition's Opening-Special Number', includes a double-page aerial view of the South Bank by G. H. Davis, 70 pages, 12th May, 1951.
£10–12 *PC*

> **Cross Reference:**
> Collectables under £5

r. A silver book match cover, with enamelled Festival of Britain logo, 1951, 2¼ by 1½in (5.5 by 4cm).
£7–8 *PC*

A postcard of the Royal Festival Hall, by Jarrold & Sons, Norwich, 1951, 3½ by 5½in (9 by 14cm).
£4–5 *PC*

A pair of commemorative tea caddy spoons: Plain bowl with enamelled colour logo, 1951, 3in (7.5cm) high. Ribbed bowl with enamelled colour logo, 1951, 3in (7.5cm) high.
£5–10 each *PC*

A postcard of 'The Islanders, South Bank Exhibition, Festival of Britain, 1951', by Raphael Tuck & Sons Ltd, 5½ by 3½in (14 by 9cm).
£2–3 *PC*

A set of 13 Collins *About Britain* guide books, sponsored by the Brewers' Society, with Festival of Britain logo, 92 pages, 1951.
£3–5 each *PC*

It is important that guides should be in good condition and in their original map covers.

A Festival of Britain proof set of coins, containing 10 coins from farthings to crowns, original price £1, maroon box, 1951.
£45–50 *PC*

These sets were sold in maroon, dark blue and turquoise cardboard boxes. Maroon examples are the most common, dark blue are comparatively rare and the turquoise box is very rare indeed.

A Poole Pottery Festival of Britain hors d'oeuvres dish, designed by Claude Smale, decorated by Gwen Haskins, in black and puce with central monogram 'FOB', a fish, an umbrella, bottles and a top hat, impressed and painted marks, 1951, 8½in (21.5cm) diam.
£150–200 *DN*

A Festival of Britain Yachting Regatta bronze medal, by Pinches, 1951, 1¾in (4.5cm) diam.
£10–12 *PC*

A pressed glass sweet dish/ashtray, with Festival logo in the centre, 1951, 5in (12.5cm) diam.
£4–5 *PC*

Fifties

A set of 3 LCM chairs, designed by Charles Eames, USA, by Evans Products Company, with birch veneer plywood seats and backs on steel rod frame, Herman Miller labels to frames, 1950s.
£650–700 *Bon*

A set of 4 kitchen chairs, covered with Sanderson's fabric, 1950s.
£5–10 *PC*

As the surrounding examples show, designer fifties furniture is already expensive. This set of chairs, purchased from a school fête for only £5, demonstrates how reasonably priced fifties collectables can be.

A black and white BBC promotional card of Buddy Holly and The Crickets, signed, mounted, framed and glazed, 1958, 8 by 10in (20 by 25cm).
£550–600 *Bon*

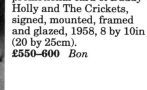

l. A rocking chair, with green upholstered seat on 2 U-shaped legs, very worn cover, c1958.
£225–300
r. A serving trolley, with two-tiers and V-shaped support, on clear Perspex front wheels and smaller back wheel on metal support, c1958.
£140–160 *Bon*

Miller's is a price GUIDE not a price LIST

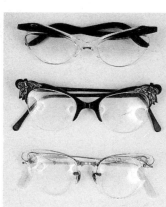

Three pairs of lady's fashion spectacles, 1950s.
£10–15 each *PC*

A pair of armchairs, by Yngve Ekstrøm, Sweden, for Swedese, each with bent laminated frame and upholstered sheepskin seat, 1950s.
£600–650
A 'Fibonacci Lamp', by Sophus Frandsen, Denmark, with white painted concentric rings, 1950s, 19in (48cm) diam.
£100–120
A circular teak coffee table, by Yngve Ekstrøm, Sweden, 1950s.
£130–160 *Bon*

A Zeiss Movikon 8, 8mm movie camera, 1952, 6in (15cm) wide.
£25–35 *HEG*

A white enamelled table lamp, by Gino Sarfatti, Italy, with brass stem and marble base, Arteluce Milano label under shade, slight damage, 1950s, 14in (35.5cm) high.
£150–180 *Bon*

A two-seater sofa, designed by Finn Juhl, Denmark, made by Niels Vodder, original navy blue upholstery with teak frame, 1950s.
£800–850 *Bon*

A pair of 'Sunrex' sunglasses, with original box, 1950s.
£3–5 *JR*

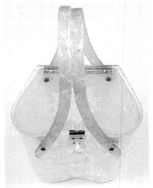

A Perspex handbag, from Miami, USA, 1950s, 6in (15cm) high excluding handles.
£85–95 *LBe*

Ceramics

An Eric Leaper studio ceramic 'Bull' charger 1950s, 7in (18cm) diam.
£14–16 *JR*

A Midwinter Stylecraft plate, Flower Mist design by Jessie Tait, c1956, 6in (15cm) diam.
£5–6 *AND*

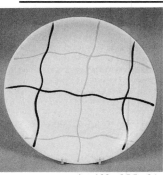

An Alfred Meakin dinner plate, 1950s, 9½in (24cm) diam.
£4–5 *GFR*

Cross Reference:
Ceramics:
Midwinter
Rye

l. A Poole Pottery free form vase, 1950s, 6½in (16.5cm) high.
£65–75 *GFR*

A Ridgeway's Homemaker pattern bowl, 1950s, 7in (18cm) diam.
£3–5 *PC*

The Homemaker pattern was designed by Enid Seeney for Ridgway Potteries in 1955 and retailed through Woolworths until the 1960s. An archetypal image of 1950s style, Homemaker tableware was decorated with emblems of contemporary taste, such as the boomerang-shaped table and two-seater sofa.

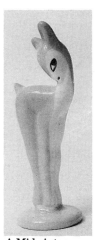

A Midwinter stylised fawn, c1950, 5in (12.5cm) high.
£30–35 *AND*

A Rosenthal porcelain coffee service, designed by Roland Peynet, 1950s, coffee pot 8in (20cm) high.
£200–250 *JES*

A Czechoslovakian china dog,
1950s, 4in (10cm) long.
£15–18 *BEV*

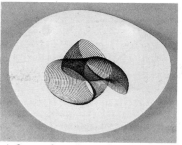

A Queensbury bone china ovoid
dish, mid-1950s, 7in (18cm) wide.
£10–14 *JR*

A ceramic sugar sifter,
unmarked, 1950s, 5in
(12.5cm) high.
£10–12 *GFR*

A Grimwades Royal Winton dish,
1950s, 10in (25cm) long.
£8–12 *PC*

l. A Royal Copenhagen vase,
with abstract design,
1950s–60s, 4½in (11cm) high.
£20–25 *YY*

Costume & Textiles

A cotton skirt, decorated with royal
blue and turquoise flowers, 1950s.
£10–15 *PC*

A Lo Roco cotton
dress and matching
jacket, printed with
red, yellow and
green abstract
design, 1950s.
£10–18 *PC*

r. A blue wool Teddy Boy suit,
with black velvet lapels, cuffs
and pockets, labelled in nape
'Rose Tailors, 19 Savile Row,
London', 1950s, and a
collection of costume.
£250–300 *CSK*

l. A cotton skirt, decorated
with red flowers, 1950s.
£20–30 *PC*

A length of Boris Wafveri fabric, Burma design by Sven Fristedt, 1950s, 120 by 50in (305 by 127cm).
£90–100 *NCA*

A length of Whitehead linen, designed by John Piper, c1950, 72 by 50in (183 by 127cm).
£175–200 *NCA*

A length of Turnbull & Stockdale cotton fabric, designed by Mary White, 1950s, 120 by 50in (305 by 127cm).
£100–130 *NCA*

Sixties

A pair of Op Art drinking glasses, one decorated in green, one black, 1960s, 5½in (14cm) high.
£1–2 each *PC*

A Troika Wheel vase, by Honor Curtis, moulded in relief with abstract geometric motifs, painted in brown and cream on a buff ground, painted marks, artist's monogram, 1960s, 6¼in (16cm) high, together with a square section and a coffin vase.
£150–180 *CSK*

A '560' green upholstered chair, designed by Pierre Paulin, France, for Artifort, with loose cushion and green stretchy jersey fabric, 1961.
£180–220
A '577' brown easy chair, designed by Pierre Paulin, France, for Artifort, 1967.
£400–450
A '437' easy chair, designed by Pierre Paulin, France, for Artifort, with a double shell of moulded wood, upholstered in polyfoam, covered in dark yellow patterned fabric, raised on a chrome-plated steel tube frame, 1959.
£350–400 *Bon*

A Portmeirion Pottery Totem coffee service, by Susan Williams-Ellis, 1960s, coffee pot 12in (30.5cm) high.
£40–55 *GFR*

A Melmac pink trio, by The Branchell Co, St Louis, USA, designed by K. La Moyne, c1960, plate 10in (25cm) diam.
£4–6 *PC*

l. A set of 5 pop star flower power Pop Art coat hangers, 1960s.
£80–100 *Bon*

Costume & Textiles

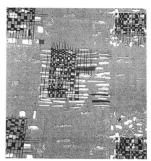

A length of Heal's textured cotton fabric, Quatro design, by Lucienne Day, 1960s, 120 by 50in (305 by 127cm).
£125–150 NCA

A length of Bevis satinized cotton fabric, Wimbold design, 1960s, 120 by 50in (305 by 127cm).
£65–75 NCA

A bolero waistcoat and matching chain mail skirt, composed of silver and gilt links, with gilt shoulder bag, late 1960s.
£160–200 CSK

A chocolate and cream checked wool suit, the short bell-shaped jacket trimmed with leather buttons, with Givenchy label, tagged '48810', 1960s.
£220–260 CSK

r. A length of Bernard Wardle cotton fabric, Naxos, Op Art design by Edward Pond, 1960s, 120 by 50in (305 by 127cm).
£85–100 NCA

A pink nylon scarf showing scenes of London, with Cirro label, 1960s, 28in (71cm) square.
£1–5 PC

l. A matching coat and dress of white gaberdine, trimmed with black leatherette squares on pockets of dress and coat, the collars and waist similarly trimmed, labelled 'FM' (Fortnum & Mason), made in France, 1960s.
£120–150 CSK

GARDEN COLLECTABLES

As gardening grows ever more popular, so demand has increased for horticultural collectables. Popular items include antique metal watering cans with brass roses, traditional tools such as trowels, forks, and the more unusual daisy grubbers and dock lifters, old garden sprinklers which were attractively shaped, and wooden wheelbarrows which are often used as planters. Once relegated to the garden shed, today these humble objects appear at the smartest metropolitan antique fairs – spotted amongst the splendid and costly treasures at the recent Fine Art Fair at Olympia was a selection of old terracotta flowerpots, with prices beginning at one pound.

One of the joys of collecting gardening items is that many of the objects are serviceable – for example, a number of the early lawnmowers illustrated in the following section are still regularly used by their enthusiastic owner. Another traditional garden object to which we devote a special feature this year is the much-loved garden gnome.

A ceramic sundial, c1900, 8½in (21.5cm) diam.
£100–120 *Ber*

An Irish peat barrow, c1860, 63in (160cm) long overall.
£150–200 *HON*

A diploma, awarded by Toogood & Sons for Excellence in Horticulture, 1912, 15 by 18in (38 by 45.5cm).
£20–30 *PC*

A Robinson's seed sower, 1920s, 4in (10cm) high.
£20–30 *PC*

A Victorian garden line and stake.
£25–30 *TaB*

r. A digging fork, with wooden T-shaped handle, early 20thC, 42in (106.5cm) long.
£12–16 *TaB*

A Haw's watering can, c1920, 29in (73.5cm) long.
£20–30 *AL*

A wooden crow scarer, late 19thC, 7in (18cm) wide.
£25–35 *TaB*

l. A cast iron pitchfork, early 20thC, 66in (167.5cm) long.
£14–16 *TaB*

A brass spray gun, early
20thC, 13in (33cm) long.
£12–15 *TaB*

A trowel, 1930s, 6½in (16.5cm) long.
£3–5 *TaB*

Two terracotta flowerpots, c1900,
smallest 1½in (4cm) diam.
£1–2 each *TaB*

A trowel and fork, 1950s,
trowel 13in (33cm) long.
£4–5 each *TaB*

r. A garden spade,
with wooden
handle, 1930s,
34in (86.5cm) long.
£12–15 *TaB*

A thistle or dock
lifter, early
20thC, 38in
(96.5cm) long.
£30–35 *TaB*

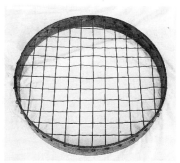

A wooden potato riddler, with
wire mesh, 1920s, 23in
(58.5cm) diam.
£12–15 *TaB*

A pair of garden bellows,
c1880, 28in (71cm) long.
£50–60 *PC*

A swan-necked
hoe, early
20thC, 60in
(152.5cm) long.
£8–10 *TaB*

Gardening

- **Cutting tools**: pruners and shears came
  in a wide range of sizes and were devised
  for different jobs. Gardening encyclopedias
  of the 19th century show shears designed
  to cut turf, verges, flowers and grapes,
  whilst an 18th century publication
  recommended the purchase of a pair of
  caterpillar shears 'for removing caterpillars
  which would otherwise destroy all'.
- **Garden lines and stakes**: used to mark
  out straight lines for creating paths and
  flower beds.
- **Rollers**: these were used to flatten lawns
  and paths. Victorian gardeners were
  advised to wear light shoes when rolling a
  path so that the smooth effect would not
  be marred by footmarks.
- **Riddler**: a coarse meshed sieve used for
  sifting, or riddling, dirt from vegetables,
  chaff from corn, sand from gravel, etc.
- **Rose**: the sprinkler attached to a
  watering can.
- **Spray guns**: designed to hold insecticides,
  these syringes or spray guns came in
  several designs, varying in size and
  fineness of spray.

Cutting & Trimming Tools

A pair of garden shears, with pruning notch, 1930s, 21in (53.5cm) long.
£8–10 *TaB*

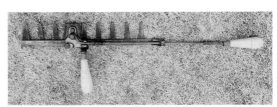

A Code Half Time hedge trimmer, c1950, 29in (73.5cm) long.
£10–15 *PC*

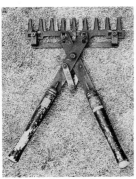

A Remex hedge trimmer, c1950, 11in (28cm) wide.
£10–15 *PC*

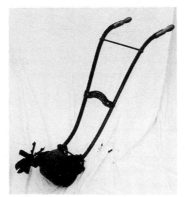

A Ransome's edge trimmer, c1930, 28in (71cm) high.
£30–50 *PC*

An Astor hedge trimmer, c1950, 9in (23cm) wide.
£10–15 *PC*

This hedge trimmer was made to a pre-war design by Flexa, and sold in the 1950s.

A pair of garden shears, with original clip, 1930s, 12in (30.5cm) long.
£8–10 *TaB*

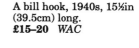

A bill hook, 1940s, 15½in (39.5cm) long.
£15–20 *WAC*

A Ridgeway's patent hedge trimmer, c1900, 18in (45.5cm) wide.
£20–40 *PC*

A Spong hedge trimmer, c1930, 15in (38cm) long.
£15–25 *PC*

Two pairs of children's garden shears, *top* 1930s, *bottom* 1950s, 10in (25cm) long.
£8–10 each *TaB*

Furniture

A folding garden table, with iron frame and pine top, 29in (74cm) high.
£40–60 *NWE*

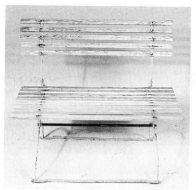

A German bench, with folding iron frame, c1900, 35½in (90cm) wide.
£80–100 *NWE*

A German bandstand chair, with folding iron frame, pine seat and back, c1900.
£15–20 *NWE*

A French wrought iron folding coaching or picnic chair, with old painted surface, c1840, 15in (38cm) wide.
£150–200 *RYA*

l. A folding park chair, c1890.
£30–35 *AL*

Miller's is a price GUIDE not a price LIST

A pair of bamboo chairs and matching table, c1920, table 20in (51cm) diam.
£325–350 *MofC*

Gnomes

The *Oxford English Dictionary* (OED) describes a gnome as 'one of a race of diminutive spirits fabled to inhabit the interior of the earth and to be the guardian of its treasures; a goblin or dwarf'. The word is first recorded in the English language in 1658, but as Ann Atkins, owner of the Gnome Reserve in Devon, points out, gnomes, goblins and 'the little people' have appeared in the mythology of cultures across the world since the dawn of time.

References to garden gnomes did not appear in the *OED* until the 1930s, when the miniature sculptures were reaching the peak of their colourful popularity. Nevertheless, according to Atkins, the German writer, Geothe, refers to gnome statues in his poem *Hermann und Dorothea* (1797), and the earliest examples discovered by Miller's in compiling this edition are believed to date from the 18th century. It was in the Victorian age, however, that the garden gnome truly planted his boots on British soil, and the man responsible for this was Sir Charles Isham.

In 1847, Sir Charles began to create his celebrated rockery at Lamport Hall, Northamptonshire. 'We have seen nothing more strange and, in a way, fascinating,' enthused *Country Life* magazine, who visited in 1898. The rock garden was designed in miniature, with tiny mountains, crystal caves and dwarf trees, and was peopled with terracotta gnomes, probably imported from Germany, fairy miners working the shining quartz, and even a group of striking miners, who had downed tools. Sir Charles was known for his whimsical sense of humour, but also, like many gnome fanciers, genuinely believed in the existence of sprites and spirits. Initially gnomes seem to have been a fairly upper class passion. Friar Park had a celebrated gnome grotto built by Sir Frank Crisp (1843–1919), and advertisements for model gnomes appeared in the *Connoisseur* magazine in 1908. As the 20th century progressed, however, the gnome became the standard ornament of the suburban garden, loved and despised equally.

l. A Victorian terracotta gnome, original colour, small repairs, fishing rod replaced, 27in (68.5cm) high.
£400–700 *GNR*

This gnome was originally in the gardens of Erdigg Hall, near Wrexham, North Wales.

r. A Victorian painted brass and bronze gnome, with umbrella, 3½in (9cm) high.
£500–600 *GNR*

An Austrian white earthenware gnome, holding a hare, 35in (90cm) high.
£750–1,500 *GNR*

This gnome was made from one of the original moulds of the now defunct Imperial State Pottery of Vienna (1718–1861).

r. A German gnome, 19thC, 14in (35.5cm) high.
£15–20 *LIB*

A set of 10 sandstone garden gnomes, 18thC, 25in (63.5cm) high.
£5,000–6,500 *HUN*

A gnome doctor, giving
medicine to a frog, by
Heissner, Germany,
late 19thC, 14in
(35.5cm) high.
£100–200 *GNR*

A Czechoslovakian
gnome, painted
white, foot
damaged, c1900,
18in (45.5cm) high.
£100–120 *GNR*

A terracotta gnome,
taking snuff, by
Heissner, Germany,
c1900, 26½in
(67.5cm) high.
£200–500 *GNR*

A gnome fishing, by
Heissner, Germany,
original paint, rod
missing, c1900,
24in (61cm) high.
£300–600 *GNR*

A terracotta sitting
gnome, hands
missing, c1900,
11in (28cm) high.
£80–100 *GNR*

A white earthenware
gnome, holding two pots,
by Heissner, Germany,
original paint, c1900,
27½in (70cm) high.
£300–600 *GNR*

A lead gnome, 28½in
(72.5cm) high.
£150–250 *GNR*

A white earthenware
gnome, smoking a
pipe, by Heissner,
Germany, c1900,
25in (63.5cm) high.
£300–600 *GNR*

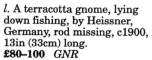

r. A terracotta group of a
sleeping gnome and a small
gnome watching, by
Heissner, Germany, late
19thC, 11in (28cm) high.
£100–200 *GNR*

l. A terracotta gnome, lying
down fishing, by Heissner,
Germany, rod missing, c1900,
13in (33cm) long.
£80–100 *GNR*

Three terracotta gnomes, 1930s, standing gnome 2¾in (7cm) high.
£10–25 each *GNR*

A pixie cake decoration with a penguin, early 1930s, 2¼in (5.5cm) high.
£10–25 *GNR*

A gnome, with no arms, c1880, 9½in (24cm) high.
£20–60 *GNR*

This gnome is believed to have been fired in a corner of a kiln when bricks were being fired, by a kiln worker and made to take home.

A terracotta gnome, with an axe, 1930s, 12in (30.5cm) high.
£30–50 *GNR*

A pair of solid lead gnomes, c1920, 5in (12.5cm) high.
£30–40 each *GNR*

l. A terracotta gnome, with a metal wheelbarrow, c1940, 10¾in (27.5cm) high.
£30–50 *GNR*

A pair of solid lead gnomes, 1930s, reclining gnome 2½in (6.5cm) long.
£30–40 each *GNR*

A terracotta gnome, sitting clutching his knees, 1940s, 15½in (39.5cm) high.
£25–35 *GNR*

Four standing gnomes, repainted, 1940s, tallest 13in (33cm) high.
£25–35 each *GNR*

r. Three terracotta gnomes, 1940s, tallest 8in (20cm) high.
£25–35 each *GNR*

A pottery gnome, listening, c1940, 6½in (16.5cm) high.
£20–30 *GNR*

A white earthenware and terracotta gnome lamp, c1940, 16½in (42cm) high.
£30–40 *GNR*

A white earthenware gnome, smoking a pipe, 1940, 8in (20cm) high.
£10–15 *GNR*

A pottery gnome, with a green pouch, c1940, 7in (18cm) high.
£15–20 *GNR*

A pair of white earthenware gnome musicians, one playing a double bass, the other a drum, 1940s, 13½in (34.5cm) high.
£20–40 each *GNR*

Miller's is a price GUIDE not a price LIST

A pixie, Puck, c1958, 14in (35.5cm) high.
£40–50 *GWo*

A gnome inkwell, 1940s, 5in (12.5cm) high.
£15–20 *GNR*

A gnome fishing, very weathered, c1968, 27in (68.5cm) high.
£20–40 *GWo*

A terracotta gnome, playing a concertina, 1950s, 8in (20cm) high.
£20–30 *GNR*

A terracotta gnome, leaning against a tree stump, 1940s, 3½in (9cm) high.
£10–20 *GNR*

A terracotta frog, c1940, 6in (15cm) long.
£10–15 *GNR*

Lawnmowers

The first lawnmower was invented by Edwin Budding in 1830. Up until this date, lawns were cut with a scythe, and generally only the wealthy had large areas of grass. Budding assured potential purchasers that his cylindrical cutter would out-perform the best human mowers, adding that 'country gentlemen may find using the machine themselves an amusing, useful and healthy exercise.'

Very early machines, before 1860, were a luxury product aimed at the gentry and are rarely found today outside museums. Far more common are machines from the 1920s onwards. Lawnmower production boomed after WWI and again after WWII, thanks to a dearth of gardeners and the rise of detached and semi-detached houses, each with its own small garden.

Today, demand for old lawnmowers is obviously select, although according to collector Christopher Proudfoot, the Lawnmower Collecting Society boasts some 150 members. Most collectors are interested in mechanics as much as gardening since many old lawnmowers need restoration. Nevertheless, once restored, according to Proudfoot, they can be perfectly operational and functional.

A Green's 8in Silens Messor lawnmower, with curved handles, c1880.
£100–150 *PC*

Early mowers were extremely noisy, and gardeners were often forbidden to use them before the family had risen in the morning. In 1859, Thomas Green patented his Silens Messor (Silent Mower), the first chain-driven lawnmower, which considerably reduced the noise and was produced virtually unchanged from the 1860s to the 1930s.

A New Excelsior 6in lawnmower, with original paint and transfer, c1890.
£350–500 *PC*

A Ransomes 11in Lion lawnmower, c1905.
£5–15 *PC*

l. An Atco 22in oval framed lawnmower, 1921.
£100–150 *PC*

Only models made in 1921, the first year of production, had this frame of oval section cast iron. Later models were O1 section malleable iron, which was less brittle.

A Ransomes 12in Patent Chain Automoton lawnmower, c1920.
£20–30 *PC*

r. A Pennsylvania 12in side-wheel lawnmower, with optional grass box and delivery plate, c1900.
£40–60 *PC*

A Ransomes 6in Anglo Paris lawnmower, with delivery plate, grass box and handle badge missing, 1902.
£80–120 *PC*

Small-bladed machines were used for mowing the borders and narrow paths which were popular in gardens at the turn of the century.

A Shanks 10in Caledonia lawnmower, with grass box, original paintwork, c1925.
£80–120 *PC*

The design for this mower dated from the 1890s. A chain-driven version was also made.

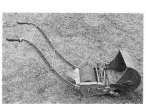

A Drummond Brothers 12in Willing Worker lawnmower, c1925.
£30–50 *PC*

Miller's is a price GUIDE not a price LIST

l. An Atco 16in Standard motor mower, carburettor replaced, c1926.
£40–60 *PC*

A Ransomes 16in Mark 5A motor mower, 1934.
£70–100 *PC*

A Flexa 18in lawnmower, with wooden-sided grass box, c1955.
£10–20 *PC*

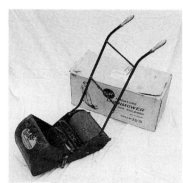

A Webb's 8in miniature lawnmower for children, with original box, c1950.
£50–80 *PC*

A Ransomes 14in Conquest lawnmower, with pressed steel body and wheels driving the cylinder via a chain, c1960.
£5–15 *PC*

A Ransomes 12in Atlas Mark I lawnmower, c1935.
£5–15 *PC*

Line Markers

A Green's line marker, c1920, 29in (73.5cm) high.
£30–50 *PC*

A Caxton line marker, with chain drive and locking control rod, c1890, 33in (84cm) high.
£40–60 *PC*

Rollers

A Victorian garden roller, adapted for towing, c1870, 19in (48.5cm) wide.
£20–40 *PC*

A Crown garden roller, by Smith & Paget, cast iron with divided rollers and solid ends for ease of turning, late 19thC, 18in (45.5cm) wide.
£20–40 *PC*

A lawn roller, 19thC, 16in (40.5cm) wide.
£65–75 *WEL*

l. A stone roller, 18thC, 23½in (59.5cm) wide.
£150–200
r. A cast iron open-ended single cylinder roller, 19thC, 18in (45.5cm) wide.
£20–40 *PC*

A garden roller, early 20thC, 20in (51cm) wide.
£100–125 *WRe*

A Lions cast iron roller, by Turtle of Croydon, c1925, 18in (45.5cm) wide.
£5–15 *PC*

A large garden roller, early 20thC, 25in (63.5cm) wide.
£200–250 *WRe*

Watering Cans

A watering can, with unusual spout and traces of old paint, c1900, 16in (40.5cm) high.
£60–70 *RYA*

A watering can, c1880, 16in (40.5cm) high.
£15–20 *MIL*

A watering can, with unusual rose, used for weed killer, c1920.
£100–120 *RYA*

A galvanised watering can, with brass rose, c1920.
£10–20 *NWE*

A polished galvanised one gallon watering can, with copper rose, 1920s, 13in (33cm) high.
£25–30 *WAC*

A French galvanised watering can, with copper rose, mid-20thC, 18in (45.5cm) high.
£30–40 *TaB*

A galvanised ¾ gallon watering can, 1920s.
£30–35 *TaB*

A galvanised watering can, with original brass rose, c1940.
£45–55 *RYA*

Two galvanised watering cans, c1920.
£10–20 each *NWE*

GLASS

A pair of glass tea caddies, engraved with the owner's initials 'M.R.', 'Bohea' and 'Green', and an exotic bird amid foliage, very good condition, with their original stoppers, 1750, 5½in (14cm) high.
£500–550 *QSA*

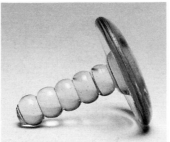

A heavy glass mushroom-top slicker stone, with five-knop handle, early 19thC, 3½in (8.5cm) high.
£100–200 *CB*

A slicker stone, or linen smoother, was used to iron and glaze the linen with a circular sweeping movement, and was made of glass, marble or lignum.

A glass hat, early 19thC, 2½in (6.5cm) high.
£50–70 *JHa*

A Stourbridge blue glass salt, c1890, 2in (5cm) wide.
£40–50 *CB*

A set of 3 Sowerby flint glass bowls, c1870, largest 8in (20cm) diam.
£60–65 *GLN*

A pair of cut glass table lustres, c1880, 10in (25cm) high.
£350–450 *CB*

A piece of Sam Herman Studio glass, 1980s, 7½in (19cm) high.
£400–600 *JHa*

Sam Herman was given permission to set up a glass studio in the Royal College of Art in 1968.

Glass – Glossary of Terms

- **Baluster glass**: drinking glass with a swelling at the base of the stem, rising in a concave curve to a narrow stem or neck.
- **Cranberry glass**: transparent, reddish-pink glass.
- **Flint glass**: alternative name for lead glass.
- **Knop**: a swelling, which can be solid or hollow, on glass stems.
- **Lead glass**: glass with a high lead content, suitable for cutting and faceting.
- **Pressed glass**: glass made by the technique of pouring molten glass into a metal mould and pressing it to the sides using a metal plunger.
- **Printies**: impressions in the glass, similar to thumbprints.
- **Rummer**: A 19thC English low drinking goblet, traditionally used for drinking rum and water (German *roemer*).
- **Satin glass**: glass with a satin finish.
- **Slag glass**: glass with a marbled or malachite effect resulting from waste slag from metal being included in glass.
- **Vaseline glass**: glass containing uranium, giving a yellowish 'vaseline' effect.

A Sowerby pressed glass jar, with cover, decorated with ferns, c1885, 8½in (22cm) high.
£30–35 *GLN*

A Continental ice glass ice pail, 1930s, 6in (15cm) high.
£25–35 *JHa*

Bottles, Decanters & Jugs

A clear engraved glass vinegar bottle, c1790, 7½in (19cm) high.
£150–170 *CB*

A pair of plain glass serving carafes, with double neck rings, c1800, 6in (15cm) high.
£100–120 *CB*

A Sheffield plate decanter stand, of trefoil form, with central posted scroll handle, the borders decorated in shells and fruiting vines, on pierced foliate shell feet, c1835, and 3 faceted octagonal mallet decanters with triple neck rings and conical stoppers, c1850.
£225–300 *N*

A cut glass carafe, with triple neck rings, 1830, 14in (35.5cm) high.
£150–180 *CB*

A rock crystal cut glass 'glug-glug' decanter, c1860, 8in (20cm) high.
£180–220 *CB*

A Webb's glass decanter, with amethyst stopper and foot, 1930s, 10½in (27cm) high.
£50–70 *JHa*

A silver plated stand, with reeded leaf-chased frame and central loop handle, containing 3 'Bristol' blue tinted glass spirit decanters and stoppers, inscribed in gilt 'Hollands', 'Brandy' and 'Rum', within gilt labels, early 19thC, 11in (28cm) high.
£450–550 *DN*

An Edwardian glass claret jug, with cut floral and hobnail decoration, silver plated rim, mask spout, shaped handle and hinged dome cover, on a star cut base, 11in (28cm) high.
£140–180 *Gam*

l. A crystal cut glass decanter and stopper, by Thomas Hawkes & Co, New York, USA, c1900, 14in (35.5cm) high.
£200–300 *CB*

Cross Reference:
Drinking

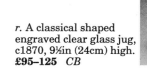

r. A classical shaped engraved clear glass jug, c1870, 9½in (24cm) high.
£95–125 *CB*

Cranberry Glass

A pair of Bohemian cranberry glass vases, with white enamel overlay, the enamel panels decorated with floral and gilt sprays and heightened with gilding, 19thC, 13in (33cm) high.
£900–1,100 *Mit*

A cranberry glass ewer, with painted blue enamel forget-me-nots, crimped clear handle and stopper, 19thC.
£70–100 *RBB*

A cranberry glass épergne, with 4 trumpet vases and dish base, crinkled rims and pinched trailed decoration, 19thC, 21in (53cm) high.
£500–550 *RBB*

A cylindrical crackled cranberry glass vase, with painted heron, insects and lakeside flowers in coloured enamels and gilt, with pedestal base, 19thC, 14in (35.5cm) high.
£300–350 *RBB*

l. A cranberry glass vase, c1890, 10in (25cm) high.
£85–95 *COL*

Glasses & Cups

An Irish dark coloured glass goblet, the round bowl engraved with a band of stars within a wrigglework border, with overall star pattern, flute cut base, on a facet cut stem and plain conical foot, c1830, 8¾in (22cm) high.
£340–380 *Som*

A glass rummer, with lemon squeezer base, c1800, 6in (15cm) high.
£80–110 *CB*

A glass rummer, engraved with monogram, c1820, 8½in (21.5cm) high.
£250–300

A glass toddy lifter, with neck ring, c1820, 5in (12.5cm) long.
£40–80 *CB*

A glass goblet, with an engraved floral band to the rim of the ogee bowl, circular cartouche with inset initials 'E. S.', surrounded by floral sprays and central bow, the reverse side with hops and barley motif, capstan stem, on a plain foot, c1810, 7in (18cm) high.
£200–250 *Som*

A set of 4 glass goblets, the round funnel bowls cut with printies, on cut baluster stems and plain conical feet, c1850, 6¼in (16cm) high.
£200–240 *Som*

Miller's is a price GUIDE not a price LIST

A petal-moulded glass rummer, c1830, 5¼in (13.5cm) high.
£80–120 *CB*

A heavy ogee glass rummer, c1840, 5in (12.5cm) high.
£35–45 *CB*

r. A French heavy facet cut and engraved glass tumbler, c1840, 3¾in (9.5cm) high.
£100–120 *CB*

l. A patent silver and green engraved mercury glass, by Hale Thomson, c1850, 4in (10cm) high.
£150–250 *JHa*

An Austrian double champagne flute and saucer, c1930, 8in (20cm) high.
£50–70 *JHa*

Custard Cups

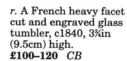

r. A pink glass custard cup, on a clear base, c1890, 4in (10cm) high.
£30–50 *CB*

l. A set of 8 glass petal-moulded custard cups, c1850, 3½in (9cm) high.
£120–150 *CB*

Gray-Stan Glass

A Gray-Stan glass two-handled cup, the top and domed foot with applied blue rim, clear body with pulled-up blue thread decoration, engraved signature, c1930, 7½in (19cm) high.
£200–250 *CMO*

Gray-Stan items were produced by the glass-making studio of Mrs Graydon-Stannus, London, c1923–32.

A Gray-Stan glass candlestick, of baluster form, the top and stem with spiral green glass threading, the domed foot edged with green, engraved signature, c1930, 11¼in (28.5cm) high.
£280–300 *CMO*

A Gray-Stan glass conical vase, with blue threads pulled into loops on a clear body, knopped base, on ribbed foot, engraved signature, c1930, 13½in (34.5cm) high.
£180–220 *CMO*

A Gray-Stan vaseline glass goblet, with applied amber trails, ribbed stem and ribbed folded foot, engraved signature, c1930, 10½in (26.5cm) high.
£350–450 *CMO*

A Gray-Stan green glass vase, with everted rim, the body with pulled-up swags, on a disc foot, engraved signature, c1930, 8½in (21.5cm) high.
£80–100 *CMO*

A Gray-Stan glass vase, of flared form and bulbous base, with green swirls on white, cased in clear glass, engraved signature, c1930, 11½in (29cm) high.
£200–250 *CMO*

A Gray-Stan pink and white glass vase, of tapering cylindrical form, with everted rim, pink festoons over white, cased in clear glass, with clear disc foot, engraved signature, c1930, 10½in (26.5cm) high.
£300–330 *CMO*

A Gray-Stan pink glass trumpet vase, decorated with red over white, cased in clear glass, on domed and folded foot, engraved signature, c1930, 15in (38cm) high.
£300–350 *CMO*

l. A Gray-Stan glass bowl, decorated with mauve over white, cased in clear glass, engraved signature, c1930, 10in (25cm) diam.
£200–250 *CMO*

r. A Gray-Stan bulbous glass vase, with everted rim, decorated with mauve swirls on white, cased in clear glass, engraved signature, c1930, 6in (15cm) high.
£160–180 *CMO*

l. A Gray-Stan bulbous vase, with 4 dimples below a cylindrical neck, decorated with blue swirls pulled down into yellow at the base over white, cased in clear glass, engraved signature, c1930, 9¼in (23.5cm) high.
£320–380 *CMO*

l. A Gray-Stan glass vase, of flared form above bulbous base, decorated with brown swirls on white, cased in clear glass, engraved signature, c1930, 7¼in (18.5cm) high.
£150–200 *CMO*

A Gray-Stan glass goblet, with ovoid body on rudimentary knopped stem on folded-over foot, decorated with blue swirls on white, cased in clear glass, engraved signature, c1930, 7¾in (19.5cm) high.
£200–300 *CMO*

Lalique

A Lalique frosted glass car mascot, Coq Nain, marked, 8in (20cm) high.
£650–750 *WL*

René Jules Lalique was the major glass designer of the Art Deco Movement. Lalique signed his works but after his death in 1945, the glassworks omitted the initial 'R' from items produced by the factory.

A Lalique opalescent peacock feather dish, c1900, 24in (61cm) diam.
£450–500 *HEM*

A Lalique frosted glass vase, Oursant, with blue staining, c1930, 5in (12.5cm) high.
£450–550 *AAV*

l. A Lalique baluster-shaped vase, Domrene, decorated with blue tinged metal, moulded in high relief, etched 'R. Lalique, France', 8½in (21.5cm) high.
£500–600 *L*

Powell Glass

A James Powell blue bowl, with thread design, 1930s, 9in (23cm) diam.
£80–120 *JHa*

A James Powell footed bowl, with blue ribbon decoration, 1930–50s, 3in (7.5cm) high.
£15–20 *JHa*

A James Powell goblet, M54 service, 1930s, 6in (15cm) high.
£25–35 *JHa*

Pressed Glass

A James Powell tumbler, 1930s, 6in (15cm) high.
£80–120 *JHa*

An amber pressed glass bowl and vase, by Jules Lang and Son, with fish handles and flower decoration, c1937, vase 11in (28cm) high.
£55–65 *BKK*

A blue pearline glass pedestal salt, by Davidsons, c1890, 2½in (6.5cm) high.
£40–50 *GLN*

A blue pearline glass plate, c1890, 8½in (21.5cm) diam.
£35–45 *GLN*

An opaque blue glass three-footed vase, by Sowerby, c1880, 3¼in (8.5cm) high.
£30–40 *GLN*

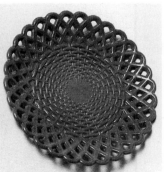

An opaque blue glass basketwork plate, by Sowerby, c1880, 8in (20cm) diam.
£30–35 *GLN*

The Sowerby glasshouse, Gateshead-on-Tyne, specialised in producing inexpensive pressed glassware in the second half of the 19thC.

l. An amber pressed glass basket, by Davidson, c1891, 7½in (19cm) wide.
£20–30 *GLN*

An opaque blue pressed glass creamer and sucrier, c1890, jug 3½in (9cm) high.
£85–95 *GLN*

A cross patch amethyst malachite pressed glass vase, c1880, 3½in (9cm) high.
£80–120 *JHa*

A malachite pressed glass beaker and vase, c1900, vase 7in (18cm) high.
Beaker **£10–15**
Vase **£30–35** *COL*

A black pressed glass vase, c1848, 3½in (9cm) high.
£20–25 *GLN*

A malachite pressed glass vase and dish, late 19thC, vase 5in (12.5cm) high.
£8–18 each *COL*

A purple slag malachite pressed glass bowl and cover, decorated with sprigs of holly, 1880, 5in (12.5cm) diam.
£60–70 *GLN*

A malachite pressed glass hat, by Greener, c1880, 3½in (9cm) high.
£80–120 *JHa*

A purple slag glass two-handled bowl, marked 'Sowerby', c1880, 2½in (6.5cm) diam.
£50–60 *GLN*

A pair of opalescent glass salts, by Sowerby, c1880, 1¼in (3cm) high.
£120–180 *JHa*

A purple slag pressed glass sucrier and cream jug, decorated with ivy leaf design, jug 3in (7.5cm) high.
£60–70 *GLN*

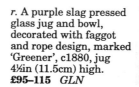

r. A purple slag pressed glass jug and bowl, decorated with faggot and rope design, marked 'Greener', c1880, jug 4½in (11.5cm) high.
£95–115 *GLN*

A white pressed glass jug and sucrier, marked 'Greener', c1876, jug 4in (10cm) high.
£85–95 *GLN*

A white pressed glass jug and bowl, by Hepple, late 19thC, bowl 3½in (9cm) high.
£100–115 *GLN*

A Queen's ivory pressed glass posy vase, c1880, 2¼in (5.5cm) high.
£140–180 *JHa*

A pressed glass pin tray, with Sowerby peacock trademark, c1880, 3in (7.5cm) diam.
£40–60 *JHa*

A pressed glass vase, decorated with a design of Old King Cole, from a Walter Crane design, c1880, 3¼in (8.5cm) high.
£100–150 *JHa*

A Queen's ivory pressed glass double-ended swan vase, after a design by Walter Crane, c1880, 5¼in (13.5cm) wide.
£120–180 *JHa*

Roman & Islamic

l. A Roman glass vessel, with 'strings' round the neck, 1st–3rd century AD, 7in (18cm) high.
£600–750 *JFG*

A Roman glass vessel, 1st–3rd century AD, 5in (12.5cm) high.
£600–700 *JFG*

l. A Roman vessel, 1st–3rd century AD, 5¼in (13.5cm) high.
£350–500 *JFG*

A Roman blue glass tear bottle, 1st–3rd century AD, 3in (7.5cm) high.
£250–300 *JFG*

r. A Persian Sasanid cut glass vessel, used for cosmetics, 4th century AD, 1in (2.5cm) high.
£70–90 *JFG*

A Roman glass vessel, 1st–3rd century AD, 6in (15cm) high.
£250–300 *JFG*

An Islamic glass vase, chipped, 6th century AD, 2½in (6.5cm) high.
£750–900 *JFG*

An Islamic glass rose water sprinkler, 8th century AD, 8¼in (21cm) high.
£1,000–1,200 *JFG*

A Roman amber glass bowl, on a low flared foot, with a folded thickened rim, base restored, 3rd–4th century AD, 7in (18cm) diam.
£750–800 *Bon*

A pair of earrings, with fragments of Roman glass mounted on sterling silver, 1½in (4cm) high.
£100–130 *JFG*

A sterling silver boat-shaped pendant, with fragments of Roman glass, 3in (7.5cm) wide.
£110–140 *JFG*

Vases

A glass celery vase, cut and engraved with birds and flowers, c1880, 8in (20cm) high.
£90–120 *CB*

r. A glass celery vase, by Molineux Webb, c1865, 10¼in (26cm) high.
£70–80 *GLN*

A trumpet-shaped glass celery vase, cut with plain and strawberry diamond pattern, scalloped rim, on a plain foot, c1825, 7½in (19cm) high.
£350–380 *Som*

A five-trumpet green vaseline glass épergne, with one central and 4 radiating trumpets each with frilled rims and applied spiralling trails, above a dish with a frilled rim, slight damage and repairs, 19thC, 19¾in (50cm) high.
£450–550 *CSK*

An opaline glass vase, enamelled with flowers, c1860, 12in (30.5cm) high.
£250–300 *CB*

r. A Pellaton pink glass posy vase, c1880, 3½in (9cm) high.
£60–80 *CB*

A pair of Stourbridge glass vases, with pale blue bodies, applied with pale amber rims, branch handles and feet, applied all-over in colours with fruiting branches, slight damage, c1880, 9½in (24cm) high.
£450–550 *CSK*

A coralene type glass vase, the body shading from pink to yellow, applied with yellow coral fronds, c1880, 10in (25cm) high.
£150–200 *Som*

A Bohemian amber and red flashed glass vase, engraved with flowers and gilded, c1890, 11½in (29cm) high.
£300–400 *CB*

An opalescent fan-shaped brocade glass, by Walsh Walsh, Birmingham, 10in (25cm) high.
£250–350 *JHa*

A similar item was illustrated in The Pottery Trade Gazette *of November 1897.*

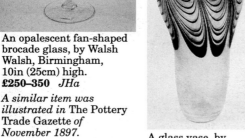

A glass vase, by Glassform Ltd, gold with black feathering, signed, marked 'No. 3158', 1986, 12in (30.5cm) high.
£100–130 *GLA*

An amethyst glass vase, by Walsh Walsh, Birmingham, engraved with a water lily and an iris, c1930, 10in (25cm) high.
£200–300 *JHa*

An opalescent vaseline glass hyacinth vase, possibly by Powell, late 19thC, 6in (15cm) high.
£60–80 *JHa*

An Orrefors glass vase, engraved with a child and flowers, c1970, 6in (15cm) high.
£30–40 *BEN*

l. A Kosta glass vase, by L. Klover, 1960s, 5½in (14cm) high.
£60–70 *HEM*

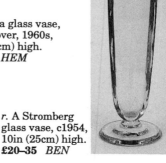

r. A Stromberg glass vase, c1954, 10in (25cm) high.
£20–35 *BEN*

Wedgwood

A Wedgwood amber glass
dolphin, c1970, 8½in
(21.5cm) wide.
£25–35 *SWB*

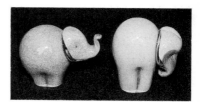

Two Wedgwood glass elephants,
1970s, largest 4in (10cm) high.
£25–30 each *SWB*

A Wedgwood glass
Scottie dog, c1970,
3½in (9cm) high.
£30–40 *SWB*

Two Wedgwood glass hedgehogs, pink
and white, and beige and brown, c1970,
3in (7.5cm) high.
£20–25 each *SWB*

Two Wedgwood glass snails, 1970s, 5¼in (13.5cm)
long. **£20–25 each** *SWB*

A Wedgwood pink glass whale,
c1970, 8½in (21.5cm) long.
£25–30 *SWB*

r. Two Wedgwood
glass otters, c1970,
6¼in (16cm) high.
£25–35 each *SWB*

A Wedgwood glass seal,
c1970, 8in (20cm) long.
£30–35 *SWB*

A Wedgwood amber
glass duck, c1970,
3½in (9cm) high.
£20–27 *SWB*

A Wedgwood glass duck,
c1970, 6¼in (16cm) high.
£30–35 *SWB*

Use the Index!

*Because certain items might fit easily
into any number of categories, the
quickest and surest method of
locating any entry is by reference to
the index at the back of the book.*

*This index has been fully cross-
referenced for absolute simplicity.*

r. A Wedgwood
glass polar bear,
c1970, 3½in
(9cm) high.
£25–35 *SWB*

Whitefriars

A pair of Whitefriars glass vases,
c1930, 5in (12.5cm) high.
£20–25 *HEM*

A Whitefriars conical glass bowl,
1930s, 8in (20cm) high.
£30–35 *HEM*

A Whitefriars trail ribbed
amethyst glass vase,
1930s, 5½in (14cm) high.
£50–70 *JHa*

l. A Whitefriars
amethyst glass vase,
1960s, 6in (15cm) high.
£15–25 *JHa*

r. A Whitefriars glass
decanter, 1930–50s,
9in (23cm) high.
£40–60 *JHa*

l. A Whitefriars 'bull's-eye' glass
vase, c1930, 6½in (16.5cm) high.
£50–80 *JHa*

A garden roller, early 20thC,
16in (40.5cm) diam.
£75–100 *WRe*

A terracotta flowerpot, with
decorative edging, early
20thC, 4in (10cm) diam.
£5–7 *TaB*

A Green's 14in Silens Messor lawn
mower, with straight handles, c1925.
£30–50 *PC*

A German iron framed
folding bandstand chair, with
pine seat and back, c1900.
£15–20 *NWE*

A watering can, with original paint,
to hold ¾ gallon, 1950s.
£20–25 *TaB*

A strawberry picker's trug, 1950s,
20in (51cm) long.
£12–15 *TaB*

A Qualcast 8in Model E lawn
mower, with grass box
and delivery plate, c1935.
£20–30 *PC*

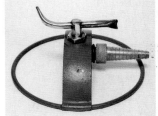

A metal, brass and copper
garden sprinkler, 1930s,
18in (45.5cm) wide.
£18–25 *TaB*

A garden trug, 1930s, 13in (33cm) long.
£25–30 *TaB*

An Abol insecticide spray gun, 1930s,
13in (33cm) long.
£7–10 *TaB*

A weather house, 1920s,
6in (15cm) high.
£28–35 *Ber*

A gnome, standing with a bear,
c1920, 14in (35.5cm) high.
£40–50 *HSA*

A gnome, holding a shell,
repainted in original colours,
1920s, 18½in (47cm) high.
£100–150 *GNR*

A terracotta gnome, fishing,
1940s, 11in (28cm) high.
£25–40 *GNR*

A gnome, with toadstool house,
1930s, 12in (30.5cm) high.
£40–50 *GNR*

A gnome, on a swing,
1900–20, 29in
(73.5cm) high.
£500–600 *GNR*

A white earthenware gnome,
on a swing, repainted, 1920s,
26in (66cm) high.
£80–100 *GNR*

A Pilshner gnome,
holding a pick, 1950–60,
6½in (16.5cm) high.
£10–20 *GNR*

A Heissner terracotta gnome,
c1900, 15in (38cm) high.
£300–600 *GNR*

A Roman glass double-handled jug, 1st–3rd century AD, 4in (10cm) high.
£1,600–1,900 *JFG*

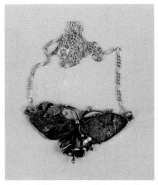

An Art Nouveau style sterling silver pendant, with Roman glass fragments, mid-20thC, 2in (5cm) wide.
£110–140 *JFG*

A pair of sterling silver earrings, with Roman glass fragments, mid-20thC, 1½in (3.5cm) long.
£100–130 *JFG*

A blue opaline glass hat, with gilt decoration, early 19thC, 2¼in high (5.5cm) high.
£60–80 *JHa*

A Roman glass vessel, 1st–3rd century AD, 4in (10cm) high.
£2,000–2,500 *JFG*

An opaline glass cornucopia, with gilded stag mount, on a marble base, c1870, 8in (20cm) high.
£200–250 *CB*

A pair of French opaline glass salts, with silver plated branch frame, c1870, 5in (12.5cm) wide.
£90–120 *CB*

A pearline glass basket, c1890, 5in (12.5cm) wide.
£30–40 *GLN*

A carnival glass mug, early 20thC, 4½in (11.5cm) diam. **£12–15** *PC*

A pearline cream jug and sucrier, by Davidson & Co, c1890, 5½in (14cm) high.
£100–125 *GLN*

A purple slag pressed glass lobed bowl, c1880, 5¾in (14.5cm) long.
£30–35 *GLN*

A pressed glass hat, possibly by Greener & Co, c1890, 3½in (9cm) high.
£20–30 *JHa*

A carnival glass bowl, early 20thC, 6in (15cm) diam.
£20–25 *PC*

An opaline vase, decorated with swans, c1880, 6½in (16.5cm) high.
£80–90 *GLN*

A Sowerby blue malachite pressed glass cauldron, c1880, 2½in (6.5cm) high.
£40–60 *JHa*

A Bohemian red glass water carafe and tumbler, early 20thC, 7in (17.5cm) high.
£25–30 *COL*

A pressed glass candle-stick, c1885, 7in (17.5cm) high. **£125–150** *GLN*

A glass dump, c1890, 4in (10cm) high.
£100–150 *CB*

A pair of pressed glass models of dogs, by Davidson & Co, c1895, 5½in (14cm) long.
£225–250 *GLN*

A Gray-Stan glass vase, 1930s, 10in (25.5cm) high.
£250–350   *JHa*

An Art Glass bowl, 1930s, 6½in (16.5cm) diam.
£40–50   *JHa*

Two tapestry glass vases, c1900, largest 5in (12.5cm) high.
£12–25 each   *COL*

A cloud glass vase, by Davidson, 1930s, 6in (15cm) high.
£20–25   *COL*

A Richardson's opaline glass vase, c1860, 10in (25.5cm) high.
£550–600   *CB*

A Gray-Stan glass vase, 1930s, 13in (33cm) diam.
£350–400   *CMO*

A Gray-Stan glass vase, 1930s, 7¼in (18.5cm) high.
£280–320   *CMO*

A pair of Stourbridge glass vases, c1880, 4½in (11.5cm) diam.
£150–200   *JHa*

A Gray-Stan ovoid glass vase, 1930s, 10in (25.5cm) high.
£250–280   *CMO*

A Gray-Stan glass vase, 1930s, 12in (30.5cm) high.
£450–500   *CMO*

A glass bowl, by Bagley, 1940s, 12in (30.5cm) diam. **£20–25**   *COL*

A glass bowl, by John Walsh Walsh, 1930s, 9in (23cm) diam. **£50–55** *COL*

A Stevens & Williams glass vase, 1930s, 11in (28cm) high. **£80–120** *JHa*

A Glassform vase, c1991, 5in (12.5cm) high. **£20–30** *GLA*

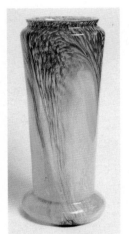

A glass vase, by Glassform Ltd, c1990, 9in (23cm) high. **£50–70** *GLA*

A Lamoirtine acid-etched vase, 1930s, 11in (28cm) high. **£150–200** *HEM*

A Gray-Stan glass vase, with engraved signature, 1930s, 10¼in (26cm) high. **£350–450** *CMO*

A Whitefriars Studio Art Glass vase, c1969, 10in (25.5cm) high. **£200–300** *JHa*

A Call of Future engraved glass bowl, 'The Warrior Dance', by Clare Henshaw, c1994, 11¼in (28.5cm) high. **£2,000–3,000** *JHa*

A glass vase, by Glassform Ltd, 1994, 5¼in (13.5cm) high. **£50–70** *GLA*

A Thomas Webb 'wavy' vase, 1930s, 7in (17.5 cm) high. **£50–70** *JHa*

A velvet and gold kid leather handbag, probably made in India for the European market, c1940, 8in (20.5cm) long.
£30–35 *LBe*

A Victorian silk woven purse, 3½in (9cm) high.
£25–35 *Ech*

A tapestry evening handbag, c1950, 8in (20cm) wide.
£10–12 *STP*

A crocodile handbag, with Art Deco chrome clasp, c1930, 10½in (27cm) wide.
£90–100 *LBe*

An American felt handbag, with a beaded front, 1940s, 12½in (32cm) wide.
£45–55 *LBe*

A French mesh evening bag, 1920s, 5in (13cm) long.
£30–50 *Ech*

A Victorian wool embroidered purse, 8in (20cm) long.
£25–35 *Ech*

A black lacquered metal and kid leather handbag, c1950, 10in (25.5cm) wide.
£75–80 *LBe*

A Victorian silver brooch, with enamelled roses, 2in (50mm) long.
£110–140 *SPE*

A Victorian 9ct gold hair brooch, with seed pearls and gold thread, 2in (50mm) wide. **£150–200** *SIG*

An enamelled silver brooch, decorated with a horse's head, 1½in (38mm) diam.
£125–150 *SPE*

A Russian gold chain, with rock crystal, gold, enamel and agate egg-shaped stones, c1860, 16in (40.5cm) long.
£600–650 *LBr*

A selection of enamelled butterfly brooches, 1914–20, largest 2in (50mm) wide.
£35–100 each *SGr*

A silver Mizpah brooch, inscribed 'Best Wishes', c1910, 2in (50mm) wide.
£35–40 *AnE*

An Art Deco diamanté bracelet, with chrome fitting, 7in (18cm) long.
£450–500 *GLT*

A selection of Christmas tree pin brooches, diamanté, glass, crystal, brass and gilt setting, some signed, 1940–60s, largest 2¾in (7cm) long.
£35–45 each *GLT*

A Victorian 15ct gold brooch and matching earrings, modelled as bugs, brooch 1½in (38mm) wide.
£300–350 *SPE*

A brooch, made for Jean Muir's 1987 collection, painted and decorated with sequins and glass, 4¼in (11cm) long.
£15–20 *PC*

A pair of Egyptian *pâte de verre* earrings, c1928.
£45–55 *LBe*

A gilt and paste necklace, in the form of a snake, c1940, 17in (43cm) long.
£110–120 *LBe*

A glass and plastic necklace, by Pierre Balmain, 1970s.
£100–120 *GBN*

This necklace still has its original shop price tag of $480 (£320).

Two pairs of brass earrings, by Joseff of Hollywood, 1940s, 3¼in (8cm) long.
£120–150 each *GLT*

A selection of plastic and resin bangles, 1930–50.
£10–15 each *GLT*

A red glass bead multi-strand necklace, by Ciner, with diamanté and gilt clasp, 1960s, 17in (43cm) long.
£350–400 *GLT*

A green glass three-strand necklace, by K.J. Lane, with diamanté crystal clasp, 1960s, 17¾in (45cm) long.
£125–145 *GLT*

A gilt metal bracelet, unsigned, 1960s, 1in (25mm) wide.
£20–25 *GBN*

A glass, crystal and gilt rope necklace, by Boucher, 1960s, 15in (38cm) long.
£200–240 *GLT*

A European dough bin, c1880, 21in (53.5cm) long.
£30–40 WCA

A copper kettle, c1880,
8in (20.5cm) high.
£70–80 WCA

A hand-operated bacon/bread slicer,
c1930, 9in (23cm) high.
£30–35 TaB

An enamel bread bin, c1920,
10in (25.5cm) high.
£20–30 WAC

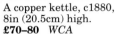

Two European enamel
cooking utensils, 1950s,
5in (13cm) diam.
£6–8 each TaB

A Nutbrown De Luxe Icing Set, in original
box, 1950–60, 5in (13cm) wide.
£4–5 WAC

l. A German coffee
grinder, c1930,
6in (15cm) high.
£15–20 WAC

A Cornish ware flour
shaker, 1950s,
5in (13cm) high.
£15–20 WAC

A raffia tea cosy, c1930,
10½in (28cm) high.
£25–35 Ber

A knife polisher, late 19thC,
10in (25.5cm) high.
£25–35 WCA

A Royal Doulton ceramic pull, with brass chain, c1920. **£60–90** *BS*

A ceramic pull, with brass chain, c1920, 5in (12.5cm) long. **£35–45** *BS*

An ebonised beech and brass pull, c1930. **£50–60** *BS*

A ceramic pull, with brass chain, c1920, 5in (12.5cm) long. **£65–75** *BS*

A ceramic pull, with brass chain, c1900, 5in (12.5cm) long. **£90–110** *BS*

A brass oil lamp, adapted for electricity, c1880, 20½in (52cm) high. **£175–195** *LIB*

A brass table lamp, with glass shade, c1920, 16½in (42cm) high. **£100–130** *LIB*

An oil lamp, c1910, 14in (35.5cm) high. **£25–30** *AL*

A brass lantern, c1920, 13½in (34.5cm) high. **£125–155** *LIB*

A copper oil lamp, early 20thC, 22¾in (58cm) high. **£70–90** *Gam*

An oil lamp, with Duplex burner, c1865, 27in (68.5cm) high. **£275–300** *LIB*

An oil lamp, with glass base and opaque shade, 1950s, 14in (35.5cm) high. **£45–55** *HEM*

A Troika pottery lamp base, c1960, 19½in (50cm) high. **£100–120** *NCA*

Two copper planters, with porcelain handles, c1880, largest 17½in (44.5cm) wide.
£25–30 each   *HEM*

A Dutch silver gilt vinaigrette, c1850, 2in (50mm) diam.
£550–600   *LBr*

A silver and agate picture frame, c1909, 1¼in (30mm) high.
£100–120   *LBr*

A pair of copper bell pulls, by Elkington & Co, 19thC, 6½in (16.5cm) long.
£250–285   *BS*

A crumb brush, with silver handle, c1904, 6in (15cm) long.
£50–60   *WN*

A cast brass plate, inscribed 'Milners Thief-Resisting Safe List 3', c1900, 8in (20cm) wide. **£50–60**   *BS*

A Russian silver plated and enamelled box, c1900, 4¼in (11cm) wide. **£250–270**   *LBr*

A set of 5 cold painted spelter figures of puppies, 4 with a frog, one with a fly, early 20thC. **£250–300**   *AAV*

A brass foot warmer, late 19thC, 17½in (44.5cm) high. **£65–75**   *AnE*

A set of 3 brass water jugs, 1900–10, largest 13in (33cm) high. **£60–70**   *MIL*

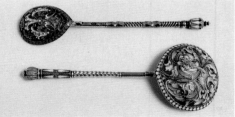

Two Russian silver and enamel spoons, c1820, 6in (15cm) long. **£150–200**   *LBr*

A carved and lacquered box, 19thC, 7in (18cm) diam. **£200–250** *ORI*

A Nanking Cargo plate, with underglaze pattern, c1750, 9in (23cm) diam. **£350–400** *RBA*

A Diana Cargo bowl, with panels decorated with petals, 1816, 6½in (16.5cm) diam. **£75–95** *CFA*

A 'longevity' dish, with *shou* character and *ruyi* lappets, c1816, 11in (28cm) diam. **£250–350** *RBA*

A Sancai glazed pottery tray, with 6 cups, Tang Dynasty, tray 10in (25.5cm) diam. **£400–500** *ORI*

A Diana Cargo tea bowl and saucer, c1816, dish 8¼in (20.5cm) diam. **£250–325** *RBA*

A pair of Chinese jardinières, on dragon mask feet, late 17thC, with later ormolu mounts, 8½in (21.5cm) wide. **£2,500–3,000** *DN*

A Cizhou Sancai glazed pottery pillow, early Ming Dynasty, 10in (25.5cm) long. **£300–400** *ORI*

An underglazed decorated bowl, early 19thC, 5½in (14cm) diam. **£450–500** *ORI*

A Japanese Imari bowl, late 19thC, 7½in (19cm) diam. **£120–140** *ORI*

A pair of Nanking Cargo sauceboats, silver shape pattern, c1750, 8¼in (21cm) wide. **£4,000–4,600** *RBA*

A Satsuma coffee set, c1870. **£250–300** *COL*

A Japanese cloisonné tripod jar, with silver top, late 19thC, 5½in (14cm) high. **£120–140** *ORI*

A kraak style Kangxi period dish, 11in (28cm) diam. **£350–400** *ORI*

A Diana Cargo storage jar, encrusted, 1816, 9in (23cm) high. **£650–750** *CFA*

A Starburst dish, c1816, 11in (28cm) diam. **£200–280** *RBA*

A collection of Diana Cargo moulded glazed toy figures, c1816, 3¾in (9.5cm) high. **£75–125 each** *RBA*

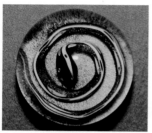

A Caithness paperweight, by William Manson, 1978, 3in (7.5cm) diam. **£275–325** *SWB*

A Whitefriars Silver Jubilee paperweight, c1977, 3in (7.5cm) diam. **£160–180** *MLa*

A Val St Lambert paperweight, c1880, 4in (10cm) diam. **£200–250** *SWB*

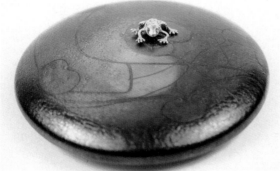

A paperweight, with lily decoration and sterling silver frog on top, 1995, 4¼in (11cm) diam. **£40–50** *GLA*

A Whitefriars Christmas paperweight, 1979, 2¾in (7cm) diam. **£300–350** *MLa*

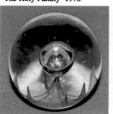

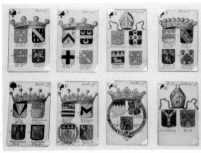

An English Heraldic pack of cards, by John Nicholson, decorated with coats-of-arms, 1688, 3½ by 2¼in (9 by 5.5cm). **£800–1,000** *PC*

A Tartan ware bridge marker, c1900, 3 by 2in (7.5 by 5cm). **£50–70** *MRW*

The Royal Cabinet of Games, by Jacks of London, the coromandel box containing an ivory chess set and other games, c1870, 12½in (32cm) wide. **£1,500–2,000** *TMi*

A French bagatelle game, 1920–30, 42in (107cm) long. **£240–270** *GD*

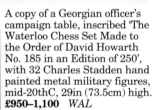

A copy of a Georgian officer's campaign table, inscribed 'The Waterloo Chess Set Made to the Order of David Howarth No. 185 in an Edition of 250', with 32 Charles Stadden hand painted metal military figures, mid-20thC, 29in (73.5cm) high. **£950–1,100** *WAL*

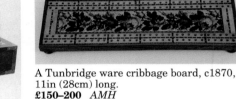

A Tunbridge ware cribbage board, c1870, 11in (28cm) long. **£150–200** *AMH*

A box containing a game of Happy Families, and a tin of Gibbs Dentifrice, cards 1940s, 2¾ by 2in (70 by 50mm). **£20–25** *PC*

A bagatelle game, c1925, 36in (91.5cm) long. **£25–35** *WCA*

A Worshipful Company of Playing Card Makers' presentation box of playing cards, 1902, 3½in (9cm) wide. **£150–200** *PC*

A box of 48 snap cards, by the Co-operative Wholesale Society, 1900, 3½ by 2½in (9 by 6.5cm). **£70–75** *PC*

GRAMOPHONES

The HMV Model 202 re-entrant gramophone (1928) made a world record sum when it was sold by Christie's South Kensington recently. It was not the neo-Gothic case that attracted bidders, but the machine itself which, with its No. 5A soundbox, represented the height of technical expertise and sound quality in the late 1920s. The price of this HMV Model 202 has been consistently rising, it appeals particularly to Japanese and Korean buyers, currently big players in this collecting field. The gramophone market remains extremely stable, attracting an international audience of dedicated enthusiasts.

A Columbia Graphophone AB phonograph, with original 5in (12.5cm) mandrel adapter for Grand cylinders, in a carved oak case, retailer's transfer 'Dulcetto, The Phono Exchange London', c1900.
£600–800 *BTA*

A Thornward phonograph, No. 47448, with type N graphophone upper chassis with bullet-shaped mandrel and endgate, type A bedplate and motor with single spring, in oak case, with banner transfer 'Montgomery Ward & Co, Chicago, ILL', now with reproduction reproducer, c1898.
£1,200–1,400 *CSK*

The Thornward was retailed by the mail order company Montgomery Ward of Chicago. The price of the N was $40 (£27) in 1895. Montgomery Ward was America's largest mail order house in the late 19thC, supplying the huge rural population with goods which were difficult, if not impossible, to obtain in remote communities. The firm is still in business, now as Chicago's premier chain of department stores rather than a low-priced mail order business.

A Victor gramophone, by Gramophone & Typewriter Ltd, with brass-belled black horn, small gooseneck tone arm, Gramophone Company exhibition soundbox, base mounted motor and oak case, with 'Gramophone' banner and G & T transfers, lacking brake, c1905.
£650–750 *CSK*

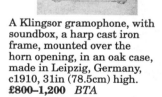

A Klingsor gramophone, with soundbox, a harp cast iron frame, mounted over the horn opening, in an oak case, made in Leipzig, Germany, c1910, 31in (78.5cm) high.
£800–1,200 *BTA*

It was alleged that when the strings of the harp were properly tuned they would respond to the frequencies being transmitted by the record and consequently enhance and give more body to the sound.

r. An Edison home phonograph, gearing for both 2 and 4 minute cylinders, Model S reproducer, restored ten panel tinplate horn, c1906.
£700–900 *BTA*

An Edison Standard Model B phonograph, with original 30in (76cm) brass horn and table stand, Model C reproducer, c1905.
£500–700 *BTA*

An Edison Standard
phonograph, with reproducer
horn, c1908, 21in (53.5cm) high.
£350–400 *OTA*

An Edison Triumph
Model B phonograph,
gearing for both 2 and
4 minute cylinders,
Model O reproducer,
Edison No. 11 tinplate
Cygnet horn in
simulated wood finish
with Edison transfer,
oak case, ivorine
retailer's plaque, c1906.
£1,500–2,000 *BTA*

A Phonogrand gramophone, with 3
wooden internal horns above tone arm
with S-neck, in mahogany case, with
fretwork apertures in sides and back
for the horns, on matching pedestal
with accessories drawer, cupboard
below and turned legs, with 'Phonogrand
Warranted London Made' plaque,
replacement soundbox in carton, c1910,
46½in (118cm) high.
£1,000–1,200 *CSK*

l. An Edison Standard Model F
phonograph, gearing for both 2 and
4 minute cylinders, Edison No. 10
Cygnet horn, Model S reproducer,
oak case, c1912.
£750–950 *BTA*

An HMV Senior Monarch horn
gramophone, exhibition soundbox, in mahogany case with
fielded panels, carved and reeded
pillars, the mahogany horn with
HMV trademark transfer, c1910.
£1,800–2,000 *BTA*

The Masters
Gramophone, in
wooden cabinet, 1920s,
40in (101.5cm) high.
£75–150 *OTA*

l. A horn Zonophone, Model HVO,
with Exhibition pattern soundbox
and a gilt-lined black Morning
Glory horn, oak case, dated on base
'1920', horn 23in (58.5cm) diam.
£950–1,200 *CSK*

An HMV Model 2A horn
gramophone, Exhibition
soundbox on gooseneck tone
arm, single 1in (2.5cm) spring
motor and mahogany case
with dealer's plaque 'Wallace
Harris Ltd, Gloucester', dated
on base '16.3.20'.
£2,500–2,800 *CSK*

*Gramophones with mahogany
horns are particularly desirable.*

An HMV Model 1 table gramophone, hornless, c1920, 14in (35.5cm) high.
£100–150 *OTA*

An HMV Model 250 gramophone, in mahogany cabinet, c1925, 35in (89cm) high.
£350–400 *OTA*

An HMV Model 32 gramophone, with quadruple spring motor, No. 5b soundbox, contemporary brass horn, oak case, c1927.
£850–1,250 *BTA*

An HMV Model 161 gramophone, by James Smith & Son Ltd, of Liverpool, with saxophone horn, in oak cabinet, c1926, 39in (99cm) high.
£250–350 *OTA*

An Academy mahogany cased gramophone, by Johnson Talking Machine Co, Liverpool and Birmingham, England, c1925.
£450–500 *BTA*

A C. A. Vandervell loudspeaker horn, c1924, 22in (56cm) high.
£60–100 *OTA*

An HMV Model 202 re-entrant tone chamber gramophone, with No. 5A soundbox, oxidised fittings and oak case, 1928, 49½in (125.5cm) high.
£15,000–16,000 *CSK*

Six tins of Songster 78rpm gramophone needles, 1920s, each tin 2in (5cm) wide.
£15–20 each *MRW*

A tin of HMV 78rpm gramophone needles, 1920s, 1¾in (4.5cm) wide.
£15–20 *MRW*

A tin of Golden Pyramid 78rpm gramophone needles, 1920s, 2½in (6.5cm) high.
£20–30 *MRW*

HANDBAGS & CASES

Handbags are once again a highly fashionable accessory, with contemporary designers, producing new and often costly designs. An alternative is to buy handbags from a bygone era. Handbags are already widely collected, particularly in the USA. The most sought after types include beaded bags from the Edwardian period and good quality examples from the 1920s–60s. 'People like interesting and whimsical shapes, Perspex bags from the 1950s, and Art Deco bags with decorative clasps and special compartments for cosmetics,' explains dealer Linda Bee.

A Victorian silk mesh purse, 4in (10cm) high.
£25–35 *Ech*

An Art Nouveau pewter bag frame, with coloured stones, c1900, 5½in (14cm) wide.
£10–15 *LBe*

A sequined evening bag, 1930s, 8in (20.5cm) wide.
£7–10 *STP*

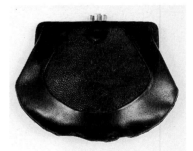

A brown leather bag, c1920, 7in (18cm) high.
£15–25 *Ech*

A silver mesh evening bag, with amethyst clasp, lined in kid leather, c1915–20, 9½in (24cm) high.
£130–140 *LBe*

An antelope suede handbag, with metal Viennese trim, by Hoffman, c1930, 8in (20.5cm) high.
£90–110 *LBe*

A sharkskin and leather handbag, with metal clasp, c1930, 8in (20.5cm) wide.
£110–120 *LBe*

A handbag, with imitation petit point panels, in mint condition, 1930s, 8in (20.5cm) wide.
£40–50 *LBe*

> **Cross Reference:**
> Costume

r. A leather handbag, with Bakelite clasp, c1930, 10in (25.5cm) wide.
£25–35 *LBe*

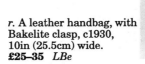

An antelope suede and gold kid leather handbag, 1930s, 11in (28cm) wide.
£45–55 *LBe*

An antelope suede handbag, with silver, lapis lazuli, marcasite and enamel frame, c1930, 8in (20.5cm) wide.
£190–200 *LBe*

A snakeskin clutch bag, 1930s, 8in (20.5cm) wide.
£15–30 *Ech*

A suede handbag, with paste clasp, and emerald green satin lining, c1930, 10in (25.5cm) wide.
£75–85 *LBe*

A black kid leather handbag, with chrome handle and Bakelite trim, c1930, 8in (20.5cm) wide.
£40–50 *LBe*

A gold sequined evening bag, c1930, 6½in (16.5cm) wide.
£30–40 *LBe*

A quilted leather handbag, by Waldy, c1940, 9in (23cm) wide.
£55–65 *LBe*

Waldy, handbag maker to the Queen, operated from a small factory in Tottenham Court Road, London.

An antelope suede handbag, with gold trim, with fitted make-up section inside, 1940s, 9in (23cm) wide.
£45–55 *LBe*

A felt handbag, with appliquéd flowers and a central handle, c1935, 8in (20.5cm) wide.
£5–6 *STP*

l. A green leather handbag, with Bakelite clasp, 1930s, 14in (35.5cm) wide.
£65–75 *LBe*

An antelope suede handbag, with metal trim and a compact compartment, 1940s, 6½in (16.5cm) high.
£45–55 *LBe*

A brown crocodile skin handbag, with chrome handle, c1940, 5½in (14cm) wide.
£80–90 *LBe*

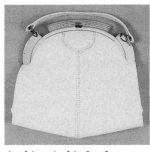

A white pigskin leather handbag, 1940s, 8½in (21.5cm) square.
£7–10 *STP*

A black leather and tortoiseshell handbag, with compact compartment, c1940, 5½in (14cm) wide.
£40–50 *LBe*

An black suede and gilt evening bag, with various compartments, possibly American or French, 1940s, 4¾in (12cm) high.
£80–90 *LBe*

An American black crocodile skin handbag, by Saks 5th Avenue, with gilt clasp and trim, c1950, 9in (23cm) wide.
£80–90 *LBe*

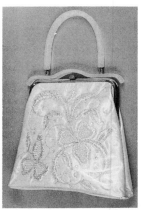

A plastic-covered quilted satin and pearl handbag, with gilt frame, Bakelite handle and top, c1950, 10in (25.5cm) high.
£65–75 *LBe*

A black velvet evening bag, with chain mail gold top, 1950s, 5½in (14cm) square.
£40–45 *LBe*

A black patent leather handbag, with chain handle, c1970, 7½in (19cm) wide.
£40–45 *LBe*

A chain metal handbag, with Perspex handle, Paco Rabanne inspired, c1960, 7½in (19cm) wide.
£45–55 *LBe*

A Victorian brown leather travelling bag, 24in (61cm) long.
£60–100 *Ech*

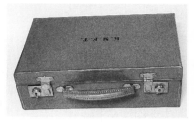

r. A leather suitcase, initialled 'K.M.F.T.', c1930, 14in (35.5cm) long.
£30–50 *Ech*

HANDCARTS

A flatbed handcart, c1880, 70¾in (180cm) long.
£125–175 *NWE*

A roadman's handcart, inscribed 'GWO Stanford KE 7262', c1900, 82in (208.5cm) long overall.
£250–300 *JUN*

A wooden handcart, with brakes and moulded decoration, c1880, 37½in (95cm) long.
£150–175 *NWE*

A Victorian wooden handcart, 31½in (80cm) long.
£75–100 *NWE*

A tradesman's handcart, c1900, 94in (239cm) long overall.
£300–350 *JUN*

A European handcart, with original paintwork, early 20thC, 24in (61cm) long.
£120–130 *TaB*

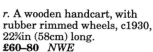

r. A wooden handcart, with rubber rimmed wheels, c1930, 22¾in (58cm) long.
£60–80 *NWE*

A wooden luggage cart, c1930, 28¾in (73cm) long.
£60–80 *NWE*

JEWELLERY

An Edwardian hinged openwork gem set bangle, with applied central heart-shaped green stone and half-pearl cluster with trefoil borders, one stone missing.
£400–500 *CSK*

A silver and gold buckle, decorated with brilliants, early 19thC, ¾in (20mm) wide.
£20–25 *EBB*

A 9ct gold fob, with carnelian stone, 19thC.
£45–55 *AnE*

Two Victorian poison rings.
l. engraved gold. **£140–160**
r. agate and engraved gold.
£195–220 *SPE*

The stone in these rings lifts to reveal a compartment reputedly for poison. These Victorian designs are based on 16thC so-called 'poison rings', whose hidden compartments were probably used to contain solid perfume or religious relics.

A gold cased carnelian fob, the seal matrix engraved with initials, the mount chased and engraved with scrolls and fox masks, 19thC.
£225–275 *CSK*

A goldstone pendant, 1930s, 1in (25mm) high.
£30–35 *AnE*

Brooches

A Victorian silver and gold hand engraved brooch, 1¼in (32mm) high.
£65–85 *SPE*

A Victorian gold filigree and aquamarine brooch.
£275–325 *HCH*

l. A Victorian gold, pearl and rose-cut diamond bar brooch, the centre with 2 pearls surrounded by diamonds and flanked by a pair of pearls.
£340–400 *HCH*

A Victorian gold and black enamel mourning ring.
£125–150 *SPE*

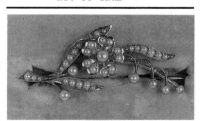

A 15ct gold and pearl brooch, in the form of a floral spray.
£80–100 *HCH*

An oval shell cameo, depicting a biblical scene, the gold brooch mount with foliate engraved scroll surround, 19thC.
£200–250 *CSK*

A gold and garnet brooch, the circular locket back body with applied rope and wirework decoration surmounted by a Bohemian garnet and cabochon garnet cluster, 19thC.
£300–350 *CSK*

A pinchbeck frame brooch, c1860, 2¼in (55mm) high.
£55–65 *AnE*

Two enamelled butterfly brooches, 1920s, largest 1½in (38mm) wide.
£35–40 each *SPE*

An Edwardian brooch and pendant, the half pearl flowerhead and crescent brooch suspending a diamond, blue enamel and half pearl heart-shaped locket back pendant.
£450–550 *CSK*

An Edwardian aquamarine and half pearl brooch, with pendant loop, the central oval aquamarine with half pearl scroll and floral openwork decoration, suspending a single pear-shaped aquamarine.
£250–300 *CSK*

A brooch, in the form of a butterfly, c1918, 3in (7.5cm) wide.
£100–120 *SGr*

A silver Mizpah brooch, 2 hearts and a bird, c1910, 1½in (38mm) wide.
£40–45 *AnE*

l. An enamelled silver butterfly brooch on a bar, 1920s, 1in (25mm) wide.
£25–28
r. An enamelled silver butterfly brooch, 1920s, 1½in (38mm) wide.
£35–40 *SPE*

A collection of enamelled dog brooches, c1930, largest 1½in (38mm) wide.
£60–90 each *SGr*

Name Brooches

Two silver name brooches, 1880–90, 1½in (38mm) diam.
£30–40 each *AnE*

r. A collection of 6 Victorian silver name brooches, 1in (25mm) diam.
£28–45 each *SPE*

A collection of Victorian silver name brooches, 1½in (38mm) wide.
£28–45 each *SPE*

A Victorian jet name brooch, 2in (50mm) long.
£25–30 *SPE*

A collection of 8 silver name brooches, c1890–1912, largest 1¾in (45mm) wide.
£25–40 each *AnE*

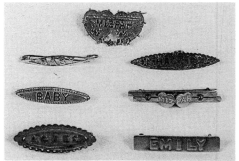

A collection of 7 gold name brooches, largest 1½in (38mm) wide.
£55–65 each *SPE*

Costume Jewellery

Twentieth century jewellery has attracted enormous interest over the last 15 years and now has an established worldwide market. Designer costume jewellery, produced from the 1930s onwards, was manufactured from non-precious materials, refined glass crystals set in electroplated base metals and contemporary plastics. Costume jewellery was created by the great names of the fashion industry, such as Chanel and Dior, as well as by specialist costume jewellers such as Joseff of Hollywood and Trifari.

According to dealer and private collector, Mike Sinclair, some 75 per cent of costume jewellery was manufactured in the USA. The Hollywood film industry provided a natural market and before WWII a number of German and European craftsmen emigrated to America, where they established their own highly successful costume jewellery businesses. The remaining 25 per cent of material was made on the Continent. Coco Chanel paved the way in creating and popularising costume jewellery, and other fashion designers soon followed suit.

Prices begin under £50, rising to £500 upwards, depending on the name of the designer, the quality of the piece and its over-all appeal. Works by major designers tend to be the most desirable and are usually signed.

A gilt metal brooch, by Marcel Boucher, in the form of seaweed and fish, 1960s, 2½in (65mm) high.
£50–60 *GBN*

A pink and green glass and gilt flower necklace, by Chanel, Bijoux des Fleurs, 1950s, necklace 15¾in (40cm) long.
£400–460 *GLT*

A blue crystal and diamanté pavé set bracelet, by Marcel Boucher, with chrome setting, 1940s, 6¾in (17cm) long.
£250–280 *GLT*

l. A white glass necklace and a pair of earrings, made by Madame Gripoix for Chanel, with metal mounts, 1930s, necklace 15¾in (40cm) long.
£650–750 *GLT*

r. A pair of white, red and turquoise, glass earrings, made by Madame Gripoix for Chanel, 1950s, 1¼in (32mm) wide.
£75–95 *GLT*

A three-strand gilt brass necklace, by Chanel Boutique, 1970s, 15¾in (40cm) long.
£150–170 *GLT*

A pair of tortoiseshell earrings, by Chanel Boutique, each with a brass plated chain and insignia, 1980s, 2¾in (70mm) high.
£75–95 *GLT*

A silver and crystal parrot brooch, by Coro, 1940s, 3in (7.5cm) high.
£150–200 *GBN*

A grey and mauve glass three-strand necklace and pair of earrings, by Christian Dior, 1950s, necklace 13¾in (35cm) long.
£150–185 *GLT*

A glass and plastic six-strand necklace, by Christian Dior, in pink, blue, green and lavender, 1960s, 15¾in (40cm) long.
£200–250 *GLT*

A necklace and ear clip set, by Christian Dior, with cabochon and brilliant cut pastes in autumnal colours, scrolling vine design, 1962.
£375–450 *CSK*

A pair of glass diamanté baroque pearl drop earrings, by K. J. Lane, 1960s, 4in (10cm) long.
£100–120 *GLT*

A blue crystal necklace and pair of earrings, by Lisner, with chrome settings, 1950s, necklace 13¾in (35cm) long.
£150–180 *GLT*

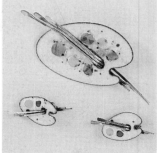

A Matisse copper brooch and pair of matching earrings, designed in the form of an artist's palette, 1950s, brooch 3in (7.5cm) wide.
£40–45 *GBN*

A green glass crystal necklace and pair of earrings, by Weiss, with gilt brass settings, 1950s, necklace 23½in (60cm) long.
£100–140 *GLT*

Unsigned Pieces

A clear diamanté crystal parure, by Weiss, with chrome settings, 1940s, necklace 13¾in (35cm) long.
£300–380 *GLT*

A pink and grey crystal necklace and pair of earrings, by Trifari, 1940s.
£100–200 *GLT*

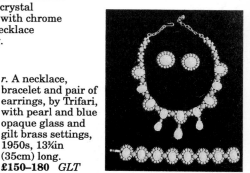

r. A necklace, bracelet and pair of earrings, by Trifari, with pearl and blue opaque glass and gilt brass settings, 1950s, 13¾in (35cm) long.
£150–180 *GLT*

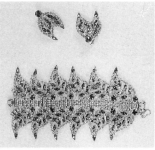

A chenille necklace, with rhinestones, Bakelite clasp, 1930s, 26in (66cm) long.
£100–120 *LBe*

An Austrian gilt metal and crystal bracelet and pair of earrings, 1950s, bracelet 7in (18cm) long.
£110–120 *GBN*

Two crystal necklaces, 1960–70s.
£8–9 each *STP*

A pair of crystal drop earrings, with chrome fittings, 1950s, 5in (13cm) long.
£150–170 *GLT*

Hair Jewellery

Hair jewellery first became popular in the 17th century and the fashion was revived in the 19th century. Human hair was set into brooches and rings, plaited as bracelets and woven for pendants. Some pieces were commemorative, using the hair of the dear departed, and others were love tokens.

Hair could be taken to a professional hair worker/jeweller to be made up, but many examples were homemade. *The Lock of Hair*, published in 1871 by Alexanna Speight, gave amateurs precise instructions and designs for hair work, and claimed that it was far better to create one's own jewellery since unscrupulous tradesmen had been known to substitute cherished family locks with hair from their general stock if there were not sufficient strands to make up a particular pattern.

A Georgian gold and enamel hair brooch, 1in (25mm) wide.
£50–100 *SPE*

A Georgian gold hair ring, ¾in (20mm) wide.
£75–100 *SIG*

A Georgian hand woven hair longuard, with gold fastener and clips, 50in (127cm) long.
£95–125 *SPE*

A gold 'Regard' hair brooch, the order of the stones from top left being ruby, emerald, garnet, amethyst, ruby, diamond, c1830, 1¼in (32mm) wide.
£450–550 *SGr*

The initial letters of the names of the stones spell out the word 'regard'.

A Georgian gold and enamel hair brooch, inscribed 'In Memory', 1½in (38mm) wide.
£50–100 *SPE*

A gold hair brooch, with hardstone cameos and rose diamonds, dated '1830', 1in (25mm) diam.
£375–475 *SGr*

A Victorian hair heart pendant, with gold fitting and chain, pendant ¾in (20mm) long.
£60–65 *SPE*

A Victorian gold hair brooch, with seed pearls and gold thread, 2in (50mm) wide.
£150–185 *SIG*

The Prince of Wales feathers was a very popular pattern in hair jewellery.

A hair bracelet, with shell cameo and gold mount, c1860, 7½in (19cm) long.
£900–1,250 *SGr*

Two gold mourning hair brooches, c1880, largest 1in (25mm) wide.
£40–45 each *AnE*

Marcasite

A silver, marcasite and rose quartz bracelet, 1920s, 8in (20cm) long.
£140–200 *SPE*

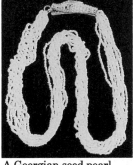

A marcasite cat and umbrella brooch, 1920s, 2in (50mm) wide.
£55–75 *SPE*

Marcasite is crystalline cubic sulphur ore, or polished iron pyrites, often known as 'fool's gold'. Cut steel jewellery is also often referred to as marcasite.

A silver marcasite ring watch, by Tissot, 1920s.
£120–140 *SPE*

Necklaces & Lockets

A Georgian seed pearl necklace, with gold Japanese shikuda fastener, 12in (30.5cm) long.
£425–475 *SPE*

A Georgian seed pearl necklace, with gold snake fastener set with turquoises, 16in (40.5cm) long.
£450–500 *SPE*

A Victorian 9ct gold and enamel locket, with seed pearls, c1850, 1½in (38mm) long.
£75–85 *AnE*

A Georgian seed pearl necklace, 20in (51cm) long.
£500–550 *SPE*

KITCHENWARE & HOUSEHOLD ITEMS

Interest in collecting kitchenware has grown in recent years. According to specialist Christina Bishop, one of the reasons is that many objects were extremely well made and having seen active service for generations, they can still be used today.

'Nothing beats cooking with old utensils,' she enthuses. 'Remember, however, they do need a bit more looking after than new ones. Take extra care with washing and drying up, and store items in a dry place where they can't get rusty.'

Collectables range from decorative jelly moulds to lethally sharp chopping instruments, from Victorian wooden rolling pins to 1950s Pyrex. Prices depend on rarity, material, condition and date, though Bishop warns that dating can sometimes be difficult since the same design may have remained in production for several years.

Apart from specialist dealers and antique shops, old kitchenware can be found at flea markets and car-boot sales, and perhaps even at home. 'Check your mother's and grandmother's cupboards,' recommends Christina Bishop. 'It is amazing what you can find in the family kitchen.'

A cast iron 6 pint kettle, by Beechill & Co, No. 1 size, late 19thC.
£50–60 *TaB*

A European wooden bowl, 19thC, 17in (43cm) diam.
£30–40 *WCA*

A cast iron 2 gallon cauldron, early 20thC, 8½in (21.5cm) high.
£25–30 *TaB*

l. A set of 12 coffee spoons, with coffee bean finials, cased, 1930s.
£10–12 *WCA*

FURTHER READING

Christina Bishop
Miller's Collecting Kitchenware
Reed Books Ltd, London 1995

A wicker shopping basket, 1950s, 13in (33cm) wide.
£10–15 *TaB*

A silver metal teapot, with strainer, c1920.
£35–45 *WCA*

A Sam Clarke's pyramid food warmer, comprising a ceramic pot and cover, with steel stand, brass candle holder, china saucer and glass cover, c1900, 12in (30.5cm) high.
£250–275 *BS*

Boards

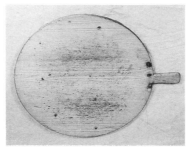

A European chopping board, c1880, 27in (68.5cm) diam.
£30–40 *WCA*

A circular pine bread board, c1900, 20in (51cm) diam.
£10–15 *NWE*

A French wooden chopping block, mid-20thC, 11 by 18in (28 by 46cm).
£15–20 *TaB*

Ceramics

A glazed earthenware cream pan, late 19thC, 18½in (47cm) diam.
£25–30 *TaB*

Two cream pans, c1880, 9½ by 5in (24 by 12.5cm).
£25–30 *AL*

l. A blue mixing bowl, c1910, 13in (33cm) diam.
£15–20 *AL*

Two gourmet boilers, No. 8 and No. 9, c1880, 6¼in (16cm) high.
£30–35 each *AL*

A Grimwade's Quick Cooker basin, with lid, one pint size, early 20thC.
£35–40 *TaB*

A Cornish ware rice jar, by T. G. Green & Co, 1950s, 5¼in (13cm) high.
£15–20 *WAC*

Three china eggs, for use with a broody hen, late 19thC.
£4–5 each *TaB*

A cream bowl, c1900, 6in (15cm) diam.
£10–15 *AL*

A German mustard pot, in the shape of a cow's head, 1920, 4in (10cm) high.
£50–60 *MRW*

A Lipton's jar, by Dundee Pottery, Glasgow, holds 4lbs, used in dairy shops for lard or margarine, c1900, 7½in (19cm) diam.
£65–75 *BS*

Choppers & Cleavers

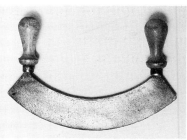

A double-handled herb chopper, c1920–30, 11in (28cm) wide.
£15–20 *WAC*

A terracotta milk bottle cooler, 1930s, 11in (28cm) high.
£12–15 *TaB*

A Cornish ware storage jar, by T. G. Green & Co, 1950s, 4¼in (11cm) diam.
£15–20 *TaB*

A butcher's cleaver, c1880, 22in (56cm) wide.
£20–30 *WCA*

A late Victorian vegetable chopper, 7 by 6in (18 by 15cm).
£15–20 *WAC*

A vegetable or herb chopper, c1940, 5 by 6in (13 by 15cm).
£15–20 *WAC*

A mid-Victorian steel herb chopper, with fruitwood handle, 6½ by 5½in (16.5 by 14cm).
£35–45 *WAC*

Egg Baskets

A wire egg or potato basket, 1930s, 13in (33cm) diam.
£14–16 *TaB*

A wire egg basket, early 20thC, 11in (28cm) high.
£12–15 *TaB*

An enamel flour bin, c1930, 10in (25.5cm) high.
£15–20 *WAC*

Enamelware

A French enamel bucket, 1950s, 10in (25.5cm) high.
£12–16 *TaB*

A French enamel coffee pot, early 20thC, 11½in (29cm) high.
£35–40 *TaB*

An enamel bread bin, with fluted lid, 1930s, 14in (35.5cm) high.
£15–20 *WAC*

Griddles

An iron griddle, 15in (38cm) wide.
£25–30 *TaB*

A griddle, c1890, 15in (38cm) diam.
£25–30 *AL*

A hand flute iron, with brass flutes on cast iron body, inscribed 'Geneva Hand Fluter Improved', American, patented 1866, 6in (15cm) high.
£250–300 *BS*

Laundry

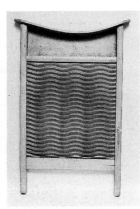

MAKE THE MOST OF MILLER'S

Condition is absolutely vital when assessing the value of any item. Damaged pieces appreciate much less than perfect examples. However, a rare, desirable piece may command a high price even when damaged.

l. A Scandinavian mangling board and roller, early 20thC, board 28½in (72cm) high.
£40–45 *TaB*

A wood and galvanised scrubbing board, 1930s, 23in (58.5cm) high.
£12–15 *TaB*

A Swedish wooden washing bat, early 20thC, 29½in (75cm) long.
£12–16 *TaB*

An American cast iron hand fluting iron, with heating block, late 19thC, 7in (18cm) long.
£200–250 *BS*

A wicker linen basket, 1920s, 26¾in (68cm) high.
£20–40 *NWE*

An American cast iron hand crimper, inscribed 'The Best', c1880–1900, 5in (12.5cm) wide.
£180–200 *BS*

An American cast iron and brass crimping machine, with original paintwork, patented 19th August 1879, 9in (23cm) wide.
£225–250 *BS*

Metal & Wooden Utensils

A European pine plunger with lid, early 20thC, 25in (63.5cm) high.
£65–75 *TaB*

A brass tally iron, on cast iron base, marked 'Bullock No. 12', poker missing, 19thC, 8in (20cm) high.
£100–115 *BS*

A wooden cheese paddle, 19thC, 40in (101.5cm) long.
£75–90 *WAC*

An iron salamander, for browning pies and pastry, mid-19thC, 27½in (70cm) long.
£35–40 *TaB*

A Victorian mechanical apple peeler, 12in (30.5cm) high.
£50–60 *AnE*

A carved wooden rack, with spoons, 1930s, 12in (30.5cm) wide.
£30–35 *TaB*

A steam-heated copper honey knife, for taking honey off hive comb, c1920, 16in (40.5cm) long.
£45–55 *BS*

A selection of knife sharpeners, c1900–30, largest 7in (18cm) long.
£7–10 each *AL*

A fish slice, c1920, 13in (33cm) long.
£10–15 *AL*

A patent crumb brush, c1920,
12in (30.5cm) long.
£10–15 *AL*

A metal nutmeg grater, early 20thC,
4½in (11cm) high.
£8–10 *TaB*

A malt spade,
19thC, 46in
(117cm) long.
£50–70 *WAC*

A lemon
squeezer,
19thC, 9½in
(24cm) long.
£20–25 *AnE*

A twisted metal
vegetable masher,
with wooden
handle, c1950,
13½in (34cm) long.
£6–8 *TaB*

Kitchenware

- Ensure kitchen scales have a complete
  set of weights – heavier weights are
  easier to find individually
- Older baking tins should not be left to
  soak in soapy water as they will rust
- Condition affects price – beware of rust,
  chipped paintwork and loose handles

A Victorian brass pastry crimper,
5in (12.5cm) long.
£18–25 *TaB*

A fruitwood meat press, c1830,
15½in (39.5cm) high.
£150–200 *AnE*

A wooden
vegetable masher,
1930s, 12½in
(32cm) high.
£6–8 *TaB*

Moulds

A set of 3 Victorian jelly moulds, largest
7in (18cm) wide.
£30–40 *TaB*

A set of 3 Father Christmas chocolate
moulds, 1920s, 5in (12.5cm) high.
£45–50 *WAC*

A pig chocolate mould, 1920s,
3in (7.5cm) high.
£35–40 *WAC*

A French pottery cheese mould,
mid-20thC, 5½in (14cm) diam.
£12–15 *TaB*

A Victorian ice cream mould,
c1890, 10in (25cm) high.
£8–10 *WCA*

r. A rabbit chocolate mould,
1920s, 4in (10cm) high.
£35–40 *WAC*

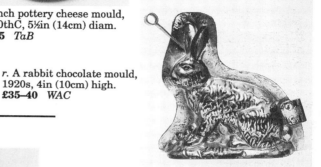

Rolling Pins

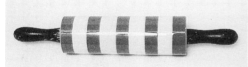

Two wooden rolling pins, c1880, 15in
(38cm) long.
£10–12 each *AL*

A Cornish ware rolling pin, by T. G. Green
& Co, 1950s, 17in (43cm) long.
£30–40 *WAC*

A Nutbrown china rolling pin, 1930s,
16in (40.5cm) long.
£12–15 *TaB*

Scales

A set of Salter's kitchen
scales, c1930, 11in
(28cm) high.
£20–25 *AL*

A set of Salter's cast iron
scales, with brass face and
detachable steel pan, to weigh
up to 14lbs, early 20thC,
12½in (32cm) high.
£70–90 *BS*

Coat & Hat Stands

A set of French wooden hat and coat hooks,
1930s, 20½in (52cm) wide.
£60–70 *LIB*

r. A beech hat and coat stand,
early 20thC, 62in (157.5cm) high.
£120–150 *WAT*

Bathroom & Washing Items

A Krauss galvanised hip bath,
early 20thC, 23¾in (60cm) high.
£30–50 *NWE*

A galvanised bath and washing
tub, c1900–20, 37½in (95cm) long.
£20–30 *NWE*

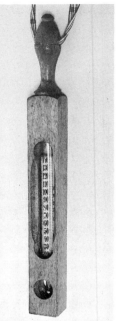

An Edwardian wood
and glass bath or dairy
thermometer, 10in
(25.5cm) long.
£10–15 *TaB*

Fireside Items

l. A set of Victorian bellows.
£80–100 *WEL*

A late Victorian copper and
iron Purdonium.
£300–400 *DaD*

*Invented by Mr Purdon in
the 19thC, this type of coal
shuttle contained a sheet
metal container for the coal
which was concealed under
the lid.*

LAMPS & LIGHTING
Hanging Lamps

A gilt-brass ceiling light, with tapering wrythen rod to circlet pierced to the underside with leaves and foliate mounts, the 6 radiating branches with leafy drip-pans, glass corona above, 20thC, 29¼in (74.5cm) diam.
£250–300 *CSK*

A hanging lamp, with pink holophane shade, 1920s, 6½in (16.5cm) high.
£80–90 *LIB*

A gilt-bronze chandelier, the polygonal baluster column cast with oval cabochons, suspension loop above, scrolling supports to square frame with fluted scroll twin-light fittings to the angles, with bud terminal, 20thC, 35½in (90cm) high.
£375–425 *CSK*

An Art Deco green and white glass hanging light, 1920s, 9½in (24cm) high.
£85–95 *LIB*

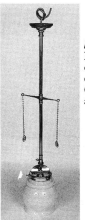

l. A brass rod hanging light, originally gas, c1900, 28in (71cm) high.
£100–120 *LIB*

An extending rod hanging light, originally gas, c1900, 32in (81.5cm) high.
£150–185 *LIB*

A hanging lamp, with engraved glass shade, c1900, 8½in (21.5cm) high.
£60–70 *LIB*

Oil Lamps

In 1850 James Young, a Scotsman, patented a refining process for producing paraffin. The fuel burned efficiently without any danger of spontaneous combustion, and its discovery lead to the massive production of oil lamps. Cheap, safe and reliable, these lamps began to replace candles as a major source of domestic lighting.

Many different designs were produced worldwide and lamps were imported to Britain from Germany and the USA. On these 19th and early 20th century examples the brass tends to be weighty whilst the glass shades can often be very light and finely made – hence the reason why many period shades no longer survive.

r. A French alabaster and gilt bronze-mounted oil lamp, the cut glass reservoir supported on a tapering column, with spreading circular base, composite capitals and entwined with leaves, on shell feet, converted for electricity, late 19thC, 21in (53.5cm) high.
£150–200 *CSK*

An oil lamp, with painted ceramic reservoir and cast iron base, 19thC, 22in (56cm) high.
£95–115 *LIB*

An oil lamp, with cast iron base, all original, c1880, 18½in (47cm) high.
£150–175 *LIB*

An oil lamp, with double burner, green glass reservoir and enamel base, c1880, 22in (56cm) high.
£250–275 *LIB*

A Victorian oil lamp, with double burner, decorated glass reservoir and cast iron base, 22in (56cm) high.
£185–200 *LIB*

l. A wall oil lamp, c1900, 15in (38cm) high.
£30–35 *AL*

A Regency style glass oil lamp, with hobnail cut and fluted hemispherical reservoir, conforming domed base, tapered octagonal faceted pillar, on gilt brass paw feet, late 19thC, 20in (51cm) high.
£450–550 *N*

A Duplex double-burner oil lamp, with blue glass reservoir, c1900, 22½in (57cm) high.
£150–175 *LIB*

A brass oil lamp, c1890,
6in (15cm) high.
£40–50 *AL*

A Duplex copper
and brass oil
lamp, c1880, 18in
(46cm) high.
£45–55 *HEM*

*A Duplex burner
has two flat wicks,
side by side,
invented by Joseph
Hinks in 1865.*

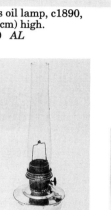

A copper oil lamp,
c1880, 16in
(40.5cm) high.
£55–65 *HEM*

A Thermidor Belcepat
brass oil lamp, 1884,
16½in (42cm) high.
£65–75 *HEM*

A brass pressure oil
lamp, by Aladdin
Industries Ltd,
Model No. 12, c1905,
23¼in (59cm) high.
£65–75 *HEM*

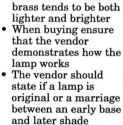

An Edwardian
brass Tilley lamp,
23in (58.5cm) high.
£80–90 *HEM*

Oil Lamps

- Good oil lamps are
  often marked on the
  burner and the
  discovery of a maker's
  name is an indication
  of quality
- A large number of
  reproduction oil lamps
  have been
  manufactured and the
  brass tends to be both
  lighter and brighter
- When buying ensure
  that the vendor
  demonstrates how the
  lamp works
- The vendor should
  state if a lamp is
  original or a marriage
  between an early base
  and later shade
- The buyer should
  always request a fully
  documented receipt

A copper and brass
oil lamp, c1880,
18in (46cm) high.
£50–60 *HEM*

r. A clear glass oil lamp,
with handle, c1900,
15in (38cm) high.
£35–45 *HEM*

l. An Edwardian brass
Tilley lamp, with
Corinthian column
stand, etched glass
shade, a fuel pump in
the base supplies
vaporised fuel to the
incandescent mantle,
24in (61cm) high.
£100–120 *HEM*

Picture Lights

A copper picture light, 1940s,
15½in (39.5cm) wide.
£75–85 *LIB*

Table Lamps

A clip-on brass picture
light, English patent
April 5, 1919, made in
USA, 6in (15cm) diam.
£95–110 *LIB*

A set of 3 brass picture lights,
each with adjustable shield,
1940s, 10in (25cm) wide.
£150–180 *LIB*

A brass table lamp,
converted to
electricity, c1875,
22⅛in (57cm) high.
£200–255 *LIB*

A brass table lamp,
with Corinthian
column stand and
decorative glass
shade, converted to
electricity, 1890s,
18½in (47cm) high.
£125–145 *LIB*

A brass table lamp,
with black ceramic base
and glass shade, c1910,
15in (38cm) high.
£100–125 *LIB*

A brass table lamp, with
white glass shade, 1920s,
13½in (34.5cm) high.
£100–130 *LIB*

An Art Deco copper
and brass lamp, with
glass shade, 1920s,
18in (46cm) high.
£120–130 *LIB*

r. A brass Pullman lamp,
with painted glass shade,
1920s, 16½in (42cm) high.
£120–140 *LIB*

A brass table lamp,
with floral decorated
glass shade, 1920s,
17½in (44.5cm) high.
£135–145 *LIB*

A silver plated table lamp,
with fabric shade, 1920s,
18in (46cm) high.
£80–100 *LIB*

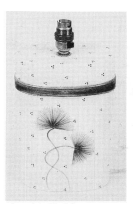

A chrome silhouette lamp, 1930s, 9½in (24cm) long.
£140–150 *GFR*

A green phenolic table lamp, with shade, 1930s, 17in (43cm) high.
£120–140 *GFR*

A black metal and chrome table lamp, with 'saturn' shade, 1930s, 22in (56cm) high.
£125–150 *GFR*

A pair of table lamp bases, 1930s, 13in (33cm) high.
£120–150 *Ber*

Wall Lights

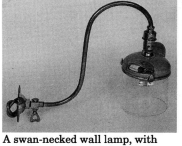

A pair of wall lights, with copper fittings, originally gas, c1900, 12½in (32cm) wide.
£200–220 *LIB*

A swan-necked wall lamp, with porcelain burner, originally gas, c1900, 11in (28cm) wide.
£85–100 *LIB*

A candelabra wall light, converted to electricity, c1875, 14in (35.5cm) high.
£85–95 *LIB*

A set of 4 brass wall lights, with holophane shades, originally gas, c1900, 9in (23cm) wide.
£400–440 *LIB*

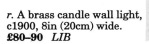

A pair of wall lights, with copper and brass fittings, originally gas, c1900, 8½in (21.5cm) wide.
£200–230 *LIB*

A pair of brass wall lights, originally gas, c1900, 9in (23cm) wide.
£185–200 *LIB*

r. A brass candle wall light, c1900, 8in (20cm) wide.
£80–90 *LIB*

A brass wall lantern, 1930s,
8½in (21.5cm) high.
£75–85 *LIB*

A brass wall lamp, with marbled glass
shade, c1900, 13in (33cm) wide.
£95–110 *LIB*

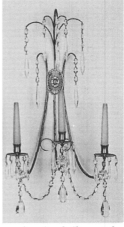

A pair of gilt-metal
wall lights, with
3 scroll branches
centred by paterae,
strung with glass
beads and hung with
faceted pendants,
20thC, 23¾in
(60.5cm) high.
£125–150 *CSK*

A pair of brass wall lights,
originally gas, with registration
mark for 1908, 10in (25.5cm) wide.
£200–230 *LIB*

A set of 3 silvered brass
Dutch style wall lights, the
twin scrolling branches
radiating from bulbous
bodies, with acorn finials
and *flambeau* terminals,
20thC, 14in (35cm) high.
£140–170 *CSK*

A pair of brass double
candle wall lights, c1910,
9in (23cm) wide.
£200–245 *LIB*

MAUCHLINE WARE

A Mauchline ware burr root
snuff box, the top printed
with a scene from a tavern
interior and verse, early
19thC, 5in (12.5cm) long.
£275–325 *SWO*

A Mauchline ware thimble
case, the top with a print
of Barmouth, containing
silver thimble, c1900,
1½in (38mm) wide.
£60–80 *MRW*

l. A Mauchline ware pincushion,
with a print of the Pump Room,
Harrogate, 1850, 1½in (38mm) long.
£40–50 *GLN*

A Mauchline ware
pincushion, shaped as a
milking stool, with a
print of Pevensey Castle
on the top, c1900, 2in
(50mm) diam.
£80–100 *MRW*

A Mauchline ware
egg cup, with print
of Skegness, 1900,
3½in (9cm) high.
£25–35 *MRW*

A Mauchline ware box, with colour
lithograph of children, c1900, 10in
(25.5cm) long.
£80–100 *MRW*

A Mauchline ware
dictionary cover,
with print of Fabyan
House, c1900, 3½in
(9cm) long.
£45–50 *MRW*

A Mauchline ware napkin
ring, with print of
Kenmore, Aberfeldy,
c1900, 1¾in (45mm) high.
£15–20 *MRW*

l. A Mauchline ware
egg timer, with a
print of the Crystal
Palace, c1900,
3in (7.5cm) high.
£60–80 *MRW*

A Mauchline ware
photograph frame, with
4 small prints of Scottish
locations, c1900, 8½in
(21.5cm) high.
£80–120 *MRW*

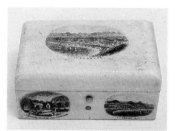

A Mauchline ware jewel box, with
various prints of Llandudno,
c1900, 4½in (11.5cm) long.
£30–40 *MRW*

A Mauchline ware
bookmark, with
print of Barmouth
Bridge, c1900,
3¾in (9.5cm) long.
£50–60 *GLN*

A Mauchline ware pincushion,
with 2 views of Windsor Castle,
c1900, 2in (50mm) diam.
£60–70 *GLN*

A Mauchline ware thimble case,
with view of Chee Tor, Buxton,
c1900, 1½in (38mm) high.
£55–65 *GLN*

MEDALS

The following section covers both military and British historical medals. As dealer Timothy Millett explains, the two fields are very different in emphasis. 'Service and military medals tend to inspire military enthusiasts and are collected for the individual name on the medal and the story behind it. Historical medals are sought after for the event celebrated and the artistry of the medal itself.' As military specialist Roy Butler enthuses, 'you read about the man, about the battle he fought and the courage it

took. There is that name inscribed on the side – you are holding his history in your hand.'

Collectors of historical medals often begin with objects of local interest, for example agricultural or exhibition medals from their area. Others might collect a particular subject, such as school prize medals or works by a particular artist or medal maker. 'It is a good idea to concentrate on a specific field,' advises Millet, 'and, as with everything else, to find a theme that really inspires you.'

Agricultural & Horticultural

A National Pig Breeders' Association silvered bronze prize, 1931, by Herbert Maryon, with inscription 'The Hillsborough Fruit Farm', the edge engraved 'Kent County Show', very good condition, 1¾in (45mm) diam.
£40–50 *BAL*

A County Dublin, North Dublin & Fingal Farming Society silver prize, 1859, by I. C. Parkes, inscribed on reverse, very good condition, 1¾in (45mm) diam.
£45–55 *BAL*

A Royal Botanic Society of London red ivory pass, legend within floral wreath, inscribed on reverse, very good condition, 1½in (38mm) diam.
£150–165 *BAL*

Exhibitions

A silver medal, inscribed 'British Empire Exhibition 1924', by E. Carter Preston, on reverse 'Make All Sure We Are One', very good condition, 2 by 3in (50 by 75mm).
£85–95 *BAL*

A Devonport Exhibition of Arts, Science and Manufacture bronze medal, with profile of Queen Victoria, the reverse with legend within a laurel wreath, very good condition, 1¾in (45mm) diam.
£35–40 *BAL*

An Eastbourne Exhibition of Sanitary Appliances and Fine Art bronze medal, by T. Hadlow, Brighton, with the figure of Minerva and exhibition centre in the distance, inscribed 'Eastbourne', very good condition, 2in (50mm) diam.
£45–55 *BAL*

Military

A group of 3 medals, Punniar Star 1843, Sutlej Campaign medal 1845–46, for Moodkee with 3 bars, Ferozeshuhur, Aliwal, Sobraon, and Army Long Service and Good Conduct medal, Victorian issue, all in good condition.
£750–850 *WAL*

A WWI pilot's group of medals: a 1914–15 Star, BWM, Victory Medal and 3 related cap badges, awarded to Lieutenant T. R. C. Birkin, Royal Flying Corps, in contemporary brass gilded glazed frame with gold plated engraved and inscribed plaque.
£475–575 *S(S)*

A Victoria India Medal, 1857–58, with Central India Bar, awarded to Surgeon J. H. Orr, 4th Cavalry, very good condition, and miniature medal.
£240–300 *WL*

l. A pewter Carmarthenshire Militia medal, 1798, good condition, 1½in (38mm) diam, in glazed case with gold rim surround.
£300–350 *S(S)*

r. A bronze specimen of the Ashanti medal, 1900, in mint condition, 4in (10cm) diam.
£300–350 *S(S)*

The Royal Mint collection does not contain a similar specimen and the origins of this particular example remain unknown.

Police

A silver Mauritius Police Department Good Conduct Medal, very good condition.
£240–280 *S(S)*

A Liverpool Police Lifesaving group comprising: a silver Liverpool Shipwreck and Humane Society, Marine medal, 3rd type, a bronze Good Service Medal and another similar in silver with 'Service Over 30 Years' clasp, all in good condition.
£225–250 *S(S)*

A group, comprising: a King's Police medal George V, 1st type, East and West Africa medal, 1887, 1 clasp, Sierra Leone 1898–99, Jubilee medal, 1887, Metropolitan Police issue, in bronze,
£260–300 *S(S)*

A Scottish Police British Empire Medal for gallantry, Civil Division, Elizabeth II, with gallantry emblem and City of Glasgow Police Bravery Medal, in gold, both in cases of issue, very good condition.
£600–700 *S(S)*

These medals were awarded to Constable Iain Harris for apprehending an armed robber who had already injured 2 civilians.

A Royal Canadian Mounted Police Long Service and Good Conduct medal, Elizabeth II issue, awarded to Superintendent C. W. J. Goldsmith, very good condition.
£425–525 *S(S)*

Political & Historical

A Lord Clive bronze medal, 1766, by J. van Nost, with bust of Clive and inscribed 'Robert Clive Baron of Plassy', very good condition, 1¾in (45mm) diam.
£85–95 *BAL*

A Dublin, York Club, silver medal, 1825, by I. Parkes, on a buckled garter, inscribed 'The Protestant Ascendancy in Church and State', very good condition, 1½in (38mm) diam.
£120–145 *BAL*

A Northumberland, Restoration of Alnwick Castle silver medal, 1766, by J. Kirk, very good condition, 1¾in (45mm) diam.
£100–125 *BAL*

A bronze Government Ministers and Members of the House of Commons medal, 1849, by Lauer, very good condition, 3¾in (9.5cm) diam.
£125–150 *BAL*

A white metal medal issued for the marriage of the Prince of Wales and Caroline of Brunswick, 1795, by W. Whitley, inscribed, very good condition, 2in (50mm) diam.
£65–75 *BAL*

Scholastic & Artistic

l. A Stonyhurst College, Lancashire, silver gilt prize medal, 1794, very good condition, 1¾in (45mm) diam.
£65–75 *BAL*

r. A Devonshire Street Academy, London, silver prize medal, inscribed 'Geography 2nd Clafs', 1810, very good condition, 1¼in (32mm) diam.
£75–85 *BAL*

The Rev W Thomas's Academy,
Enfield, silver prize medal, 1817,
very good condition,
2in (50mm) diam.
£125–145 *BAL*

An Edinburgh silver
prize medal, 1840, by
C. H. Farquaharson,
very good condition,
1½in (36mm) wide.
£85–95 *BAL*

A Royal Academy Antique
School ivory pass, 1844,
very good condition,
2in (50mm) diam.
£150–180 *BAL*

Sporting

r. A Dunlop Jubilee
International Race
Meeting at Brooklands
silver medal 1938, by
W. J. Carroll, very
good condition, in
original case of issue,
1½in (38mm) diam.
£95–115 *BAL*

A Machar Golf Club
silver medal, for the
Jamieson Monthly
Handicap, 1881,
2¾in (70mm) diam.
£825–900 *C(S)*

A Warwickshire,
Meriden, Woodmen
of Arden, lady's
silver brooch, 1858,
by I. W. & F. Thomas,
with monogram of
the Society, very
good condition,
2in (50mm) wide.
£200–225 *BAL*

l. A Duke of
Cornwall's Light
Infantry silver prize
medal, 1885, very
good condition,
1¾in (45mm) diam.
£75–85 *BAL*

METALWARE

A French white metal napkin ring, c1890, poinçon marks, 1½in (38mm) high.
£100–125 *SHa*

Two gilded metal curtain tie-backs, with opaline glass lilies, c1880, 8in (20cm) high.
£120–150 *CB*

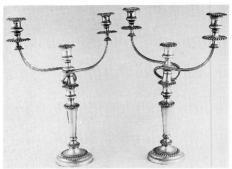

A pair of Sheffield plate two-branch candelabra, with reeded columns, leaf-chased capitals and stepped bases, early 19thC, 17½in (44.5cm) high.
£400–450 *DN*

l. A silver leaf dish, by Hukin & Heath, c1930, 8¼in (21cm) diam.
£40–45 *HEM*

An Edwardian enamelled German street sign, 24in (61cm) long.
£40–80 *MCh*

Animals & Hunting

r. A nickel dog collar, with key fastener to adjust size, and plaque with name and address of owner, c1900.
£55–65 *BS*

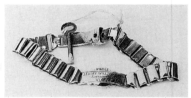

A steel and galvanised Everitt rat trap, made by H. Lane, c1900.
£65–75 *BS*

> **Miller's is a price GUIDE not a price LIST**

l. An iron saddle rack, early 20thC, 16in (40.5cm) long.
£30–35 *TaB*

A wire rat trap, 19thC, 12in (30.5cm) wide.
£70–80 *AnE*

A steel gin trap, for rabbits, 1900–20.
£9–10 *BS*

r. A steel chain dog collar, with key fastener to adjust size, 19thC.
£85–95 *BS*

Cutlery

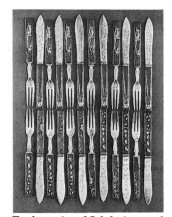

A pair of silver dolphin pattern ladles, by G. Adams, London 1845, 7½in (19cm) long.
£250–275 *AMH*

Twelve pairs of fish knives and forks, with Japanese bronze handles decorated in Komei style, with lobsters, shellfish, and figures in boats, the electroplated blades and tines engraved with fish and shells, in a fitted oak case, slight damage, 19thC.
£700–750 *HSS*

> **MAKE THE MOST OF MILLER'S**
> Condition is absolutely vital when assessing the value of any item. Damaged pieces appreciate much less than perfect examples. However, a rare, desirable piece may command a high price even when damaged.

A pair of Russian enamelled silver tongs, c1900, 5½in (14cm) long.
£120–150 *LBr*

Menu Holders

A set of 6 silver fan-shaped menu holders, by Wang Hing, chased with flowering prunus, butterflies and bamboo, with strut supports, 3in (7.5cm) high.
£275–325 *DN*

A set of 4 enamelled silver game bird menu holders, by S. Mordan & Co, depicting a pheasant, mallard, pigeon and partridge, Chester 1905.
£650–700 *DN*

Penknives

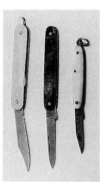

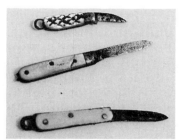

Three miniature penknives, c1900, largest 1in (25mm) long.
£30–60 each *MRW*

Three mid-Victorian mother-of-pearl, tortoiseshell and celluloid penknives, largest 1¾in (45mm) long.
£12–20 each *MRW*

A mid-Victorian mother-of-pearl penknife, in the form of a boot, 2in (50mm) long.
£25–40 *MRW*

Pomanders & Boxes

A silver egg pomander, possibly Russian, c1830, 1¼in (32mm) long.
£250–270 *LBr*

Two handmade silver miniature boxes, in the form of walnuts, oxidised to give black grooves, hallmarked, early 20thC, 1½in (38mm) long.
£65–75 *EaJ*

A German silver pomander, in the form of a gourd, c1740, 3in (7.5cm) long.
£800–850 *LBr*

r. An ivory and gold pomander, possibly Dutch, c1700, 1in (25mm) diam.
£250–270 *LBr*

Sculpture

A gilt bronze wall appliqué, cast in the form of a classical figure on acanthus leaf scroll, 20thC, 12½in (32cm) high.
£150–175 *CSK*

A bronze bust of a lady in a ball gown, signed 'Charles Masse', on a brass mounted stepped red marble base, 19thC, 16½in (42cm) high.
£850–1,000 *AH*

A German bronze cigar-smoking man, with walking stick, wearing clogs, on a green marble base, signed 'G. Jaeger', 19thC, 12¾in (32.5cm) high.
£200–250 *DA*

A bronze figure of a young tennis player, on a drum-shaped base, 20thC, 13¼in (33.5cm) high.
£175–225 *DN*

A pair of French bronzed spelter groups, each with a woman standing in a chariot being drawn by a pair of horses, on a stepped base, late 19thC, 11in (28cm) wide.
£75–95 *Gam*

Security Items

A pressed brass plate, from a Milners' Fire-Resisting Strong Holdfast Safe, c1900, 7in (18cm) diam.
£40–50 *BS*

A steel bicycle chain and lock, with key, c1900.
£40–50 *BS*

A collection of keys, c1790–1867.
£15–60 each *CS*

A pair of steel handcuffs, by Hiatt, Birmingham, with key, c1900.
£50–60 *BS*

r. A pair of steel fixed position handcuffs, by Hiatt, Birmingham, with key, c1900.
£100–125 *BS*

A cast brass plate, from a Milners' Fire-Resisting Strong Holdfast Safe, c1900, 10in (25cm) diam.
£50–60 *BS*

Silver

A pair of Scottish silver and agate salt and pepper pots, c1920, 1¼in (32mm) high.
£100–120 *LBr*

A pair of Scottish silver and agate mustard spoons, c1897, 2¼in (57mm) long.
£60–90 *LBr*

A silver porringer, London 1766, 5¼in (13.5cm) high.
£900–1,000 *WAC*

A silver four-piece tea service, comprising: teapot, hot water jug, sugar basin and cream jug, London 1929.
£550–650 *Mit*

A silver cake basket, by John Terrey, with fluted bowl, swing handle, elaborately chased and pierced vine leaf detachable rims, on a collet foot, London 1825, 30oz.
£300–350 *WL*

A Regency silver three-piece tea set, comprising: teapot with domed lid, foliate shell rim, leaf capped loop handle and spout, gadrooned body and lions' paw feet, London 1814, 11¼in (28.5cm) wide, and matching sugar bowl and milk jug, 46oz 12dwts.
£550–650 *AH*

A silver three-piece tea service, by Walker & Hall, Sheffield 1922, 40oz.
£375–450 *Mit*

A solid silver hump-back whale, with grooved underbelly, 1994, 4in (10cm) long, 12oz.
£550–600 *EaJ*

A George II silver baluster-shaped mug, with double scroll handle, by George Hunter I, London 1750, 3¾in (9.5cm) high, 5½oz.
£300–350 *DN*

A silver cream jug, in the shape of a garage oil can, 1920s.
£120–160 *BCA*

r. A pair of silver plated on copper bell winds, by Elkington & Co, 19thC, 6½in (16.5cm) high.
£250–285 *BS*

> **Miller's is a price GUIDE not a price LIST**

Toast Racks

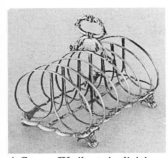

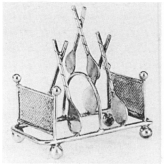

A George IV silver six-division toast rack, with crested leaf chased handle and feet, by Joseph Angell, repaired, London 1828, 7oz.
£150–200 *DN*

A William IV silver six-division toast rack, the leaf and serpent handle with monogram, on shell chased feet, by George Burrows II and Richard Pearce, London 1833, 8¼oz.
£250–300 *DN*

An electroplated four-division novelty toast rack, the handle and bars formed as tennis rackets, the end bars as nets, supported on ball feet, c1900, 3½in (9cm) wide.
£450–550 *CSK*

MILITARIA

Militaria has been growing in popularity in recent years. According to dealers and auctioneers, interest in the field is often stimulated by media coverage of military subjects in books, films and on television. For example, ever since the film *Zulu*, starring Michael Caine, was released in the 1960s, objects connected with Zulu wars have been particularly desirable, and children who first saw the film in the cinema have grown up to become specialist collectors. Another subject currently proving highly successful in the auction rooms is military headgear from the period 1750–1914, with prices at the top end of the scale running to approximately £10,000.

Militaria can be extremely expensive, but for those with less money to spend, cap badges are a good subject to start collecting. As Roy Butler of Wallis & Wallis explains, 'in the 1950s and early '60s these could be picked up for between a shilling and half a crown. Today prices begin at around £8 and go up to about £150 for rarer items.' He does, however, add a word of warning. Growing interest in cap badges has led to the appearance of reproductions. Unscrupulous traders have been known to distress these and pass them off as originals. It is always advisable to buy from a reputable and knowledgeable dealer or auction house.

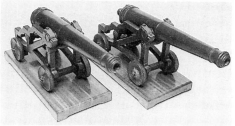

A pair of late Georgian iron cannons, on original iron carriages, barrels 30½in (77.5cm), on mahogany plinths.
£1,600–1,800 *WAL*

A watercolour, by P. W. Reynolds, showing types of the 2nd Dragoons (Royal Scots Greys), 1681–1905, signed, 12 by 17in (30.5 by 43cm), mounted and framed.
£225–275 *WAL*

P. W. Reynolds was a historian and painter of military figures. He is well known through his book illustrations, in particular Records and Badges of the British Army, *by Chichester and Burges-Short, 1895.*

A collection of 9 novelty composition figures, possibly French, including types of French army cavalry, infantry and colour bearer, c1900, 4in (10cm) high.
£100–125 *P*

A set of 50 John Player & Sons cigarette cards, Army Corps and Divisional Signs, 1924.
£10–20 *ACC*

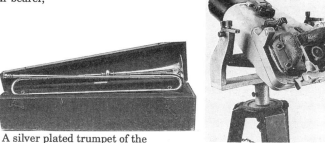

A silver plated trumpet of the Household Cavalry, by Henry Potter & Co, central knop to stem, mouthpiece with beaded bands, 27in (68.5cm) long, in baize lined wooden case.
£550–650 *WAL*

A pair of WWII German military pattern long range binoculars, probably by Zeiss, maker's label, with tripod.
£600–700 *CSK*

Ammunition & Cartridge Loading Tools

Three Bergmann rimless grooveless cartridges, c1894.
l. 5mm. **£10–15**
c. 6.5mm. **£8–12**
r. 8mm. **£1,000–1,400** *PC*

A brass 12 bore Perfect cartridge crimper, c1900, 6½in (16.5cm) long.
£150–185 *BS*

A box of 50 .38 rim fire Long Revolver cartridges, by the American Metallic Cartridge Company, USA, c1900.
£60–70 *PC*

A brass and boxwood 12 bore cartridge reloading tool, by Dixon & Co, Sheffield, registered date 'April 2 1873'.
£50–60 *BS*

A box of 10 Kynoch .303 Air Service pattern cartridges, c1926.
£6–7 *PC*

A brass 12 bore cartridge reloading tool, with horn grips, W. Hawksley patent, 19thC, 9in (23cm) long.
£95–110 *BS*

MAKE THE MOST OF MILLER'S

Condition is absolutely vital when assessing the value of any item. Damaged pieces appreciate much less than perfect examples. However, a rare, desirable piece may command a high price even when damaged.

A box of 20 Eley 7.63mm Mannlicher Auto cartridges, c1910.
£35–40 *PC*

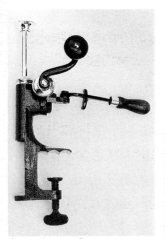

A cast iron 12 bore cartridge reloading tool, with brass fittings and wooden handles, c1900.
£75–85 *BS*

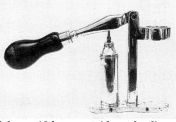

A brass 12 bore cartridge reloading tool, for removing and replacing firing cap, c1900, 6in (15cm) long.
£45–55 *BS*

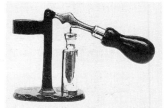

A Brags cartridge loader, c1900, 6in (15cm) wide.
£45–55 *BS*

Cap Badges

A Victorian Sussex Artillery Volunteer's silver helmet plate, 4in (10cm) high.
£100–120 *PC*

A bronze cap badge of the Drake Battalion, Royal Naval Division, WWI.
£35–40 *PC*

An officer's silver cap badge of the Duke of Cornwall's Light Infantry, hallmarked 'Birmingham 1927', with brooch pin.
£50–60 *WAL*

r. A brass cap badge of The 19th P.W.O. Hussars, 1900, 2in (50mm) wide.
£25–30 *PC*

A white metal cap badge of The Royal Armoured Corps, 1953.
£4–5 *PC*

A cap badge of the Jewish Battalion, The Royal Fusiliers, WWI.
£60–70 *WAL*

An officer's die struck silver plated cap badge of the 1st Volunteer Battalion The Welsh Regiment, blade fasteners.
£65–75 *WAL*

An officer's gilt and silver plated crossed rifles cap badge of the 3rd County of London Yeomanry (Sharp Shooters).
£70–80 *WAL*

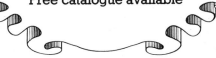

Edged Weapons

A German hunting sword, the curved blade etched with scenes from the chase, gilt brass hilt cast in high relief, short quillons formed as hunting dogs, the guard decorated with rococo designs of a stag, an eagle and a huntsman in mid-18thC dress, lion's head pommel, fluted horn grip, late 18thC, blade 19¾in (50cm) long.
£750–850 *S(S)*

A Bowie knife, by Moseley & Son, 7 & 18 New St, Covent Garden, London, the blade double-edged at the point, both sides ridged, iron disc guard, stag horn grip, iron cap and collar, c1870, 15¼in (38.5cm) long.
£550–650 *S(S)*

A left-handed dagger, probably German, in excavated condition, with tapering double-edged blade, spirally fluted wooden grip with later wire binding and Turks' heads, c1560–80, 15½in (39.5cm) long.
£600–700 *S(S)*

The incorporation of 3 additional bars for catching the opponent's blade is rare.

Military Headgear

A German burgonet, with two-piece skull extending to a peak and neck guard and joined by a narrow comb, studded with rows of lining rivets on pewter rosette washers, hinged cheek pieces, turned edges, lamination and light pitting, early 17thC, 10¼in (26cm) high.
£900–1,000 *S(S)*

An Imperial German officer's pickelhaube of the 1st Grand Ducal Hessian Leibgarde Infantry No. 115, silvered helmet badge with Star of the Order of St. Louis, scroll with date '1621', leather-backed silvered chinscales, both cockades, brass spike base mount, and front peak mount, fluted silver tall spike with black yak hair parade plume, leather and silk lining, with interchangeable fluted plated spike.
£1,400–1,600 *WAL*

l. An Imperial Prussian M 1915 Ersatz infantryman's pressed metal pickelhaube, brass helmet plate and spike, blackened roughened skull finish, both cockades, leather lining and chinstrap.
£375–450 *WAL*

A Victorian other ranks blue cloth spiked helmet of a Volunteer Battalion, The Duke of Wellington's (West Riding Regiment), white metal top mount and spike, leather-backed chinchain, ear rosettes, and helmet plate with scarlet centre backing, leather lining.
£475–575 *WAL*

Oriental

A Turkish silver inlaid sword yataghan, with 2 Arabic inscriptions dated 'AH 1222', cartouche with foliage, inlaid floral design, gilt ferrules and gripstrap with fluted corals, two-piece walrus ivory grips, swollen ear-shaped pommel, in its silver mounted leather covered embossed scabbard, 1807, blade 22in (56cm) long.
£700–800   *WAL*

Pistols & Revolvers

A double-barrelled sword pistol, by Sanders, the curved, single-edged blade cut down to 17in (43cm), turn-off cannon barrels with rotating tap, border engraved locks, swan-necked cocks, steel guard pierced with entwined foliage, stag horn grip with eagle's head pommel, 18thC.
£1,800–2,000   *S(S)*

l. A Persian Qjar garniture of helmet, shield and arm guard, the Khulah Khud bowl of one-piece, etched with seated figures surrounded by potted plants separated by gold damascened cartouches within shaped borders, adjustable nasal bar, twin plume sockets, square top spike, camail of butted steel and brass rings, 18in (45.5cm) dhal with brass reinforced border, slight wear, 19thC.
£1,300–1,600   *WAL*

r. A George III trooper's pistol.
£330–360
A pepperpot overhammer pistol, mid-19thC.
£220–260   *DaD*

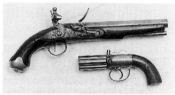

A 38 bore Queen Anne flintlock pistol, by I. Tarlys, turn-off, rifled, cannon barrel with 7in (18cm) hinged link, part-rounded, foliate engraved lock with swan neck cock and unbridled frizzen, half-stocked with pierced serpent sideplate and reeded butt cap with engraved tangs.
£2,800–3,200 *S(S)*

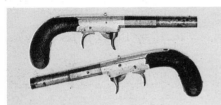

A pair of 80 bore white metal framed boxlock percussion underhammer bootleg pistols, made for the American market, ½ octagonal turn-off 4in (10cm) barrels, Birmingham proved, foliate engraved frames, chequered walnut grips, hinged cap boxes in buttcaps, slight wear, 9in (23cm) long.
£450–550 *WAL*

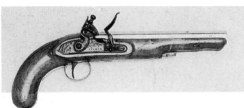

A 20 bore brass-barrelled flintlock holster pistol, Birmingham proved, top flat script engraved 'Bristol', fullstocked, foliate engraved stepped lock with 'Fisher', roller bearing frizzen spring, foliate engraved pineapple finialled brass trigger guard, barrel 13in (33cm) long.
£500–600 *WAL*

Shotguns, Fowling Pieces & Rifles

A Holland & Holland 12 bore hammer Paradox double barrel shot and ball gun, No. 15683, marked 'Nitro Paradox, Fosbery Patent', restocked in walnut, steel barrels 28in (71cm) long.
£425–500 *Bri*

Powder & Shot Flasks

A German musketeer's powder flask, with curved triangular wooden body bound with strips of iron, fitted with iron belt hook, 5 suspension rings, iron top with spring cut-off, spring nozzle closure, struck with maker's mark and Nuremburg mark, early 17thC, 12¾in (32.5cm) long.
£550–650 *S(S)*

An Austrian tooled leather shot flask, with curved drop-shaped body decorated on both sides with a running pattern of flowering foliage in relief on a stippled ground, applied with small leather hunting trophies, expanded flowerheads, loops for suspension, and a leather-covered horn shot measure also forming the nozzle plug, slight damage, c1900, 11in (28cm) long.
£120–150 *S(S)*

A pump-up air rifle, by G. & J. Deane, with interchangeable 80 bore rifle barrel and 36 bore shot barrel, both barrels browned twist and engraved, 29¼ and 46¾in (74.5 and 119cm) long, in green felt-lined oak case.
£1,200–1,500 *WAL*

A Swedish flintlock fowling piece, by Nils Lorens Björkman, with sighted slender two-stage barrel engraved and gilt with flowers and designs of gilt military trophies and flowering urns at the breech, signed, repaired, c1780, barrel 41in (104cm) long.
£900–1,000 *S(S)*

A flintlock light fowling piece, by Edward Bate, Brownlow Street, Long Acre, London, with sighted rebrowned, slender barrel formed in 2 stages, signed silver panel inlaid at the breech, repaired, c1775, barrel 32in (81.5cm) long.
£850–950 *S(S)*

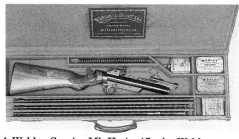

A Webley Service Mk II air rifle, by Webley & Scott Ltd, Birmingham, No. S1623, with 3 interchangeable stamped barrels, swivel locking arm with adjustable flip-up rearsight, each barrel 29½in (75cm) long, in canvas covered felt-lined case with pellet and oil containers.
£1,500–1,800 *WAL*

Uniforms

A Victorian trooper's full dress uniform of the Queen's Own Oxfordshire Hussars, comprising: fur busby, blue tunic with purple facings, white cord trim, pearl buttons, Austrian knots to cuffs and waist, and a pair of overalls with double purple stripe, dated '1897'.
£750–850 *WAL*

A late Georgian officer's full dress scarlet coatee of the South Salopian Yeomanry, black velvet facings and turnbacks to skirts, gilt loop and button to collar and cuffs, button on gilt lace diamond skirt ornaments, 8 buttons to chest, minor wear and repairs.
£425–525 *WAL*

l. An officer's green cloth peaked forage cap of The Duke of Cornwall's Light Infantry, tailor's label 'Brooks', slight damage.
£275–325

A late Victorian major's (reserve) full dress scarlet tunic of The Duke of Cornwall's Light Infantry, with gilt lace and braid trim, and a pair of matching overalls, name inside tunic 'Maj W L Harvey, 2/D of C.L. Inf. 7.6.99'.
£240–280 *WAL*

William Lueg Harvey, commissioned 46th Foot, 1878, Lieutenant 2nd Bn DCLI 1881, served in Egypt 1882, and Sudan 1884–85, Major 1894, awarded DSO in 1901 for services during the Boer War.

A Victorian officer's full dress embroidered pouch of the Volunteer Artillery, silver lace border to flap, embroidered crown over 3 solid cannon within wreath, silver plated mounts, with its red velvet-lined foul weather cover.
£350–400 *WAL*

A Georgian officer's universal pattern copper gilt gorget, engraved with crowned GR cypher and wreath.
£275–325 *WAL*

A Victorian officer's full dress embroidered sabretache of The Royal Artillery, gilt lace border embroidered Royal Arms, motto scrolls and wreath with solid gilt cannon, in its crimson velvet-lined leather foul weather cover.
£325–375 *WAL*

MINIATURE ITEMS

A mid-Victorian apprentice's mahogany chest of drawers, 11in (28cm) wide.
£450–600 *MRW*

A miniature canterbury, with a set of miniature volumes of Shakespeare, c1900, 6in (15cm) high.
£150–200 *WN*

A mid-Victorian miniature mahogany chest of drawers, c1860, 12in (30.5cm) wide.
£220–260 *TMi*

A Swiss miniature bone china tea set, c1950, tray 4½in (11.5cm) wide.
£60–80 *MRW*

A miniature longcase clock, early 20thC, 19in (48.5cm) high.
£250–300 *DaD*

A Victorian miniature papier mâché snuff box, 1½in (38mm) wide.
£25–30 *MRW*

An early Victorian miniature ivory dice holder, 1in (25mm) long.
£40–50 *MRW*

A pair of mid-Victorian metal novelty flies, ¼in (7mm) long.
£10–20 each *MRW*

Four miniature books, c1900, largest 1in (25mm) long.
£8–15 each *VB*

Three miniature Stanhopes, late 19thC, ¾in (19mm) long.
£20–50 each *MRW*

MAKE THE MOST OF MILLER'S

Price ranges in this book reflect what you should expect to *pay* for a similar example. When selling, however, you should expect to receive a lower figure. This will fluctuate according to a dealer's stock and saleability at a particular time. It is always advisable, when selling a collectable, to approach a reputable dealer or an auction house which has specialist sales.

MONEY BOXES

A pottery money box, modelled as a blue tiled house with Gothic windows, the 2 doors flanked by cherub figures and with sponged decoration to the roof ridge, inscribed 'Saving Bank', 19thC, 6¾in (17cm) high.
£575–650 *HSS*

A cast iron money box, late 19thC.
£350–400 *DaD*

l. A child's silver plated money box, c1950, 4in (10cm) high.
£38–45 *Ber*

A money box, named 'Dinah', painted in yellow and naturalistic colours, impressed name to back, early 20thC, 6½in (16.5cm) high.
£130–160 *WIL*

l. An American cast iron mechanical bank, by Shepard Hardware, depicting 2 bricklayers building a wall, some paint chipped, c1880.
£1,800–2,000 *Bon*

A novelty clockwork 'Coffin Bank', 1960s, 6½in (16.5cm) high.
£20–30 *COB*

A Beswick money box, 'Saving for a Rainy Day', Model 2802, c1983.
£50–75 *TP*

MUSICAL COLLECTABLES

A jug, probably by Meigh, moulded with 'The Distin Family – The Sax Horn Performers', the 5 figures within scroll moulded lavender ground panels, printed name, coat-of-arms and 'No. 136' in black, 6in (15cm) high.
£110–130 *MSW*

A piano accordian, by Galizi & Bros, New York, once owned by Mary Honri, used c1936–70s, cased, together with an ammunition box.
£120–150 *Gam*

Mary Honri was reputedly the first Entertainments National Services Association artist to cross the Rhine in 1945.

A jukebox, by Ami Jensen, with 40 record selections, finished in red and black, chrome window frames, top mounted speaker and record selection panel, incomplete, 31½in (80cm) wide.
£600–800 *Bon*

l. A pine violin case, c1900, 31in (78.5cm) long.
£30–40 *OPH*

Two Duo-Art pianola rolls, 'Fox Trot' and 'Always', c1926, 12in (30.5cm) long.
£5–7 each *PIA*

An Eastonola Minor pianola, unrestored, c1932, 54in (137cm) wide.
£600–650 *PIA*

ORIENTAL

An Oriental rice serving plate, decorated in blue and white with a central tree, hand coloured floral sprays in enamelled colours and gilding, 19thC, 24in (61cm) diam.
£850–1,000 *Mit*

A Chinese etched gourd, depicting a monkey legend, 19thC, 2¼in (57mm) high.
£200–250 *ORI*

A soapstone libation cup, with chilong dragon handles, 19thC, 2½in (64mm) diam.
£40–60 *ORI*

A pair of Japanese cloisonné baluster-shaped vases, brightly decorated with flowering branches and birds on a turquoise ground, within decorative borders, late 19thC, 11¾in (30cm) high.
£450–550 *DN*

Four Japanese scrolls of figures and scenes, signed 'Sakurai', 'Hyashi', 'Aien' and 'Nakamaro'.
£150–180 *DN*

A Japanese bronze vase, of compressed bottle shape, decorated with applied copper, silver and gold chrysanthemums, signed on base, c1880, 7⅜in (19.5cm) high.
£250–285 *QSA*

A pair of Chinese sleeve panels, cream silk embroidered with figures in garden landscapes, late 19thC, each panel 20 by 4½in (51 by 11.5cm).
£145–165 *PBr*

A pair of Chinese sleeve panels for a summer robe, cream coloured gauze embroidered with figures and pavilions, late 19thC, each panel 20 by 4½in (51 by 11.5cm).
£200–225 *PBr*

Four Chinese soapstone lion dog choc seals, c1920, largest 2in (50mm) high.
£100–150 *SHa*

Chinese Ceramics

A Chin Dynasty grey
pottery tile, 1115–1234 AD,
11 by 6½in (28 by 16.5cm).
£250–300 *ORI*

A Song Dynasty blue/grey glazed
pottery dish, 1127–1278 AD,
7½in (19cm) diam.
£450–500 *ORI*

A Yuan Dynasty brown
glazed earthenware
jar, Honan Province,
1275–1368 AD,
5½in (14cm) high.
£120–150 *ORI*

A Song Dynasty blue/green six-
lobed incised dish, 1127–1278 AD,
8in (20cm) diam.
£500–600 *ORI*

Two Chin Dynasty grey
pottery tiles, 1115–1234 AD,
7½ by 6½in (19 by 16.5cm).
£100–125 each *ORI*

A Kangxi period blue
and white prunus
design jar, c1700,
5½in (14cm) high.
£250–300 *ORI*

A Ming Dynasty Chinese
Provincial ware dish, c1600,
7in (18cm) diam.
£60–80 *ORI*

Chinese Marks

- The reign marks found on
  Chinese porcelain and
  other works of art record
  the dynasty and the
  emperor's name.
- They should be regarded
  with caution as Chinese
  potters often added early
  marks to later pieces as a
  mark of veneration for
  their ancestors.
- Square seal marks are
  sometimes used instead
  of the more usual
  character marks.
- Character marks should
  be read from the top right,
  downwards. Therefore,
  with a six-character
  mark, the first is the
  symbol for 'great', the
  second records the
  dynasty, the third and
  fourth marks are the first
  and second names of the
  emperor, and the fifth and
  sixth the period in which
  the piece was made.

An early Ming Dynasty
brown glazed stem cup,
3½in (9cm) high.
£120–150 *ORI*

A Kangxi period blue and
white prunus design plate,
c1700, 6¼in (16cm) diam.
£80–100 *ORI*

A pair of Kangxi period baluster-shaped wall vases, enamelled in *famille verte* with vases, flowers and foliage, damaged, 8¾in (22cm) high.
£475–550 *HSS*

A Kangxi period blue and white tea bowl and saucer, c1720, saucer 3¼in (8.5cm) diam.
£100–120 *ORI*

A Qianlong period bowl, *famille rose* decorated, c1840, 8in (20cm) diam.
£200–300 *ORI*

A Chinese Provincial ware blue and white dish, early 19thC, 10in (25cm) diam.
£60–80 *ORI*

A Chinese bowl, the interior and exterior decorated in *famille verte* with panels of figures and birds, within flower and trellis borders, 19thC, 13¼in (33.5cm) diam.
£450–500 *DN*

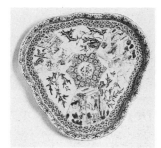

A Canton dish, 19thC, 10½in (26.5cm) wide.
£120–140 *ORI*

A Kangxi period blue and white vase, c1710, 7½in (19cm) high.
£400–450 *ORI*

A Cantonese vase and cover, decorated in typical Canton colours with panels of figures, flowers and butterflies, 19thC, 19½in (49.5cm) high.
£340–380 *Mit*

Japanese Ceramics

l. An Arita tapering square section sake bottle, with pine branch knop and square spout, decorated in underglaze blue and enamels with trees and a river landscape, chipped, probably late 17thC, 7½in (19cm) high.
£1,800–2,000 *DN*

r. An earthenware ovoid vase, brightly enamelled with a procession of figures within decorative borders, signed, late 19thC, 11in (28cm) high.
£475–575 *DN*

Imari

Imari is the Western name for Japanese porcelain made in or around Arita from the late 17th century onwards and shipped to Europe from the port of Imari.

Imari ware is richly decorated and has distinctive colours of red, blue and gold, sometimes accompanied by other colours, such as turquoise, purple, yellow and green. The term 'brocade Imari' is applied to ceramics covered with floral patterning, reminiscent of textile design.

A pair of Imari dishes, decorated with quails, late 19th, 6in (15cm) wide.
£90–100 *ORI*

r. An Imari bowl, late 19thC, 7½in (19cm) diam.
£100–140 *ORI*

An Imari figure of a seated child, dressed in Imari coloured clothing, 19thC.
£350–400 *Mit*

An Imari charger, late 19thC, 18½in (47cm) diam.
£400–450 *ORI*

Miller's is a price GUIDE not a price LIST

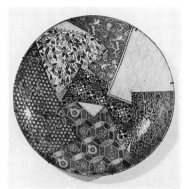

A Fukagawa brocade Imari wall plaque, decorated in polychrome enamels with overlapping panels of birds and flowers, signed in red enamel on reverse, repaired, 24½in (62cm) diam.
£375–420 *WIL*

An Imari vase, decorated with birds and flowers, late 19thC, 18in (45.5cm) high.
£300–350 *ORI*

An Imari vase, decorated with tigers in panels, on a ground of swirling green dragons, neck cracked, late 19thC, 31in (78.5cm) high.
£550–600 *MJB*

Kutani

Kutani was a small ceramics factory at Kutani Mura, west Honshu, Japan, active in the 1670–80s. Kutani ware was boldly decorated and richly coloured showing the influence of both Chinese and Arita porcelain. The Kutani factory was revived in 1823 by Iidaya-Hachiroemon and survived for some years producing imitations of the early porcelain wares as well as producing pieces decorated with gold on a red enamel ground.

A pair of Kutani baluster-shaped vases, decorated with birds and flowering branches within iron red decorative borders, late 19thC, 13¾in (35cm) high.
£500–600 *DN*

r. A Kutani porcelain melon-fluted ovoid vase and cover, painted with panels of deities within a tendril and key pattern border, in iron red and gilt, the domed cover with pomegranate finial, signed, damage, 13in (33cm) high.
£350–450 *HSS*

Satsuma

The Satsuma province in south west Kyushu, Japan, was a major area of ceramic production. From the 19th century onwards much Satsuma ware was made for export to the West. Pieces often have a crackle glaze brightly painted with gold and coloured enamels. Sometimes ceramics would be artificially aged and discoloured by exposing them to smoke or immersing them in tea.

r. A pair of Satsuma vases, decorated with panels of figures in typical Satsuma colours, 19thC, 7½in (19cm) high.
£375–450 *Mit*

A Satsuma tea set, comprising: teapot, sucrier, cream jug and 6 cups and saucers, decorated with dragons and figures.
£120–150 *RBB*

A Satsuma ovoid vase, the deep blue ground decorated in coloured enamels and gilt with brocading and foliage in gilt, painted with 2 panels of geishas in garden settings, red mark, 8¾in (22cm) high.
£575–675 *HSS*

A pair of Satsuma vases, all-over decorated with butterflies and flowers, 19thC, 6½in (16.5cm) high.
£220–250 *Mit*

A pair of Satsuma miniature vases, decorated with figures in Satsuma colours heightened with gilding, 19thC, 3½in (9cm) high.
£110–140 *Mit*

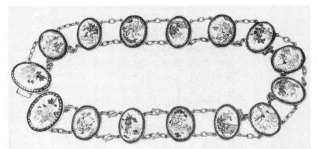

A Satsuma pottery belt, consisting of 15 oval tablets detailed alternately with figures and landscapes, within blue borders and white metal settings, c1920, in original box.
£375–425 *WIL*

A pair of Satsuma baluster-shaped vases, decorated with figures in garden settings, signed, late 19thC, 15in (38cm) high.
£650–750 *HCC*

Sculptures

A Western Han
Dynasty green pottery
figure of a horse's head,
202 BC–6th century AD,
10in (25cm) high.
£500–700 *ORI*

An Eastern Han Dynasty
part-glazed pottery figure of
a dog in a kennel, 25–220 AD,
5½in (14cm) wide.
£450–500 *ORI*

A Western Han Dynasty grey
pottery figure of a chicken,
202 BC–6th century AD,
5in (12.5cm) high.
£150–200 *ORI*

A Tang Dynasty grey
pottery figure of a horse
and rider, 618–906 AD,
16½in (42cm) high.
£1,800–2,000 *ORI*

An early Tang
Dynasty cream
earthenware
figure of a lady,
11in (28cm) high.
£500–700 *ORI*

A Japanese ivory
figure of a lady with a
basket of fruit, signed,
7¾in (19.5cm) high.
£275–300 *DN*

A pair of terracotta figures of
Samurai warriors, their
costumes painted in coloured
enamels, late 19thC, largest
11in (28cm) high.
£275–325 *RBB*

A Japanese sectional carved
ivory group of a rice farmer, a
boy, a faggot gatherer and a
seated basket maker, Meiji
period, largest figure 6½in
(16.5cm) high, on an ebonised
wood platform.
£450–550 *P(S)*

A Tang Dynasty
red pottery figure
of an attendant,
8in (20cm) high.
£80–100 *ORI*

A pair of wooden temple
figures, with black, red
and gilt colouring, early
19thC, 18in (45.5cm) high.
£500–550 *ORI*

A Chinese carved
ivory tusk figure
of a female deity
holding a sword
in each hand, a
quiver of arrows
at her side, Ming
Dynasty marks,
19thC, 13½in
(34.5cm) high.
£480–520 *MJB*

OSBORNES

Osborne plaques were produced in Faversham, Kent, between 1899–1965. The plaques show highly detailed relief representations of buildings, historical events and personalities. They were handmade from plaster, finished with wax and then hand painted. The finish was given the trade name Ivorex.

Arthur Osborne founded the business after his return from America in 1898. Most Osbornes carry the mark '© AO' on the face of the plaque, but after Arthur Osborne's death in 1943 some new editions were issued under the guidance of Walter Davis, when 'WD' was substituted.

Early plaques from 1906–1930 feature mainly brown shades but in the 1930s greens were added, and around 1940 blue tones were introduced. Some collectors concentrate on works from one period only. Approximately 660 different designs have been identified, including figurines, and some very early circular plaques relating to Dickens and buildings in Canterbury.

An Osborne plaque, inscribed 'Burns' Birthscene', c1910, 6¾ by 9¾in (17 by 24.5cm).
£45–55 *JMC*

An Osborne plaque, inscribed 'Burns' Cottage, Alloway, Ayr', c1913, 3¼ by 4½in (8.5 by 11.5cm).
£17–22 *JMC*

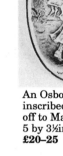

An Osborne plaque, inscribed 'Welsh Peasant off to Market', c1920, 5 by 3½in (12.5 by 9cm).
£20–25 *JMC*

An Osborne plaque, inscribed 'The Old Windmill', 6¼ by 9¼in (16 by 23.5cm).
£18–25 *JMC*

An Osborne plaque, inscribed 'The *Mayflower* as it entered Plymouth Harbour 1620 bringing the first New England Settlers', 6¼ by 9¼in (16 by 23.5cm).
£38–45 *JMC*

An Osborne plaque, inscribed 'The Return of the *Mayflower*', 4½ by 6½in (11.5 by 16.5cm).
£35–42 *JMC*

An Osborne plaque, inscribed 'Durham Cathedral', 7¼ by 9½in (18.5 by 24cm).
£42–48 *JMC*

An Osborne plaque, inscribed 'Landing of the Pilgrims 1620', 6¼ by 9¼in (16 by 23.5cm).
£38–45 *JMC*

An Osborne plaque, inscribed 'The March of Myles Standish', 4¼ by 7½in (11 by 19cm).
£38–45 *JMC*

An Osborne plaque, inscribed 'King Charles Tower, Chester', 8 by 6in (20 by 15cm).
£35–45 *JMC*

An Osborne plaque, inscribed 'Lincoln Cathedral', marked '© AObl', 6 by 8in (15 by 20cm).
£22–28 *JMC*

Two Osborne plaques, inscribed 'Buckingham Palace', c1936, and 'Tower of London', c1920, 3¼ by 4½in (8.5 by 11.5cm).
£20–25 each *JMC*

r. Two Osborne plaques, inscribed 'Wells Cathedral from Tor Hill', c1924, and 'Bath Abbey', 3¼ by 4½in (8.5 by 11.5cm).
£15–28 each *JMC*

An Osborne plaque, inscribed 'The Guildhall, Faversham', marked '© AO' 7 by 9in (17.5 by 23cm).
£35–45 *JMC*

An Osborne plaque, inscribed 'Houses of Parliament, London', marked '© AO', 7½ by 11½in (19 by 29cm).
£45–55 *JMC*

An Osborne plaque, inscribed 'Tenterden Church', 6 by 7¼in (15 by 18.5cm).
£40–45 *JMC*

An Osborne plaque, inscribed 'The Little Chapel, Guernsey', c1931, 4½ by 3¼in (11.5 by 8.5cm).
£28–32 *JMC*

Two Osborne plaques, inscribed 'Houses of Parliament, London', c1921, and 'Windsor Castle', c1918, 3¼ by 4½in (8.5 by 11.5cm).
£20–25 each *JMC*

An Osborne plaque, inscribed 'The Houses of Parliament, Ottawa, Canada', 7¼ by 9½in (18.5 by 24cm).
£38–45 *JMC*

PAPER MONEY
China

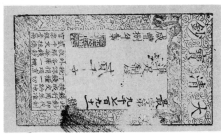

A Tai-Ping Rebellion Bank 2,000 cash note, 1858.
£80–100 *NAR*

Cuba

An El Tesoro de la Isla de Cuba 50 pesos note, 1891.
£150–200 *NAR*

Great Britain

An emergency WWII blue/pink one pound note, c1939–45.
£8–10 *WP*

A Fisher second-type United Kingdom of Great Britain and Ireland one pound note, c1922.
£40–50 *WP*

l. A Bank of England twenty pounds note, 1937.
£250–350 *NAR*

A one pound note, signed by John Bradbury, 1914.
£200–250 *NAR*

A ten pounds error note, with the Chief Cashier's signature missing.
£100–150 *NAR*

A Newcastle-upon-Tyne five pounds note, 1803.
£25–40 *NAR*

Channel Islands

A States of Guernsey WWII occupation sixpence note, dated '1st January, 1943'.
£30–40 *WP*

The States of Jersey one pound note, dated '9th May, 1995'.
50p–£1 *WP*

l. A States of Jersey WWII occupation one shilling note, 1942.
£10–15 *NAR*

A States of the Island of the Jersey five pounds interest bond, dated '1st September, 1840'.
£30–35 *WP*

Russia

A Russian 500 roubles note, with a vignette of Peter the Great, 1912.
£5–8 *NAR*

A specimen Russo-Asiatic Bank three roubles note, 1917.
£100–150 *NAR*

Scotland

A Bank of Scotland first series five pounds note, dated '1st November, 1968'.
£40–50 *WP*

The Union Bank of Scotland Limited five pounds note, dated '5th January, 1953'.
£30–35 *WP*

A Bank of Scotland twenty pounds note, dated '11th June, 1956'.
£50–60 *WP*

The Commercial Bank of Scotland one pound note, dated '3rd Jan'y, 1922'.
£60–100 *NAR*

MAKE THE MOST OF MILLER'S

Condition is absolutely vital when assessing the value of any item. Damaged pieces appreciate much less than perfect examples. However, a rare, desirable piece may command a high price even when damaged.

USA

l. A Confederate States of America 100 dollars note, 1868.
£30–40 *NAR*

A Treasury of United States of America one silver dollar note, Education series, 1896.
£200–250 *NAR*

A Bank of Lexington five dollars private bond, 1860.
£10–15 *NAR*

PAPERWEIGHTS

An American miniature double clematis paperweight, in the manner of Nicholas Lutz, with pointed dark red petals and yellow stamens, on a stem with 3 serrated leaves set above a white latticinio ground, 1¾in (45mm) diam.
£300–350 *P*

An American blue poinsettia paperweight, the flower with deep blue pointed petals around a central copy of a Clichy rose, on a short stem with 2 large and 3 small serrated leaves, 2¾in (70mm) diam.
£375–425 *P*

A Baccarat miniature buttercup paperweight, with 6 outer pink cupped petals and 5 inner white petals with a yellow stardust centre, set on a pointed stem with 5 bright green leaves, star-cut base, 1¾in (45mm) diam.
£400–450 *P*

A Baccarat paperweight, with a snail set in a dark ground amongst various leaves and flowers, limited edition of 300, 1977, 2¾in (70mm) diam.
£250–275 *SWB*

An American paperweight, by Rick Ayotte, with 3 mallards, limited edition of 50, signed, 1992, 4in (10cm) diam.
£850–900 *SWB*

A Baccarat pansy paperweight, set with a large flower with deep purple and ochre petals, on a stem with 2 leafy branches and a bud at one side, star-cut base, 2¾in (70mm) diam.
£225–250 *P*

A Baccarat paperweight, with a cobra, limited edition of 300, 1979, 3in (7.5cm) diam.
£250–300 *SWB*

A Delmo Tarsitano fruit and flower paperweight, set with an open white blossom and a black berry on a stem with 5 leaves, star-cut base, signed with an indistinct 'DT' cane, 2in (50mm) diam.
£120–150 *P*

A Clichy paperweight, with 5 C-scrolls in different coloured millefiori, 5 facets, star-cut base, central pink rose, c1850, 2¾in (70mm) diam.
£600–680 *SWB*

Three Glassform Ltd paperweights, with trail and feathered patterns, signed, c1994, 3½in (9cm) diam.
£30–40 each *GLA*

A series of ten Perthshire hollow blown paperweights, enclosing a lamp-worked swan, seal, squirrel, penguin and bald eagle with various coloured flashes, all faceted, editions of 250–400, 1973–87, largest 3½in (9cm) diam.
£300–450 each *SWB*

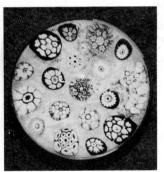

An American paperweight, by Paul Stankard, 'St Anthony's Fire', orange flowers on pale blue ground, edition of 75, 1978, 3in (7.5cm) diam.
£825–875 *SWB*

An American paperweight, 'Beta Fish', from the Lundberg Studio, signed 'Daniel Salazar', c1994.
£140–180 *MLa*

A Perthshire faceted flat bouquet paperweight, with a white double clematis, a red and white wild rose and 3 blue flowers with stardust centres, with green leaves and stems, cut with 9 windows, the base star-cut, signed with a 'P' cane, 3in (7.5cm) diam, with certificate No. 1 from an edition of 450 issued in 1979, boxed.
£175–225 *P*

A Scottish paperweight, by Paul Ysart, with spaced millefiori on muslin, 'PY' cane and circular sticker, c1970, 3in (7.5cm) diam.
£400–435 *SWB*

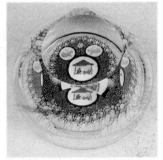

A Whitefriars paperweight, 'The Crib', 1977, 3in (7.5cm) diam.
£280–300 *MLa*

l. Two Belgian paperweights, by Val St Lambert, flashed in blue and red, faceted and heavily cut, base also heavily cut, c1880, 4in (10cm) diam.
£200–250 each *SWB*

A Whitefriars paperweight, commemorating the 25th anniversary of the reign of Queen Elizabeth II, 1978, 3in (7.5cm) diam.
£160–180 *MLa*

A Bush TR82 portable transistor radio, c1959, 12in (30.5cm) wide.
£10–20 *OTA*

The Bakelite casing for an Ekco Type AD 65 radio, designed by Wells Coates, with Harrods supply label, damaged, c1932, 15½in (39.5cm) diam.
£3,250–3,750 *CSK*

A Philco People's Set radio, Model A527, 1937, 12in (30.5cm) wide.
£250–300 *OTA*

A Westminster PWR 2/1 radio, with Bakelite case, c1947, 19½in (49.5cm) wide.
£60–100 *OTA*

A microphone, c1952, 8½in (21.5cm) high.
£40–70 *COB*

A Goblin Time Spot, radio/alarm clock, c1948, 17in (43cm) wide.
£30–60 *OTA*

An RAP table model radio, with mahogany veneered cabinet, c1946, 20in (51cm) wide.
£60–100 *OTA*

A Ekco U319 radio, c1956, 14in (35.5cm) wide.
£5–10 *OTA*

A KB Radio cardboard counter display sign, c1952, 9 by 11in (23 by 28cm). **£40–60** *COB*

A Pye battery valve portable radio, c1956, 8in (20cm) wide. **£5–10** *OTA*

A German 'Tel Tape' tape recorder, 1960s, boxed.
£8–10 *JON*

A GWR nameplate, for the Bulldog class 4-4-0 locomotive GWR 3732, 1909, 60in (152.5cm) wide. **£4,100–4,500** *SRA*

A gauge O clockwork LSWR M7 0-4-4T engine, No. 109, by Bing for Bassett-Lowke, c1914. **£800–900** *SRA*

A Great North of Scotland Railway poster, 1900. **£425–475** *SRA*

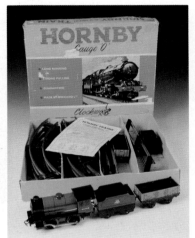

A Hornby gauge O clockwork train set, with original box and instructions, c1950. **£125–155** *WCA*

A one inch scale spirit-fired live steam traction engine, The Prince of Wales, 1981, 20½in (52cm) wide. **£950–1,200** *S(S)*

A brass steam engine boiler, 1890, 10in (25.5cm) wide. **£100–120** *COB*

A Southern Railway Schools Class locomotive nameplate, 1930, 30in (76cm) wide. **£6,500–7,000** *SRA*

A British Railways totem station sign, 1950s. **£1,500–2,000** *SRA*

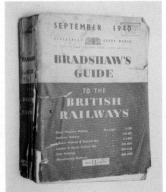

Bradshaw's Guide to the British Railways, September 1940, 7 by 5in (18 by 12.5cm). **£5–10** *COB*

A British Railways locomotive headboard, 'The Thames-Clyde Express', 1950s. **£2,500–3,000** *SRA*

A station vending machine, 1920s. **£300–400** *SRA*

The Beatles, 'Pantomime',
Flexidisc, with Fan Club
newsletter, Christmas 1966.
£30–40 *BTC*

The Beatles, 'Sgt Pepper's
Lonely Hearts Club Band', mono
LP, with cut-out insert and red
inner sleeve, 1967. **£20–30** *PC*

John Barry, 'Stringbeat',
mono LP, 1961.
£25–30 *ED*

The Beatles, album sleeve of
'Let It Be', 1960s, framed, 17in
(43cm) square. **£90–120** *CNY*

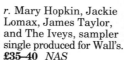

Elvis Presley, 'Blue Hawaii',
mono LP, 1961.
£15–20 *ED*

Fields, 'Fields', LP, 1971.
£10–12 *ED*

l. The Rolling Stones,
'Black and Blue',
LP, c1976.
£7–8 *ED*

r. Mary Hopkin, Jackie
Lomax, James Taylor,
and The Iveys, sampler
single produced for Wall's.
£35–40 *NAS*

Cliff Richard, 'Expresso Bongo',
mono EP, 1959.
£12–15 *ED*

Nazareth, 'Loud 'n' Proud',
LP, 1973.
£8–10 *ED*

Tommy Steele, 'The Tommy
Steele Story', 10in LP, 1957.
£18–20 *ED*

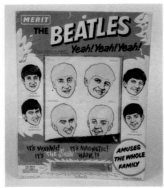

A Beatles magnetic hair game, by Merit, 1960s, 10½ by 8in (26.5 by 20cm). **£100–150** *BTC*

The Beatles Flip Your Wig game, by Milton Bradley, c1964, 11½ by 17¾in (29 by 45cm). **£100–140** *CTO*

The Beatles Big Beat toy guitar, by Selcol, 1960s, 21in (53.5cm) long. **£200–250** *BTC*

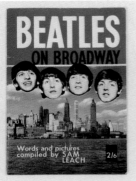

Beatles on Broadway magazine, 1964, 12 by 8in (30.5 by 20cm). **£10–15** *CTO*

A Beatles toy drum, 1960s, 14in (35.5cm) diam. **£100–150** *BTC*

l. A cork stopper, in the shape of Ringo Starr's head, 1960s, German, 5in (12.5cm) high. **£150–250** *BTC*

A Beatles Big 6 guitar, by Selcol, 1960s, 31in (80cm) long. **£300–400** *TOY*

A Beatles calendar, 1960s, 5in (12.5cm) square. **£80–100** *BTC*

A set of 4 barrel tumblers, with pictures of The Beatles, by J & L Co. Ltd, 1960s, 4in (10cm) high. **£150–200** *BTC*

Four Beatles nodding head dolls, by Carmascot, 1960s, 8in (20cm) high. **£150–200** *BTC*

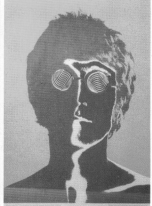

A set of 4 Beatles psychedelia-photos, for the *Daily Express*, by Richard Avedon, 1968, 31½ by 22⅛in (80 by 57cm).
£150–200 *BTC*

A Donny Osmond string puppet, in original box, 1970s, 11in (28cm) high.
£40–50 *BTC*

A Freddie Mercury Japanese embroidered 'Happy Jacket Kimono', 1980s.
£2,750–3,250 *Bon*

A framed gold disc, 'Lucy in the Sky with Diamonds', by Elton John, 1975, 10in (25.5cm) wide.
£200–240 *COB*

Frank Zappa's first Fender Stratocaster electric guitar, 1966.
£7,500–8,000 *CNY*

Seven Victor Moscoso and Neon Rose psychedelic posters, 1967.
£700–800 *Bon*

A guitar strap used by Jimi Hendrix, and 2 colour photographs, c1960.
£7,500–8,000 *CNY*

Two Michael Jackson dolls, in original boxes, 1980s, 14in (35.5cm) high.
£70–80 each *BTC*

A pair of Madonna's shoes, by Dolce & Gabbana, 1980s.
£3,750–4,250 *CNY*

A Bohemian cut glass scent bottle, with stopper, c1860, 9in (23cm) high.
£150–200 *LBr*

A cut glass scent bottle, with silver mount, Birmingham 1910, 4in (10cm) high.
£40–50 *WN*

A glass scent bottle, with brass finger chain, c1880, 1¼in (32mm) high.
£180–200 *LBr*

A Venetian glass scent bottle, c1860, 13in (33cm) high.
£200–250 *LBr*

A Venetian glass scent bottle, with brass stopper and finger chain, c1880, 2¾in (70mm) high.
£240–260 *LBr*

A painted porcelain scent bottle, with gold screw top, c1800, 2¼in (57mm) high.
£250–270 *LBr*

An American glass scent spray, decorated with a flower, c1920, 3¼in (8.5cm) high.
£60–80 *LBr*

A Roger & Gallet glass scent bottle, c1910, 4in (10cm) high.
£30–35 *LBr*

A glass double-ended scent bottle, with silver tops, c1880, 5in (12.5cm) long.
£150–200 *LBr*

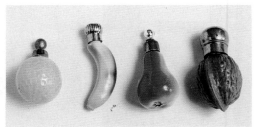

Four porcelain novelty scent bottles, in the form of a lemon, banana, pear and walnut, c1900, 2½in (64mm) long. **£125–150 each** *LBr*

A Czechoslovakian atomiser and powder bowl, in original box, c1920, 8½in (21.5cm) square.
£500–600 *LBr*

An iridescent glass scent bottle, 1993, 5in (12.5cm) high.
£35–45 *GLA*

A pair of stands, in the form of cats, holding bottles of 'Indiscreet' and 'Primitive' scent, by Max Factor, c1950, 4¼in (11cm) high.
£10–15 each *LBe*

A vaseline glass scent bottle, c1930, 3¼in (8.5cm) high.
£60–80 *LBr*

Three novelty gifts, containing 'Soir de Paris' scent, by Bourjois, c1930, 4½in (11.5cm) high.
£75–90 each *LBe*

r. A Bakelite and glass 'Jockey Club' scent bottle, retailed by Woolworths, c1930, 2in (5cm) high.
£20–25 *LBe*

A glass scent bottle, c1930, 5in (12.5cm) high.
£80–90 *LBr*

A 'Californian Poppy' scent bottle, c1930, in Bakelite case, 3in (7.5cm) high. **£40–50** *LBe*

A scent bottle, by Vigney, in the form of a golly, c1930, 3½in (9cm) high, in original box.
£300–350 *LBr*

A Bakelite top hat, containing a bottle of 'Mischief', by Saville, c1940, 3¾in (9.5cm) high, in original box.
£55–65 *LBe*

A six-sided embroidered pincushion,
c1900, 3¾in (9.5cm) wide.
£20–25 *MRW*

A late Victorian silk
and lace pincushion,
8½in (21.5cm) square.
£15–25 *Ech*

A gold needle
holder, c1850,
2½in (64mm) long.
£325–350 *GLN*

A Japanese metal-bound sewing box,
with marquetry inlay and lacquered
panels, c1890, 15in (38cm) high.
£175–200 *WCA*

A turned mahogany
sewing clamp, with
pincushion top, 19thC,
5½in (14cm) high.
£50–65 *GLN*

A tooled leather needle case,
c1830, 2in (5cm) wide.
£40–50 *GLN*

A metal thimble, contained in a Tartan
ware fitted box, c1850, 1½in (4cm) long.
£75–85 *GLN*

A needle holder, decorated with glass beads over
ivory, 19thC, 3¾in (9.5cm) long.
£50–60 *GLN*

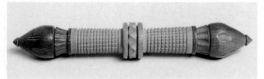

A turned wood needle holder, 19thC,
4in (10cm) long.
£20–25 *GLN*

A silver pincushion, in the form of a turtle,
Birmingham 1906, 3in (7.5cm) long.
£200–220 *WAC*

PHOTOGRAPHS

A sepia photograph, on card, by
E. Ireland, 25 Lr. Mosley St,
Manchester, c1860, 6½ by 4in
(16.5 by 10cm).
£10–15 *MRW*

A photograph, by Charles
Lutwidge Dodgson, (Lewis
Carroll 1832–98), mounted
as a visiting card, 3½ by
2½in (9 by 6.5cm).
£1,500–2,000 *DW*

r. A view of Naples Harbour,
c1870, 8 by 10in (20 by 25cm).
£15–20 *DW*

A Victorian *carte de visite*
viewer, marked 'Souvenir de
Paris', 8 by 5in (20 by 12.5cm).
£50–75 *MRW*

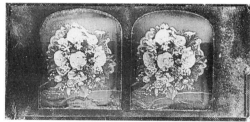

A stereoscopic daguerreotype, of Still Life of
Summer Flowers, by T. R. Williams, with
painted black arched top surround, paper taped
with printed credit label verso, mid-1850s.
£375–475 *Bon*

*Thomas Williams (1825–1871) was among the
top British daguerreotypists of the 1850s.*

A stereoscopic daguerreotype, A Baby Asleep,
by T. R. Williams, hand coloured, signed on the
black painted arched top 'T.R.W. 236 Regent
St', with printed credit label verso, mid-1850s.
£3,500–4,000 *Bon*

A view of a harbour, possibly in Scotland, c1880, 8 by 10in (20 by 25cm).
£5–10 *DW*

As with postcards, topographical photographs including people, transport, etc, are popular.

A albumen print of a view of Constantinople harbour, c1880, 8 by 10in (20 by 25cm).
£10–15 *DW*

A photograph of Leamington Spa Cycle Club, c1900, 10 by 12in (25 by 30.5cm).
£20–30 *MRW*

Photographs

- Stereograph – two almost identical pictures which, when viewed through a special glass or stereoscope, form a single three-dimensional image
- Daguerreotype – one of the earliest photographic processes in which the image was produced on iodine-sensitized silver and developed in mercury vapour

A mid-Victorian *carte de visite* album, with original cards depicting an aristocratic Yorkshire family, 9in (23cm) wide.
£80–120 *MRW*

A photograph album, containing photographs of views of the Lake District, each with pen and ink drawn borders, c1880.
£440–480 *DW*

A *carte de visite* photograph album, bound in leather with a clasp, with chromolithographic decoration on the birds, c1880–90.
£30–40 *DW*

Such albums usually contain 8 decorated pages, and another 8 to 12 blank pages with cut-outs for photographs.

A 9ct gold pendant, with a photograph of a young lady, c1906, 1in (25mm) diam.
£40–50 *AnE*

r. A Woodbury type cabinet photograph of Buffalo Bill's Wild West Show, depicting John Nelson, who performed for Buffalo Bill, c1890, 6½ by 4in (16.5 by 10cm).
£70–80 *DW*

JOHN NELSON,
Scout, Interpreter and Guide.

BUFFALO BILL'S WILD WEST.

PLAYING CARDS & BOARD GAMES

Probably originating in the Middle East, playing cards are not recorded in the West until the 14th century. First appearing in Italy, they rapidly spread across Europe, their popularity aided by the invention of printing in the 15th century.

Designs and suitmarks varied from country to country. The earliest known Islamic packs show how court cards were represented by arabesques since religion forbad the portrayal of the human figure. Italian court cards were all male – king, knight and jack – and suitmarks included swords, cups, coins and batons. In Germany, the queen was introduced

and suit marks were standardized as hearts, hawkbells, leaves and acorns, which are still in use today. The now familiar symbols, hearts, clubs, diamonds and spades, were devised in France around 1480. The French soon became the largest producers and exporters of playing cards, and it is from their model that the traditional English pack of cards, the standard international deck, derives.

Interest in card collecting has been growing steadily. The English Playing Card Society was founded in 1984 to promote the study of English playing cards and card games, their makers and designers.

A non-standard pack of cards, by Rowley & Co, comprising: King of Trefoils, in green, representing Spain and the peasants, Queen of Lozenges, in yellow, representing Prussia and the nobles, Jack of Chalices, in red, representing England and the clergy, King of Pikes, in black, representing France and the citizens, and Ace of Pikes, dated '23 June 1765', 3½ by 2½in (9 by 6.5cm).
£650–750 *PC*

A Piques pack of cards, by Gibson, Hunt & Son, in full colour, 1801, 3¼ by 2¼in (8.5 by 5.5cm).
£200–250 *PC*

The ace of spades is known as a 'Garter Ace' because it is similar to a garter (Order of the Garter), and shows the amount of tax that had to be paid to the Commissioners of Stamps for each pack produced. Here it is 2s per pack.

The game of The Golden Egg, by E. & M. A. Ogilvy, pack of 32 cards and a 'golden' egg, with illustrated wooden box, 1860, 5½ by 8in (14 by 20cm).
£75–100 *PC*

A standard pack of cards, by De La Rue & Co, second design, 52 cards in full colour, 1834, 3¾ by 2½in (9.5 by 6.5cm).
£200–250 *PC*

A pack of cards, by Goodall & Son, 1862, 3¾ by 2½in (9.5 by 6.5cm).
£200–250 *PC*

The reverse side of these cards is full colour showing the coat-of-arms of the Prince of Wales, and the court cards are 'double-ended'.

A game of The Muddled Menagerie, by Valentine, 52 cards in full colour, 1900, 3½ by 2¾in (9 by 7cm).
£20–25 *PC*

The game of Newmarket,
by Multum in Parvo, 1900,
3½ by 2½in (9 by 6.5cm).
£40–50 *PC*

A game of Happy Families,
by John Jaques & Son, 1900,
3¾ by 2¾in (9.5 by 7cm).
£20–25 *PC*

A double pack of cards, by Goodall
& Son, produced in full colour for
the Coronation of King George V
and Queen Mary, 22 June 1911,
3¾ by 2½in (9.5 by 6.5cm).
£90–100 *PC*

A boxed set of 4 packs of cards, by
Universal Playing Card Co Ltd,
produced for the Prince Line
Services shipping company, the ace
of spades showing Prince of Wales'
feathers, 1920, 3½in (9cm) long.
£90–100 *PC*

A Waddington's first design
pack of cards, showing an
anonymous ace of spades,
with 'Spratts Dog & Puppy
Cakes' on reverse, 1922,
3½ by 2½in (9 by 6.5cm).
£65–75 *PC*

A British Legion pack of cards,
produced by the Universal
Playing Card Co Ltd, the ace
of spades and court cards in
full colour, the reverse black
and white on red, 1930,
3½ by 2½in (9 by 6.5cm).
£8–10 *PC*

Board Games

r. A pack of Congress
playing cards, by the
US Playing Card Co,
Cincinnati, Ohio,
c1930, 4 by 2½in
(10 by 6.5cm).
£8–10 *LBe*

A set of engraved bone
and bamboo Mah-Jongg,
with money counters, teak
racks and set of rules, in a
teak case, c1900, 18in
(45.5cm) wide.
£200–250 *QSA*

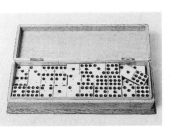

A bone and ebony nine-point
domino set, late 19thC,
box 11in (28cm) wide.
£50–70 *TMi*

A bone and coromandel
cribbage board, 1880s,
11in (28cm) long.
£60–80 *MRW*

Chess

A Staunton pattern ebonised and boxwood weighted chess set, used by G. F. Anderson, c1900, king 4in (10cm) high.
£100–150 *TMi*

l. The Rose Chess set, lead pieces in original box, c1940, king 2½in (6.5cm) high.
£50–70 *TMi*

The Waterloo Chess set, by Franklin Mint, alloy, with table, 1984, king 2¼in (5.5cm) high.
£300–400 *TMi*

Chess

- Chess sets have been commanding high prices in the current market, and there are now specific auctions devoted to chess.
- Condition and completeness are all important, as are quality of carving and material. High prices can be gained by antique sets over 100 years old, in bone and ivory, which often originated in the East.
- British chess sets from the 19th and early 20thC are very collectable. Manufacturers to look out for include John Jaques & Sons, Staunton, Calvert, Fisher and William Lund.

A Regent's pattern aluminium chess set, c1930, king 2in (5cm) high.
£30–50 *TMi*

Twenty-four red and green tinted glass chessmen, some damage, 20thC, 3½in (9cm) high.
£140–170 *DN*

Dice

Three late Victorian wooden dice, largest ½in (12.5mm) square.
£8–12 each *MRW*

r. Three Victorian blue, white and black glass dice, largest ¼in (6.5mm) square.
£5–10 each *MRW*

Nine Victorian bone and ivory dice, largest ¼in (6.5mm) square.
£5–10 each *MRW*

RADIOS, RECORDING & TELEVISIONS
Radios

An Ekco Type A22 All Electric radio receiver, the circular silvered wave band indicator enclosing speaker, with 3 control knobs below, in a Bakelite drum case, on arched rectangular base, c1930, 14in (35.5cm) high.
£400–450 *P(HSS)*

An Osram Music Magnet kit radio, c1928, 9in (23cm) high.
£50–80 *OTA*

An Edison Bell twin crystal set, c1924, 7in (18cm) high.
£150–200 *OTA*

An Ultra Coronation Twin mains/battery portable radio, with Bakelite case, 1953, 7½in (19cm) high.
£40–80 *OTA*

A Zetavox Model A radio, with a veneered and solid wood cabinet, c1932, 19in (48.5cm) high.
£300–400 *OTA*

A Ferranti 145 radio, with Bakelite case, 1946, 18in (45.5cm) high.
£150–200 *OTA*

A Philips 462A radio, with Bakelite case, c1948, 11in (28cm) high.
£60–80 *OTA*

A Bush DAC 90A radio, with brown Bakelite case, c1950, 9in (23cm) high.
£40–60 *OTA*

An Ekco M23 radio, with Bakelite case, c1933, 16in (40.5cm) high.
£180–220 *OTA*

Recording

r. A Meico microphone, 1920–30s, 3¾in (9.5cm) diam.
£40–60 *JON*

A Reslo ribbon microphone, 1960s, 2¼in (6cm) high.
£40–50 *JON*

A Simon Cadenza ribbon microphone, 1960s, 6½in (16.5cm) high.
£40–50 *JON*

> **Miller's is a price GUIDE not a price LIST**

l. A Swiss Nagra III tape recorder, 1960s, 14in (35.5cm) wide.
£550–600 *JON*

Televisions

r. A Bush 22 television, in Bakelite case, c1952, 15in (38cm) wide.
£150–200 *OTA*

l. A GEC BT1091 television/bookcase, c1949, tube 9in (23cm).
£80–100 *OTA*

RAILWAYANA

Train spotters are renowned for their tireless devotion to their subject, and certainly railwayana auctions achieve consistently strong results. Objects tend to sell to private collectors, rather than dealers for sums which would no doubt astonish the original railwaymen who once used these formerly humble items. Recent success stories include a GWR brass cabside numberplate '4000', carried by the ex-Star Class 4-4-2 locomotive No. 40, the North Star, between 1906–12. Extremely rare because of the three noughts in the number, this plate was described by the *Antiques Trade Gazette* as the railwayana equivalent of the Maltese Falcon. Lost for many years, it was finally discovered in Australia, shipped back to Britain and made an impressive auction price of over £7,000. Another fortunate find, featured in the Colour Review (page 346), is the nameplate 'Bullfinch'. Discovered blocking up a fireman's fence near Shrewsbury, this 1909 Great Western Railway nameplate was sold at auction for over £4,000.

A London, Brighton and South Coast Railway clothes brush, c1890, 14¼in (36cm) long.
£50–60 *Sol*

l. A Southern Railway steel and alloy electric train intermediate single line key token machine, by Tyer & Co Ltd, c1945, 20¾in (53cm) high.
£250–300 *Sol*

A GWR cast iron signal finial, c1930, 23½in (60cm) high.
£20–25 *Sol*

A London, Brighton and South Coast Railway guard's hand lamp, made at Brighton works, restored, dated '1887', 13¾in (35cm) high.
£60–80 *Sol*

A Great Western Railway carriage door brass hinge, c1930, 3in (7.5cm) high.
£13–15 *COB*

A Southern Railway copper 'Sugg' gas lamp, from Fareham station, c1940, 16¼in (41cm) high.
£30–40 *Sol*

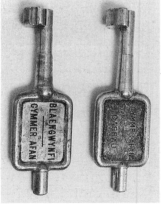

Two GWR alloy single line key tokens, from the Welsh valleys, c1900, 7¾in (19.5cm) long.
£30–40 *Sol*

Ephemera & Pictures

A black ink and coloured drawing of Locomobile Rousser, signed 'Bonnet', 16¼ by 19¾in (41.5 by 50cm), framed and glazed, and another, depicting a French 2-2-2 locomotive No. 33, signed 'Bonnet Eng', with parts notation, 11 by 16in (28 by 40.5cm).
£150–175 *CSK*

A Union-Castle Line Royal Mail Service poster, early 1920s.
£400–500 *SRA*

A London Midland and Scottish Railway poster, 'The Peak District', 1930s.
£400–500 *SRA*

l. An oil on canvas of LNER 4472, the Flying Scotsman, on the turntable, signed 'Alan Fearnley', 20thC, 20 by 30in (51 by 76cm).
£950–1,200 *CSK*

r. A collection of London Transport maps, 1920s–60s, all folding to various sizes.
£2–3 each *DW*

Model Locomotives

A 5in gauge coal-fired model of an LMS 2F tank locomotive with valve gear, supplied with display track and finished in LMS black with '11270' to tank sides, 27½in (70cm) long.
£2,500–2,750 *AH*

A GWR King Class 3½in gauge model locomotive, 1950s.
£4,000–5,000 *SRA*

Nameplates

An LNER nameplate, 'Grimsby Town', 1930s, 45in (114.5cm) long.
£10,000–12,000 *SRA*

A GWR Castle Class nameplate, 'Hampden', 1940s, 60in (152cm) long.
£10,000–12,000 *SRA*

A London Midland and Scottish Railway Jubilee Class nameplate, 'Palestine', 1930s, 38in (96.5cm) long.
£4,000–4,500 *SRA*

Numberplates

An ex-War Department cast iron smokebox numberplate, '90067', 1943–64, 22in (55cm) long.
£120–130 *Sol*

A Western Railway cast iron smoke box numberplate, '1607', 1949–65, 20in (51cm) long.
£110–130 *Sol*

Signals

r. A block signalling instrument, by L. Clark, Muirhead & Co, Telegraph Engineers, Regency Street, Westminster, with a varnished wood case, 17½in (44.5cm) high.
£100–150 *CSK*

Signs

A LSWR cast iron warning sign, 'Stop Look & Listen Before Crossing the Line', c1900, 32in (81.5cm) wide.
£50–60 *Sol*

l. A LB & SCR paper warning notice, on original board, c1904, 33in (84cm) high.
£40–50 *Sol*

ROCK & POP

The first rock and pop auction was held in 1981, and sales now form a regular part of the auction calendar in Britain and the USA. Some of the more curious objects that have been collected in the past include Elvis Presley's nail clippings, a piece of toast discarded by George Harrison and, perhaps the most bizarre of all, a unique selection of authentic casts of pop stars private parts, taken from life over the years by the infamous and dedicated Ms Cynthia 'Plastercaster'. Most enthusiasts, however, are happy to satisfy themselves with an autograph or some slightly less intimate piece of memorabilia.

Items associated with The Beatles are undoubtedly the most collectable. Other sought after objects include those associated with Buddy Holly and Elvis Presley from the 1950s, and 1960s groups such as the Jimi Hendrix Experience, the Rolling Stones and the Doors. Signatures of stars who are no longer alive tend to be the most desirable and the recent deaths of Kurt Cobain, Frank Zappa and the Grateful Dead's Jerry Garcia have brought material associated with them into the saleroom. Memorabilia connected with great living rock stars is also collectable, but who will be the names to look out for in the future?

'Contemporary Britpop bands such as Blur, Oasis, and Pulp have inspired a whole new generation of fans who, in 15 years' time, might well go to a rock and pop auction to buy back a piece of 1990s nostalgia,' advises Jon Lewin, producer of Soundbite, BBC Radio One's rock magazine show. 'Hang on to promotional material and if possible get things signed.'

A colour photograph of Sam Cooke, mounted with a gold disc of 'You Send Me', and a piece of paper signed 'Lots of Luck Sam Cooke', 11½ by 15½in (29 by 39.5cm).
£385–425 *CNY*

A presentation multi-platinum disc and cassette award for 'Slippery When Wet', by Bon Jovi, RIAA certified, strip plate format, presented to Polygram Records, 19½ by 15½in (49.5 by 39.5cm)
£385–425 *CNY*

A silkscreen poster for the Cream playing at the Ricky-Tick, Windsor on 7.1.1967, 30 by 20in (76 by 51cm).
£350–400 *Bon*

r. A 'Dead in Vermont' T-shirt, with inscriptions and signatures of members of The Grateful Dead.
£385–425 *CNY*

l. A black and white photograph of Jim Morrison, mounted with a Willie Mitchell 'Live' advertisement, signed 'J. Morrison', 14¼ by 19¼in (36 by 49cm).
£385–425 *CNY*

A Marine Band Hohner harmonica, signed by
Bob Dylan in black felt pen, with case.
£1,500–2,000 *Bon*

Billy Fury's desk diary, 1964,
photographic folder, personal letters,
lyrics, postcards and other items
collected by him, all lyrics and letters
in his handwriting.
£2,000–2,500 *Bon*

A black and white photograph
of Buddy Holly playing guitar,
signed by him in black biro,
mounted, framed and glazed,
8½ by 6½in (21.5 by 16.5cm).
£300–350 *Bon*

A yellow, blue and
white check suit,
tailor-made for
Elton John.
£800–1,000 *Bon*

A black and white
photograph of Jimi Hendrix
in performance at the
Carousel Theatre,
Farmington, Massachusetts,
1968, signed 'Leonard J.
Eisenberg Carousel, MA.
August 26, 1968', 19¾ by
15¼in (50 by 38.5cm).
£275–320 *CNY*

r. A colour advertisement for
the Eurythmics' 'They've Got
The Golden Touch' tour, signed
in blue felt pen 'Annie Lennox',
19 by 15½in (48 by 39.5cm).
£160–200 *CNY*

A black and white
promotional poster of Jimi
Hendrix, by Track Record,
together with a double-sided
handbill for The Newport
Festival at Devonshire
Downs, 20th June 1969.
£600–700 *Bon*

A Michael Jackson
signature, on a sheet of
Hilton Hotel notepaper,
good condition.
£50–60 *VS*

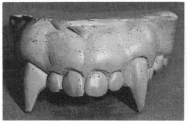

The mould used for the animal
'fangs' to fit Michael Jackson
in the video *Thriller*.
£350–380 *CNY*

A colour billboard advertisement for Madonna, 'Ciao Italia: Live From Italy', inscribed and signed in gold felt pen 'Madonna', 18½ by 15½in (47 by 39.5cm), framed.
£280–320 *CNY*

A colour poster for Mama Cass and Her Musicians, and The Debbie Reynolds Show, at the London Palladium, and another for 'Mama' Cass Elliot and Paper Lace, largest 30 by 20in (76 by 51cm).
£175–200 *CNY*

A concert poster for The Move and The Nice at Town Hall, Torquay, c1967, 30 by 20in (76 by 51cm), mounted, framed and glazed.
£500–600 *S*

The gold award for the Queen single 'Crazy Little Thing Called Love', presented to Paul Prenter, in original envelope.
£275–325 *Bon*

A blue vinyl Nirvana album, with jacket Incesticide, signed on the cover 'Kurt', 'Chris' and 'David', 1992.
£620–700 *CNY*

A colour advertisement for Queen – The Works, signed across the front 'Freddie Mercury', 19½ by 15½in (49.5 by 39.5cm), framed.
£425–500 *CNY*

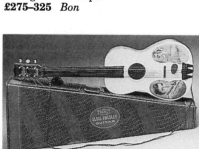

An Elvis Presley musical toy guitar, with transfers of Elvis and 'You ain't nothin' but a hound dog', and 'Love Me Tender' logo, with original carboard box, 1950s, 31½in (80cm) long.
£675–750 *CNY*

A silver ring, custom-designed for Elvis Presley in 1976, with images of 10 people in compromising positions.
£5,000–5,500 *CNY*

A silkscreen poster for The Rolling Stones at the Ricky-Tick Club, Windsor, c1963, 20 by 30in (51 by 76cm).
£1,000–1,200 *Bon*

A black and white poster for the final concert of The Velvet Underground, at Max's Kansas City, New York, 1968.
£325–375 *Bon*

A poster for the Sex Pistols' Anarchy in the UK Tour at The 400 Ballroom, Torquay, 1976, small tear, 29 by 19¾in (74 by 50cm).
£150–200 *S*

A Gary Moore Ibenez Roadstar II guitar, made c1983 and owned by Gary Moore for 10 years, signed in silver felt pen.
£2,750–3,000 *Bon*

Used on numerous live appearances between 1983 and 1984, also on Ibenez guitars' promotional poster from 1984.

A cream felt stetson with feather trim, worn on stage by Dave Hill of Slade and signed 'Best Wishes, Dave Hill' on the inside, with a black and white photograph of Noddy Holder and Dave Hill wearing the hat, also signed.
£225–275 *Bon*

A photograph of The Yardbirds, a ticket for a Blackpool gig, 11th Sept, 1965, and a full set of signatures, all in common mount.
£280–320 *Bon*

> **Miller's is a price GUIDE not a price LIST**

A pair of cowboy boots once owned by Keith Moon of The Who, in tan leather and skin, size 9A, labelled 'Sheplers Inc. The World's Largest Western Stores', 1970s.
£500–600 *S*

These boots were given by Keith to John Wolff, a member of the band's road crew, as they were uncomfortably narrow. Wolff also found the same problem so they have been worn very little.

A half-length colour photograph of Queen star Freddie Mercury, 12 by 8½in (30.5 by 21.5cm).
£150–180 *VS*

A music song sheet for 'My Generation' by The Who, signed by all group members, mounted, framed and glazed.
£340–400 *Bon*

Beatles

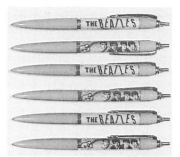

A collection of 15 pens, in red plastic and chrome, printed with images of The Beatles, 1960s.
£225–265 *Bon*

A Beatles headscarf, by Blackpool Publishers, 1960s, 26in (66cm) square.
£30–50 *BTC*

Two signed ceramic tiles, made by Carter Tiles, of Paul McCartney and Ringo Starr, 1960s, 6in (15cm) square.
£30–50 each *BTC*

A Beatles Li-Lo Air Bed, 54in (137cm) long.
£250–300 *BTC*

A Paul McCartney doll, with rooted hair, 1960s, 4½in (11.5cm) high.
£40–50 *BTC*

l. A morning suit, made for John Lennon by Doug Millings for the film *A Hard Day's Night*, 1960s.
£3,500–4,000 *Bon*

A Beatles handkerchief, 1960s, 10in (25.5cm) square.
£40–50 *BTC*

Four pairs of Ballito Beatles stockings, with coloured heads around the welt and Beatles heads and guitars woven throughout the legs, all unopened and in original packaging.
£300–350 *Bon*

A lamp shade, decorated with prints of The Beatles' heads and their music, 1960s, 6½in (16.5cm) high.
£150–200 *BTC*

Four sweet dishes, each with a head-and-shoulders print of one of The Beatles, made by Washington Pottery, 1960s, 4½in (11.5cm) diam.
£150–200 *BTC*

A road stud removed from the famous zebra crossing in Abbey Road, and 2 photographs of the re-surfacing and removal of the crossing on 5th March 1994.
£400–450 *Bon*

l. A metal beetle brooch enclosing a photograph of The Beatles, 1960s, 1½in (38mm) high.
£80–100 *PC*

A 'New Sound Guitar', made by Selcol, decorated with prints of The Beatles, 1960s, 23in (58.5cm) long.
£75–100 *BTC*

A pillow, with prints of The Beatles' heads, 1960s, 10in (25.5cm) square.
£60–80 *BTC*

A white cotton T-shirt, worn by John Lennon, featuring a yellow grapefruit over a body, inscribed to the right 'Yoko Ono', mounted with a colour photograph of John Lennon, 35¾ by 24in (91 by 61cm), framed.
£380–420 *CNY*

A Rickenbacker Model 1996 short scale guitar, imported by Rose Morris, 1964.
£1,500–2,000 *CTO*

An original poster for Rory Storm, with The Beatles as support band, Hamburg, c1961.
£375–450 *Bon*

A brick from The Cavern, with plaque of authenticity and original box and bag, one of 5,000 sold by Royal Life in 1983, when the site was developed.
£125–150 *CTO*

A Beatles lined notepad, US copyright, 1964, 10 by 8½in (25 by 21.5cm)
£25–30 *CTO*

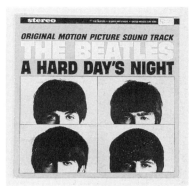

An LP of the soundtrack of *A Hard Day's Night*, United Artists label, 1964.
£25–35 *CTO*

Signatures

Beatles signatures were often faked by the group's associates in order to keep up with the huge demand from fans. According to Rock and Pop specialist Stephen Maycock, 'in the 1960s the one way to be sure that a signature was genuine was to see the band member signing it in person'. Today, only experience enables the enthusiast to distinguish the true item from the imitation. Maycock recommends that collectors should obtain a guarantee from the vendor stating that the purchase price will be returned should a signature prove to be a forgery.

l. A 'With The Beatles' album, Parlophone Records, signed on the front cover by all 4 members of the group, 1963.
£1,500–1,800 *CSK*

r. A single record, 'Love Me Do', Parlophone Records, signed on the label by all 4 members of the group, 1962.
£2,400–2,800 *CSK*

'Love Me Do' was The Beatles' first UK Top Twenty hit.

A black and white photograph, signed in black felt pen by Paul McCartney, George Harrison and Ringo, 1960s, 7 by 5in (18 by 12.5cm).
£1,000–1,200 *CNY*

An early publicity postcard, signed and inscribed on reverse, April 5th, 1962, 4 by 6in (10 by 15cm), and a membership card for The Cavern Club, 1961.
£340–400 *CSK*

A Nelson Tipped cigarette packet, signed on the inside in 3 different coloured inks by Paul McCartney, George Harrison and John Lennon, c1962, 5¾ by 2¾in (14.5 by 7cm).
£600–650 *CSK*

Records

The Beatles, 'Revolver', LP, in mint condition, 1966.
£20–25 *PC*

The Beatles, 'Rubber Soul', LP, in mint condition, 1966.
£18–25 *PC*

The Beatles, 'Sgt. Pepper's Lonely Hearts Club Band', double EP, Top 4 label, 1967.
£95–100 *ED*

This album was possibly a bootleg copy.

The Beatles, 'Help!', LP, 1965.
£18–25 *PC*

The Beatles, 'Magical Mystery Tour', LP, USA only, 1967.
£25–30 *ED*

Birds Birds, 'Say Those Magic Words', 45rpm single, 1966.
£125–150 *ED*

Miller's is a price GUIDE not a price LIST

Jack Bruce, 'Harmony Row', LP, 1971.
£8–10 *ED*

Eddie Cochran, 'The Eddie Cochran Memorial Album', LP, 1960.
£40–50 *CTO*

Bobby Darin, 'Things & Other Things', LP, 1962.
£18–20 *ED*

l. The Birds, 'No Good Without You Baby', 45rpm single, 1965.
£45–50 *ED*

The Doors, 'The Doors',
LP, 1971.
£6–8 *ED*

The Spencer Davis Group,
'Their First LP', 1965.
£20–25 *ED*

The Diamonds', Tell The
Truth', 45rpm single,
USA only, 1960.
£10–12 *ED*

Foggy, 'Patchwork Album',
LP, 1973.
£25–30 *ED*

Everly Brothers, EP, on the
London Records label, 1958.
£12–15 *ED*

The Earls, 'Remember Then',
45rpm single, 1963.
£10–15 *ED*

l. Jimmi Hendrix
Experience, 'Are
You Experienced',
his first LP, 1967.
£20–30 *CTO*

Records

To fetch a good price both the record and its
cover should be in fine or mint condition.
Rarity is crucial. Look out for test pressings,
promotional records, limited edition releases
and examples with a mistake that makes
them unusual such as an error on the label
or a mis-pressed record.

Fusion Orchestra, 'Skeleton
in Armour', LP, 1973.
£55–60 *ED*

Rory Gallagher, 'Tattoo',
LP, 1973.
£6–7 *ED*

Buddy Holly, 'Heartbeat',
45rpm single, 1960.
£6–7 *ED*

Mary Hopkin, 'Think About Your Children', 45rpm single, 1970.
£6–8 *ED*

The Jam, 'Snap!', LP, 1990.
£8–10 *ED*

Man, 'Be Good to Yourself at Least Once a Day', LP, 1972.
£10–12 *ED*

r. Mountain, 'Nantucket Sleighride', LP, 1971.
£18–20 *ED*

Elvis Presley, 'Aloha from Hawaii via Satellite', LP, 1973.
£12–15 *ED*

Roy Orbison, 'Love Hurts', EP, 1965.
£10–12 *ED*

Billy Preston, 'The Most Exciting Organ Ever', LP, 1967.
£30–35 *ED*

Cliff Richard, '21 Today', LP, 1961.
£20–25 *ED*

Various artists, 'R & B Chartmakers', EP, 1964.
£35–40 *ED*

Cliff Richard, 'Cliff's Hit Album', LP, 1963.
£12–15 *ED*

Queen, 'Sheer Heart Attack', LP, c1974.
£8–10 *ED*

The Rolling Stones, 'Big hits (high tide and green grass)', LP, in mint condition, 1966.
£10–18 *PC*

Mike Sarne, 'Come Outside', LP, 1962.
£20–25 *ED*

Sex Pistols, 'Anarchy', 7in single, first issue, 1976.
£15–20 *CTO*

Small Faces, 'Roots', autographed single album, with cuttings and original ticket, 1977.
£125–150 *CTO*

Them, 'The Angry Young Them', LP, 1965.
£25–30 *ED*

Stray, 'Mudanzas', LP, 1973.
£10–12 *ED*

Stone The Crows, 'Teenage Licks', LP, 1970.
£12–15 *ED*

Jesse Lee Turner, 'Shake, Baby, Shake', 45rpm single, 1959.
£45–50 *ED*

Led Zeppelin 4, lilac vinyl LP, Atlantic label, 1978.
£30–35 *CTO*

r. The Who, 'The Last Time', 45rpm single, 1967.
£20–25 *ED*

SCALES & BALANCES

A diamond scale, by
De Grave & Son, Aldgate,
London, with a steel beam,
brass pans and set of
weights, diamond scoop and
label, in mahogany case,
19thC, 5in (12.5cm) wide.
£150–175 *CSK*

A set of brass scales, on
mahogany base with drawer,
by Parnell & Sons, Bristol,
used by grocers and chemists,
late 19thC, 33in (84cm) wide.
£250–275 *BS*

A set of scales, with brass pans and cast
iron base, c1900, 17in (43cm) wide.
£150–180 *BS*

A decorative brass postal balance,
the pans pierced with scrolls and
palm trees, the beam and supports
engraved with foliate scrolls, the
shaped walnut base with
5 weights, signed on the beam
'S. Mordan & Co, London', late
19thC, 8¾in (22cm) wide.
£375–425 *CSK*

A set of confectionery scales, with brass
pans and cast iron base, by J. Farquharson
& Sons, c1920, 14in (35.5cm) wide.
£100–125 *BS*

l. A Salter's brass
balance, to take
40lbs, early 20thC,
15in (38cm) long.
£25–35 *MIL*

A brass
balance, to take
20lbs, early
20thC, 23in
(58.5cm) long.
£30–35 *MIL*

Two Salter's brass
balances, early 20thC,
7in (18cm) long.
£8–10 *MIL*

Cross Reference:
Kitchenware

l. A set of brass, steel and
cast iron confectionery
scales, by Day & Millward
Ltd, Birmingham, c1900,
13in (33cm) wide.
£120–150 *BS*

A brass and
iron balance,
to take
150lbs, used
for weighing
carcasses, early
20thC, 19in
(48.5cm) long.
£65–75 *MIL*

SCENT BOTTLES

It was only in the 20th century that it became commonplace to buy perfume and bottle together as a complete package. Previously a lady would have her own personal bottles into which the scent she bought from the perfumer or made for herself was decanted.

Shapes of bottles have over the years been influenced by many different factors. Nineteenth century flacons, for instance, were produced in a wide range of sizes, materials and shapes, for both decorative and practical purposes. Because of their corsets, Victorian women were prone to fainting, and double-ended scent bottles were designed to contain perfume in one half and sponge soaked in aromatic vinegar, ie smelling salts, in the other. Miniature bottles, worn like jewellery, enabled ladies to keep their scent with them at all times.

By the early 1900s customers were giving up mixing their own perfume in favour of buying named brands. The 20th century saw the massive commercial expansion of the perfume industry dominated by couturiers such as Chanel and Dior. Whereas for enthusiasts of Victorian bottles, the individual bottle is enough, the collector of 20th century commercial scent bottles wants the whole package: the specific bottle designed for a named scent, complete with labels, stickers, box and ideally still containing at least some of the original perfume, known as the juice.

As examples in the following section show, design of commercial scent bottles became extremely inventive as the great fashion houses competed to gain a share of the luxury market. At the top end of the range, prices for scent bottles can run to thousands of pounds – in 1990 a bottle designed by René Lalique fetched a record £38,000. At the other end of the scale, the simpler Victorian and Edwardian bottles can be purchased for under £50 and commercial bottles can still be found at reasonable prices.

A brass fish scent bottle, c1700, 3½in (9cm) long.
£100–120 *LBr*

An Irish glass double-ended scent bottle, with prism and diamond cutting and plain silver mounts, c1790, 5¼in (13.5cm) high.
£350–400 *Som*

A carved nut scent bottle, possibly Persian, c1800, 4in (10cm) high.
£150–200 *LBr*

A clear glass four-compartment scent bottle, cut with strawberry diamonds, fan cut stoppers, star-cut base, c1820, 3¾in (9.5cm) high.
£450–500 *Som*

Two brass scent bottles, fish c1800, 5¼in (13.5cm) long, bird c1830, 2½in (65mm) high.
£100–150 each *LBr*

r. Two glass scent bottles, c1830, largest 1½in (38mm) high.
£60–75 each *LBr*

A hobnail glass scent flask, with silver neck and top, c1830, 10in (25cm) long.
£180–220 *LBr*

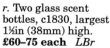

A silver scent bottle, possibly German, c1820, 3½in (9cm) high.
£450–500 *LBr*

Two scent bottles and a silver funnel, in shagreen case, c1820, 3¼in (8.5cm) high.
£300–350 *LBr*

Two glass scent rings, with silver tops, c1840, largest 1½in (38mm) diam.
l. **£115–125**
r. **£250–280** *LBr*

A porcelain scent bottle, c1840, 5½in (14cm) high.
£70–80 *LBr*

A clear glass double-ended scent bottle, with plain silver gilt mounts, c1860, 5in (12.5cm) long.
£100–130 *Som*

A clear glass double-ended scent bottle, with silver tops, c1880, 5in (12.5cm) long.
£80–120 *LBr*

A cut glass scent bottle, with a gold top, c1840, 4in (10cm) high.
£250–300 *LBr*

A Viennese hand painted porcelain scent bottle, c1880, 2½in (65mm) high.
£200–220 *LBr*

A silver scent bottle, c1880, 3¼in (8.5cm) high.
£80–120 *LBr*

A horn-shaped glass scent bottle, with a whistle at one end, finger chain missing, c1880, 3in (7.5cm) long.
£260–280 *LBr*

A nut scent bottle, c1850, 2in (50mm) diam.
£100–120 *LBr*

A blue glass scent bottle, with silver top, c1880, 3¼in (8.5cm) high.
£120–180 *LBr*

r. A cut glass double-ended scent bottle, with plain silver gilt mounts, c1880, 4¾in (12cm) long, in fitted case.
£100–150 *Som*

A French gilt metal scent
bottle, c1900, 4in (10cm) high.
£100–120 *LBr*

Two perfume bottles, in the
form of a White Hart Scotch
Whisky bottle, and a
Guinness Extra Stout bottle,
c1910, 3in (7.5cm) high.
£40–50 each *LBr*

A Royal Worcester scent
bottle, commemorating
Queen Victoria's Golden
Jubilee, the metal cover in
the form of the Imperial State
Crown, the bottle with a
portrait of the Queen within a
garland of roses, shamrocks
and thistles entwined with a
dated and inscribed banner,
the reverse inscribed with the
principal overseas
possessions, the blush ivory
ground enriched in pale blue
and gilt, printed marks,
c1887, 3½in (9cm) high.
£1,500–1,800 *CSK*

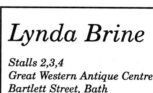

r. A silver brooch
scent bottle, inlaid
with coloured
stones, c1910,
2¼in (55mm) high.
£100–120 *LBr*

A glass scent
bottle, with silver
top, c1900, 3½in
(9cm) high.
£50–70 *WN*

A silver flask, by
Mappin & Webb,
with enamel
inlay, c1913, 3¼in
(8.5cm) high.
£100–125 *LBr*

r. Two Art Nouveau glass
scent bottles, decorated
with gold painted fuchsias,
c1900, 6½in (16.5cm) high.
£120–150 *LBr*

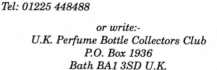

Five American miniature scent bottles, from a dime store, c1910, largest 3½in (9cm) high.
£60–80 each *LBr*

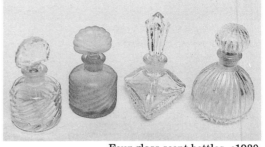

Four glass scent bottles, c1930, largest 3½in (9cm) high.
£20–30 each *LBr*

A Czechoslovakian silver and glass scent bottle brooch, c1930, 1½in (38mm) high.
£70–80 *LBr*

A pair of wooden perfume wax dice, c1930, ¾in (20mm) wide.
£40–60 each *LBr*

A Lalique Coty 'L'Aimant' scent bottle, c1930, 3¼in (8.5cm) high.
£100–150 *LBr*

A cut glass scent bottle, with silver top, Birmingham 1919, 6in (15cm) high.
£50–60 *WN*

A bottle of 'Carnet de Bal' scent, by Ravillon, Paris, 1930–40, 2¼in (55mm) high.
£85–95 *LBe*

This bottle, when turned upside down, looks like a glass of brandy.

An American pair of scent bottles, in the form of binoculars, with metal tops, c1930, 2½in (64mm) wide.
£30–60 *LBr*

A pair of American gilt metal scent bottles, c1940, 11½in (29cm) high.
£280–350 *LBr*

l. A 'Maderas de Oriente', by Myrurgia, scent bottle, in a wooden case with a tassel, c1930, 6in (15cm) high.
£90–100 *LBe*

A scent bottle, 'Saison', by Muriel, Paris, with a Stanhope in the plastic top, showing scenes of Paris, c1960, 3¼in (8.5cm) high.
£10–15 *PC*

SCIENTIFIC INSTRUMENTS

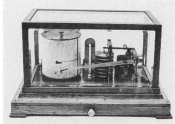

A barograph, by Negretti and Zambra, London, the French 8-day movement driving the chart drum, a pen to the side controlled by a stack of 7 vacuum discs, also fitted with a thermometer, the plinth containing a chart drawer with bone knob, in a glazed oak case, 14in (35.5cm) wide.
£475–550 *WIL*

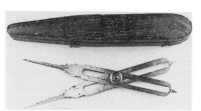

A brass proportional compass, with engraved scales for circles and lines, in plush lined shaped morocco leather case, c1800, 6¼in (16cm) wide, a folding ivory and brass 12in ruler, and a set of 3 Stanley compass bows, in fitted case.
£275–325 *Bon*

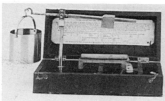

A lacquered brass chondrometer, with sliding weight, finely turned pillar and bucket, operating instruction label, signed on beam 'Rubidge, London', in mahogany case, late 19thC, 9in (23cm) wide.
£210–240 *CSK*

A trough compass, with engraved compass rose, blued and burnished steel needle with agate cap, 2 supplementary engraved copper scales 0°–30° (x2), signed on the paper card 'LNr', for Lenoir, Paris, in a glazed mahogany case with cover slide, late 18thC, 6¼in (16cm) long.
£250–300 *CSK*

A gilded brass pocket compass, with white enamelled dial divided in 4 quadrants, blued steel needle on jewelled pivot, with needle clamp and suspension loop, 19thC, 2¼in (57mm) diam.
£175–225 *CSK*

A Florentine desk compass, with silvered compass card, scale from 0°–360°, flat needle and clamp, in an octagonal embossed paper case, mid-19thC, 5½in (14cm) diam.
£120–150 *Bon*

A copper and brass natural siphon recording rain gauge, by Negretti and Zambra, 1940s, 31in (78.5cm) high.
£350–400 *RTw*

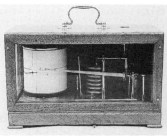

A barograph, by Wilson, Warden & Co, with time marker, ink dipper and pen arm drawer, 1943, 12in (30.5cm) wide.
£250–350 *RTw*

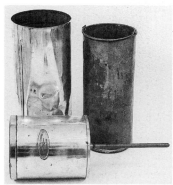

A copper rain gauge, by Negretti and Zambra, with inner water container, c1950, 16½in (50cm) high.
£30–50 *RTw*

A Stockert pattern diptych
dial, with coloured paper
cards, blued iron needle,
string gnomon, the cover
pasted with a label of 48
Continental cities and towns,
19thC, 2¾in (70mm) long.
£250–300 *CSK*

A large pattern thermograph,
by Short and Mason, with cast
iron base, 1950s, 10½in
(26.5cm) wide.
£140–180 *RTw*

> **Miller's is a price GUIDE
> not a price LIST**

A thermo-hygrograph, by
Negretti and Zambra, with
cast iron base, and glazed
copper lid, c1935, 10in
(25cm) wide.
£175–225 *RTw*

A Philips' 4in terrestrial Graphic
Globe, with 12 printed colour gores
and 2 polar calottes, on brass
tripod stand, early 20thC, 8in
(20cm) high, in maker's carton.
£250–300 *CSK*

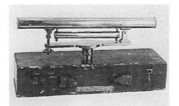

A lacquered brass surveying
level, with draw-tube focusing,
knurled screw vertical
adjustment, in a pine case,
19thC, 14¼in (36cm) wide.
£120–150 *CSK*

A wet and dry bulb thermometer,
by Newman, London, with ivory
scales, brass stand and jar, the
sales slip inscribed 'To Wet and
Dry bulb Thermometer
compared by Mr Glaisher of the
Royal Observatory Greenwich',
indistinctly signed, in fitted
mahogany case, 19thC, 6in
(15cm) wide.
£250–280 *CSK*

A thermograph, by Negretti and
Zambra, with cast iron base and
glazed copper lid, c1925, 10in
(25cm) wide.
£170–220 *RTw*

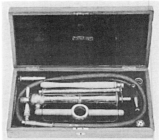

A lacquered brass veterinary
syringe, with accessories, in
plush lined fitted mahogany
case with label, inscribed in gilt
'Millikin & Lawley, 165 Strand,
London', the lid inset with brass
plaque engraved 'R. Forster,
Veterinary, Morpeth', 19thC,
19in (48.5cm) wide.
£325–375 *CSK*

A mercury
thermometer,
by N. Hughes
& Son, early
20thC, 10in
(25cm) high.
£20–25 *RTw*

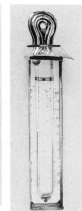

A copper
cased max/min
thermometer,
1930s, 12in
(30.5cm) high.
£35–45 *RTw*

Medical & Dental

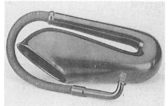

A burnished steel and ivory handled trepanning brace, with spring clip for holding the trepanning crowns or perforators, signed 'Renaud' on the upper shank, 18thC, 10½in (26.5cm) long.
£300–350 *CSK*

A brass and steel phrenological measure, each division divided into quarters, engraved 0–10, early 19thC, 9⅛in (23.5cm) long, and a coquilla nut nutmeg or spice grater, with engine turned decoration, the interior with ivory mounted grater, 3⅛in (8.5cm) long.
£60–75 *CSK*

A composition ear trumpet, with oval section horn and conversation tube, 19thC, 21in (53.5cm) long.
£275–325 *CSK*

A tooth key, with cranked shaft, detachable claw and lignum vitae handle, early 19thC, 5½in (14cm) long, and 2 dental elevators with chequered ebony handles, stamped 'Svendsen', and a pair of forceps, by C. Nyrop.
£200–250 *CSK*

A French orthopaedic artificial arm, by Emile Haran, Paris, the leather limbs with chamois leather lining, nickel plated iron bracing, carved fruitwood hand with sprung articulated thumb, late 19thC, 24½in (62cm) long.
£250–300 *CSK*

A dentist's mahogany cabinet, with 5 drawers containing implements, a steriliser and a box of dressings, cabinet marked 'G. C. Webster', 19thC.
£450–500 *WIL*

Microscopes

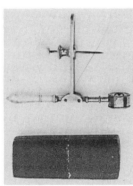

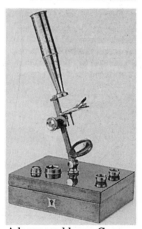

A pocket microscope, the folding brass frame with magnifier, specimen holder and ivory handle, in simulated fishskin covered case, 19thC, 3⅛in (8.5cm) long.
£230–280 *CSK*

A bone flea glass, the lens held by an iron retaining ring set in wood, with threaded spike, c1770, 2in (50mm) diam.
£200–250 *Bon*

A brass microscope lamp, with glass reservoir and chimney, ceramic shade inscribed 'R. Bailey, 14 Bennett's Hill, Birmingham', in pine case, 19thC, 12¾in (32.5cm) high.
£375–425 *CSK*

A lacquered brass Cary-type compound monocular pocket microscope, with rack-and-pinion focusing, stage with slide clamp and swivel mirror, with 3 objectives and other accessories, 19thC, in mahogany case, 6in (15cm) wide, the lid with mounting socket.
£250–300 *CSK*

SCRIPOPHILY
Austria

A Schuldverschreibung 4% loan
certificate, 5,000 crowns, pink and
white, 1902.
£20–22 *GKR*

Eastern Europe

A City of Warsaw Bond for 100 Roubles,
brown, dated '1903'.
£20–25 *SCR*

Great Britain

A share certificate of The
Eccles Rubber & Cycle Co Ltd,
blue and yellow, dated '1898'.
£10–12 *GKR*

China

A £100 bond certificate
of Shanghai Hangchow
and Ningpo, brown, blue,
green and red, 1936.
£65–75 *GKR*

A Hukuang Railway £20
bond certificate of
the Imperial Chinese
Government, French issue,
green and black, dated '1911'.
£30–37 *GKR*

Egypt

A share certificate of the Société Cooperative
de Consommation des Fonctionnaires du
Gouvernement, issued in Alexandria 1910.
£25–30 *SCR*

A share certificate of
The Pandora Theatre
Limited, dated '1882'.
£40–45 *SCR*

l. A share certificate of
Bernard Hughes Ltd, green,
beige, red and gold, 1894.
£12–15 *GKR*

A £100 debenture, The Moss
Hall Coal Company Ltd, with
affixed red seal, issued c1898.
£8–9 *GKR*

France, Belgium & Colonies

r. A share certificate of Compagnie des Claridges Hôtels, with vignette of ship and train, dated '1921'.
£90–100 *GKR*

l. A share certificate of Chaux & Ciments Portland Artificiels de l'Aisne, with vignette, 1920.
£45–50 *GKR*

Ottoman Empire & Turkey

South & Central America

l. A £100 debenture of The Costa Rica Railway Company Limited, red, dated '1889'.
£12–15 *SCR*

This was a famous railway constructed by the American entrepreneur, Minor Cooper Keith.

A share certificate of The Ottoman Railway, dated '1905'.
£55–65 *GKR*

USA Companies

A share certificate of the Elkhorn Gold and Silver Mining Company, red and blue, dated '1863'.
£115–120 *SCR*

l. A share certificate of the Playboy Enterprises, Inc, with vignette.
£115–125 *SCR*

USA Railroads

A Sandusky & Columbus Short Line Railway $1,000 bond, rust brown and black, dated '1891'.
£25–30 *SCR*

A Baltimore & Drum Point Railroad Company $1,000 bond, with loco vignette, green and black, dated '1888'.
£40–45 *SCR*

USSR (Former)

A City of Moscow 5% loan bond, orange and brown, 1908.
£10–12 *GKR*

With all the changes in the former Soviet Union this is becoming a very collectable area. Outside capital was used to finance gas and water supply systems and other municipal works, interest payments terminating with the fall of the Czar in 1917.

Lottery Tickets

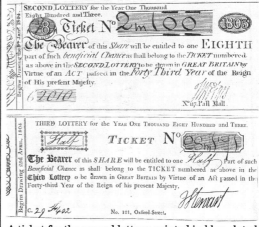

A ticket for the second lottery, printed in blue, dated '1803', with a further ticket for the third lottery, 1803.
£12–15 each *DW*

SEWING

The 19th century was perhaps the most prolific period for the production of sewing tools, and the following examples are predominantly Victorian. Needlework was both a necessity and a popular female pastime. During social occasions, it was commonplace for ladies to sew as they sat and chatted, and as their needlework tools were on public display they were often extremely decorative. Accessories were widely available from specialist shops and travelling traders, and were often purchased as gifts. Many were made as souvenirs, and much can be found in Tunbridge ware and Mauchline ware.

Today, some collectors specialise in specific items (thimbles and needle cases are popular), others buy more generally, perhaps to fill up an empty sewing box. Because of the range of materials used, sewing implements can appeal to collectors in different fields. 'Collectors of ceramics often buy porcelain thimbles, and there is much available for the treen enthusiast,' says dealer Mrs Shirley Burgan. At the top of the range objects can be expensive, although thimbles, for example, can still be found for as little as 50p. 'It is a good idea to begin by buying cheaply and to work your way up,' advises Mrs Burgan.

Baskets & Boxes

A hazelnut cased étui, possibly French, 1830, 1in (25mm) high.
£1,000–1,200 *LBr*

A sewing nécessaire, in the form of a miniature cylinder bureau, the front and sides inlaid with cube parquetry, the tambour cylinder opening to reveal a pincushion, a spring-operated drawer to the left, on slender turned ivory legs, early 19thC, 5½in (14cm) wide.
£375–450 *L*

A lacquered sewing/writing box, decorated with Oriental figures, with carved ivory fittings, 1840, 14in (35.5cm) wide.
£375–400 *GLN*

A basket weave sewing table, with 2 drawers, late 19thC, 19in (48cm) high.
£125–150 *MofC*

A harewood and satinwood work box, set with printed flowers, views and shells, with marquetry husk borders and two brass handles, 19thC, 11¼in (28.5cm) wide.
£125–150 *DN*

A sewing basket, 19thC, 9in (23cm) high.
£80–90 *Ber*

Bodkins & Stilettos

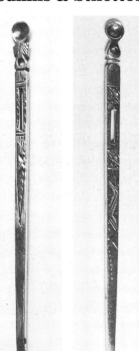

A silver bodkin, with mark for Joseph Wilmore, c1800, 2½in (6.5cm) long.
£100–115 *GLN*

A steel stiletto, c1810, 2½in (6.5cm) long.
£20–25 *GLN*

A silver-handled stiletto, 19thC, 4in (10cm) long.
£20–25 *GLN*

A carved mother-of-pearl stiletto, late 19thC, 2½in (6.5cm) long.
£30–40 *GLN*

A mother-of-pearl stiletto, c1830, 2in (5cm) long.
£45–50 *GLN*

An engraved silver bodkin and ear scoop, c1656, 7in (18cm) long.
£450–470 *GLN*

Stilettos were used for making eyeholes, and bodkins for piercing holes in cloth. Tape or cord was fed through the bodkin's eyehole and then drawn through the material.

A silver bodkin and ear scoop, c1700, 4¾in (12cm) long.
£325–350 *GLN*

A rosewood sewing clamp, with pincushion top, 19thC, 4½in (11.5cm) high.
£60–75 *GLN*

Clamps

A carved wooden hemming clamp, with pincushion top, 19thC, 6in (15cm) high.
£75–95 *GLN*

r. A painted Tunbridge ware sewing clamp, with tape measure, c1820, 4¼in (11cm) high.
£95–100 *AMH*

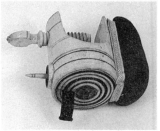

Needle Cases

A bright cut silver needle holder, 18thC, 3in (7.5cm) long.
£40–55 *GLN*

An ivory and steel mirror needle holder, 19thC, 3½in (9cm) long.
£30–35 *GLN*

l. A red leather needle packet box, in the form of a book, c1820, 1¾in (4.5cm) wide.
£40–50 *GLN*

A plain painted turned wooden needle holder, c1820, 2½in (6.5cm) long.
£20–25 *GLN*

A turned ivory stiletto needle holder, 19thC, 3¼in (8.5cm) long.
£20–25 *GLN*

A turned ivory needle holder, 19thC, 3½in (9cm) long.
£40–50 *GLN*

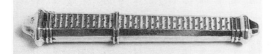

A French silver needle holder, 19thC, 2½in (6.5cm) long.
£200–230 *GLN*

A silver needle case, marked 'M. Linwood', c1810, 2½in (6.5cm) long.
£100–115 *GLN*

A carved acorn vegetable ivory needle holder, 19thC, 2¾in (7cm) long.
£45–50 *GLN*

A carved ivory needle holder, late 19thC, 3¼in (8.5cm) long.
£30–40 *GLN*

A French gilt needle holder, 19thC, 2½in (6.5cm) long.
£150–185 *GLN*

A turned ribbed ivory needle holder, 19thC, 3½in (9cm) long.
£40–50 *GLN*

A silver cannon barrel needle holder, c1830, 2½in (6.5cm) long.
£60–75 *GLN*

A French gold needle holder, 19thC, 2½in (6.5cm) long.
£275–300 *GLN*

Pincushions

A steel pincushion, in the form of an acorn, c1800, 1½in (4cm) long.
£25–35 *GLN*

A mother-of-pearl pincushion, 19thC, 1½in (4cm) diam.
£20–25 *GLN*

A cream and blue silk pincushion, embroidered with 2 ladies, one seated with a parakeet perched on one hand, the other seated on an anchor, in a landscape with a castle beyond, flanked by trees and foliage, with tassel fringes to the corners, worked in coloured silk thread in long and short stitch, with silvered coloured metal thread, original sequins missing, some wear, 17thC, 6½in (16.5cm) wide.
£1,800–2,000 *HSS*

A Tunbridge ware stickwork emery pincushion, c1860, 1¼in (3cm) diam.
£50–60 *GLN*

r. A comb case with pincushion, with alternate cream and blue silks inset, with shaped mirrors and embellished with coloured foils, beads and silver thread, probably Austrian or German, c1800, 19in (48cm) long.
£110–130 *CSK*

l. A Tunbridge ware pincushion, 1850s, 1¾in (4.5cm) diam.
£85–95 *GLN*

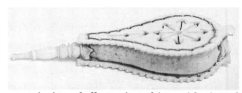

An ivory bellows pincushion, with pierced decoration, c1800, 2¾in (7cm) high.
£40–50 *GLN*

A silver shoe pincushion, London 1891, 4¼in (11cm) long.
£140–150 *WAC*

A stained bone and cut steel pincushion, 19thC, 1½in (4cm) high.
£35–45 *GLN*

A silk pincushion, 'Welcome Lovely Babe', early 20thC, 7½in (19cm) wide.
£50–55 *LB*

This type of cushion was made in various sizes, up to 18in (46cm) wide.

A Mauchline ware sewing box/pincushion, inscribed with 'Tibbie Shiel's Cottage, St Mary's Loch', c1900, 2¼in (5.5cm) high.
£40–60 *MRW*

A silk pyramid pincushion, with glass beads, late 19thC, 1in (25mm) high.
£18–25 *GLN*

An officer's cap pincushion, with silver peak, c1914, 2in (5cm) diam.
£120–140 *WAC*

A French fabric pincushion, c1920, 3½in (9cm) wide.
£12–16 *MRW*

l. A silver parrot pincushion and ring tree, Birmingham 1921, 2½in (6.5cm).
£130–150 *WAC*

Scissors

A pair of Victorian steel folding scissors, 2in (5cm) long.
£20–25 *GLN*

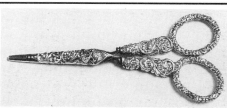

A pair of decorated scissors, with silver handles, mid-19thC, 6in (15cm) long.
£50–55 *GLN*

A pair of Edwardian steel scissors, inscribed 'J. Rogers & Sons', 4in (10cm) long.
£30–35 *GLN*

A pair of steel scissors, with file edge, early 20thC, 3¾in (9.5cm) long.
£10–12 *GLN*

A pair of elaborately decorated steel scissors, late 19thC, with case, 6in (15cm) long.
£35–40 *GLN*

A pair of Sheffield steel scissors, inscribed
'G. Platts & Son', early 20thC, 3½in (9cm) long.
£5–6 *GLN*

A pair of silver handled scissors, 1910,
3¼in (8.5cm) long.
£30–35 *GLN*

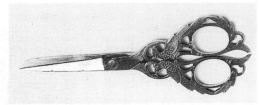

l. A pair of steel scissors, with decorative
handles, early 20thC, 6in (15cm) long.
£40–50 *GLN*

Tapestry Frames

A mahogany tapestry frame, with
adjustable stretcher on trestle base,
mid-19thC, 36in (91.5cm) wide.
£250–300 *WIL*

Thimbles

l. A gilt-metal
thimble, the sides
cast and pierced to
simulate filigree,
incorporating an
oval vacant
cartouche, early
19thC, 1¼in
(32mm) high.
£275–325 *CSK*

A French silver and
enamel thimble, c1880.
£40–50 *GLN*

An Imari pattern thimble,
marked inside with
Stevenson-Hancock mark
for Derby Factory, c1890,
¾in (20mm) high.
£500–600 *THi*

A silver thimble,
with milled
border applied
with a band of
holly leaves and
berries enamelled
in green and red,
the rim bright-cut
on a milled ground
and stamped
with 'Registration
No. 212114,
James Fenton,
Birmingham 1893',
1in (25mm) high.
£210–250 *CSK*

l. to r. A Russian silver gilt and enamel thimble,
marked on the rim with Kokochnik, silver standard
mark of 875, post-Revolution, ¾in (20mm) high.
£650–750
An enamel on silver thimble, with moonstone top,
marked 'Sterling' inside, German or US export,
c1890, ¾in (20mm) high. **£125–150**
An enamel on silver thimble, with moonstone top,
mark inside apex, probably Scandinavian, c1890,
¾in (20mm) high. **£150–170**
A Russian silver gilt and enamel thimble, mark
inside apex, post-Revolution, ¾in (20mm) high.
£700–800 *THi*

Thimbles

- Thimbles were produced in a wide range of different materials:
  - Metal and silver are the most commonplace. Before the late 19thC silver thimbles were not hallmarked.
  - Other more decorative materials used include gold, enamel, tortoiseshell, mother-of-pearl, filigree examples and thimbles bearing precious or semi-precious stones.
  - Porcelain thimbles, though fragile, were considered useful because they would not catch on delicate materials. Many were produced by Royal Worcester, as well as other factories (check for a mark inside the thimble). Old examples tend to be rare and costly but ceramic thimbles are still being produced today.
  - Ivory thimbles are comparatively unusual, since the material has always been expensive. Take care not to confuse them with ivory-coloured plastics.
- Look out for advertising and commemorative thimbles, and examples bearing the maker's name for these are highly sought after.
- Thimble cases are made in a variety of materials and shapes. Fine examples can be found in both Tunbridge ware and Mauchline ware.

A silver thimble, Birmingham 1896.
£40–50 GLN

A silver thimble, Chester 1899.
£20–23 GLN

l. to r. A silver thimble, with waffle shaped indentations, no rim, c1901, ¾in (20mm) high.
A silver thimble, with waffle shaped indentations, no rim, c1910, ¾in (20mm) high.
A silver thimble, with round indentations, decorated rim, c1898, ¾in (20mm) high.
A silver thimble, with round indentations, no rim, c1908, ¾in (20mm) high.
£14–25 each *THi*

Thimble Cases

l. A sterling silver thimble, marked 'H.G. & S', c1900.
£15–18 GLN

r. A gold thimble, inscribed 'Alice, Jan 1st 1920'.
£125–140 GLN

A Mauchline ware thimble case, decorated with 'Burns Mausoleum Dumfries', c1900, 1¾in (45mm) wide.
£40–50 GLN

Sewing Machines

A turned rosewood acorn thimble and case, 19thC, 2in (50mm) high.
£80–90 GLN

A toy sewing machine, c1900, 7in (18cm) wide.
£30–40 WaH

A Victorian Express hand sewing machine, with gilt floral decoration, on a rectangular base, 4 spreading scroll and scallop feet, 11¾in (30cm) overall.
£80–100 Gam

SHELLS, FOSSILS & NATURAL HISTORY

Since the earliest times, shells have been gathered for decorative and practical purposes, using them for ornament, tools and money. In the West, shell collecting reached its height of popularity in the 18th and 19th centuries. The expansion of trade in the Pacific and China and the discovery of new lands led to the importation of a host of unfamiliar shells. A knowledge of natural science – like a knowledge of the arts – was considered the mark of a gentleman. Shells were collected in much the same way as stamps, coins and small antiquities. Catalogued and carefully labelled with their Latin names, they would often be kept in collecting cabinets.

Shell auctions were popular in the 19th century and high prices were paid for perfect specimens. Less rare shells were used by the Victorians to make shell work pictures and the elaborate and labour-intensive table displays, which were a popular centrepiece of the 19th century drawing room. Shells were used extensively in the button industry and large quantities of mother-of-pearl were also imported to Birmingham to be used as inlay for papier mâché furniture. Today the hobby of shell collecting is again growing in popularity and we include a selection of contemporary shells imported from across the globe, as well as fossils and natural history collectables.

Shell Pictures & Ornaments

A shell picture frame, with a photograph of General Sir Redvers Buller, c1900, 10in (25.5cm) diam.
£30–40 *OO*

A Victorian shell picture frame, with marine print background, 6in (15cm) diam.
£50–60 *GHA*

An Arnwreath purse of woven reed and pierced shells, with black and red pigment, 19thC, 5in (12.5cm) wide.
£100–125 *LHB*

A pair of Neapolitan figures, wearing traditional costumes encrusted with shells, one carrying a basket of shells, 19thC, 11½in (29cm) high.
£550–650 *P*

A Victorian sea shell and coral floral arrangement, in a glass case, 16¼in (41cm) high.
£30–40 *P(B)*

A Victorian shell collection, contained in a mahogany case, 18in (45.5cm) square.
£140–150 *PC*

Shells

A conch shell, c1990,
13in (33cm) long.
£10–15 *PC*

Two bull's mouth shells,
5in (12.5cm) wide.
£2–10 each *ShS*

Two blood mouth conch
shells, 2in (50mm) long.
15p–£1 each *ShS*

A fluted clam shell,
9in (23cm) wide.
£18–20 *ShS*

A collector's shell,
3in (7.5cm) diam.
£15–20 *ShS*

Two green turban shells,
largest 5½in (14cm) wide.
l. **£20–30**
r. **£25–35** *ShS*

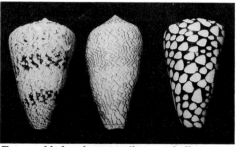

Two marbled and one textile cone shells,
2½in (64mm) long.
£1–5 each *ShS*

An auger, a giant screw shell,
6in (15.5cm) long.
50p–£1 *ShS*

A branched murex shell,
8in (20cm) wide.
£10–20 *ShS*

A mushroom shell,
2½in (64mm) diam.
£1–5 *ShS*

A harlequin top shell,
2in (50mm) long.
£40–50 *ShS*

A scallop shell,
5in (12.5cm) diam.
15p–£1 *ShS*

An imperial volute shell,
5in (12.5cm) long.
£20–30 *ShS*

A queen conch shell,
11in (28cm) long.
£10–15 *ShS*

An orchid spider shell,
4½in (11.5cm) wide.
£1–2 *ShS*

A sea urchin shell,
collected in Cornwall,
1990s, 4in (10cm) diam.
£2–3 *PC*

A scorpion shell, 9in (23cm) long.
£5–10 *ShS*

A purple prupe shell,
1½in (38mm) diam.
£1–2 *ShS*

A star shell, 2in (50mm) diam.
£1–5 *ShS*

A thorny oyster on a hammer
oyster shell, 6in (15cm) long.
£5–10 *ShS*

Two sundial shells, 1½in (38mm) diam.
50p–£2 each *ShS*

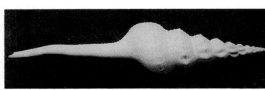

A spindle shell, 5½in (14cm) long.
£2–5 *ShS*

Two top shells:
l. polished, 2½in (64mm) diam.
£5–10
r. unpolished.
£80p–£2 *ShS*

A brown stem coral,
11in (28cm) wide.
50p–£2 *ShS*

A venus combe murex shell,
6in (15cm) long.
£15–20 *ShS*

l. A precious winkle trap shell,
2in (50mm) wide.
£10–15 *ShS*

A collection of shells, from
Continental beaches, 1930s.
£5–10 *PC*

Fossils & Natural History

A Madagascan great elephant
bird egg, aepyornis maximus,
15in (38cm) long.
£15,000–18,000 *Bon*

*Aepyornis was in appearance
very much like a gigantic and
ponderous ostrich, its eggs
being the largest ever known.
Until 1851, when 3 eggs were
brought back to France by
Capt Abadie, there had only
been one other reported
sighting, by Madagascar's first
French Governor, Etienne de
Placourt in 1658. However, he
was killed returning to France
without elaborating the
account. Aepyornis is likely to
have been extinct well before
the turn of the 19thC.*

A sea scorpion fossil, eurypterus
remipes, showing masticatory
appendages, swimming paddles,
abdomen and spine, U. Silurian,
Herkimer Co., NY, USA, well
preserved, 4in (10cm) long.
£175–225 *Bon*

A hippopotamus skull, with
full tusks, c1900.
£800–1,000 *HnT*

An American bison skull, 1920s,
26in (66cm) wide.
£200–300 *HnT*

A sperm whale tooth,
physeter macrocephalus,
mounted on a turned ivory
stand, pale creamy patina,
early 19thC, the tooth
4½in (11.5cm) long.
£1,200–1,400 *Bon*

SHIPPING

A Massey presentation ship's log, in its original box, c1865.
£500–600 *Tem*

A brass-cased aneroid barometer, c1900, 8½in (21.5cm) high.
£150–170 *Tem*

A ship's brass and glass companionway lamp, c1960, 6in (15cm) diam.
£45–50 *Tem*

A wooden mooring buoy, shaped as a barrel, c1850, 10in (25.5cm) diam.
£90–100 *Tem*

An enamel badge of the *Queen Mary*, 1950s.
£6–8 *MRW*

r. A shipping agents' brass sign, 1914, 10in (25.5cm) square.
£50–60 *COB*

A pair of brass chart dividers, c1940, 7in (18cm) radius.
£20–25 *Tem*

S.S. UGANDA

S.S. CANBERRA

S.S. NEVASA

A selection of Merchant Navy cap ribbons, c1960, 37in (94cm) long.
£3–5 each *COB*

r. A brass porthole, fitted with deadlight, c1960, 17in (43cm) diam.
£100–120 *Tem*

Ephemera

A certificate of admittance for William Jacobs as a free and qualified waterman, 3rd January 1733, printed document with manuscript insertions, papered wax seal of the Company of Watermen, signed by 4 of the 'overseers and rulers of all the wherry-men, watermen and lightermen . . . between Gravesend Bridge and Windsor Bridge, Berkshire', with an apprenticeship document on vellum for William Jacobs, son of William Jacobs, mariner, to apprentice himself as a tallow chandler to Robert Wyrill, 1723, signed by Wyrill and another.
£25–35 *DW*

Two shipping line menus, largest 10 by 7½in (25.5 by 19cm): *l.* Holland America Line, 1949 *r.* Union Castle Line, 1962.
£3–5 each *COB*

Thirty-one press photographs of the various craft and powerboat records of Mrs Bruce, each approx 6¾ by 8¼in (17 by 21cm).
£90–110 *ONS*

Mrs Bruce broke the long distance record on the water covering 672 nautical miles in 24 hours without relief. She was also holder of the Dover to Calais and back record with a small outboard motor driving alone.

A Canadian Pacific menu, depicting the Château Frontenac, Old Quebec, 1953, 10 by 7½in (25.5 by 19cm).
£2–5 *COB*

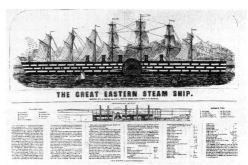

THE GREAT EASTERN STEAM SHIP.

A wood engraved illustration of the *Great Eastern*, fully rigged, T. Goode, machine printer, Clerkenwell, c1850, 29½in (75cm) wide.
£150–170 *DW*

A pack of 32 cards, entitled 'The Loss of the Titanic', 1990s.
£12–14 *MAP*

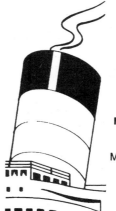

A brochure for the Ocean Terminal, Southampton Docks, 1953, 5½ by 8¾in (14 by 22cm).
£5–15 *COB*

A selection of various shipping companies baggage labels, 1950s and 60s, largest 6in (15cm) diam.
£2–5 each *COB*

A shipwright's model of the Brixham trawler *Ibex*, c1960, 35in (89cm) long.
£350–400 *Tem*

A model of the yacht *Bluenose*, c1920, 11½in (29cm) wide.
£150–175 *Tem*

l. A hand built 1:78 scale wooden model of HMS *Victory*, in a glazed mahogany framed case, 61in (155cm) wide.
£625–725 *HSS*

SILHOUETTES & MINIATURES

A silhouette print of King Ferdinand of Sicily, c1791, 9¼ by 7¾in (23.5 by 19.5cm).
£55–65 *STA*

A silhouette print of Queen Sophie Charlotte of England, c1791, 9 by 7¾in (23 by 19.5cm).
£55–65 *STA*

A painting on glass, attributed to Mrs Barrett, of a woman, c1810, 2¾in (7cm) high.
£200–250 *BlA*

A painting on glass, by Mrs Isabella Beetham, of a gentleman, with *verre églomisé* border, trade label on reverse, in a turned wood frame, 18thC, 3½in (9cm) high.
£350–400 *CSK*

A painting on glass, by Beale, of Dr Jowett's daughter, c1840, 9¼in (23.5cm) high.
£500–600 *BlA*

A cut-out paper silhouette, by Baron Scotford, c1909, 14in (35.5cm) high.
£200–250 *BlA*

A cut-out paper silhouette, by Baron Scotford, impressed mark, c1925, 13¾in (35cm) high.
£40–60 *BlA*

A miniature watercolour, by an unknown artist, of a boy in a top hat, c1815, 3½in (9cm) high.
£200–250 *BlA*

A miniature watercolour, by an unknown artist, of a young woman, c1830, 5in (12.5cm) high.
£400–500 *BlA*

A miniature watercolour, by Adam Buck, of a young woman, c1822, 5in (12.5cm) high.
£600–800 *BlA*

SMOKING & SNUFF TAKING
Smoking

An Ally Sloper pipe, c1890.
£10–15 *WCA*

A European pine pipe rack, 19thC,
18in (45.5cm) wide.
£35–45 *OPH*

A Victorian cigarette rolling
machine, 15in (38cm) wide.
£75–85 *JHW*

A set of scales, with copper
pans, used for weighing
tobacco, made in Bristol,
c1880, 14in (35.5cm) wide.
£100–135 *LIB*

r. A Langley tobacco jar, c1905,
7in (18cm) high.
£40–45 *WCA*

Cigar Smoking

A cigar cutter, with Egyptian decoration,
19thC, 1¾in (45mm) high.
£50–60 *GLN*

A silver-mounted cigar cutter, Birmingham 1951,
5¾in (14.5cm) long.
£50–60 *GLN*

A bronze cigar cutter, in the form of a
bulldog, c1880, 4in (10cm) wide.
£300–350 *GLN*

An amber and silver meerschaum cigar and
cheroot holder, c1896, 2½in (64mm) long, in
original box.
£30–35 *WCA*

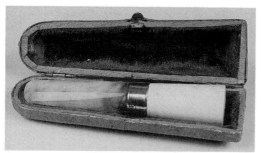

An ivory cigarette holder, c1920, 5in (12.5cm) long.
£25–40 *Ech*

An amber and silver cigar holder, c1900,
2in (50mm) long, in original box.
£18–20 *WCA*

An amber, gold and sapphire cigarette holder, 1930s,
3¾in (9.5cm) long.
£45–65 *Ech*

Lighters, Matchbox Covers & Vesta Cases

A French cold metal vesta case,
late 19thC, 3¼in (8.5cm) long.
£80–100 *MRW*

A Victorian owl vesta
case, 2in (50mm) high.
£75–85 *WCA*

A Prince Albert safety vesta
holder, c1851, 4in (10cm) diam.
£30–35 *WCA*

l. An embossed table
lighter, Edward Jones,
Birmingham 1910.
£250–300 *SHa*

A metal tinder striker and cigar
cutter, 19thC, 2in (50mm) wide.
£75–85 *GLN*

Two book match covers,
l. with enamelled cover,
r. onyx style, 1920–30,
2¼ by 1½in (57 by 38mm).
£15–25 each *PC*

Two cloisonné matchbox covers, c1920,
2½ by 1½in (64 by 38mm).
£15–20 each *AnE*

Snuff Taking

A William IV silver snuff box, the lid decorated with a classical scene, the interior gilded, marked 'London 1837', 3½in (9cm) wide.
£350–400 QSA

A brass and copper snuff shoe, 19thC, 4½in (11.5cm) wide.
£300–350 JCr

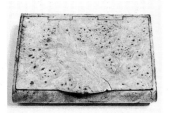

A wooden snuff box, 19thC, 4¾in (12cm) wide.
£20–30 Ech

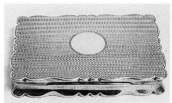

A silver snuff box, with engine-turned decoration, hallmarked for Chester 1915, 3½in (9cm) wide.
£250–300 QSA

A lacquered and inlaid snuff shoe, 19thC, 2½in (64mm) wide.
£45–60 VB

A silver snuff bottle, with gold neck, possibly German, c1910, 1¼in (32mm) high.
£60–90 LBr

SOUVENIRS

l. A selection of silver plated Butlin's items, c1948.
£5–12 each PC

r. A Torquay ware cruet set, c1950, 3in (7.5cm) high.
£12–15 COL

l. A collection of plaster fishermen and fisherwomen, made in France for seaside towns both in France and England, c1920, largest 7in (18cm) high.
£20–50 each AND

A glass swan, containing different coloured sand from Alum Bay, Isle of Wight, 1950s, 4in (10cm) high.
£10–15 TAR

SPECTACLES & OPTICAL EQUIPMENT
Lorgnettes

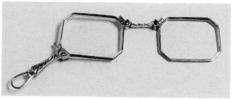

A pair of Art Deco chrome lorgnettes, 4in (10cm) wide.
£40–70 *Ech*

A pair of tortoiseshell lorgnettes, c1860, 4in (10cm) wide.
£25–40 *Ech*

r. A pair of mother-of-pearl and silver lorgnettes, c1910, 4in (10cm) wide.
£120–150 *LBe*

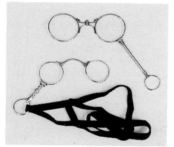

Two pairs of gold coloured metal lorgnettes, 4in (10cm) wide.
top late 19thC. **£45–55**
bottom early 19thC.
£100–125 *PC*

Pince-Nez

A pair of Chinese folding pince-nez, with metal bridge, temple rest and silk ties, pale amethyst lenses, 19thC, 2in (50mm) diam, in carved hardwood carrying case.
£325–375 *CSK*

A pair of Chinese folding pince-nez, with metal rims and temple rest, replacement cord ties, in hardwood case, the lid carved with a lady, rabbit and flowers, the reverse with a deer on a rocky outcrop, 19thC, 5in (12.5cm) long.
£300–350 *CSK*

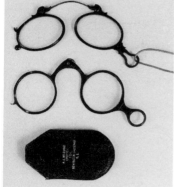

Two pairs of tortoiseshell folding pince-nez, one with case, c1830, 4in (10cm) wide.
£35–45 each *PC*

r. A pair of gold folding pince-nez, c1850, 4in (10cm) wide.
£85–100 *PC*

Quizzes

l. & r. Two tortoiseshell quizzes, 19thC, 2 and 2½in (50 and 64mm) long.
£15–25 each
c. A gold metal quiz, c1830, 2¼in (57mm) long.
£75–100 *PC*

Spectacles

Two pairs of steel spectacles, late 19thC and a pair of spectacles, glazed with quartz pebble lenses, white metal with imitation hallmark, late 18thC.
£15–25 each *PC*

Three pairs of gentleman's tortoiseshell spectacles, *bottom* acetate with cataract lens and 'earjoy' sides, 1950s.
£15–25 each *PC*

A pair of George III silver spectacles, with loop ends, plain oval lenses with matching green-tinted folding side lenses, in part case, and a pair of shooting blued steel wire spectacles, with one pale blue tinted lens and one with adjustable sight volvelle, in leather case.
£225–275 *CSK*

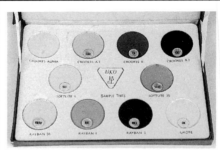

A boxed set of demonstration Health Service lens tints, Softlite and Crookes, 6½ by 9in (16.5 by 23cm).
£10–15 *PC*

Spy, Field & Opera Glasses

l. A lady's spy glass, c1880, 2¼in (57mm) long, in original case.
£50–60 *PC*

A pair of aluminium miniature opera glasses, by Aitchison of London, with unusual slide focusing, 2½in (64mm) high.
£15–20 *PC*

l. A pair of German civilian field glasses, 1930–40, 4½in (11.5cm) high.
£20–25 *PC*

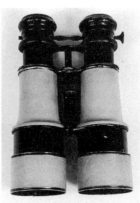

A pair of leather-covered field/theatre/marine glasses, c1910, 7½in (19cm) extended.
£45–50 *PC*

A miniature telescope, 1920s,
2½in (64mm) long.
£20–25 *PC*

Two pairs of double extending field glasses,
with ray shields, c1900.
l. leather covered enamelled brass,
5in (12.5cm) extended.
r. leather-covered aluminium,
7¼in (18.5cm) extended.
£45–55 each *PC*

Miscellaneous

r. A pair of
Bakelite toy
opera glasses,
by ESL, 1950s,
3in (7.5cm) high.
£8–10 *PC*

Three ceramic eye baths, c1920,
l. & r. white, 1¾in (45mm) high.
£10–15
c. pink, 2¼in (57mm) high.
£25–30 *PC*

Three glass eye baths, 1960s, 1½in (38mm) high.
Coloured **£3–5 each**
White **£10–20** *PC*

Two blown glass eye baths, c1870,
largest 3in (7.5cm) high.
£30–50 each *PC*

l. Two glass eye
baths, c1915,
largest 2½in
(64mm) high.
£10–15 each *PC*

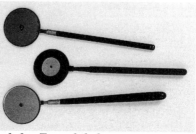

l. & r. Two ophthalmascopes,
c. a retinscope, c1910, 7in (18cm) long.
£8–10 each *PC*

SPORTING

Sporting collectables continue to score high results in the salerooms. In 1995 an astonishing world record auction price of £17,000 was set for a 19th century feathery golf ball, signed by maker D. Marshall. Golf balls are becoming ever more desirable, and not just Victorian examples. Early 20th century dimple golf balls can fetch £50 upwards at auction and boxed sets, from as late as the 1960s, are now attracting collectors.

Sales devoted to golfing memorabilia have been established for over ten years, but 1995 saw the first specialist auctions of cricket and tennis items at Sotheby's and Christie's South Kensington. In the cricketing field, runs of *Wisden's Almanack* have been making strong prices, as have cricketing pictures and ephemera. Christie's tennis auction was a near sell-out with private enthusiasts and specialist museums bidding keenly for early equipment, mascots and collectables.

Football memorabilia is growing in popularity, and Bonham's regularly feature a strong selection of football material in their sporting sales. Thanks largely to television, interest in American sports continues to develop in Britain and in this edition we illustrate a small selection of baseball cards.

Finally, we have devoted a special section to fishing. Angling was a favourite pastime with Victorian gentlemen, including Prince Albert. The variety of equipment available was enormous, specific tools were developed for every conceivable aspect of the sport and objects were often beautifully crafted. Today's collectors can not only buy antique tackle but even become proud owners of fish that were landed perhaps a century ago. The ultimate way of commemorating a notable catch was to have it stuffed and mounted. Cased fish are included in our section on taxidermy.

Rudyard Kipling, *An Almanac of Twelve Sports*, illustrated by William Nicholson, 12 colour woodblock illustrations, original picture boards with linen backstrip, 1898, slim 4to.
£220–250 *DW*

A Doulton stoneware silver mounted sporting tyg, moulded in relief with 3 sportsmen, against a slip trailed ground of green, blue and brown flowers, the silver mount inscribed and dated '1904', 6in (15cm) high.
£275–325 *N*

A mahogany billiard scoreboard, by George Wright & Co, the central blackboard with brass scorers above and below, flanked by sliding coloured ball indicators, early 20thC, 39in (99cm) wide.
£350–400 *S*

'The Rules and Order of Cocking' (cock fighting), in a glazed frame with various spurs, thong and hood and a collection of feathers, 18thC.
£240–280 *S*

A boxed set of 3 billiard balls, by Thos Padmore & Sons, c1900, box 7¼in (18.5cm) long.
£30–40 *MSh*

A croquet mallet putter, with lined face and leaded weighted sole, c1910.
£210–250 *C(S)*

A pair of leather
stirrups, c1870.
£40–60 *MSh*

A wooden decoy bird, hand
carved and painted, c1860,
9in (23cm) wide.
£200–220 *RYA*

A large collection of photographs of
rugby footballers, 1931–51,
including England, Wales, Scotland,
France and the All Blacks.
£475–575 *S*

l. A pair of WMF
pewter water sports
figures, c1920,
9½in (24cm) high.
£100–135 *HEM*

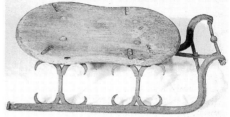

A wood and iron sleigh, handle and back rest
missing, c1880, 26in (66cm) long.
£40–60 *NWE*

A leather 'leg of mutton' gun case, c1920.
£60–80 *MSh*

A wooden sledge, 1920s, 41in (104cm) long.
£20–40 *NWE*

Baseball

A Topps No. 300 baseball card
of Mickey Mantle, mint
condition, 1961.
£425–475 *S(NY)*

A Bowman Color No. 117
baseball card, of Duke Snider,
near mint condition, 1953.
£540–600 *S(NY)*

A Topps baseball card set,
including the 660 and 44 set,
in near mint and mint
condition, 1974.
£320–375 *S(NY)*

Cricket

An England touring team cricket blazer for the 1933–34 Tour of India, with raised embroidered badge, England touring team cap, sweater and tie, a scarf and neckerchief in MCC colours.
£500–600 *MCA*

The property of W. H. V. 'Hopper' Levett, Kent wicket keeper of the 1930s, celebrated for his high number of stumpings.

A Bussey cricket bat, with patent leather grip, 1905, 34½in (87.5cm) long.
£80–120 *MSh*

A scoresheet for a five-day cricket match between Northern and Southern Counties of England, August, 1836, printed by J. Hicklin, Nottingham, slight damage, 10 by 8in (25.5 by 20cm).
£300–350 *CSK*

The Northern Counties were comprehensively beaten in this match, thanks to the bowling of Lillywhite and Cobbett and an extraordinary century of 125, by Alfred Mynn in his second innings for the Southern Counties.

A cast iron pub table, the wooden top supported by an ornate tripod frame with 3 portrait masks of W. G. Grace, with pierced stretcher, late 19thC, 29in (74cm) high.
£1,100–1,500 *S*

A photograph of the Australian cricket team, by E. Hawkins & Co, of Brighton, at Sheffield Park, 1884, 9½ by 11½in (24 by 29cm).
£480–520 *S*

Football

A Mitre Mercury leather football, with approximately 40 ink signatures including Busby Babes, Matt Busby, Tom Finney, Bert Troutman, Don Revie, Billy Wright and Frank Swift, late 1950s.
£350–400 *Bon*

A spelter figure of a footballer, on black marble base, c1910, 7in (18cm) high.
£120–180 *MSh*

A 78rpm 1932 Cup Final souvenir record, of the Arsenal and Newcastle United teams, Regal label, in original printed sleeve.
£220–260 *DW*

Programmes

An official souvenir programme for England v. Scotland, Wembley, April 5th, 1930, folds.
£60–80 *Bon*

An official souvenir programme of the FA Cup Final, Bolton Wanderers v. Portsmouth, April 27th, 1929, torn.
£200–240 *Bon*

FURTHER READING
Duncan Chilcott, *The Hamlyn Guide to Football Collectables*, Reed Books, London, 1995.

An official programme for England v. Scotland, Wembley, April 9th, 1932, folds.
£40–60 *Bon*

An official programme of the FA Cup Final, Manchester City v. Portsmouth, April 28th, 1934, torn.
£140–170 *Bon*

l. An Arsenal Football Club programme for England v. Hungary, Highbury, December 2nd, 1936, folds.
£75–100 *Bon*

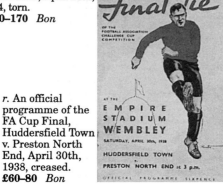

r. An official programme of the FA Cup Final, Huddersfield Town v. Preston North End, April 30th, 1938, creased.
£60–80 *Bon*

Fishing
Reels

An Allcock 4½in Match
Aerial reel, 1939.
£200–240 *ND*

An Allcock 4in Aerial lever
check reel, c1925.
£380–440 *ND*

An Allcock 6in Commodore
heavy duty stainless steel
sea reel, c1960.
£25–40 *DDO*

An Allcock 3½in Aerial
Popular reel, c1927–62.
£150–180 *GHA*

An Allcock 4½in Record Breaker
alloy trotting reel, c1965.
£30–60 *DDO*

A Coxon 4in Aerial reel,
with mahogany back and
alloy drum, c1925.
£500–550 *ND*

A C. Farlow 4in brass
Patent Lever salmon
reel, script engraving
of company name and
address, c1910.
£60–100 *DDO*

A C. Farlow 2in brass
crank wind reel, with
turned ivory handle on
curved crank arm, c1870.
£150–200 *DDO*

Two Hardy 3½in and 4in Eureka reels, 1922–55.
£130–200 each *PC*

A Hardy 3in Silex Major alloy
bait casting reel, with smooth
brass foot and ivorine casting
trigger, c1925.
£120–160 *DDO*

A Hardy Altex Mk I fixed spool
reel, with 'duck's foot', c1932.
£300–400 *PC*

A Hardy 3/0 Cascapedia
reel, 1935.
£5,500–6,000 *ND*

A brass faced Hardy 4in Perfect
reel, with smooth brass foot,
ivorine handle, face with
straightline logo, 'Rod-in-Hand'
mark, initials 'G.H.', regulator
guard with locking nut, 1906.
£300–350 *S(S)*

A Hardy Altex Mk IV No. 3 reel,
with fixed spool, 1935–65.
£100–150 *PC*

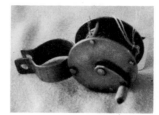

A Victorian 1¾in simple brass
clamp reel.
£90–110 *ND*

l. A Victorian
1½in wide drum
brass pole winch,
with perforated
collar, turned
bone handle and
drum locking
lever, c1850.
£300–400 *DDO*

A Malloch Erskine 3¼in Multiplying
Sidecaster, c1900.
£220–260 *ND*

Painted & Wooden Fish

A carved wooden model, by Farlows, London, of a 46lbs salmon caught by Victor Bonney at Eden, on the Deveron, Scotland, c1928.
£2,500–3,000 *HnT*

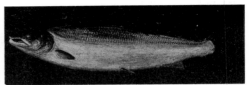

An oil painting on board, entitled 'Salmon Fresh Run Blue Colour', signed 'J. A. H.', board inscribed 'H.W.', 18 by 54in (45.5 by 137cm).
£340–380 *ND*

The fish was caught on 28th May, 1924, was 49in (124.5cm) long, and weighed 47lbs. 'H.W.' was Harry Woolliams, a gilly on the Wye.

Tackle

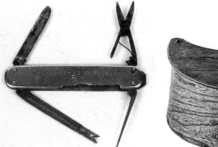

An angler's knife, by Shaw's, Ely, 1892–1914, 3¾in (9.5cm) long.
£100–120 *PC*

A Victorian wooden fishing creel, 15in (38cm) wide.
£220–250 *ND*

Three Victorian clearing rings, 2⅜in diam.
£60–80 each *PC*

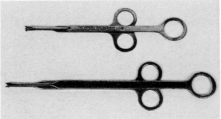

r. A Hardy The 'Houghton' leather cast case, c1940.
£20–40 *DDO*

A Hardy Lambeth brass disgorger, c1929, 7¼in (18.5cm) long.
£50–80 *PC*

A Jeffery disgorger, by S. Allcock & Co Ltd, patent No. '311616', 1928, 7½in (19cm) long.
£80–120
An unnamed disgorger, 9½in (24cm) long.
£60–80 *PC*

A Victorian Malloch patent black japanned swing leaf fly box, with gut eyed flies, 7 by 4in (18 by 10cm).
£260–300 *ND*

A Farlow's keeper ring, c1930, 1½in (4cm) diam.
£20–30 *PC*

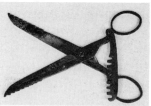

A pike gag, by S. Alcock & Co Ltd, c1898, 6in (15cm) long.
£120–200 *PC*

A telescopic gaff, with turned wooden handle, brass shaft and steel head, early 20thC.
£40–70 *DDO*

A Hardy Wardle fly fisher's magnifier, 1924–70, 3½in (9cm) long.
£20–30 *DDO*

A Hardy Zane Grey grease gun, c1950.
£200–250 *PC*

A Foster's Anglers' Thumb Magnifier, in original box, box 3¾in (9.5cm) wide.
£50–60 *PC*

A combined pocket microscope and line box, 'The Verette', c1930, 1½in (3.5cm) long.
£90–100 *PC*

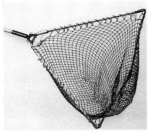

An Allcock's Lockfast landing net, with bamboo shaft, brass fittings and hickory arms, c1915.
£30–70 *DDO*

A Hardy Boomeranc, inscribed, c1911, 6in (15cm) long.
£200–250 *PC*

This multi-purpose tool was used to keep a fish's mouth open in order to remove the hook.

A Hardy angler's thermometer, the outer casing of brass or nickel silver, 1950s.
£10–25 *DDO*

An ebony priest, dated '1797', 9½in (24cm) long.
£125–200 *PC*

A Hardy Gem priest and disgorger, 1940–60, 5in (12.5cm) long.
£10–20 *PC*

A brass eyed hook threader, for tying on hooks and flies in poor light, possibly by Army & Navy, 2in (5cm) long.
£30–60 *DDO*

A Victorian string-bound priest, with brass end, 8½in (21.5cm) long.
£60–90 *PC*

A Hardy trout priest, wood with brass end, c1950, 7in (18cm) long.
£15–25 *DDO*

A rule, inscribed 'The Angler's First Rule', and 'Return all undersized fish to the water immediately', the reverse with 'Guide to Identify Species', 1930s, 18in (45.5cm) extended.
£20–30 *PC*

Golf

A feather-filled golf
ball, c1840.
£1,900–2,200 *C(S)*

Three boxes of golf balls, 1920–30,
7in (18cm) wide.
£100–200 each *MSh*

A gutta-percha golf ball,
with mesh pattern,
stamped 'P. McEwan',
c1880, 1½in (4cm) diam.
£500–600 *MSh*

A steel-headed
cylindrical putter,
by George Sayers
of Scotland,
with hickory
shaft and leather
grip, 20thC.
£250–300 *C(S)*

A collection of club makers'
stamps, including Arthur Lees,
Sunningdale, various dates.
£600–700 *S*

A smooth moulded gutta-
percha golf ball, c1850.
£1,800–2,000 *C(S)*

A glass decanter,
engraved with golfers,
with silver neck band
and top, 1920, 12in
(30.5cm) high.
£400–500 *MSh*

FURTHER READING
Sarah Fabian-Baddiel,
Miller's Golf Memorabilia,
Reed Books, London, 1994.

An untitled sepia photogravure, of ladies playing golf,
by Michael Brown, published by the Life Association
of Scotland, c1900, 9 by 15in (23 by 38cm).
£275–325 *DW*

Tennis

A cast iron tennis ball cleaner, c1910.
£80–120 *MSh*

A chrome-plated British car mascot, by A. E. Lejeune, modelled as a female tennis player about to serve, 1930s, racket later, 5½in (14cm) high.
£500–600 *CSK*

A Spartan tennis racket, made by Harry C. Lee, New York, open throat construction with box trebling and two-tone strings, green and gold trim, patented slotted shaft and octagonal handle, c1910.
£280–330 *CSK*

A lawn tennis racket, with tilted head, original coarse gut strings, walnut convex wedge with initials 'HS' carved on one side, circular walnut handle, mid-1870s.
£1,200–1,500 *CSK*

r. A steel tennis racket, made by Dayton, with piano wire strings and wooden octagonal handle with rubber sleeve, in canvas bag, c1920.
£80–100 *Bon*

A tennis press, made by Geo Bussey & Co, London, 1900–10, 12¾in (32.5cm) square.
£15–30 *MSh*

Soloman Charles Frederick Peile, *Lawn Tennis,* William Blackwood, Edinburgh & London, 1885.
£400–450 *CSK*

A. Wallis Myers, *Lawn Tennis At Home & Abroad,* first edition, 1903.
£60–80 *DW*

A triple card programme, for 'The Lawn Tennis Championships, 1914', with advertisements on the back.
£300–350 *DW*

A shell, with silver inlay, c1880, 1¾in (4.5cm) long.
£120–130 *LBr*

A blue abalone shell, 8in (20cm) long.
£10–15 *ShS*

A Victorian dressing table mirror, the frame decorated with shells.
£40–50 *P(B)*

A Victorian free-standing shell picture frame, with marine watercolour, 8½in (21.5cm) high.
£100–120 *GHA*

A piece of natural red coral, 2½in (6.5cm) wide.
£3–10 *ShS*

A collection of polished and carved silver mouth turban shells, 2½in (6.5cm) wide.
60p–£2 each *ShS*

A pair of Caribbean sailor's Valentine shell collages, 19thC, 18in (46cm) wide.
£2,000–2,200 *Bri*

A pair of Victorian sea shell displays, in the form of flowers and foliage, on circular bases, 20in (51cm) high.
£70–80 *P(B)*

A lamp conch shell, 9½in (24cm) wide.
£15–20 *ShS*

Two sea urchin shells, 5in (13cm) diam.
£3–5 each *ShS*

A gilt bronze plaque of two footballers, by Lemoine, c1910, 8in (20cm) diam.
£120–160 *MSh*

Forty-six Mecca prizefighter's cards, from a set of 50.
£450–500 *S(NY)*

A set of 8 miniature golf clubs, by Auchterlonie, c1920, longest 14½in (37cm).
£1,500–1,800 *MSh*

A jar of Hardy's Preserved Baits, Loach, with original box, c1930, 5½in (14cm) high.
£50–60 *PC*

A brass line twister, with crank handle, 1930s, 7in (18cm) long.
£300–350 *PC*

l. A Hardy 6in reel, 1934–56.
£400–500

A Dartmouth pottery mug, c1948, 5¼in (13.5cm) high.
£55–65 *WN*

A golf advertising figure, 'We play Dunlop', 1920s, 15½in (39.5cm) high.
£450–550 *MSh*

A Hardy's anglers pipe and reamer, with original box, c1960, pipe 6½in (16.5cm) long.
Pipe **£100–150**   Reamer **£20–30** *PC*

A wicker fishing basket, with long carrying handle, c1950, 14in (35.5cm) wide.
£12–15 *TaB*

A leather 'Grasshopper' rugby ball, c1950.
£15–25 *MSh*

A set of 5 Kilncraft mugs, commemorating the Olympic Games, c1984, 3½in (9cm) high.
£20–30 *BCO*

A Coalport Olympic figure, 1984, 8¼in (21cm) high.
£65–75 *BCO*

A beech and brass snooker cue re-tipping tool, 1918, 7in (18cm) lon
£50–60 *BS*

A pudding basin by Gibson & Sons Ltd, Burslem, decorated with tennis players, c1910, 4in (10cm) high. **£80–120** *MSh*

A Granger hockey advertising stand, late 1930s, 34in (86.5cm) high. **£190–220** *S(NY)*

A wooden sledge, made by Naether, c1920, 37½in (95cm) long.
£20–40 *NWE*

A Schoenhut golf toy, 1920s, figure 5in (12.5cm) high.
£100–160 *MSh*

A lob-sided lawn tennis racket, c1880, 26½in (67.5cm) long.
£800–1,200 *MSh*

A pair of Continental ceramic tennis figures, c1900, 9½in (24cm) high.
£80–120 *MSh*

Three boxes of tennis balls, by MacLellan, F. H. Ayres, and Wisden, 1930–50, 8in (20cm) long.
£20–50 each *MSh*

A pied blackbird, mounted
in a picture frame case, by
Murray of Carnforth, c1900,
12in (30.5cm) high.
£150–250 *HnT*

A bittern, by Rowland Ward,
mounted in a new case, 19thC,
19in (48.5cm) square.
£450–485 *BS*

A rabbit, dressed in an
Alice in Wonderland
style tunic, early
20thC, 30in (76cm) high.
£250–300 *HnT*

A roach and tench, mounted in a glazed case, labelled
'Preserved by F. W. Anstiss, 23 First Street, London, S.W,
Caught in Bushy Park', 1920s, 27in (68.5cm) wide.
£375–475 *Gam*

A wild boar, mounted by Rowland
Ward, 19thC, 20in (60cm) wide.
£1,000–1,200 *BS*

A hare mask, by P. Spicer,
Leamington Spa, c1929,
9in (23cm) high.
£100–150 *HnT*

A collection of tropical birds
in a glass domed case,
c1880, 26in (66cm) high.
£300–400 *HnT*

A fox's mask, mounted on a stirrup
leather, by Peter Spicer & Sons,
Leamington Spa, c1955.
£120–150 *HnT*

A Hermann teddy bear, c1950, 12in (30.5cm) high. **£80–120** *BaN*

A House of Nisbet teddy bear, c1950, 8in (20cm) high. **£50–60** *Ber*

A Merrythought Noddy, c1958, 12in (30.5cm) high. **£80–100** *TED*

A Schuco bear, c1959, 2¾in (7cm) high. **£250–300** *TED*

A Japanese Winnie the Pooh, 1964, 6½in (16.5cm) high. **£50–60** *TED*

A Farnell chimpanzee, c1930, 18in (46cm) high. **£150–200** *BaN*

Twin plush bears, late 1960s, 18in (46cm) high. **£20–55** *B&F*

A teddy bear, bandaged arm, 1930s, 27½in (70cm) high. **£120–135** *Ber*

A golden mohair teddy bear, Max, with felt pads, c1965, 19in (48cm) high. **£70–120** *B&F*

A Merrythought Cheeky art silk plush bear, with a bell in each ear, 1950s, 15in (38cm) high. **£200–250** *TED*

A Chad Valley mohair teddy bear, Tim, 1950s, 15½in (39.5cm) high. **£70–150** *B&F*

A mohair teddy bear, with growler, c1950, 26in (66cm) high. **£60–135** *B&F*

A Schuco yes/no teddy bear, 1920s, 18in (45.5cm) high. **£650–750** *DOL*

A Bing teddy bear, with shoe button eyes and hump on back, c1910, 16in (40.5cm) high. **£450–500** *DOL*

A fully jointed mohair teddy bear, c1930, 19in (48.5cm) high. **£130–220** *B&F*

A plush teddy bear, c1960, 21in (53.5cm) high. **£25–65** *B&F*

A telephone, No. 26, c1905,
10in (25.5cm) high.
£900–1,100 *TL*

A candlestick No. 2
telephone, c1910,
21in (53.5cm) high.
£175–225 *TL*

A Danish pay phone,
20thC, 22in (56cm) high.
£120–160 *TL*

*Only a few were produced
for trial purposes.*

A brass intercom mouthpiece, with
whistle, c1900–20, 2⅝in (6.5cm) long.
£50–75 *BS*

A Bakelite telephone, 1930s,
6½in (16.5cm) high.
£175–225 *SCA*

BT Phoneday phonecard, 1995,
Christmas 1988 phonecard cover,
and Youth Series phonecard, 1993.
50p–£3 each *JMC*

A Jersey Telecoms
phonecard, Battle of
Flowers 1990.
£15–30 *JMC*

A wooden telephone, in the form of a boat, c1970,
12½in (32cm) long.
£30–40 *COB*

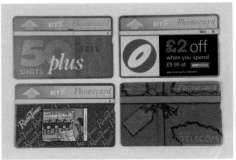

Four BT phonecards, 1988–94.
Used **50p–£1 each**
Mint **£3–6.50 each** *JMC*

A Victorian tile, with floral design, 6in (15cm) square.
£15–20 *BAS*

A dust pressed tile, with transfer printed pattern and hand coloured underglaze, c1900, 6in (15cm) square.
£8–12 *GR*

A Victorian Derwent Foundry tile, 8 by 6in (20 by 15cm).
£35–45 *BAS*

A panel of 8 William de Morgan tiles, with 'Persian' glaze and blue carnation motifs, c1870, each tile 8in (20cm) square.
£1,100–1,400 *Bon*

An encaustic floor tile, c1870, 6in (15cm) square.
£9–12 *GR*

l. A set of 10 Victorian fireplace tiles, 30 by 6in (76 by 15cm).
£200–300 *BAS*

Three hand painted tiles, by Packard & Ord, 'Fantastic Birds', 1930s, 18 by 6in (46 by 15cm).
£70–80 *GFR*

A panel of 'Atlantic Avenue' hand painted tiles, from a restaurant, c1936, 40 by 60in (101.5 by 152.5cm).
£600–750 *COB*

A pair of Victorian tiles, 12 by 6in (30.5 by 15cm).
£30–40 *BAS*

A panel of 4 Copeland tiles, c1880, 32 by 8in (81.5 by 20cm).
£150–195 *GR*

A Gemini friction-driven rocket, 1960s, 4in (10cm) wide.
£35–45 *COB*

A wooden horse and cart, by Lines Bros, pre-WWII, 39in (99cm) long.
£400–425 *JUN*

A Fisher-Price wooden pull-along hen, 1940s, 9½in (24cm) high.
£10–15 *OPH*

A clockwork tinplate drummer, one stick missing, c1930, 9¼in (23.5cm) high.
£50–75 *MRW*

A tinplate clockwork bird, c1930–40, 7in (18cm) wide.
£10–12 *AnE*

l. Two Japanese tinplate robots, c1960, 11½in (29cm) high.
£150–200 each
TOY

A Comet wooden 'Model Airplane' kit, c1944, 11in (28cm) long.
£10–15 *COB*

A tinplate train and track, mounted on a board, 1950s, 14in (35.5cm) wide.
£20–25 *WCA*

An Indian wooden puzzle bus, 1950s, 18in (45.5cm) long.
£8–10 *FAL*

A Corgi Toys No. 1110 Mobilgas
Petrol Tanker, c1959.
£75–100 *WN*

A set of 3 Days-Gone trucks, boxed, 1990s, each
truck 3½in (9cm) long.
£8–10 *FAL*

A Dinky Toys van, c1948,
3in (7.5cm) long.
£16–18 *FAL*

A Dinky Toys Hillman Minx
Saloon car, c1958, 3½in
(9cm) long. **£75–85** *FAL*

A toy fire engine, Duke Express, 1930s,
28in (71cm) long.
£100–150 *WCA*

A Corgi Toys *The Man from U.N.C.L.E.* Gun Firing
Thrush-Buster, c1966, mint and boxed.
£60–90 *WN*

Two tinplate clockwork vans, c1930,
3½in (9cm) long.
£100–150 *MRW*

A Corgi Toys 'Black Beauty' Crime Fighting Car,
from *The Green Hornet*, 1967, boxed.
£175–200 *WN*

A Corgi Toys No. 261 James Bond Aston Martin DB5,
from *Goldfinger*, c1967, mint and boxed.
£70–100 *WN*

A Chinese battery-operated 'Photoing on
car' camera, c1990, 12in (30.5cm) long.
£50–70 *VCL*

A Sutcliffe Nautilus clockwork submarine, 1950, 10½in (27cm) long.
£100–150 *TOY*

A Lincoln International remote-controlled Stingray, 1960s, box 13½in (34.5cm) long.
£150–200 *TOY*

A set of 4 *Thunderbirds* postcards, published by Engale Marketing and Athena, 1980s.
80p–£1 each *JMC*

A Captain Scarlet Escape & Capture game, c1967, box 16in (40.5cm) long.
£200–300 *TOY*

A Captain Scarlet puppet, from the original TV series, 1967, 23in (58.5cm) high.
£21,000–23,000 *P*

A Peter Pan Series Pop-Eye, Pipe and Ring Game, c1929, box 15in (38cm) long.
£60–80 *TOY*

A Pedigree Joe 90 doll, c1968, 19in (48.5cm) high.
£80–100 *CTO*

A set of Mazda 'Bambi' Disneylights, 1950s, box 16in (40.5cm) wide.
£80–120 *TOY*

A Lady Penelope puppet, from the original *Thunderbirds* TV series, 1965, 21in (53.5cm) high.
£35,000–40,000 *P*

A Pedigree Captain Scarlet doll, 1960, 11½in (29cm) high.
£150–200 *TOY*

The Dalek Oracle quiz game, by
Bell, c1965, 16in (40.5cm) wide.
£100–150 *TOY*

Three Aurora all-plastic assembly
kits, 1960s, 13in (33cm) high.
£100–150 each *TOY*

A Star Wars *Return of the Jedi*
X-wing fighter, by Palitoy,
c1983, 14in (35.5cm) wide.
£35–45 *TOY*

Two bionic man dolls,
by Denys Fisher, 1970s,
14in (35.5cm) high.
£40–80 each *TOY*

A Star Trek *The Next Generation*
model kit, by Geometric, Japanese,
1980s, 12in (30.5cm) high.
£50–80 *ALI*

A diecast string puppet, Mr. Turnip,
The Children's Favourite Television
Puppet, 1950s, 7in (18cm) high.
£50–70 *TOY*

A Marvel Comics
Super Heroes lunch
box, 1974, 8in (20cm)
wide. **£15–20** *COB*

A Billiken tinplate mechanical
toy, The Joker, c1989,
9in (23cm) high.
£75–85 *TOY*

A Noddy battery-operated projector, with
35mm film strips, 1980s, 8in (20cm) wide.
£10–12 *HEG*

A Comic Action Heroes game, by Denys
Fisher, c1976, 18in (45.5cm) wide.
£10–20 *ALI*

A 9ct gold pocket watch, by
John Forrest, fusee movement,
1908, 2¼in (55mm) diam.
£500–600 *BWC*

A Buren gold plated pocket
watch, c1930.
£75–100 *BWC*

A marcasite and silver
watch/ brooch, c1920,
2¼in (55mm) diam.
£200–250 *SPE*

A Swiss watch, the cover in the
form of a mesh pattern golf
ball, c1920, 1½in (38mm) diam.
£180–200 *MSh*

A Rodonia watch,
with 17 jewels,
manual wind, c1950.
£65–80 *BWC*

A Snoopy wrist-
watch, 1970s.
£45–55 *BWC*

A Seiko Bellmatic
stainless steel wristwatch,
with 17 jewels, 1960–70.
£75–100 *BWC*

A Russian submarine
commander's watch, c1980.
£60–75 *BWC*

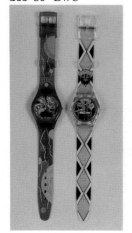

Two Power Ranger watches,
from Burger King, 1995.
£5–6 each *PC*

A Swatch 'Happy
Fish' watch, c1991.
£175–200 *BWC*

An Omega Genève
automatic watch, 1970s.
£175–200 *BWC*

A pocket vesta watch,
1930s, 2¾in (70mm) long.
£80–100 *MRW*

A George VI postbox, with key, 20in (51cm) high.
£400–450 *BS*

A wall-mounted postbox, c1912–50, 33in (84cm) high.
£150–175 *WEL*

A postbox, with key, c1912–50, 20in (51cm) high.
£350–400 *BS*

An Edward VII cast iron pillar box, with lock and key, 81in (205.5cm) high.
£1,400–1,500 *BS*

A Salter Standard Patent Improved No. 6 typewriter, with vertical typeface, early 20thC.
£110–140 *MAW*

An oak inkstand, with two glass bottles, c1890, 10in (25.5cm) wide.
£125–150 *WCA*

r. An Edward VII wall-mounted post box, with lock and key, c1901–11.
£400–450 *BS*

A Victorian pillar box, pre-1900, 81in (205.5cm) high.
£1,400–1,500 *BS*

An ink bottle, with wicker covering and handle, early 20thC, 7in (18cm) high.
£10–15 *TaB*

A Tunbridge ware inkstand, c1850–60, 11in (28cm) wide.
£675–750 *AMH*

A collection of pencil sharpeners, in the form of
cameras and viewers, 1950–90, largest 3½in (9cm) long.
£1–5 each *HEG*

An American scarf, c1950,
40in (101.5cm) square.
£3–5 *PC*

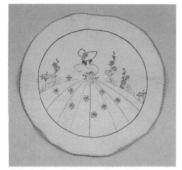

A hand embroidered cushion
cover, 1930s, 13in (33cm) diam.
£1–3 *PC*

A ceramic plate, unmarked,
1950–60, 7in (18cm) diam.
50p–£1 *PC*

A McVitie's biscuit tin, 1990s,
5in (12.5cm) long.
£4–5 *FAL*

A set of 4 drinking glasses, decorated with
pirates, 1960s, 2in (50mm) high.
50p–£1 each *PC*

A collection of French sugar sachets, 1990s.
1–2p each *PC*

A collection of flower brooches, 1950–60.
£4–5 each *STP*

A collection of plastic eye baths, 1980–90,
1½in (40mm) high.
£1–2 each *PC*

A pair of Dr Martens boots, 1995.
£35–40 *PC*

A decorative twist on a classic design, and a good example of 1990s style.

Led Zeppelin II, LP, 1969, signed by Robert Plant and Jimmy Page in 1995.
£80–100 *PC*

Although this is an old record, its value is enhanced by the recent signatures of the original artists.

A press pack for the launch of Gerry Anderson's *Space Precinct* sci-fi series for Sky Television, the silver 'transfer cylinder' with light sensitive device that bleeps when tube is opened, March 1995.

Although originally distributed free its value will be determined when sold. *PC*

A collection of Tetley Teafolk Houses, given away with packets of Tetley's teabags, 1995.
£3–4 each, including teabags *PC*

Jan Pienkowski, *ABC Dinosaurs*, a pop-up book, published by Heinemann, 1993.
£13 *PC*

There are many fine examples of pop-up books produced today, and perfect specimens could become collectable in the future.

A selection of small format books, published to commemorate Penguin Books' 60th anniversary, 1995, and could become collectables of the future.
60p each *TBo*

A collection of Limoges hand painted pill boxes, in the form of vegetables, with gilt metal mounts, signed, 1990s, largest 4in (10cm) long.
£50–100 each *JPr*

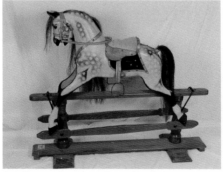

A tulip wood and poplar reproduction rocking horse, by Stevenson Brothers, from an original design by F. H. Ayres, 1987.
£1,800–2,000 *STE*

STANHOPES

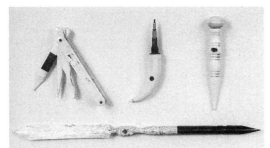

Four bone Stanhopes, with various views, c1900, lace pricker 2¾in (7cm) long.
£25–30 each *PC*

An ivory Stanhope needle case, showing erotic pictures, c1890, 3in (7.5cm) long.
£175–195 *MLa*

A mother-of-pearl Stanhope watch fob, c1890, 4in (10cm) long.
£150–170 *MLa*

A metal and wire Stanhope needle case, with views of Swanage, c1890, 2¾in (7cm) long.
£100–125 *MLa*

A brass Stanhope bookmark, with views of Brightlingsea, c1890, 4¼in (11cm) long.
£120–140 *MLa*

A Stanhope in the form of a pig, made from bog oak, c1880, ½in (12.5mm) long.
£40–45 *PC*

r. A Stanhope magnifying glass, with views of Sutton Coldfield, c1890, 2¾in (7cm) long.
£180–200 *MLa*

A coquilla nut Stanhope basket, with views of the Bridge of Allan, Scotland, c1900, 2½in (6.5cm) high.
£180–200 *MLa*

Two pairs of gold metal Stanhope binoculars, one as a key ring, c1900, largest 1½in (4cm) long.
£15–18 each
A pair of bone Stanhope binoculars, and a bone Stanhope monocular, c1900, binoculars 1in (25mm) long.
£25–30 each *PC*

Stanhopes

- Stanhopes are small trinkets or souvenirs made from materials such as ivory, wood and bone.
- They contain a photographic transparency, mounted on a minute microscope lens.
- The lens itself was invented in the late 18thC by the Earl of Stanhope. In 1853 David Brewster conceived the idea of placing the tiny photograph and lens within a piece of jewellery, thus creating the first Stanhope.
- The main period of manufacture was from the 1860s to 1920s, mostly in England and France. Popular subjects depicted topographical scenes, famous people and public events.
- Look out for early examples and unusual images such as Royalty, nudes and views outside England and France. Hand-tinted photographs and any object containing more than one Stanhope are also desirable.

TAXIDERMY

Although taxidermy can appear strange, or even somewhat distasteful today, in the 19th century having a stuffed animal in the drawing room was no more peculiar than hanging a picture on the wall. The Victorian and Edwardian periods were the great age of taxidermy and, ruled by an animal loving queen, the British public was fascinated by animals, in every possible contradictory sense. On the one hand, pet ownership sprang up, natural history was a popular hobby, and museums and zoos were opened to the public. On the other hand, hunting was the national sport, fur and feathers were indispensable fashion accessories and every family drawing room had its glass case of stuffed birds.

Taxidermy can be divided into three major categories: scientific, hunting and decorative. For the 19th century naturalist, stuffing an animal was often the only way to preserve it for research and natural history museums today still display these zoological specimens. With hunting trophies, taxidermists specialised in a given field. Peter Spicer of Leamington Spa (1839–1934) was famous for fox masks, Rowland Ward (1848–1912) concentrated on big game throughout the British Empire and Cooper's of London (active until the 1950s) was the master of cased fish. Taxidermy designed for predominantly decorative purposes, includes cases of exotic birds and bizarre anthropomorphic creations in which small animals (rabbits, rodents, even frogs) were dressed up and often displayed in miniaturized domestic tableaux.

The stuffed animals illustrated in this section are all old or antique. The laws governing the sale of taxidermy are strict. Dealers must be registered with the Department of the Environment and full records of each item must be preserved.

Animals

Two antelopes' heads, mounted by Rowland Ward. **£250–300** *Bon*

An African gnu's head, mounted by Rowland Ward, No. 6901, c1880, 49in (124.5cm) high. **£800–900** *BS*

A red stag's head, mounted on a wooden shield, by P. Spicer & Sons, Leamington Spa, c1913, 56in (142cm) high. **£250–350** *HnT*

A Vaddacachi Ceylon deer's head, mounted by Rowland Ward, c1908, 44in (112cm) high. **£300–345** *BS*

l. A ram's head, mounted by J. E. Massey of Malton, c1900, 15in (38cm) high. **£200–250** *HnT*

r. A head of an antelope, from N. W. Rhodesia, mounted by Rowland Ward, c1911, 15in (38cm) high. **£120–150** *HnT*

A pair of East African gazelles' horns, c1900, 26in (66cm) high.
£60–70 *BS*

l. A fox's mask, mounted on a wooden shield, and a brush, by P. Spicer & Sons, Leamington Spa, c1927.
£75–150 *HnT*

r. A Colobus monkey, mounted on a base, by James Gardner, c1900, 24in (61cm) high.
£400–500 *HnT*

An Indian pangolin, with extended tail, c1900, 38in (97cm) long.
£600–700 *Bon*

Three bird-eating spiders, in glazed case, c1950, 20in (51cm) wide.
£100–150 *HnT*

l. A collection of spiders and bugs, in glazed case, c1950, 12in (30.5cm) square.
£40–60 *HnT*

Two horses' hooves, by Rowland Ward of Piccadilly, in the form of ashtrays, one inscribed 'Josephine II, 1904–1927', the other 'Pierrot', late 1920s.
£50–150 each *HnT*

Birds

A white domestic dove, by
J. Cooper, mounted in a
bowfronted case, c1910,
14in (35.5cm) wide.
£200–300 *HnT*

A green Amazon parrot, by
James Gardner, London,
mounted in a wall dome, c1920.
£250–300 *HnT*

A whimbrel, c1900, mounted in
a new case, 19in (48.5cm) high.
£400–450 *BS*

An African great horned owl,
perched on a stump, mounted by
Rowland Ward, in a glass case.
£650–750 *Bon*

A pair of barn owls, perched
amidst ferns and grasses,
inscribed on reverse 'Shot by
J. G. Abram, March 18th,
1903', 21in (53.5cm) wide.
£120–150 *DA*

An English puffin, c1900,
mounted in a new case,
15in (38cm) high.
£350–365 *BS*

An immature tawny owl,
c1900, mounted in a new case,
14in (35.5cm) high.
£250–275 *BS*

A peregrine falcon,
c1900, mounted in a new
case, 26in (66cm) high.
£1,400–1,600 *BS*

A sulphur crested cockatoo,
c1880, mounted in a new
case, 26in (66cm) high.
£600–650 *BS*

Fish

Five roach, by J. Cooper & Sons, in a bowfronted case, c1884, 35in (89cm) wide.
£2,000–2,500 *HnT*

A tench, amidst reeds, taken by Mr Butler, September 15th, 1908, preserved by W. F. Homer, 157 Forest Lane, Forest Gate, London, in glazed case, 22in (56cm) wide.
£225–300 *Oli*

Two roach, by F. T. Williams & Co, 10 Queen Street, London WC, entitled 'Roach Taken by Gus Elen from the Avon, Fordingbridge, 22 July, 1904, weights 1lb 10ozs and 1lb 5ozs', 26in (66cm) wide.
£700–800 *Mit*

A carp, by W. F. Homer, in a bowfronted glass case, c1919, 28½in (72.5cm) wide.
£1,000–1,200 *HnT*

A salmon, by J. Cooper & Sons, caught in the Battery Pavilion Water, Melrose, November 15th, 1912, LWM, 28½lbs, 48½in (123cm) wide.
£1,200–1,400 *DN*

A perch, by J. Cooper, mounted in a bowfronted glass case, 1937, 11in (28cm) wide.
£800–1,000 *HnT*

A brown trout, 7¼lbs, caught in Windermere Lake, 1937, with label on reverse 'H. Murray & Son, Naturalists & Specialists in Pictorial Taxidermy, Bank Buildings, Carnforth'.
£500–600 *Mit*

A carp, 4½lbs, caught at Rainham 30.11.50 by P. Mayes, preserved by Homers, 105 Woodgrange Road, Forest Gate, London, mounted in a bowfronted glazed case, 25¾in (65.5cm) wide.
£500–550 *Oli*

MAKE THE MOST OF MILLER'S

Price ranges in this book reflect what you should expect to *pay* for a similar example. When selling, however, you should expect to receive a lower figure. This will fluctuate according to a dealer's stock and saleability at a particular time. It is always advisable, when selling a collectable, to approach a reputable dealer or an auction house which has specialist sales.

TEDDY BEARS & SOFT TOYS

As early teddy bears grow ever more expensive, collectors have been turning to bears from the 1950s and '60s, the teddies that they themselves might have owned as children. 'This is a very good period for anybody who wishes to start collecting,' notes dealer Ian Pout. 'There are a lot of bears available within the £50–200 bracket and values will certainly go up in the future.' As with early bears, Steiff examples from the 1950s and '60s are the most desirable and attract an international market.

Also very popular are bears by English companies, such as Merrythought and Farnell, which have now become collectable across the world. With bears from this period, the presence of a label is crucial and good condition is all-important. Related booklets, packaging or a contemporary photograph showing the bear with its original child owner will also enhance its value. In the field of contemporary bears, Ian Pout recommends Steiff limited editions as a good bet for a collectable of the future. Judging from past evidence, parents who choose to invest in a Steiff or any other modern soft toy, would do well to photograph their children with it, thus giving their bear that little bit of background history that could enhance its potential interest.

A Bing teddy bear, with shoe button eyes and hump, c1910, 14in (35.5cm) high.
£400–500 *DOL*

A straw-filled teddy bear, possibly Farnell, early 20thC, 12in (30.5cm) high.
£350–400 *BaN*

A straw-filled plush teddy bear, worn, replaced pads, c1910, 18in (46cm) high.
£200–250 *BaN*

A Knickerbocker straw-filled teddy bear, with black mohair, orange and black glass eyes, gold embroidered nose and mouth, fully jointed, velvet cloth pads, worn, c1920, 18in (45.5cm) high.
£250–350 *Bon*

A Bing golden mohair teddy bear, large brown and black glass eyes, clipped snout, black stitched nose, mouth and claws, swivel head, jointed shaped limbs, felt pads and hump, worn and damaged, c1920, 19in (48.5cm) high.
£475–575 *CSK*

A German soccer playing teddy bear, possibly by Bing, with jointed arms, c1910, 5½in (14cm) high.
£500–600 *TED*

The wind-up clockwork ball rotates moving the bear along as though he is kicking it forward.

A Schuco yes/no teddy bear, with head that moves up-and-down and from side-to-side, c1924, worn, 23in (58.5cm) high.
£1,200–1,500 *TED*

The value of this bear is increased by the accompanying photograph of the bear with his original owner in 1925.

A lilac mohair teddy bear, no label, c1930, 21in (53.5cm) high.
£250–300 *TED*

A Chad Valley fully jointed golden mohair teddy bear, c1950, 14in (35.5cm) high.
£100–150 *B&F*

An Invicta Toys Ltd teddy bear, no label, c1945, 12in (30.5cm) high.
£80–100 *TED*

A cotton plush teddy bear, stuffed with wood shavings, 1950s, 9in (23cm) high.
£45–50 *TED*

This bear is believed to have been made in Eastern Europe and was a popular design during the 1950s, but seldom, if ever, found with original maker's label.

A Chad Valley teddy bear, Harry, original labels, c1940, 27in (68.5cm) high.
£300–400 *B&F*

A fully jointed mohair teddy bear, c1940, 12in (30.5cm) high.
£100–165 *B&F*

A Chad Valley teddy bear, Sam, c1950, 15in (38cm) high.
£50–90 *B&F*

r. A Chiltern teddy bear, Henry, no label, late 1950s, 13in (33cm) high.
£90–165 *B&F*

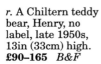

A Pedigree mohair teddy bear, Simon, c1950, 11in (28cm) high.
£60–120 *B&F*

A Twyford's fully jointed mohair teddy bear, c1950, 14in (35.5cm) high.
£70–145 *B&F*

A Schuco miniature teddy
bear, fully jointed, c1950,
3½in (9cm) high.
£100–120 *TED*

*This bear, with original
red, white and blue silk
ribbon, was made for the
American market.*

A Schuco teddy bear, with
growler, no label, c1955,
20in (51cm) high.
£150–175 *TED*

A Pedigree teddy bear,
Douglas, c1960, 13½in
(34.5cm) high.
£85–145 *B&F*

A teddy bear, Bert, c1960,
16in (40.5cm) high.
£40–90 *B&F*

A Chiltern teddy bear, Archie,
c1960, 16in (40.5cm) high.
£40–95 *B&F*

A Steiff teddy bear,
Jasmine, c1960,
15in (38cm) high.
£300–375 *B&F*

Soft Toys

A terrier toy dog, c1930,
5½in (14cm) high.
£40–50 *MRW*

A Steiff gold plush lioness,
with cup-shaped ears, black
and amber glass eyes, red
and black stitched snout with
white muzzle, moving limbs,
stitched claws, long tail and
button to ear, 9in (23cm) high.
£250–300 *P(HSS)*

A knitted golly, c1950,
12½in (32cm) high.
£8–10 *SP*

TELEPHONES & PHONECARDS
Telephones

A Danish black telephone, with crest inscribed 'JYDSK', c1909, 13in (33cm) high.
£90–100 *PIA*

A Danish white telephone, with horn, 1908, 10in (25.5cm) wide.
£185–285 *TL*

These telephones were generally produced in black so white examples are more valuable.

An L. M. Ericsson & Co skeleton telephone, No. 16, c1900, 11in (28cm) high.
£400–600 *TL*

r. A Danish telephone, with crest, c1915, 10in (25.5cm) high.
£90–130 *TL*

MAKE THE MOST OF MILLER'S

Condition is absolutely vital when assessing the value of any item. Damaged pieces appreciate much less than perfect examples. However, a rare, desirable piece may command a high price even when damaged.

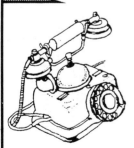

A Strowger telephone, 1930,
5½in (14cm) high.
£150–185 *TL*

*This telephone was used by
the Independent Hull
Telephone Company.*

A French candlestick telephone,
c1920, 12in (30.5cm) high.
£175–225 *TL*

A candlestick telephone, c1931,
13in (33cm) high.
£180–200 *PIA*

A Bell metal telephone,
1930s, 6in (15cm) high.
£60–80 *TL*

A Bell wall telephone, 1930s,
9in (23cm) high.
£60–80 *TL*

A green telephone, No. 232F,
c1938, 9in (23cm) wide.
£450–500 *PIA*

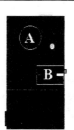

A white Bakelite telephone, No. 232, c1940, 9in (23cm) wide.
£275–325 *TL*

A Siemens black Bakelite wall telephone, 1940s, 9in (23cm) wide.
£60–70 *TL*

A black 300 series telephone, c1943, 9in (23cm) wide.
£60–75 *PIA*

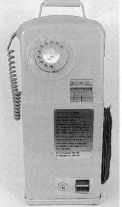

l. A coin-operated red telephone, No. 725, c1966, 18½in (47cm) high.
£60–75 *PIA*

r. A button A and B coin collecting box, No. 32, for telephone kiosk, c1950, 13in (33cm) high.
£160–180 *PIA*

r. A red telephone, No. 706, c1964, 9in (23cm) wide.
£40–50 *PIA*

Intercoms

A lignum vitae and brass tube intercom, with silk-covered hose and whistle, 19thC, 14½in (37cm) long.
£100–125 BS

A lignum vitae and brass mouthpiece intercom, with whistle, 19thC, 2½in (6.5cm) long.
£50–65 BS

Phonecards

Six BT private commission cards.
£25–75 each PC

Phonecards in mint condition are the most desirable, commanding higher sums than used cards.

Four commemorative Mercurycards, 1991.
£10–20 each JMC

A Mercurycard, one of a set of six cards issued by Boots.
£4–6 PC

20,000 of these cards were produced.

r. A Manx Telecom phonecard, Series 9, 3rd TT Races, showing Geoff Duke, 1990.

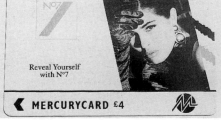

r. A Mercurycard, in support of The Prince's Trust, showing Harry Enfield and Phil Collins, c1991.
£2–3 each JMC

TILES

In the past, as today, tiles were predominantly made for architectural purposes, to be placed on floors, walls and fireplaces, although they were also used to decorate furniture. Tile making in Britain dates back to the Middle Ages, but the principle periods for collectors are the 18th century and, more commonly, the Victorian and Edwardian eras, the great age of the British tile.

In the 18th century the English potters, inspired by Dutch examples, began to produce delftware tiles. Main centres of manufacture included Lambeth, Bristol and Liverpool where, in 1756, John Sadler perfected the technique of transferring engraved prints on to white tiles. Cheap and quick to produce, transfer printed tiles were much used in the following century.

The Victorian building boom led to a huge increase in demand of tiles. Major 19th century producers include Minton's, Maw & Co, Pilkington's and Wedgwood, as well as a host of other firms.

The manufacturer's name and/or trademark often appear on the underside of a tile. Registration marks can provide a date and pencilled builder's instructions can occasionally be found on tile backs.

Designs of Victorian tiles cover a huge range of styles and subjects. One of the greatest names in the field is leading Arts and Crafts potter, William de Morgan (1839–1917), whose tiles can fetch hundreds or even thousands of pounds. Tiles associated with Morris & Co are always in demand, as are decorative examples from the Art Nouveau period. At the lower end of the scale, individual Victorian and Edwardian tiles can be purchased for under £10, and antique tiles can still cost less than modern examples.

17th & 18th Century

Four blue tin glazed tiles, probably London, depicting biblical subjects, 18thC, 5in (12.5cm) square.
£180–240 *Bon*

A Dutch polychrome tin glazed tile, painted with a dromedary in blue, orange and green, 17thC, 5¼in (13.5cm) wide.
£225–275 *Bon*

Four tiles, probably Bristol, 2 with figures, 2 with floral designs, chips and flakes, c1700, 5in (12.5cm) square.
£90–110 *Bon*

A transfer printed tin glazed tile, by John Sadler, depicting 'The Lion and the Frog', from *Aesop's Fables*, c1770.
£80–100 *JHo*

A transfer printed tin glazed tile, by John Sadler, depicting 'The Geese and the Cranes', from *Aesop's Fables*, c1770.
£220–240 *JHo*

A set of 6 London delft tiles, each decorated in blue, green and manganese with a vase of flowers and leaves, the blue powdered ground with manganese carnation corners, c1730–50, in two modern oak frames.
£110–150 *DN*

19th & Early 20th Century

An Art Nouveau tile, unmarked, c1900, 6 by 3in (15 by 7.5cm).
£15–20 *BAS*

An Art Nouveau tile, unmarked, c1900, 6 by 3in (15 by 7.5cm).
£15–20 *BAS*

Two Chinese hand painted tiles, c1860, 5in (12.5cm) square.
£100–120 each *BAS*

l. A dust pressed tile, with moulded abstract pattern in Art Nouveau style, unmarked, c1900, 6in (15cm) square.
£8–12 *GR*

A Victorian Derwent Foundry tile, marked on reverse, 6 by 8in (15 by 20cm).
£35–45 *BAS*

A dust pressed tile, probably by Edge Malkin & Co, transfer printed with a pattern depicting 'Youth', c1880, 6in (15cm) square.
£30–40 *GR*

l. A Victorian tile, by Minton & Co, 6in (15cm) square.
£12–15 *BAS*

A tile panel, by Minton & Co, made up of encaustic blue, black and brown tiles, decorated with anthemion scrolls, in a frame, 17½in (44.5cm) square.
£110–150 *Bon*

A Victorian tile, by Minton & Co, from a set of 6 round a fireplace, 6in (15cm) square.
£12–15 *BAS*

Minton

The Minton porcelain factory was founded in 1793 in Stoke-on-Trent, Staffordshire, by Thomas Minton. Tile production began c1830 under his son, Herbert Minton, who experimented with new tile making techniques and collaborated with leading designers of the day, such as Owen Jones and Gothic architect A. W. N. Pugin, on commissions that included the flooring of the House of Commons in 1852. In 1845 Michael Daintry Hollins joined the company and between 1845 and 1868 the firm traded as both Minton & Hollins and Minton & Co. The partnership split in 1868 and Hollins established his own tile business, known as Minton Hollins & Co.

A panel of 12 tiles, by Minton & Hollins, hand painted with the months of the year, sunflowers replacements, one tile repaired, c1870, 24 by 18in (61 by 45.5cm).
£400–450 *Bon*

Two Wedgwood tiles, one depicting Plymouth Rock, c1907, the other New Building Corner, Boston, 1915, with advertising calendars on reverse, 4¾ by 3¼in (12 by 8.5cm).
£60–75 each *MLa*

A tile panel, by Minton & Hollins, made up of polychrome, hand painted tiles, depicting Jesus flanked by disciples and children, one tile repaired, c1880, 12 by 18in (30.5 by 45.5cm).
£275–325 *Bon*

A Qajar type tile, brightly decorated with courtly figures in a landscape with flowers, animals and buildings, floral borders, 19thC, some damage, 14 by 13in (35.5 by 33cm).
£300–400 *DN*

A Victorian embossed tile, maker unknown, 6in (15cm) square.
£6–8 *GFR*

A Wedgwood blue and white tile, depicting the month of June, c1870, 6in (15cm) square.
£40–45 *WAG*

TOOLS

A French silversmith's hammer, with steel head and boxwood handle, c1900, 9in (23cm) long.
£45–55 *BS*

A Victorian claw hammer, 7in (18cm) long.
£30–50 *MRW*

A fret drill, with ebonised grips, 19thC, 8in (20cm) long.
£45–55 *BS*

This drill works on the Archimedean principle, with the bits contained inside a narrow grip.

A weaving shuttle, c1900, 15in (38cm) long.
£3–5 *WCA*

A steel screw gauge, 19thC, 4½in (11.5cm) long.
£18–25 *BS*

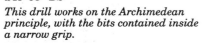

r. Two wooden carders, with metal teeth, used for teasing wool, early 20thC, 9½in (24cm) wide.
£25–30 *TaB*

A carpet fitting tool, with ash handle, early 20thC, 25½in (65cm) long.
£15–20 *WAC*

A nickel and cast iron device for measuring the inside of a hat, c1900, 6in (15cm) diam.
£70–80 *BS*

A yarn wheel, c1880, 29in (73.5cm) wide.
£50–60 *WCA*

TOYS

A lithographed paper and board toy theatre, inscribed 'The Theatrette', depicting *Snow White and the Seven Dwarfs,* with paper label 'The Martin Studios Inc, Hartford, Connecticut', lithograph board figures, props, scenery and curtains, the wood and metal stands electrified, theatre surround damaged, late 19thC, 22in (56cm) high.
£200–225 *SK(B)*

A suede leather-covered toy model of a cow, wearing a cowbell, the head articulated and mooing when moved, with mahogany grained four-wheel base, early 20thC, 13in (33cm) high.
£330–380 *N*

A Japanese battery-operated musical mobile car, The Monkees, 1960s, 13½in (34cm) long.
£300–350 *NTM*

A ventriloquist's dummy, with 2 spare heads, c1920.
£500–550 *AAV*

A terracotta Felix the cat, 1930s, 5in (13cm) high.
£300–350 *TOY*

A pair of handpainted pottery footballing gollies, c1960, 2¼in (5.5cm) high.
£10–12 each *TAC*

Gollies were produced in several different footballing positions. Plastic examples were made in the 1970s and are worth £3–5 each.

A French flock covered carton Boston terrier, white with black markings, moving head with glass eyes, painted pink mouth which opens and growls on a chain pull, bristle ruff and red flock covered collar, on casters, early 20thC, 18in (45.5cm) long.
£700–800 *WW*

The high price range reflects the fact that this dog is in good condition, with its barking mechanism still intact.

A Mickey Mouse candle holder, 1930s, 5in (13cm) high.
£200–250 *TOY*

A trio of Schoenhut hand-carved Felix the cat wooden figures, with articulated limbs, original leather ears, 1930s, tallest 8in (20cm) high.
£450–500 *CNY*

A clockwork toy camera, with walking mechanism, 20thC, 2½in (6.5cm) high.
£2–3 *HEG*

Two Japanese battery-operated toys, 'Good Time Charley' and 'Picnic Bear', c1950, 12in (30.5cm) high.
£100–200 each *TOY*

A celluloid model frog riding a duck, c1930, 2in (5cm) wide.
£8–10 *LBe*

A Bowman's model rubber speedboat, *Aeroboat II*, the wooden hull with brass gearbox fittings, finished in blue and cream, some paint peeling, c1934, 30in (76cm) long, with original box.
£130–150 *AH*

A Bowman's spirit-fired steam boat, *Snipe*, with single cylinder engine spirit burner and boiler, wooden hull with brass fittings, finished in blue and cream, c1935, 23in (58.5cm) long, in original box with instructions.
£200–250 *AH*

A Hornby No. 5 cabin cruiser, *Viking,* with clockwork mechanism, finished in blue and cream with red lining, 1930s.
£140–170 *Bon*

Diecast Toys

l. A Revell Porsche 930 turbo, in original box, c1992, 9in (23cm) long.
£14–16 *FAL*

r. An Ertl Classic Vehicles '68 G.T.O., in original box, c1992, 4½in (11.5cm) long.
£4–6 *FAL*

Corgi Toys

A Corgi No. 200M Ford Consul Saloon, with friction motor, 1950, 4in (10cm) long.
£80–90 *NTM*

A Corgi No. 421 Bedford 12cwt Van 'Evening Standard', 1960s, 3½in (9cm) long.
£80–120 *NTM*

A Corgi No. 239 Volkswagen 1500 Karmann Ghia, 1960s, 4in (10cm) long.
£40–50 *NTM*

A Corgi gift set No. 23 Chipperfields Circus, including crane truck, 2 animal cages, a Bedford tractor unit, an elephant cage and a Land Rover, together with a plastic elephant, 2 polar bears, 2 lions and 2 giraffes, animals still in original plastic bags, 1964.
£380–430 *Bon*

A Corgi No. 1120 Midland Red Motorway Express Coach, 1950s, 6in (15cm) long.
£90–110 *NTM*

A Corgi No. 275 Rover 2000 TC, painted white, 1960s, 5in (13cm) long.
£75–85 *NTM*

A Corgi Set No. 511 Chipperfields Performing Poodles, in original box, 1960s, box 4in (10cm) long.
£375–425 *NTM*

A Corgi No. 153 Proteus Campbell 'Bluebird' Record Car, 1950s, 5¼in (13.5cm) long.
£40–50 *NTM*

Dinky Toys

A Dinky No. 25k fire engine, with 6 tinplate firemen, 1930s, 1930s, 4in (10cm) long.
£200–250 *NTM*

A Dinky No. 28 Kodak Film van, in yellow livery, with solid wheels, worn, pre-WWII.
£425–500 *WAL*

A Dinky No. 160 Austin A30 Saloon, 1950s, 3½in (9cm) long.
£75–90 *NTM*

A Dinky No. 27k Hay Rake, 1950s, 3½in (9cm) long.
£20–25 *NTM*

A Dinky No. 482 Bedford 10cwt Van, 1950, 3½in (9cm) long.
£90–100 *NTM*

A Dinky bus, c1950, 3½in (9cm) long.
£20–24 *FAL*

A Dinky car, c1946, 4in (10cm) long.
£18–20 *FAL*

A Dinky car, post-WWII, 4in (10cm) long.
£30–35 *FAL*

A Dinky Castrol oil tanker, c1950, 4½in (11.5cm) long.
£18–20 *FAL*

A Dinky Supertoys No. 666 Missile Erector Vehicle, with corporal missile and launching platform, together with packing card, instructions and original box, some wear, box dated '12.59'.
£200–250 *WIL*

A Matchbox Series No. 33 Ford Zodiac, 1950s, 1½in (4cm) long.
£30–35 *NTM*

A Dinky No. 305 David Brown Tractor, 1960s, 2¼in (5.5cm) long.
£50–60 *NTM*

A Dinky No. 197 Morris Mini-Traveller, in dark green with beige woodwork, with yellow interior, in original box, c1959.
£650–700 *WAL*

A Dinky National Benzole oil tanker, c1950, 4½in (11.5cm) long.
£18–20 *FAL*

A Dinky car, post-WWII, 4in (10cm) long.
£28–32 *FAL*

Matchbox

A Matchbox Series No. 62 TV service van, 1960s, 1½in (4cm) long.
£35–40 *NTM*

r. A Matchbox Series No. 75 Ferrari Berlinetta, 1960s, 1½in (4cm) long.
£30–35 *NTM*

A Matchbox Series No. 63
Army ambulance, 1960s,
1½in (4cm) long.
£16–20 *NTM*

A Matchbox Series No. 56 trolly
bus, 1960s, 1½in (4cm) long.
£40–50 *NTM*

A Matchbox Series No. 7
horse-drawn milk float,
1950s, 1½in (4cm) long.
£45–55 *NTM*

Model Figures & Soldiers
Britains

A Britains set No. 195 British Infantry, in
khaki with rifles on the trail, one officer and
7 soldiers, in original box, c1930.
£120–150 *WAL*

A Britains set No. 144 Royal Field Artillery collar
harness gun team, first version, comprising: 6
horses with bucket seats, 3 seated men, one
mounted officer, khaki finish to gun and limber,
some damage, in original box, 1914.
£650–750 *P(Ba)*

A Britains set No.23 9th
Queens Royal Lancers, first
version, fixed arm figures with
officer, in original illustrated
box, complete with
partitioning, 1899.
£225–300 *P*

A Britains set No. 36 The Royal Sussex
Regiment, comprising: one mounted officer,
with 6 soldiers marching with rifles at the
slope, in original box, c1915.
£120–150 *WAL*

A Britains figure of a
village idiot, with light
brown hat, beige
smock, dark brown
trousers, yellow socks
and brown boots, some
wear, pre-WWII.
£90–110 *WAL*

Two Britains 'Baby Boys on
Sleigh', No. 26X, the sleigh
missing, 1940.
£100–120 *P(Ba)*

A Britains set No. 211 The 18in
Heavy Howitzer, comprising a
howitzer, limber, 10 horses,
5 mounted, together with traces,
ammunition and loading mechanism,
in original box, pre-WWI.
£1,700–2,000 *WAL*

A Britains set No. 319 police figures, comprising: one mounted, 6 on foot, 2 directing traffic and 4 standing to attention, in original Fred Whisstock box, pre-WWII.
£250–300 *WAL*

A Britains set No. 439 Soldiers on Parade, The Middlesex Regiment, comprising: 8 men with rifles at the slope, with an officer, in original Parade Series box, one helmet missing, 1932.
£290–340 *CSK*

A Britains set No. 2062 The Seaforth Highlanders, in original box.
£400–450 *CSK*

A Britains set No. 1291 Band of the Royal Marines figures, comprising: band master and 11 musicians marching, all complete in original Fred Whisstock box with card insert, pre-WWII.
£220–250 *WAL*

A Britains part-set No. 2085 Musical Ride, comprising: 4 state trumpeters, kettle drummer, 3 Life Guards and 3 horse guards, strung in unmarked factory box with insert, 1954.
£325–375 *CSK*

l. A set of 12 Britains Boy Scouts, in uniform, 2 versions with yellow and green scarves, poles and flags, 1909.
£300–350 *WAL*

r. A Britains set No. 9406 Mounted Band of the Lifeguards, in original box, 1962.
£375–450 *CSK*

A Britains set No. 27 Band of the Line figures, first version, comprising: slotted arm oval base musicians and drum major, square base side drummer and bass drummer, with additional cornet player, all tied to base card, c1896–1911.
£225–275 *CSK*

These figures were found tied into a cardboard Easter egg, possibly assembled by the retailer. The egg dated from 1908.

MAKE THE MOST OF MILLER'S

Condition is absolutely vital when assessing the value of any item. Damaged pieces appreciate much less than perfect examples. However, a rare, desirable piece may command a high price even when damaged.

Figures & Animals

A complete set of 3 figures UN Police Commandos, by Eaglewall/Kentoy Plastic Character, for the *Eagle*, Dan Dare comic strip, 1955.
£100–150 *P*

A Heyde No. 2 size Indian prince seated on a camel, with his son perched in front of him waving a sword, 1930.
£250–300 *P(Ba)*

A Walt Disney Mickey Mouse, by Stoddart, 1932.
£140–160 *P*

Two lead figures of cave children riding dinosaurs, possibly German, 1930.
£200–250 *P*

A collection of 4 Beatrix Potter figures, for use with the Peter Rabbit Race Game, comprising: Peter Rabbit, Jemima Puddleduck, Jeremy Fisher and Squirrel Nutkin, 1954.
£160–200 *P*

A German 40mm scale group of firemen, together with a burnt-out building constructed of flat lead and wood, 1895.
£375–425 *P*

A collection of German 100mm scale composition or bisque African Colonial Dress Infantry figures, comprising: 5 soldiers with rifle at the slope and an officer, figures standing on their feet without bases, 3 hands damaged, 1905.
£325–350 *P*

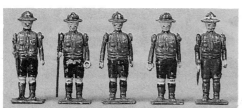

Five Hanks Boy Scouts, 4 standing at attention and a scoutmaster, movable arms, 1912.
£70–90 *P*

A boxed set of 7 Infantry guards, by M & S, 1920.
£100–140 *P*

Pedal Toys

A child's penny farthing bicycle, 1950s, 38in (96.5cm) high.
£200–300 *TOY*

r. An American pressed steel pedal aeroplane, inscribed 'Red Wing', c1930, 50in (127cm) long.
£325–375 *SK(B)*

Cross Reference:
Bicycles

l. A wooden pedal car, with tandem seats, 1910, 62in (157.5cm) long.
£800–1,000 *JUN*

A Tan-Sad pedal scooter, 1950s, 43in (109cm) long.
£350–400 *TOY*

Rocking Horses

A Victorian rocking horse, 56in (142cm) wide.
£650–750 *PEN*

A mid-Victorian fairground horse, converted to a rocking horse, 48in (122cm) wide.
£150–200 *AF*

A painted rocking horse, with rocker, 19thC, 78in (198cm) wide.
£750–850 *Mit*

A folk art rocking horse, c1860, 33in (83.5cm) wide.
£275–300 *PEN*

An American painted and decorated rocking horse, with leather saddle and bridle, mounted on a green painted rocker, 19thC, 34in (86.5cm) wide.
£1,100–1,400 *CNY*

A rocking horse, by C. & J. Lines, London, with thistle trademark on chest, 1906, 52in (132cm) wide.
Unrestored **£700–800**
Restored **£1,800–2,000** *STE*

l. A dapple grey carved rocking horse, with horse hair mane and tail, red leather saddle with studded saddle cloth and bridle, on trestle base with turned supports, early 20thC, 50in (127cm) wide.
£600–700 *DN*

r. A dapple grey rocking horse, with raised seat, on turned column stand, unrestored, early 20thC, 45¼in (115cm) high.
£450–550 *WL*

A rocking horse, by F. H. Ayres, sold by Selfridges, c1910, 50in (127cm) wide.
Unrestored **£600–700**
Restored **£1,700–1,900** *STE*

A German rocking racehorse, by Zoo, 1920s, 52½in (133.5cm) wide.
£750–850 *STE*

The wooden wheels and chocks underneath the rockers allow the horse to move forward. The pulling of one rein brakes the wheels one side enabling the rider to steer.

A rocking horse, by J. Collinson, c1955, 54in (137cm) wide.
£250–300 *STE*

Collinson's horses have studs for eyes, rather than glass, and red corduroy saddle cloths. When restoring horses, Collinson's would leave their mark by painting the metal bars red, using square posts and diamond-shaped plates. Collinson's have now ceased trading.

A rocking horse, 1930s, 38in (96.5cm) wide.
£100–120 *Ber*

l. A plush-covered rocking horse, by Pegasus, with leather saddle and harness, 1950s, 47in (119.5cm) wide.
£200–300 *TOY*

Sci-Fi Film/TV Toys

A *Man from U.N.C.L.E.* rifle set, 1960s, 14½in (37cm) wide.
£100–125 *NTM*

An unmade Airfix model kit of James Bond and Odd Job, 1960s, 9in (23cm) wide.
£75–90 *NTM*

A Corgi No. 270 The New James Bond Aston Martin DB5, with opening roof and ejector seat, rear bullet screen, telescopic overriders, retractable machine guns, revolving number plates, plated bumpers and radiator with tyre slasher blades, complete with 2 sets of operating instructions, 3 ejector seat figures, 2 lapel badges, with original box, 1960s.
£120–140 *Mit*

r. A Corgi No. 497 *Man from U.N.C.L.E.* car, with Waverly ring, original box, 1960s, 6in (15cm) long.
£150–175 *NTM*

A Highway Patrol Suit, 1950s, 10in (25.5cm) wide.
£100–150 *TOY*

A Hank's Bagatelle game, by Chad Valley, 1950s, 15½in (39.5cm) wide.
£80–100 *TOY*

A Corgi No. 267 Batmobile, with original box, c1965.
£100–120 *WN*

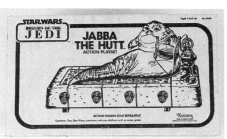

A Kenner action playset, *Return of the Jedi*, 1970s, 8in (20cm) wide.
£35–45 *TOY*

A *Star Wars* model figure of Darth Vader, made in Hong Kong, 1970, 9in (23cm) high.
£25–35 *TOY*

A Palitoy scout walker vehicle, *Return of the Jedi*, 1982, 8½in (21.5cm) wide.
£25–35 *TOY*

l. A Nightmare Before Christmas ceramic cookie jar, inscribed 'Jack Skellington R.I.P.', 1993, 16in (40.5cm) high.
£80–100 *TOY*

r. A selection of Tim Burton's Nightmare Before Christmas model figures, in original packaging, 1990s, 7in (18cm) wide.
£25–55 each *TOY*

Trains

A Bowman spirit-fired 4-4-0 steam locomotive and tender, LMS No. 13000, finished in LMS red, c1930.
£175–225 *AH*

A Hornby clockwork 4-4-2 Great Western tank locomotive, finished in green with gold lining, some parts added and replaced, c1930.
£75–100 *AH*

A Hornby clockwork 4-4-0 Yorkshire locomotive and tender, LNER No. 234, finished in green with black and white lining, some damage, c1930.
£325–400 *AH*

A Hornby three-rail electric tank locomotive, class 4-4-2, LMS No. 2180, finished in maroon with gold lining, paint chipped, c1933.
£140–180 *AH*

A Wrenn 00 gauge Coronation Class 4-6-2, 'Duchess of Rutland', No. 6228, maroon LMS livery with gold lining and lettering, with original box, packing and instruction book, c1985.
£900–1,100 *WAL*

A Hornby Trains No. 3 station, finished in cream, with printed sides and red tiled roof, with original box, 1939.
£60–80 *AH*

A Lionel electric gauge 027 train set, steam outline loco 2-6-2, including 30 pieces of track, points and auto uncoupler, multi-control transformer, and a tin of accessories, c1950.
£225–300 *AAV*

Wooden Toys

A German lithographed paper on wood Noah's ark, with lift-up roof and removable side, together with 65 painted wooden animals, late 19thC, 45in (114.5cm) long.
£1,700–1,900 *SK(B)*

A carved wood and painted hunting set, comprising: 8 horses with riders, 5 hounds, 2 foxes, 6 standing figures, 4 seated figures, horse-drawn gypsy caravan, 3 trees, and a painted board backdrop house, some damage, c1920.
£350–450 *S(S)*

r. A Fisher-Price Snoopy dog, 1960s, 14in (35.5cm) long.
£18–20 *OPH*

l. A child's measuring wheel, retailed by Woolworths, c1925.
£18–22 *WCA*

A Robot Bomb wooden model kit, by Miniature Ship Models Inc, 1944, 8¾in (22cm) long.
£10–15 *COB*

TUNBRIDGE WARE

Four Tunbridge ware
stamp boxes, c1850,
largest 3¼in (8.5cm) wide.
£100–200 each *AMH*

A mid-Victorian Tunbridge
ware handkerchief box,
6in (15cm) square.
£120–140 *WAC*

A Tunbridge ware box,
decorated with a moth,
c1840, 4¼in (11cm) wide.
£200–220
A Tunbridge ware box,
decorated with a bird, c1870,
3½in (9cm) wide.
£180–200
A Tunbridge ware box,
decorated with a butterfly,
c1860, 3½in (9cm) wide.
£130–160 *AMH*

A Tunbridge ware humming
top, c1860, 3½in (9cm) wide.
£400–450 *AMH*

A Tunbridge ware tea caddy,
decorated with a picture of Tonbridge
Castle, c1880, 10in (25cm) wide.
£750–825 *WAG*

l. A Tunbridge
ware tea caddy,
by Robert Russell,
with Tunbridge
Wells marquetry
decoration, c1860,
12in (30.5cm) wide.
£900–1,000 *WAG*

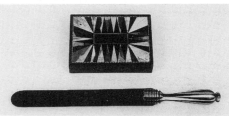

A Tunbridge ware paperweight, decorated
with Vandyke pattern, c1850,
4¼in (11cm) wide.
£175–200
A Tunbridge ware letter opener, with
stickware handle, c1860, 8in (20cm) long.
£80–90 *AMH*

l. A Tunbridge ware
box, containing
scent bottles, box
made from bird's-
eye maple, c1840,
9½in (24cm) wide.
£800–850 *AMH*

A Tunbridge ware pin table, by Thomas Barton, c1870, 4in (10cm) high.
£300–350 *AMH*

A Tunbridge ware caddy spoon, c1860, 3¾in (9.5cm) long.
£200–250 *AMH*

A Tunbridge ware thimble case, c1880, 2in (5cm) long.
£130–150 *WAG*

A mid-Victorian Tunbridge ware chamber stick, 3¼in (8.5cm) diam.
£165–185 *WAC*

A Tunbridge ware spinning top, c1870, 4in (10cm) long.
£350–400 *WAG*

WALKING STICKS

A mahogany knob-handled walking stick, c1900, 35in (89cm) long.
£23–27 *GHA*

A hazel wood walking stick, 1920s, 35in (89cm) long.
£12–14 *TAC*

A malacca walking stick, the silver handle in the form of a horse's head with inset glass eyes, inscribed 'M. M. Merceron', London 1911 by Louis Blumfeld.
£350–400 *DN*

A walking cane, the ivory handle carved as a mountain lion about to engage a rattle snake, bamboo shaft, late 19thC, 39in (99cm) long.
£425–500 *S(S)*

A late Victorian walking stick, the head depicting Ally Sloper, 57in (145cm) long. **£70–100** *MRW*

A hand carved walking stick, from Vermont, USA, the top carved as the head of a boxer dog, c1954, 35½in (90cm) long. **£30–35** *VL*

A bamboo market stick, with pine inner rod showing measurements in hand intervals, a metal pull-out rod to place on an animal's withers, level missing, 1940s, 36½in (92.5cm) long. **£45–50** *VL*

A handmade walking stick, with a horn handle, 1992, 48½in (123cm) long. **£15–20** *KT*

WATCHES

According to Tony Woolven, founder of the British Watch and Clock Collector's Association, objects currently most sought after include 1940s watches, both wartime and just post-war, and items by Omega, a name which is beginning to match Rolex in terms of desirability. Russian watches, originally supplied to the USSR armed forces in the 1980s and bearing the red Soviet star on the dial, are also fashionable today. Like other Russian artefacts, these have been making their way into Europe and have escalated in value.

Watch collecting is growing in popularity and Woolven offers collectors the following advice.

Gain all the knowledge you can from reference books and by visiting auction houses and dealers. Beware of fakes, many of which are produced in the Far East. Unless you are experienced, these can be very hard to detect. Handle the watch – the majority of fakes will not have the weight of the original item, and when opened will reveal the wrong movement.

Always carry a magnifying glass or jeweller's loupe. Examining under a glass the quality and lettering of a dial can detrmine whether or not a watch is faked. Condition is very important. Always buy the best you can afford from a reputable source.

l. A George III open face pair cased pocket watch, the fusee verge movement signed 'Richard Fenner, London, No. 1789', the white enamel dial with gilt hands, gilt metal case with japanned outer case decorated with a woman in a garden, some damage to the outer case and dial, 2in (50mm) diam. **£325–375** *DN*

A brass carrying case for a watch, c1900, 1½in (38mm) diam. **£40–50** *BS*

A silver pocket watch, with verge escapement, signed 'Edward Banks', with rare subsidiary seconds dial, c1811, 2¼in (55mm) diam.
£400–450 *BWC*

A pocket watch, by Elgin, c1910, 2in (50mm) diam.
£65–85 *BWC*

A Columbia dollar watch, 1908, 2¼in (57mm) diam.
£75–100 *BWC*

An Edwardian silver nurse's fob watch, 1½in (38mm) diam.
£175–200 *BWC*

l. A silver, enamel and marcasite brooch watch, 1920s, 2in (50mm) long.
£140–180 *LBe*

A gilt and Bakelite bracelet, with a watch one end, and a photograph frame at the other end, c1940, 3½in (9cm) diam.
£140–150 *LBe*

An ex-Royal Navy issue Cymra Navystar wristwatch, with porcelain dial, 1939–45, 1in (25mm) diam.
£150–200 *BWC*

A Rolex Standard lady's wristwatch, the oval dial with Arabic numerals enclosing a movement set with 17 rubies, in a Watch Star Case Co 10ct gold plated silver case, inscribed 'To Betty from Dutch', No. 5382501, on a leather strap, c1920.
£125–175 *Gam*

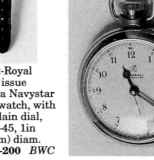

An Edwardian lady's 18ct gold fob watch, 1¼in (32mm) diam.
£150–175 *BWC*

l. An Ingersoll Chronostop pocket watch, c1940, 2in (50mm) diam.
£30–40 *BWC*

r. An Encar chronograph wristwatch, with Val Joux movement, c1970, 1¾in (45mm) diam.
£175–200 *BWC*

l. A Jaeger le Coultre pink gold automatic wristwatch, the silvered dial with raised quarter Arabic numerals, centre seconds and power reserve sector, signed, the nickel movement in a polished case with horn-shaped lugs, c1960, 1½in (38mm) diam.
£550–650 *Bon*

A Ralco stainless steel mechanical wristwatch, 1950s, 1½in (38mm) diam.
£75–100 *BWC*

l. A Longines stainless steel chronograph wristwatch, the silvered dial with gilt baton and Arabic numerals, outer timing scale, signed, subsidiary for running seconds and 30-minute recording, fly back centre seconds, the 19 jewel nickel movement in a polished case with stepped lugs and gilt push button, c1960, 1½in (38mm) diam.
£550–700 *Bon*

An Eros 9ct gold wristwatch, c1944, ¾in (19mm) diam.
£200–250 *BWC*

A CWC military wristwatch, c1985, 1½in (38mm) diam.
£75–100 *BWC*

A Bernex gold plated Masonic wristwatch, 1980–90, ¾in (19mm) diam.
£75–100 *BWC*

A Task Commander's wristwatch, 1980–90, 1¾in (45mm) diam.
£60–75 *BWC*

A Longines gentleman's 9ct gold bracelet watch, on a Milanese strap, case No. '14397', 1960.
£130–160 *Gam*

WRITING

A Persian monochrome pencil box, 19thC, 8½in (21.5cm) long.
£300–350 *JFG*

A Russian silver-topped inkwell, c1800, 10in (25cm) long.
£300–350 *WCA*

A Spanish tin glazed lobed drum-shaped earthenware inkwell, with 6 quill holders around a central well, with stylised flower motifs and vermiculated bands, inscribed in blue, restored, 18thC, 7½in (19cm) diam.
£300–350 *DN*

A table writing slope, with secret compartments, drawer to side, early 19thC, 20in (51cm) wide.
£450–500 *TMi*

A Victorian satinwood and ebonised stationery box and inkwell, the fitted stationery box behind 2 square glass inkwells and a glass pin tidy over a single drawer, on 4 bun feet, 10in (25cm) wide.
£180–220 *DA*

An ormolu figure of a lion, on a felt pen wiper, 2¾in (70mm) diam.
£20–25 *GLN*

A horse's hoof pen stand and inkwell, by Rowland Ward, c1915.
£100–150 *HnT*

A children's pine writing box, c1920, 12in (30.5cm) wide.
£25–30 *OPH*

A box of stationery, featuring 'The Three little Pigs', by Powers Paper Co, c1930, 9¾in (25cm) wide.
£200–300 *TOY*

A Carlton Ware pen tray and holder, with a yellow bird with green wings, c1930, 6in (15cm) long.
£60–70 *WTA*

A Conway Stewart display stand, mid-1950s.
£60–80 *Bon*

l. An American black 51 Vacumatic pen, engraved 'Bud Cusgrove', early 1950s, together with a winner's plaque for the annual 'Playboy Editorial Award', awarded to John le Carré, 1977.
£100–120 *Bon*

Bud Cusgrove was an aide to Hugh Heffner, founder of the Playboy empire.

r. A wooden display pen, with blue lacquer finish, varnished clip and band, brass nib, 34¾in (88cm) long.
£150–170 *Bon*

Post Boxes

A Victorian pillar box.
£5,000–6,500 *BHE*

A wall-mounted cast iron letter box, with enamel plate and lock and key, 1912–50, 28in (71cm) high.
£300-350 *BS*

A George V pillar box.
£480–500 *WEL*

A George V pillar box, c1935.
£1,500–2,500 *BHE*

l. A wall-mounted cast iron letter box, with a door in the back and front, with keys, 1912–50, 33in (84cm) high.
£275–300 *BS*

r. A wall-mounted cast iron letter box, with lock and key, c1930–50, 33in (84cm) high.
£275–300 *BS*

A George VI letter box, 33in (84cm) high.
£150–200 *WEL*

COLLECTABLES UNDER £5

There are still plenty of collectables available for under £5. Car-boot sales, charity shops and local fêtes provide endless opportunities for the bargain hunter, equally many antique shops will have a selection of low-priced pieces to entice collectors, including children. All the items illustrated below can be purchased for pocket money prices. Some might well increase in value, but when objects cost only a few pounds one can afford to buy for pleasure rather than investment. Collectables in this section are, above all, for fun.

Ceramics

Ceramics, particularly table-ware, have been produced in such quantity that many inexpensive items can still be found. For example, tea plates from the 1950s and earlier can cost less than a pound and make a decorative and useful themed collection.

A side plate, marked 'Barratt's Delphatic White Tableware', 1950–60, 7in (18cm) diam.
50p–£1 PC

A side plate, marked 'Blue Caribbean', c1950s, 7in (18cm) diam.
50p–£1 PC

l. A Royal Tudor ware side plate, by Barker Bros, marked 'Fiesta', 1960s, 6½in (16.5cm) diam.
50p–£1 PC

A ceramic cruet set, modelled as a boy and a girl, 20thC, 3¾in (9.5cm) high.
£3–4 HEM

Two white mugs, with Andy Capp cartoons, 1990s, 3½in (9cm) high.
£4–5 each FAL

Drinking Glasses

These decorated glasses date from the 1950s and '60s. As emphasised in this edition of *Miller's Collectables Price Guide*, interest in this period is expanding and values are set to rise.

A glass tumbler, decorated with yellow, white and blue bands and gold stars, 1950–60, 5½in (14cm) high.
50p–£1 PC

A glass tumbler, decorated with a cockerel on a weathervane, and red, yellow and blue patterns, 1950–60, 4in (10cm) high.
£1–2 PC

Jewellery

Bargain boxes in collectors' markets are often a good place to find low-priced costume jewellery. Prices can be considerably less than for contemporary examples.

A pair of white polished bone flower earrings, 1930–40.
£3.50–4 *STP*

Miller's is a price GUIDE not a price LIST

Key Rings

Key rings are often popular with automobilia enthusiasts who, for little outlay, can form a very varied collection.

A collection of key rings, 1960–70s, largest 2½in (6.5cm) long.
£2–3 each *COB*

Two key rings, 1950s, 2in (50mm) high.
£2–5 each *FAL*

Linen

Embroidered tray cloths and cushion covers can be bought for literally pennies in charity shops around Britain. They might not all be great works of art but they are handmade, sometimes beautifully embroidered and have a uniquely British charm.

r. A hand embroidered cushion cover, 1930–40, 18in (45.5cm) square.
£1–2 *PC*

Sugar Lumps & Sachets

These examples form part of a large private collection. They show that any object can have its enthusiasts and prove that you don't have to be wealthy to be a collector.

Three sugar sachets, from Majorca.
1–2p each *PC*

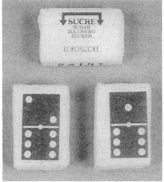

Three packets of sugar lumps, from France, depicting different dominoes.
1–2p each *PC*

A hand embroidered linen cushion cover, 1930s, 17 by 18in (43 by 45.5cm).
£1–2 *PC*

A sugar sachet, from Fauchon, Paris.
1–2p *PC*

DIRECTORY OF SPECIALISTS

(A) Auctioneers
(A&A) Arms & Armour
(A&C) Arts & Crafts
(A&M) Arms & Militaria
(AD) Art Deco
(ADC) Art Deco Ceramics
(ADJ) Art Deco Jewellery
(Ae) Aeronautica
(AN) Art Nouveau
(Au) Automobilia
(B) Boxes
(Ba) Barometers
(BC) Baby Carriages
(BH) Button Hooks
(Bks) Books
(BM) Beer Mats
(Bot) Bottles
(BP) Baxter Prints
(Bu) Buttons
(C) Costume
(Ca) Cameras
(CaC) Card Cases
(CC) Cigarette Cards
(Ce) Ceramics
(Co) Comics
(Cns) Coins
(Col) Collectables
(Com) Commemorative
(Cor) Corkscrews

(D) Doulton
(DH) Dolls Houses
(DHF) Dolls House
  Furniture
(Do) Dolls
(DS) Display Stands
(E) Ephemera
(F) Fishing
(Fa) Fans
(G&CC) Goss & Crested
  China
(G) Glass
(Ga) Games
(Gar) Gardening
(GC) Greetings Cards
(Gn) Gnomes
(Go) Golfing
(Gr) Gramophones
(H/HP) Hairdressing &
  Hat Pins
(I) Inkwells
(J) Jewellery
(Ju) Jukeboxes
(K) Kitchenalia
(L) Lighting
(L&K) Locks & Keys
(L&L) Linen & Lace
(LB) Le Blond Prints
(M) Metalware

(Ma) Matchboxes
(MB) Money Boxes
(Me) Medals
(MP) Moorcroft Pottery
(Mus) Musical
(O) Oriental
(OAM) Old Amusement
  Machines
(OP) Oriental Porcelain
(P) Pottery
(Pa) Paperweights
(PaM) Paper Money
(PB) Perfume Bottles
(PF) Photograph Frames
(PH) Props Hire
(Pia) Pianolas
(PL) Pot Lids
(PM) Papier Mâché
(PMem) Police Memorabilia
(Po) Postcards
(Pos) Posters
(R) Radios
(R&C) Rugs & Carpets
(Ra) Railwayana
(RB) Reference Books
(Re) Records
(RH) Rocking Horses
(RP) Rock & Pop
(S) Silver

(S&MI) Scientific & Medical
  Instruments
(SC) Scottish Collectables
(Scr) Scripophily
(Sew) Sewing
(Sh) Shipping
(She) Shells
(Sm) Smoking
(SP) Staffordshire Pottery
(Sp) Sporting
(St) Stereoscopes
(T&MS) Tins & Metal Signs
(T) Textiles
(Ta) Tartanware
(TB) Teddy Bears
(Te) Telephones
(Ti) Tiles
(TO) Tools
(To) Toys
(TP) Torquay Pottery
(Tr) Treen
(TV) Televisions
(TVCol) TV Collectables
(TW) Tunbridge Ware
(Tx) Taxidermy
(W) Watches
(Wr) Writing
(WS) Walking Sticks

London

20th Century Glass,
291 Westbourne Grove,
W11 2QB
Tel: 0181 806 7068
(G)

Academy Costumes Ltd
(Hire & Make),
50 Rushworth Street,
SE1 0RB
Tel: 0171 620 0771
(T, C)

Act One Hire Ltd,
2a Scampston Mews,
Cambridge Gardens,
W10 6HX
Tel: 0181 960 1456/1494
(T)

Angling Auctions,
P O Box 2095, W12 8RU
Tel: 0181 749 4175
(F)

Baldwin, A H, & Sons Ltd,
Numismatists,
11 Adelphi Terrace,
WC2N 6BJ
Tel: 0171 930 6879
(Cns, Com, Me)

Bee, Linda,
Art Deco Stand J20-21,
Grays Antique Market,
1-7 Davies Mews, W1Y 1AR
Tel: 0171 629 5921
(C, PB)

Beverley,
30 Church Street, NW8 8EP
Tel: 0171 262 1576
(AD)

Bishop, Christina,
Kitchenware,
Westway,
Portobello Road Market,
W11 2QB
Tel: 0171 221 4688
(K)

Bloomsbury Book Auctions,
3/4 Hardwick Street,
Off Rosebery Avenue,
EC1R 4RY
Tel: 0171 833 2636
(A, Bks)

Books For Cooks,
4 Blenheim Crescent,
W11 1NN
Tel: 0171 221 1992/8102
(Bks)

Bridge, Christine,
78 Castelnau,
SW13 9EX
Tel: 0181 741 5501
(G)

British Collectables,
1st Floor,
9 Georgian Village,
Camden Passage,
Islington
N1 8DU
Tel: 0171 359 4560
(Com, G&CC)

BT Museum,
The Story of
Telecommunications,
14 Queen Victoria Street,
EC4V 4AT
Tel: 0171 248 7444
(Te)

Button Queen,
19 Marylebone Lane,
W1M 5FF
Tel: 0171 935 1505
(Bu)

Cameron, Jasmin,
J6 Antiquarius,
131-141 King's Road,
SW3 5ST
Tel: 0171 351 4154
(Wr, G)

Childhood Memories,
Teapot Arcade,
Portobello Road,
W11 2QB
(Do)

Classic Collection,
Pied Bull Yard,
Bury Place,
WC1A 2JR
Tel: 0171 831 6000
(Ca)

Collector, The,
Tom Power,
9 Church Street,
Marylebone NW8 8EE
Tel: 0171 706 4586
(P, Ce)

Coronets & Crowns,
(Robert Taylor)
Tel: 01689 875022
(Com)

Davies Antiques,
40 Kensington Church St,
W8 4BX
Tel: 0171 937 9216
(Ce)

De Fresne, Pierre,
'Beaux Bijoux',
Q9/10 Antiquarius,
135 King's Road,
SW3 5ST
Tel: 0171 352 8882
(ADJ)

Decodence,
Gad Sassower,
Shop 13, The Mall,
Camden Passage,
N1 8DU
Tel: 0171 354 4473/
0181 458 4665
(AD)

Didier Antiques,
58-60 Kensington Church
Street, W8 4DB
Tel: 0171 938 2537/
0836 232634
(J, S)

Donay Antiques,
35 Camden Passage,
N1 8EA
Tel: 0171 359 1880
(Ga)

Eastgate Antiques,
Alfies Antique Market,
13-25 Church Street,
NW8 8DT
Tel: 0171 724 5650
(G, Ca)

Gallery of Antique
Costume & Textiles,
2 Church Street,
Marylebone
NW8 8EP
Tel: 0171 723 9981
(T)

Gee, Rob,
The Fleamarket,
Pierrepont Row,
Camden Passage, N1 8DU
Tel: 0171 226 6627
(Wed & Sat)
(Bot, PL)

German, Michael,
38B Kensington Church
Street, W8 8EP
Tel: 0171 937 2771
(A&A, WS)

Gibbon, Richard,
(Costume Jewellery),
Alfies Antique Market,
13-25 Church Street,
NW8 8DT
Tel: 0171 723 0449
(J)

Goldsmith & Perris,
Stand 327 Alfies Antique
Market, 13-25 Church
Street, NW8 8DT
Tel: 0171 724 7051
(S)

Gordon, Ora,
J27 Grays in the Mews,
1-7 Davies Mews, W1Y 1AR
(Ce)

Groombridge, Sarah,
Stand 335, Grays Market,
58 Davies Street,
W1Y 1LB
Tel: 0171 629 0225
(J)

Harbottle, Patricia,
Geoffrey Vann Arcade,
107 Portobello Road,
W11 2QB
Tel: 0171 731 1972
Saturdays
(Cor, Bot)

Harrington Bros,
The Chelsea Antiques
Market,
253 Kings Road,
SW3 5EL
Tel: 0171 352 5689/1720
(Bks)

Hayhurst, Jeanette,
Fine Glass,
32a Kensington Church
Street, W8 4HA
Tel: 0171 938 1539
(G)

Hayloft Woodwork,
Box Dept,
3 Bond St,
Chiswick W4 1QZ
Tel: 0181 747 3510
(B)

Hayman & Hayman,
Antiquarius M15/L3,
135/7 Kings Road,
SW3 4PW
Tel: 0171 351 6568/
0181 741 0959
(PF, PB)

Heritage Antiques,
Unit 14, Georgian Village,
Camden Passage,
N1 8DU
Tel: 0171 226 9822
(Ce, P)

J T Antiques,
16 Christchurch House,
Christchurch Road,
SW2 3UA
Tel: 0181 671 2354
(Col)

Jaertelius, Monica,
The Mall,
Camden Passage, N1 8DU
Tel: 0181 546 2807
(Bu)

Jafar Gallery,
24H Grays in the Mews,
Davis Mews, W1Y 1AR
Tel: 0171 409 7919/
0181 300 2727
(G, J)

Jessops,
65 Great Russell Street,
WC1B 3BN
Tel: 0171 831 3640
(Ca)

Keith, Old Advertising,
Unit 14,
155a Northcote Road,
Battersea SW11 6QB
Tel: 0171 228 0741/6850
(T&MS)

King & Country,
Unit 46 Alfies Antique
Market,
13-25 Church Street,
NW8 8DT
Tel: 0171 724 3439
(Go)

Langham, Marion,
Tel: 0171 730 1002
(Ce, Pa, P)

Lawson, Enid, Gallery,
Antiques Centre, 36a
Kensington Church Street,
W8 4DB
Tel: 0171 376 0552/
0171 937 9559
(G, Ce)

Memories,
18 Bell Lane,
Hendon NW4 2AD
Tel: 0181 203 1772/202 9080
(Po)

Murray Cards
(International) Ltd,
51 Watford Way,
Hendon Central
NW4 3JH
Tel: 0181 202 5688
(E, CC)

Narbeth, Colin, & Son Ltd,
20 Cecil Court, Leicester
Square, WC2N 4HE
Tel: 0171 379 6975
(PaM)

New Century Antiques,
69 Kensington Church
Street, W8 4BG
Tel: 0171 376 2810
(P, T)

Norman, Sue,
Stand L4 Antiquarius,
135 King's Road,
SW3 5ST
Tel: 0171 352 7217
(C)

Old Amusement Machines
Tel: 0181 889 2213 or
01782 680667/813621
(OAM)

Oosthuizen, Jacqueline,
23 Cale Street,
Chelsea SW3 3QR
Tel: 0171 352 6071
(SP, TP)

Oosthuizen, Pieter,
De Verzamelaar, Georgian
Village, Camden Passage,
N1 8DU
Tel: 0171 359 3322/376
3852
(P, Com, Ce)

Pearce, Stevie,
Antique Costume
Jewellery,
G144 Alfies Antique
Market, 13-25 Church
Street, NW8 8DT
Tel: 0171 723 1513
Home: 0171 724 9319
(J)

Pieces of Time,
Grays Mews, 1-7 Davies
Street, W1Y 1AR
Tel: 0171 629 2422
(W)

Pleasures of Past Times,
11 Cecil Court,
WC2N 4EZ
Tel: 0171 836 1142
(Bks, GC)

Poultney, Doug
Tel: 0181 330 3472
(Co)

Powell, Sylvia,
Decorative Arts,
18 The Mall,
Camden Passage, N1 0PD
Tel: 0171 354 2977/
0181 458 4543
(Ce, P)

Power, Annette
The Collector,
9 Church Street,
Marylebone NW8 8EE
Tel: 0171 706 4586
(Col)

Purple Shop, The,
Antiquarius,
135 Kings Road,
Chelsea, SW3 5ST
Tel: 0171 352 1127
(J)

Randall, L,
J16 Grays in the Mews,
1-7 Davies Mews,
W1Y 1AR
(J)

Rastall, John,
Stall GO47/8
Alfies Antique Market,
13-25 Church Street,
NW8 8DT
Tel: 0171 723 0449
(Col)

Robinson, Geoffrey
(Lighting & China),
GO 75-78, GO 91-92
Alfies Antique Market,
13-25 Church Street,
NW8 8DT
Tel: 0171 723 0449
(L, Ce)

Rogers de Rin,
76 Royal Hospital Road,
SW3 4HN
Tel: 0171 352 9007
(P, B)

Royal Academy Shop,
Royal Academy of Arts,
Piccadilly W1V 0DS
Tel: 0171 439 7438
(Col)

Rumours Decorative Arts,
10 The Mall, Upper
Street, Camden Passage,
Islington N1 0PD
Tel: 01582 873561
(MP)

Samii Antiques, H,
S 102/3 Alfies Antique
Market,
13-25 Church Street,
NW8 8DT
Tel: 0171 723 573
(Col)

Scripophily Shop,
Britannia Hotel,
Grosvenor Square,
W1A 3AN
Tel: 0171 495 0580
(Scr)

Shades of the Past,
Unit 1, Northcote Road
Antiques Market,
SW11 6QB
Tel: 0171 228 6580
(Col)

Shapiro & Co,
Stand 380,
Grays Antique Market,
58 Davies Street,
W1Y 1LB
Tel: 0171 491 2710
(AN, S, J)

Smale, Claire &
Rosemary,
Alfies Antique Market,
13-25 Church Street,
NW8 8DT
Tel: 0171 723 6066
(Col)

Spectrum, Sylvie,
Stand 372, Grays Market,
58 Davies Street,
W1Y 1LB
Tel: 0171 629 3501
(J)

Stone, Barbara,
Rare Books,
Antiquarius,
135 King's Road,
SW3 5ST
Tel: 0171 351 0963
(Bks)

Susie Cooper Ceramics
(Art Deco),
GO70-4 Alfies Antique
Market, 13-25 Church
Street, NW8 8DT
Tel: 0171 723 0449
(ADC)

Talking Machine, The,
30 Watford Way,
NW4 3AL
Tel: 0181 202 3473
(R, Gr)

Terrace Antiques,
10 & 12 South Ealing Road,
W5 4QA
Tel: 0181 567 5194/
567 1223
(Col)

Travellers Book Shop,
25 Cecil Court,
WC2N 4EZ
Tel: 0171 836 9132
(Bks)

Trio (Theresa Clayton),
Grays Mews,
1-7 Davies Mews,
W1Y 1AR
Tel: 0171 629 1184
(PB)

Vintage Cameras Ltd,
254 & 256 Kirkdale,
Sydenham,
SE26 4NL
Tel: 0181 778 5416/5841
(Ca)

Walker, Pat,
Georgian Village,
Camden Passage,
N1 8DU
Tel: 0171 359 4560/
435 3159
(Do)

West, Mark J,
Cobb Antiques Ltd,
39a High Street,
Wimbledon Village
SW19 5YX
Tel: 0181 946 2811
(G)

White, John,
Alfies Antique Market,
13-25 Church Street,
NW8 8DT
Tel: 0171 723 0449
(ADC)

Yesterday Child,
Angel Arcade,
118 Islington High Street,
N1 8EG
Tel: 0171 354 1601/
01908 583403
(Do)

Young, Robert, Antiques,
68 Battersea Bridge Road,
SW11 3AG
Tel: 0171 228 7847
(P, K)

Yvonne,
Kensington Church St
Antique Centre,
W8 4DB HY
Tel: 0171 376 0425
(Fa)

Zeitgeist,
58 Kensington Church
Street, W8 4DB
Tel: 0171 938 4817
(AN, M)

Avon

Bath Dolls' Hospital,
2 Grosvenor Place,
London Road,
Bath BA1 6PT
Tel: 01225 319668
(Do)

Brine, Lynda,
Scent Bottles & Smalls,
Great Western Antique
Centre,
Bartlett Street,
Bath BA1 2QZ
Tel: 01225 837932/448488
Mobile: 0860 105600
(PB, J)

Cashman, Peter & Sonia,
Bartlett Street Antique
Centre,
Bath BA1 2QZ
Tel: 01225 310457
(Col)

Collectable Costume,
The Great Western
Antique Centre,
Bartlett Street,
Bath BA1 2QZ
Tel: 01225 428731
(C)

Glenville Antiques,
120 High Street,
Yatton BS19 4DH
Tel: 01934 832284
(Col, Ce, S, Sew)

Glitterati,
Great Western Antique
Centre, Bartlett Street,
Bath BA1 2QZ
Tel: 01225 333294
(J)

Great Western Toys,
Great Western Antique
Centre, Bartlett Street,
Bath BA1 2QZ
(To)

Hale, Graham,
Great Western Antique
Centre, Bartlett Street,
Bath BA1 2QZ
Tel: 01225 446322
(Col)

Jessie's Button Box,
Great Western Antique
Centre, Bartlett Street,
Bath BA1 2QZ
Tel: 01225 310388
(Bu)

Linen & Lace,
(Jo Watson & Maggie
Adams), The Great Western
Antique Centre,
Bartlett Street,
Bath BA1 2QZ
Tel: 01225 310388
(L&L, C)

Millard, Tim,
Antiques,
Stand 31-32 Bartlett Street
Antique Centre,
Bartlett Street,
Bath BA1 2QZ
Tel: 01225 469785
(B, Ga)

Nashers Music Store,
72 Walcot Street,
Bath BA1 5DD
Tel: 01225 332298
(Re)

Payne, David,
Bartlett Street Antiques
Market, Bartlett Street,
Bath BA1 2QZ
Tel: 01225 330267
(Sm)

Proops, Joanna,
Antiques and Textiles,
No 3 Saville Row,
Bath BA1 2QP
Tel: 01225 310795
(TB)

Quiet Street Antiques,
3 Quiet Street,
Bath BA1 2JG
Tel: 01225 315727
(P, Ce)

Rees, Mark, Tools,
Tel: 01225 837031
(TO)

Scott's,
Bartlett Street Antiques
Centre, Bartlett Street,
Bath BA1 2QZ
Tel: 01225 625335
(Ce)

Somervale Antiques,
6 Radstock Road,
Midsomer Norton,
Bath BA3 2AJ
Tel: 01761 412686
(G, PB)

Twort, Richard,
Tel: 01934 641900
(S&MI)

Bedfordshire

Something Old
Antiques & Collectables,
52a Shortmead Street,
Biggleswade SG18 0AP
Tel: 01767 627564
(Col)

Berkshire

Below Stairs,
103 High Street,
Hungerford RG17 0NB
Tel: 01488 682317
(K, TX, TO)

Mostly Boxes,
92 High Street,
Eton SL4 6AF
Tel: 01753 858470
(B, I, TW)

Special Auction Services,
The Coach House,
Madgham Park,
Reading RG7 5UG
Tel: 01734 712949
(A, P, Ce)

Buckinghamshire

Ella's Button Box,
South View,
Twyford MK18 4EG
Tel: 01296 730910
(Bu)

Neale, Gillian A,
PO Box 247,
Aylesbury HP20 1JZ
Tel: 01296 625335
(Ce)

Sykes, Christopher,
Antiques,
The Old Parsonage,
Woburn, Milton Keynes
MK17 9QM
Tel: 01525 290259
(Cor, S&MI)

Cambridgeshire

Fuller, James, & Son,
51 Huntingdon Road,
Chatteris P16 6JE
Tel: 01354 692740
(Wr)

Warboys Antiques,
High Street, Warboys,
Huntingdon PE17 1NH
Tel: 01487 823686
(Sp, Col)

Cheshire

Avalon,
1 City Walls/Rufus Court,
Northgate Street,
Chester CH1 2JG
Tel: 01244 318406
(Po)

Collector's Corner,
29-31 Lower Bridge Road,
Chester CH1 1RS
Tel: 01244 346736/
01260 270429
(Co, Re, RP)

Dollectable,
53 Lower Bridge Street,
Chester CH1 1RS
Tel: 01244 344888/679195
(Do)

Eureka Antiques,
7a Church Brow,
Bowdon,
Altrincham WA14 2SF
Tel: 0161 926 9722
(CaC, J, Ta)

Nantwich Art Deco &
Decorative Arts,
87 Welsh Row,
Nantwich CW5 5ET
Tel: 01270 624876
(AD)

On The Air,
42 Bridge Street Row,
Chester CH1 1NN
Tel: 01244 348468
(R, TV, Gr)

Sweetbriar Gallery,
Sweetbriar House,
Robin Hood Lane,
Helsby WA6 9NH
Tel: 01928 723851
(Pa)

Cornwall

Gnome World,
Indian Queens,
Nr Saint Columb TR9 6HN
Tel: 01726 860812
(Gn)

Millcraft Rocking Horse Co,
Lower Trannack Mill,
Wendron,
Helston TR13 0LT
Tel: 01326 573316
(To, RH)

Cumbria

Banking Memorabilia,
PO Box 14,
Carlisle CA3 8EW
Tel: 016974 76465
(PaM)

Domino Restorations
Ceramic Restorers,
129 Craig Walk,
Windermere LA23 3AX
Tel: 015394 45751
(Ce)

Derbyshire

What Now,
Cavendish Arcade,
The Crescent,
Buxton SK17 6BQ
Tel: 01298 27178/23417
(Col)

Devon

Bampton Telephone &
General Museum of
Communication and
Domestic History,
4 Brook Street, Bampton,
Tiverton EX16 9LY
(Te, Sh)

Gnome Reserve,
West Putford,
Nr Bradworthy
EX22 7XE
Tel: 01409 241435
(Gn)

Great Western Antiques
inc Temeraire,
The Torre Station,
Newton Road,
Torquay TQ5 2DD
Tel: 01803 200551
(Sh)

Hill, Jonathan,
2-4 Brook Street,
Bampton EX16 9LY
Tel: 01398 331532
(R)

Shambles,
22 North Street,
Ashburton TQ13 7QD
Tel: 01364 653848
(Col)

Shell Shop, The,
9 The Quay,
Brixham TQ5 8AW
Tel: 01803 852039
(She)

Taylor, Brian, Antiques,
24 Molesworth Road,
Plymouth
PL1 5LZ
Tel: 01752 569061
(Gr)

Dorset

Books Afloat,
66 Park Street,
Weymouth DT4 7DE
Tel: 01305 779774
(Bks)

Nautical Antiques,
Old Harbour Passage,
3a Hope Square
(opposite Brewers Quay),
Weymouth
DT4 8TR
Tel: 01305 777838/
783180 (eves)
(Sh)

Old Button Shop,
Lytchett Minster,
Tel: 01202 622169
(Bu)

Essex

GKR Bonds Ltd,
PO Box 1,
Kelvedon
CO5 9EH
Tel: 01376 571711
(Scr)

Old Telephone Company,
The Old Granary,
Battlesbridge Antiques
Centre,
Nr Wickford
SS11 7RF
Tel: 01245 400601
(Te)

Gloucestershire

Acorn Antiques,
Sheep Street,
Stow-on-the-Wold
GL54 1AA
Tel: 01451 831519
(Ce)

Bland, Judi,
Durham House Antique
Centre, Sheep Street,
Stow-on-the-Wold
GL54 1AA
Tel: 01451 870404/
01295 811292
(P)

Corinium Galleries,
25 Gloucester Street,
Cirencester GL7 2DJ
Tel: 01285 659057
(A, Po)

Harden, Judy & Brian,
Antiques
Tel: 01451 810684
(P, B)

Oriental Gallery,
The Malthouse,
Digbeth Street,
Stow-on-the-Wold GL54 1BN
Tel: 01451 830944
(O)

Park House Antiques,
Park Street,
Stow-on-the-Wold
GL54 1AQ
Tel: 01451 830159
(Do, DHF, TB)

Specialised Postcard
Auctions,
25 Gloucester Street,
Cirencester GL7 2DJ
Tel: 01285 659057
(A, Po)

Telephone Lines Ltd,
339 High Street,
Cheltenham GL50 3HS
Tel: 01242 583699
(Te)

Trumpet, The,
West End,
Minchinhampton
GL6 9JA
Tel: 01453 883027
(Col)

Greater Manchester

A S Antiques,
26 Broad Street,
Pendleton,
Salford M6 5BY
Tel: 0161 737 5938
(AD, AN)

Toy Store, The,
Unit 32-34 Corn Exchange,
Manchester Centre
M4 3BW
Tel: 0161 839 6882
(Do, To)

Hampshire

Bona Arts Decorative,
19 Princes Mead Shopping
Centre,
Farnborough
GU14 7TJ
Tel: 01252 372188
(AD)

Cobwebs,
78 Northam Road,
Southampton SO2 0PB
Tel: 01703 227458
(Ae, Au, Sh)

Goss & Crested China Ltd,
62 Murray Road,
Horndean
PO8 9JL
Tel: 01705 597440
(G&CC)

Solent Railwayana,
31 New Town Road,
Warsash SO31 9FY
Tel: 01489 578093/
584633 (eve)
(Ra)

Tarrant, Lorraine,
Antiques,
7-11 Market Place,
Ringwood
BH24 1AN
Tel: 01425 461123
(Col, Au)

Toys Through Time,
Tel: 01329 288678
(Do)

Hereford & Worcester

BBM Jewellery & Coins
(W. V. Crook),
8-9 Lion Street,
Kidderminster
DY10 1PT
Tel: 01562 744118
(I, J, Cns)

Button Museum, The,
Kyrle Street,
Ross-on-Wye
HR9 7DB
Tel: 01989 66089
(Bu)

Platform 6,
11A Davenport Drive,
The Willows,
Bromsgrove
B60 2DW
Tel: 01527 871000
(A, To)

Russ-Welch, Malcolm,
Worcester Antiques
Centre,
Reindeer Court,
Mealcheapen Street,
Worcester
WR1 4DF
Tel: 0131 667 1407
(Col)

Hertfordshire

Ambeline Antiques,
By George Antique Centre,
St Albans AL3 4ES
Tel: 01727 53032/
0181 449 8307
(H/HP)

Forget Me Knot Antiques,
By George Antique
Centre, 23 George Street,
St Albans AL3 4ES
Tel: 01727 53032/
01923 261172
(J, Ce)

Magic Lantern
(Josie Marsden),
By George Antique
Centre, 23 George Street,
St Albans AL3 4ES
Tel: 01727 53032
(L)

Stateside Comics Plc,
125 East Barnet Road,
Barnet EN4 8RF
Tel: 0181 449 5535
(Co)

Humberside

Marine Art Posters,
Harbour Way,
Merchants Landing,
Victoria Dock,
Port of Hull HU9 1PL
Tel: 01482 321173
(Pos)

Isle of Wight

Nostalgia Toy Museum,
High Street,
Godshill PO38 3HZ
Tel: 01983 730055/840181
(To)

Kent

Amelia Dolls,
Pantiles Spa Antiques,
The Pantiles,
Tunbridge Wells TN4 8HE
Tel: 01892 541377/
01342 713223
(Do)

Amherst Antiques,
23 London Road,
Riverhead,
Sevenoaks TN13 2BU
Tel: 01732 455047
(Tr)

Badgers Antiques,
The Weald Antiques
Gallery,
106 High Street,
Tenterden TN30 6HT
Tel: 01580 762939
(Col)

Bears Galore,
8, The Fairings,
High Street,
Tenterden TN30 6QX
Tel: 01580 765233
(TB)

Beatcity
Tel: 01634 865428
(RP)

Berry Antiques,
Kay Parkin,
The Old Butchers Shop,
Goudhurst TN17 1AE
Tel: 01580 212115
(K, Col)

Candlestick & Bakelite,
PO Box 308,
Orpington BR5 1TB
Tel: 0181 467 3743
(Te)

Canterbury Bookshop, The,
37 Northgate,
Canterbury CT1 1BL
Tel: 01227 464773
(Bks)

Collectables,
PO Box 130,
Chatham ME5 0DZ
Tel: 01634 828767
(Col)

Dolls House Workshop,
54a London Road,
Teynham ME9 9QN
Tel: 01795 522445
(DHF)

Dowson, Dick
Tel: 01580 714072
(F)

Eaton and Jones,
120 High Street,
Tenterden
TN30 6HT
Tel: 01580 763357
(J)

Falstaff Antiques
(Motor Museum),
63-67 High Street,
Rolvenden
TN17 4LP
Tel: 01580 241234
(Au)

Heggie, Stuart,
14 The Borough,
Northgate,
Canterbury
CT1 2DR
Tel: 01227 470422
(Ca, St)

Heirloom Antiques,
68 High Street,
Tenterden
TN30 6AU
Tel: 01580 765535
(Col)

Hiscock & Hiscock
Antiques,
47 High Street,
New Romney TN28 8AH
Tel: 01797 364023
(TB, P)

J & D Collectables
Tel: 01227 452873
(Ce, P)

J & M Collectables
Tel: 01580 891657
(E)

Lace Basket,
116 High Street,
Tenterden TN30 6HT
Tel: 01580 763923/763664
(L&L, H/HP, C)

Magpie's Nest, The,
14 Palace Street,
Canterbury CT1 2DZ
Tel: 01227 764883
(Do, DHF)

Newman, Barbara Ann,
The Weald Antiques Gallery,
106 High Street,
Tenterden TN30 6HT
Tel: 01580 762939
(Do)

Radio Memories & Vintage
Wireless,
203 Tankerton Road,
Whitstable CT5 2AT
Tel: 01227 262491
(R)

Serendipity,
168 High Street,
Deal CT14 6BQ
Tel: 01304 369165/366536
(Ce, SP)

Stevenson Brothers,
The Workshop,
Ashford Road,
Bethersden,
Ashford TN26 3AP
Tel: 01233 820580/820363
(RH)

Variety Box,
16 Chapel Place,
Tunbridge Wells
TN1 1YQ
Tel: 01892 531868/521589
(BH, G&CC, Fa, G, H/HP,
Sew, S, TW)

Weald Antiques Gallery,
106 High Street,
Tenterden TN30 6HT
Tel: 01580 762939
(Col)

Wooden Chair Antiques
Centre,
Waterloo Road,
Cranbrook TN12 0QG
Tel: 01580 713671
(Col)

Woodville Antiques,
The Street,
Hamstreet,
Ashford TN26 2HG
Tel: 01233 732981
(TO)

Lancashire

Aspinall, Walter, Antiques,
Pendle Antique Centre,
Union Mill, Watt Street,
Sabden BB7 9ED
Tel: 01282 778642
(Col)

British Heritage
Telephones,
11 Rhodes Drive,
Unsworth,
Bury BL9 8NH
Tel: 0161 767 9259
(Te)

Bunn, Roy W, Antiques,
34-36 Church Street,
Barnoldswick,
Colne
BB8 5UT
Tel: 01282 813703
(Ce, SP)

Roberts Antiques
Tel: 01253 827794
(T, Ce)

Leicestershire

Brooks, Pamela
Tel: 0116 230 2625
(T)

Charnwood Antiques,
Tel: 0116 283 8530
(BP, Ce)

Jessop Classic
Photographica,
98 Scudamore Road,
Leicester
LE3 1TZ
Tel: 0116 232 0033
(Ca)

Pooks Motor Bookshop,
Fowke Street,
Rothley
LE7 7PJ
Tel: 01533 376222
(Bks, Au, T&MS)

Lincolnshire

20th Century Frocks,
65 Steep Hill,
Lincoln LN2 1LR
Tel: 01522 545916
(T)

Art Nouveau Originals,
c/o Stamford Antiques
Centre,
The Exchange Hall,
Broad Street,
Stamford PE9 1PX
Tel: 01780 62605
(AN)

Junktion,
The Old Railway Station,
New Bolingbroke,
Boston
PE22 7LB
Tel: 01205 480087/480068
(To, T&MS, Au)

Middlesex

Albert's Cigarette Card
Specialists,
113 London Road,
Twickenham
TW1 1EE
Tel: 0181 891 3067
(CC)

Anderson, Joan & Bob,
Calvers Collectables
of Ruislip,
156 High Street,
Ruislip HA4 8LJ
Tel: 0181 561 4517
(P)

Hobday Toys,
44 High Street,
Northwood
HA6 2XY
Tel: 01923 820115
(To)

Ives, John,
5 Normanhurst Drive,
Twickenham
TW1 1NA
Tel: 0181 892 6265
(Bks)

Norfolk

Bluebird Arts,
1 Mount Street,
Cromer NR27 9DB
Tel: 01263 512384/78487
(Po)

Bradbury, Roger, Antiques,
Church Street,
Coltishall NR12 7DJ
Tel: 01603 737444
(OP)

Howkins, John,
1, Dereham Road,
Norwich
NR2 4HX
Tel: 01603 627832
(J)

Howkins, Peter & Valerie,
39, 40 & 135 King Street,
Great Yarmouth
NR30 2PQ
Tel: 01493 844639
(J)

Winstanley Cats
Cat Pottery,
1 Grammar School Road,
North Walsham
NR28 9JH
Tel: 01692 402962
(P)

Yesteryear Antiques,
24D Magdalen Street,
Norwich NR3 1HU
Tel: 01603 622908
(Ce, D)

Northamptonshire

Shelron,
9 Brackley Road,
Towcester NN12 6DH
Tel: 01327 50242
(Po)

Nottinghamshire

Barlow, Catherine,
14 Windsor Road,
Selston,
Nottingham NG16 6JJ
Tel: 01773 860933
(Ce)

Barlow, Stuart,
14 Windsor Road, Selston,
Nottingham NG16 6JJ
Tel: 01733 860933
(To)

Keyhole, The,
Dragonwyck, Far Back
Lane, Farnsfield,
Newark NG22 8JX
Tel: 01623 882590
(L&K)

Neales,
192-194 Mansfield Road,
Nottingham NG1 3HU
Tel: 0115 962 4141
(A, E, Sp)

Reflections of a Bygone Age,
15 Debdale Lane,
Keyworth NG12 5HT
Tel: 01607 74079
(Po)

Vennett-Smith, T,
11 Nottingham Road,
Gotham,
Nottingham NG11 0HE
Tel: 0115 983 0541
(A, E, Po, Sp)

Vintage Wireless Shop,
The Hewarths, Sandiacre,
Nottingham NG9 8EX
Tel: 0115 939 3138
(R, TV)

Oxfordshire

Comics & Showcase,
19-20 St Clements Street,
Oxford OX4 1AB
Tel: 01865 723680
(Co)

Dauphin Display
Cabinet Co,
PO Box 602,
Oxford OX44 9LU
Tel: 01865 343542
(DS)

Huntercombe Manor Barn,
Henley-on-Thames,
Oxon RG9 5RY
Tel: 01491 641349
(Col)

Manfred Schotten,
The Crypt Antiques,
109 High Street,
Burford OX18 4RG
Tel: 01993 822302
(Sp)

Teddy Bears of Witney,
99 High Street,
Witney OX8 6LY
Tel: 01993 702616
(TB)

Thames Gallery,
23 Thameside,
Henley-on-Thames
RG9 2LJ
Tel: 01491 572449
(S)

Shropshire

Antiques on the Square,
2 Sandford Court,
Sandford Avenue,
Church Stretton
SY6 6DA
Tel: 01694 724111
(ADC)

Manser, F C, & Son Ltd,
53-54 Wyle Cop,
Shrewsbury
SY1 1XJ
Tel: 01743 351120
(Col, S, G, T, J, P, Ce)

Rocking Horse Workshop,
Ashfield House,
The Foxholes,
Wem SY4 5UJ
Tel: 01939 32335
(RH)

Teme Valley Antiques,
1 The Bull Ring,
Ludlow SY8 1AD
Tel: 01584 874686
(Ce, S)

Tiffany Antiques,
Unit 1, Welsh Bridge
Antique Centre,
135 Frankwell,
Shrewsbury
SY3 8JX
Tel: 01270 257425/
01743 248822
(Col, K)

Somerset

Cains Antiques,
Littleton House,
Littleton,
Nr Somerton TA11 6NP
Tel: 01458 72341
(P)

Gilbert & Dale Antiques,
The Old Chapel,
Church Street,
Ilchester,
Nr Yeovil BA22 8LA
Tel: 01935 840444
(Col)

Heads n' Tails,
Bourne House,
41 Church Street,
Wiveliscombe,
Taunton TA4 2LT
Tel: 01984 623097
Fax: 01984 624445
(Tx)

London Cigarette
Card Co Ltd,
Sutton Road,
Somerton TA11 6QP
Tel: 01458 273452
(CC)

Milverton Antiques,
Fore Street,
Milverton,
Taunton TA4 1JU
Tel: 01823 400597
(Col)

Staffordshire

Davies, Peggy, Ceramics,
28 Liverpool Road,
Stoke-on-Trent
ST4 1VJ
Tel: 01782 848002
(Ce)

Fletcher, Nick,
PO Box 411,
Longton,
Stoke-on-Trent,
ST3 4SS.
(Col)

Gordon The 'Ole
Bottleman,
25 Stapenhill Road,
Burton-on-Trent
DE15 9AE
Tel: 01283 567213
(Bot)

Keystones,
PO Box 387,
Stafford ST16 3RX
Tel: 01785 256648
(Ce)

Midwinter Antiques,
31 Bridge Street,
Newcastle under Lyme
ST5 1HF
Tel: 01782 712483
(T)

Suffolk

Crafers Antiques,
The Hill,
Wickham Market
IP13 0QS
Tel: 01728 747347
(Ce, SP, Sew)

Hoad, W L,
9 St. Peter's Road,
Kirkley,
Lowestoft NR33 0LH
Tel: 01502 587758
(CC)

Tartan Bow, The,
Tel: 01379 783057
(K, Gar)

Surrey

Aldous-Cook, David,
PO Box 413,
Sutton SM3 8SZ
Tel: 0181 642 4842
(RB)

Burns, David,
116 Chestnut Grove,
New Malden
KT3 3JT
Tel: 0181 949 7356
(S&MI)

Childhood Memories,
The Farnham Antique
Centre,
27 South Street,
Farnham
GU9 7QU
Tel: 01252 724475
(Do)

Church Street Antiques,
15 Church Street,
Godalming
GU7 1EL
Tel: 01483 860894
(ADC, Com)

Foster, David,
87 Foxley Lane,
Purley
CR8 3HP
Tel: 0181 668 1246
(Col)

New Ashgate Gallery,
Waggon Yard,
Farnham
GU9 7PS
Tel: 01252 713208
(Col)

Nostalgia Amusements,
22 Greenwood Close,
Thames Ditton
KT7 0BG
Tel: 0181 398 2141
(Ju)

Richard Joseph
Publishers Ltd,
Unit 2,
Monk's Walk,
Farnham
GU9 8HT
Tel: 01252 734347
(Bks)

West Promotions,
PO Box 257,
Sutton
SM3 9WW
Tel: 0181 641 3224
(PaM)

Sussex

Bartholomew, John &
Mary,
The Mint Arcade,
71 The Mint,
Rye TN31 7EW
Tel: 01797 225952
(Po)

Bears & Friends,
32 Meeting House Lane,
The Lanes,
Brighton
BN1 1HB
Tel: 01273 202801
(TB)

Beech, Ron,
Brambledean Road,
Portslade,
Brighton
BN41 1LP
Tel: 01273 423355
(Ce, PL)

Birdham Antiques,
The Old Bird & Ham,
Main Road,
Birdham,
Chichester
PO20 7HS
Tel: 01243 51141
(M, Col)

Bygones,
Collectors Shop,
123 South Street,
Lancing
BN15 8AS
Tel: 01903 750051/763470
(Col, Po)

Children's Treasures,
17 George Street,
Hastings
TN34 3EG
Tel: 01424 444117/422758
(To)

Elite Designs
Tel: 01424 434856
(E, Col, RP)

Horsley, Tony
Tel: 01273 732163
(Col, Ce)

Keiron James Designs,
St Dominic's Gallery,
4 South Street,
Ditchling
BN6 8UQ
Tel: 01273 846411
(TB)

Kinloch, Clare
Tel: 01424 870364
(Do)

Libra Antiques,
81 London Road,
Hurst Green,
Etchingham
TN19 7PN
Tel: 01580 860569
(L)

Lingard, Ann,
Ropewalk Antiques,
Ropewalk,
Rye TN31 7NA
Tel: 01797 223486
(K, Ti)

Pearson, Sue,
13 Prince Albert Street,
Brighton
BN1 1HE
Tel: 01273 329247
(Do, TB)

Pianola Shop, The,
134 Islington Road,
Brighton
BN2 2SH
Tel: 01273 608999
(Pia)

Recollect Studios,
Dept. M,
The Old School,
London Road,
Sayers Common,
BN6 9HX
Tel: 01273 833314
(Do)

Rin Tin Tin,
34 North Road,
Brighton
BN1 1YB
Tel: 01273 672424/733689
(Col, T&MS)

Russell, Leonard,
21 King's Avenue,
Mount Pleasant,
Newhaven
BN9 0NB
Tel: 01273 515153
(Ce, Com, P)

Sussex Commemorative
Ware Centre, The,
88 Western Road,
Hove
BN3 1JB
Tel: 01273 773911
(Ce)

Trains,
67 London Road,
Bognor Regis
PO21 1DF
Tel: 01243 864727
(To)

Wallis & Wallis,
West Street Auction
Galleries,
Lewes, BN7 2NJ
Tel: 01273 480208
(A)

Webb, Graham,
59A Ship Street,
Brighton
BN1 1AE
Tel: 01273 321803
(Mus)

Westhill Antiques,
22A Wilton Road,
Bexhill-on-Sea
TN40 1HX
Tel: 01424 731000
(Porc, S)

Witney and Airault,
Prinny's Gallery,
3 Meeting House Lane, The
Lanes,
Brighton
BN1 1HB
Tel: 01273 204554
(ADC)

Tyne & Wear

Sharp, Ian, Antiques,
23 Front Street,
Tynemouth NE30 4DX
Tel: 0191 2960656
(Ce, P)

Warwickshire

Arbour Antiques Ltd,
Poet's Arbour,
Sheep Street,
Stratford-on-Avon
CV37 6EF
Tel: 01789 293453
(A&M)

Art Deco Ceramics,
The Stratford Antique
Centre,
Ely Street,
Stratford-upon-Avon
CV37 6LN
Tel: 01789 297496/299524
(ADC)

Bowler, Simon,
Smith Street Antique
Centre,
Warwick
CV34 4HU
Tel: 01926 400554/
0121 783 8930
(O)

Central Antique Arms &
Militaria,
Smith Street Antique
Centre,
7 Smith Street,
Warwick
CV34 4JA
Tel: 01926 400554
(A&M)

Lions Den,
11 St Mary's Crescent,
Leamington Spa
CV31 1JL
Tel: 01926 339498
(ADC, P)

Midlands Goss &
Commemoratives,
The Old Cornmarket
Antique Centre,
70 Market Place,
Warwick
CV34 4SO
Tel: 01926 419119
(Ce, Com)

Old Pine House,
16 Warwick Street,
Royal Leamington Spa
CV32 5LL
Tel: 01926 470477
(Col)

Paull, Janice,
Beehive House,
125 Warwick Road,
Kenilworth
CV18 1HV
Tel: 01926 55253/
0831 691254
(P, LB)

Rich Designs,
1 Shakespeare Street,
Stratford-upon-Avon
CV37 6RN
Tel: 01789 261612
(AN, AD)

Tim's Spot,
Ely Street Antique
Centre,
Stratford-upon-Avon
CV37 6LN
Tel: 01789 297496/204182
(G, Ce)

Time Machine,
198 Holbrook Lane,
Coventry CV6 4DD
Tel: 01203 663557
(To)

Wigington, James
Tel: 01789 261418
(F, A&M)

West Midlands
Dog House, The,
309 Bloxwich Road,
Walsall WS2 7BD
Tel: 01922 30829
(K, Col)

Nostalgia Comics,
14-16 Smallbrook
Queensway,
City Centre,
Birmingham B5 4EN
Tel: 0121 643 0143
(Co)

Wiltshire
Coppins of Corsham
Repairs,
1 Church Street,
Corsham
Tel: 01249 715404
(J)

North Wiltshire Exporters,
Farmhill House
Brinkworth SN15 5AJ
Tel: 01666 824133/510876
(Col)

Relic Antiques,
Brillscote Farm,
Lea, Malmesbury SN16 9PG
Tel: 01666 822332
(T&MS)

Wells, David,
Salisbury Antique &
Collectors Market,
37 Catherine Street,
Salisbury SP1 2DH
Tel: 01425 476899
(Po, To, Col)

Winter, Dominic,
Book Auctions,
The Old School,
Maxwell Street,
Swindon SN1 5DR
Tel: 01793 611340
(A)

Worcestershire
Chapman, Michael,
Priorsleigh,
Mill Lane,
Cleeve Prior
WR11 5JZ
Tel: 01789 773897
Mobile 0831 392542
(Au)

Yorkshire
Crested China Co, The,
The Station House,
Driffield
YO25 7PY
Tel: 01377 257042
(G & CC)

BBR Auctions & British
Bottle Review,
2 Strafford Avenue,
Elsecar, Barnsley
S74 8HJ
Tel: 01226 745156
(A, Bot)

Clarke, Andrew,
42 Pollard Lane,
Bradford
BD2 4RN
Tel: 01274 636042
(To)

Danby Antiques,
61, Heworth Road,
York YO3 0AA
Tel: 01904 415280
(B, Wr)

Haley, John & Simon,
89 Northgate,
Halifax
HX1 1XF
Tel: 01422 822148
(To, MB)

Hewitt, Muir,
Halifax Antiques Centre,
Queens Road Mills,
Queen's Road/Gibbet
Street, Halifax HX1 4LR
Tel: 01422 347377
(ADC)

Holmfirth Antiques
(Ken Priestley)
Tel: 01484 686854
(Gr)

Sheffield Railwayana
Auctions,
43 Little Norton Lane,
Sheffield S8 8GA
Tel: 0114 274 5085 &
0860 921519
(A, Ra)

Tomlinson, Shirley,
Halifax Antiques Centre,
Queens Road,
Halifax
HX1 4LR
Tel: 01422 366657
(T, C)

Ireland
Stacpoole, Michelina &
George,
Main Street,
Adare,
Co Limerick
Tel: 00 353 6139 6409
(P, Ce, S)

Scotland
Barge, Chris, Antiques,
5 Southside Place,
Inverness IV2 3JF
Tel: 01463 230128
(Cor)

Black, Laurance,
45 Cumberland Street,
Edinburgh
EH3 6RA
Tel: 0131 557 4543
(Ta)

Bow-Well Antiques,
103 West Bow,
Edinburgh
EH1 2JP
Tel: 0131 225 3335
(Gr, SC, P, S)

Brown, David,
23 Claude Street,
Larkhall,
Lanarkshire
ML9 2BU
Tel: 01555 880333
(K)

Caithness Glass Ltd,
Inveralmond,
Perth PH1 3TZ
Tel: 01738 37373
(G)

Edinburgh Coin Shop,
2 Polwarth Crescent,
Edinburgh EH11 1HW
Tel: 0131 229 2915/3007
(Cns)

Maitland, Stephen,
Now & Then (Toy Centre),
7&9 West Crosscauseway,
Edinburgh
EH8 9JW
Tel: 01592 890235 & 0131
668 2927
(To, Te)

McEwan, Rhod –
Golf Books,
Glengarden,
Ballater,
Aberdeenshire
AB35 5UB
Tel: 013397 55429
(Bks)

Otterswick Antique
Telephones,
6 Lady Lawson Street,
Edinburgh EH3 9DS
Tel: 0131 228 3690
(Te)

Stockbridge Antiques,
8 Deanhaugh Street,
Edinburgh EH4 1LY
Tel: 0131 332 1366
(Do, T)

Timeless Tackle,
1 Blackwood Crescent,
Edinburgh EH9 1QZ
Tel: 0131 667 1407
(F)

USA
Postcards International,
Vintage Picture Postcards,
PO Box 2930,
New Haven,
CT 06515-0030
Tel: 001 203 865 0814
(Po)

Wales
APES Rocking Horses,
Ty Gwyn,
Llannefydd,
Denbigh LL16 5HB
Tel: 01745 540365
(RH)

Ayers, Brindley John,
8 Bay View Drive,
Milford Haven
SA73 3LJ
Tel: 01646 698359
(F)

Corgi Collector Club,
PO Box 323,
Swansea
SA1 1BJ
Tel: 01792 476902
(To)

Gibbs, Paul, Antiques,
25 Castle Street,
Conwy,
Gwynedd
LL32 8AY
Tel: 01492 593429
(P, ADC)

Howards Antiques,
10 Alexandra Road,
Aberystwyth,
Dyfed
SY23 1LE
Tel: 01970 624973
(P)

Watkins, Islwyn,
1 High Street,
Knighton,
Powys
LD7 1AT
Tel: 01547 520145
(P)

If you require a valuation for an item, it is advisable to check whether the dealer or specialist will carry out this service and if there is a charge. Please mention Miller's when making an enquiry. Having found a specialist who will carry out your valuation it is best to send a description and photograph of the item to the specialist together with a stamped addressed envelope for the reply. A valuation by telephone is not possible. Most dealers are only too happy to help you with your enquiry, however, they are very busy people and consideration of the above points would be welcomed.

DIRECTORY OF MARKETS & CENTRES

London

Alfies Antique Market,
13-25 Church Street,
NW8 8DT
Tel: 0171 723 6066

Angel Arcade,
116-118 Islington High St,
Camden Passage,
N1 8EG

Antiquarius Antique
Market,
131/141 King's Road,
Chelsea SW3 5ST

Antiques & Collectors
Corner,
North Piazza,
Covent Garden,
WC2E 8HB

Bermondsey Antiques
Warehouse,
173 Bermondsey Street,
SE1 3UW
Tel: 0171 407 2040/4250

Bond Street Antiques
Centre,
124 New Bond Street,
W1Y 9AE
Tel: 0171 351 5353

Chelsea Antiques Market,
253 King's Road, SW3 5EL
Tel: 0171 352 5689/1720

Chenil Galleries,
Enigma Z2,
Pamela Haywood Z3,
Persifage Z5,
Forthergill Crowley D11-12,
181-183 King's Road,
SW3 5EB

Corner Portobello
Antiques Supermarket,
282, 284, 288, 290
Westbourne Grove,
W11 2PS
Tel: 0171 727 2027

Cutler Street Antiques
Market,
Goulston Street,
Nr Aldgate End,
E1 7TP

Dixons Antique Centre,
471 Upper Richmond
Road West, East Sheen,
SW14 7PU

Franklin's Camberwell
Antiques Market,
161 Camberwell Road,
SE5 0HB
Tel: 0171 703 8089

Georgian Village Antiques
Market,
100 Wood Street,
Walthamstow,
E17 3HX

Good Fairy Open Market,
100 Portobello Road,
W11 2QD
Tel: 0171 351 5950/
221 8977

Grays Antique Market,
58 Davies Street,
W1Y 1LB
Tel: 0171 629 7034

Grays Mews,
1-7 Davies Street,
W1Y 1LL
Tel: 0171 629 7034

Grays Portobello,
138 Portobello Road,
W11 2DZ
Tel: 0171 221 3069

Hampstead Antique
Emporium,
12 Heath Street,
Hampstead,
NW3 6TE

Kensington Antique
Centre,
58-60 Kensington Church
Street, W8 4DB
Tel: 0171 376 0425

Mall Antiques Arcade,
359 Upper Street,
Islington,
N1 0PD

Northcote Road
Antiques Market,
155a Northcote Road,
Battersea, SW11 6QB
Tel: 0171 228 6850

Old Crowther Market,
282 North End Road,
Fulham SW6 1NH
Tel: 0171 610 3610

Peckham Indoor Market,
Rye Lane Bargain Centre,
48 Rye Lane,
Peckham SE15 5BY
Tel: 0171 246 3639

Pierrepoint Arcade,
Camden Passage,
N1 8DU
Tel: 0171 359 0190

Rochefort Antique
Gallery,
32/34 The Green,
Winchmore Hill, N21 1AY

Roger's Antiques Gallery,
65 Portobello Road,
W11 2QB
Tel: 0171 351 5353

Steptoe's Yard West
Market,
52a Goldhawk Road,
W12 8DH
Tel: 0171 602 2699

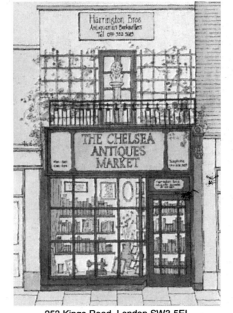

World Famous
Portobello Market,
177 Portobello Road,
W11 2DY
Tel: 0171 221 4964

York Arcade,
80 Islington High Street,
N1 8EQ
Tel: 0171 833 2640

Avon

Bartlett Street Antique
Centre,
Bartlett Street,
Bath BA1 2QZ
Tel: 01225 466689

Bristol Antique Market,
St Nicholas Markets,
The Exchange,
Corn Street,
Bristol BS1 1HQ

Clifton Antiques Market,
26/28 The Mall, Clifton,
Bristol BS8 4DS
Tel: 0117 974 1627

Great Western Antique
Centre,
Bartlett Street,
Bath BA1 2QZ
Tel: 01225 424243

Bedfordshire

Dunstable Antique
Centre,
38a West Street,
Dunstable LU6 1TA
Tel: 01582 696953

Woburn Abbey Antiques
Centre,
Woburn Abbey
MK43 0TP
Tel: 01525 290350

Berkshire

Hungerford Arcade,
26 High Street,
Hungerford RG17 0NF
Tel: 01488 683701

Lodden Lily Antiques,
1 High Street,
Twyford RG10 9AB
Tel: 01734 342161

Reading Emporium,
1a Merchant Place,
(off Friar Street),
Reading RG1 1DT
Tel: 01734 590290

Buckinghamshire

Amersham Antique
Collectors Centre,
20-22 Whielden Street,
Old Amersham
HP7 0HT
Tel: 01494 431282

Antiques at Wendover,
The Old Post Office,
25 High Street,
Wendover HP22 6DU
Tel: 01296 625335

Bell Street Antiques Centre,
20/22 Bell Street,
Princes Risborough
HP27 0AD
Tel: 01844 43034

Market Square Antiques,
20 Market Place,
Olney MK46 4BA
Tel: 01234 712172

Olney Antiques Centre,
Rose Court off Market Sq,
Olney MK46 4BA
Tel: 01234 712172

Tingewick Antiques
Centre,
Main Street,
Tingewick MK18 4NN
Tel: 01280 847922/848219

Winslow Antique Centre,
15 Market Square,
Winslow MK18 3AB
Tel: 01296 714540/714055

Cambridgeshire

Collectors Market,
Dales Brewery,
Gwydir Street
(off Mill Road),
Cambridge CB1 2LJ

Fitzwilliam Antiques
Centre,
Fitzwilliam Street,
Peterborough PE1 2R
Tel: 01733 65415

Willingham Antiques &
Collectors Market,
25-29 Green Street,
Willingham CB4 5JA
Tel: 01954 260283

Cheshire

Davenham Antique Centre,
461 London Road,
Davenham,
Northwick CW9 8NA
Tel: 01606 44350

Nantwich Antique Centre,
The Manor House,
7 Beam Street,
Nantwich CW5 5LR
Tel: 01270 610615

Cornwall

New Generation Antique
Market,
61/62 Chapel Street,
Penzance TR18 4AE
Tel: 01736 63267

Waterfront Antique
Complex,
1st Floor, 4 Quay Street,
Falmouth TR11 3HH
Tel: 01326 311491

Cumbria

Carlisle Antique & Craft
Centre,
Cecil Hall, Cecil Street,
Carlisle CA1 1NT
Tel: 01228 21970

Derbyshire

Derby Antique Centre,
11 Friargate,
Derby DE1 1BU
Tel: 01332 385002

Derby Antiques Market,
52-56 Curzon Street,
Derby DE1 1LP

Glossop Antique Centre,
Brookfield,
Glossop SK13 9JE
Tel: 01457 863904

Devon

Abingdon House Antiques,
136 High Street,
Honiton EX14 8UP
Tel: 01404 42108

Barbican Antiques
Centre,
82-84 Vauxhall Street,
Barbican,
Plymouth PL4 0EX
Tel: 01752 266927

Barnes House Antiques
Centre,
11a West Row,
Wimborne Minster,
BH21 1LA
Tel: 01202 886275

Dorset

Antiques Centre,
837-839 Christchurch
Road, East Boscombe,
Bournemouth BH7 6AR
Tel: 01202 421052

Bridport Antique Centre,
5 West Allington,
Bridport DT6 5BJ
Tel: 01308 25885

Gold Hill Antiques &
Collectables,
3 Gold Hill Parade,
Gold Hill,
Shaftesbury SP7 8LY
Tel: 01747 54050

Sherborne Antique
Centre,
Mattar Arcade,
17 Newlands,
Sherborne DT9 3JG
Tel: 01935 813464

Wimborne Antique
Centre,
Newborough Road,
Wimborne BH21 1RB
Tel: 01202 841251

Essex

Battlesbridge Antiques
Centre,
Maltings Road,
Battlesbridge,
Wickford SS11 7RF

Essex Antiques Centre,
Priory Street,
Colchester CO1 2PY
Tel: 01206 871150

Grays Galleries Antiques
& Collectors Centre,
23 Lodge Lane,
Grays RM17 5RY
Tel: 01375 374883

Townsford Mill Antiques
Centre,
The Causeway,
Halstead CO9 1ET
Tel: 01787 474451

Trinity Antiques Centre,
7 Trinity Street,
Colchester CO1 1JN
Tel: 01206 577775

Gloucestershire

Antiques Emporium,
The Old Chapel,
Long Street,
Tetbury GL8 8AA
Tel: 01666 505281

Charlton Kings Antique
Centre,
199 London Road,
Charlton Kings,
Cheltenham
GL52 6HU
Tel: 01242 510672

Cheltenham Antique
Market,
54 Suffolk Road,
Cheltenham GL50 2AQ
Tel: 01242 529812

Cirencester Antique
Market,
Market Place,
Cirencester GL7 2PY
Tel: 0171 262 5003 (Fri)

Cotswold Antiques
Centre,
The Square,
Stow-on-the-Wold
GL54 1AB
Tel: 01451 31585

Durham House Antiques
Centre,
Sheep Street,
Stow-on-the-Wold
GL54 1AA
Tel: 01451 870404

Gloucester Antiques
Centre,
Severn Road,
Gloucester GL1 2LE
Tel: 01452 529716

Painswick Antique
Centre,
New Street,
Painswick GL6 6XH
Tel: 01452 812431

Tolsey Antique Centre,
Tolsey Lane,
Tewkesbury GL20 5AE
Tel: 01684 294091

Windsor House Antiques
Centre,
High Street,
Moreton-in-Marsh
GL56 0AH
Tel: 01608 650993

Greater Manchester

Antiques Gallery,
Royal Exchange Shopping
Centre,
St Anne's Square,
Exchange Street M2 7DB

Hampshire

Creightons Antique
Centre,
23-25 Bell Street,
Romsey SO51 8GY
Tel: 01794 522758

Folly Antiques Centre,
Folly Market,
College Street,
Petersfield GU31 4AD
Tel: 01730 265937

Kingsley Barn Antique
Centre,
Church Road, Eversley,
Wokingham RG27 0PX
Tel: 01734 328518

Lymington Antiques
Centre,
76 High Street,
Lymington SO41 9AL
Tel: 01590 670934

Squirrel Collectors
Centre,
9 New Street,
Basingstoke RG21 1DE
Tel: 01256 464885

Hereford & Worcester

Galleries Antiques
Centre,
Pickwicks,
503 Evesham Road,
Crabbs Cross,
Redditch B97 5JJ

Hereford Antiques Centre,
128 Widemarsh Street,
Hereford HR4 9HN
Tel: 01432 266242

Leominster Antiques
Market,
14 Broad Street,
Leominster HR6 8BS
Tel: 01568 612189

Worcester Antiques
Centre,
Reindeer Court,
Mealcheapen Street,
Worcester WR1 4DF
Tel: 01905 610680

Hertfordshire

Bushey Antiques Centre,
39 High Street,
Bushey WD2 1BD
Tel: 0181 950 5040

By George Antique
Centre,
23 George Street,
St Albans AL3 4ES
Tel: 01727 53032

Humberside

New Pocklington
Antiques Centre,
26 George Street,
Pocklington,
York YO4 2DQ
Tel: 01759 303032

Kent

Antiques Centre,
120 London Road,
Sevenoaks
TN13 1BA
Tel: 01732 452104

Beckenham Antique
Market,
Old Council Hall,
Bromley Road,
Beckenham BR3 2JE
Tel: 0181 777 6300

Bromley Antique Market,
Widmore Road,
Bromley BR1 1RL

Burgate Antiques Centre,
10 Burgate,
Canterbury CT1 2HG
Tel: 01227 456500

Castle Antiques Centre,
1 London Road,
Westerham TN16 1BB
Tel: 01959 562492

Cranbrook Antique
Centre,
High Street,
Cranbrook TN17 3DN
Tel: 01580 712173

Heirloom Antiques
Centre,
68 High Street,
Tenterden TN30 6AU
Tel: 01580 765535

Hythe Antique Centre,
5 High Street,
Hythe CT21 5AB
Tel: 01303 269043/269643

Malthouse Arcade,
Malthouse Hill,
Hythe CT21 5BW
Tel: 01303 260103

Noah's Ark Antiques
Centre,
5 King Street,
Sandwich CT13 9BT
Tel: 01304 611144

Paraphernalia Antiques &
Collectors Centre,
171 Widmore Road,
Bromley BR1 3BS
Tel: 0181 318 2997

Sandgate Antiques
Centre,
61-63 High Street,
Sandgate CT20 3AH
Tel: 01303 248987

Tenterden Antique
Centre,
66-66A High Street,
Tenterden TN30 6AU
Tel: 01580 765655/765885

Thanet Antiques Trade
Centre,
45 Albert Street,
Ramsgate CT11 9EX
Tel: 01843 597336

Tudor Cottage Antiques
Centre,
22-23 Shipbourne Road,
Tonbridge TN10 3DN
Tel: 01732 351719

Tunbridge Wells Antique
Centre,
Union Square,
The Pantiles,
Tunbridge Wells
TN4 8HE
Tel: 01892 533708

Weald Antiques Gallery,
106 High Street,
Tenterden TN30 6HT
Tel: 01580 762939

Lancashire

Bolton Antiques Centre,
Premier Stores,
Central Street,
Bolton BL1 2AB
Tel: 01204 362694

Bygone Times,
Times House, Grove Mill,
The Green,
Eccleston PR7 5PD
Tel: 01257 453780

Darwen Antique Centre,
Provident Hall,
The Green,
Darwen BB3 1PW
Tel: 01254 760565

GB Antiques Centre,
Lancaster Leisure Park,
Wyresdale Road,
Lancaster LA1 3LA
Tel: 01524 844734

Memory Lane Antique
Centre,
Gilnow Lane, off Deane Rd,
Bolton BL3 5EL
Tel: 01204 380383

Pendle Antique Centre,
Union Mill, Watt Street,
Sabden BB7 9ED
Tel: 01282 776311

Preston Antique Centre,
The Mill,
New Hall Lane,
Preston PR1 5UH
Tel: 01772 794498

Leicestershire

Boulevard Antique &
Shopping Centre,
The Old Dairy,
Western Boulevard,
Leicester LE2 7BU
Tel: 0116 254 1201

Oxford Street Antiques
Centre Ltd,
16-26 Oxford Street,
Leicester LE1 5XU
Tel: 01533 553006

Lincolnshire

Aswell Street Antique
Centre,
Louth LN11 9HP
Tel: 01507 600366

Boston Antiques Centre,
12 West Street,
Boston PE21 8QH
Tel: 01205 361510

Eastgate Antiques Centre,
6 Eastgate,
Lincoln LN2 1QA
Tel: 01522 544404

Hemswell Antiques
Centre,
Caenby Corner Estate,
Hemswell Cliff,
Gainsborough DN21 5TJ
Tel: 01427 668389

Lincolnshire Antiques
Centre,
26 Bridge Street,
Horncastle LN9 5HZ
Tel: 01507 527794

Portobellow Row Antiques
Centre,
93-95 High Street,
Boston PE21 8TA
Tel: 01205 369456

Stamford Antiques Centre,
The Exchange Hall,
Broad Street,
Stamford PE9 1PJ
Tel: 01780 62605

Merseyside

Hoylake Antique Centre,
128-130 Market Street,
Wirral L47 3BX
Tel: 0151 632 4231

Middlesex

Calvers Collectables
of Ruislip,
156 High Street,
Ruislip HA4 8LJ
Tel: 0181 561 4517

Hampton Village Antiques
Centre,
76 Station Road,
Hampton TW12 2AX
Tel: 0181 979 5871

Jay's Antique Centre,
25/29 High Street,
Harefield UB9 6BX
Tel: 01895 824738

Norfolk

Angel Antique Centre,
Pansthorn Farmhouse,
Redgrave Road,
South Lopham,
Diss IP22 2HL

Cloisters Antiques Fair,
St Andrew's & Blackfriars
Hall,
St Andrew's Plain,
Norwich NR3 1AU
Tel: 01603 628477

Coltishall Antiques Centre,
High Street,
Coltishall NR12 7AA
Tel: 01603 738306

Fakenham Antique Centre,
Old Congregational Chapel, 14 Norwich Road,
Fakenham NR21 8AZ
Tel: 01328 862941

Gostling's Antique Centre,
13 Market Hill,
Diss IP22 3JZ
Tel: 01379 650360

Old Granary Antique & Collectors Centre,
King Staithe Lane,
off Queens Street,
King's Lynn PE30 1LZ
Tel: 01553 775509

St Mary's Antique Centre,
Duke Street,
Norwich NR3 3AF
Tel: 01603 612582

Wells Antique Centre,
The Old Mill,
Maryland NR23 1LX
Tel: 01328 711433

Wymondham Antique Centre,
No 1 Town Green,
Wymondham NR18 0PN
Tel: 01953 604817

Northamptonshire

Antiques & Bric-a-Brac Market,
Market Square,
Town Centre,
Wellingborough
NN8 1AR
Tel: 01905 611321

Finedon Antiques Centre,
Church Street, Finedon,
Wellingborough
NN9 5NA
Tel: 01933 681260

Village Antique Market,
62 High Street,
Weedon NN7 4QD
Tel: 01327 42015

Colmans of Hexham,
15 St Mary's Chare,
Hexham NE46 1NQ
Tel: 01434 603811/2

Nottinghamshire

Castle Gate Antiques Centre,
55 Castle Gate,
Newark NG24 1BE
Tel: 01636 700076

Newark Antique Warehouse,
Kelham Road,
Newark NG24 1BU
Tel: 01636 74869

Newark Antiques Centre,
Regent House,
Lombard Street,
Newark NG24 1XP
Tel: 01636 605504

Nottingham Antique Centre,
British Rail Goods Yard,
London Road,
Nottingham NG2 3AE
Tel: 0115 950 4504/5548

Top Hat Antiques Centre,
66-72 Derby Road,
Nottingham NG1 5FD
Tel: 0115 941 9143

Oxfordshire

Antique & Collectors Market,
Town Hall,
Thame OX9 3DP
Tel: 01844 28205

Chipping Norton Antique Centre,
Ivy House, Middle Row,
Chipping Norton
OX7 5NH
Tel: 01608 644212

Cotswold Gateway Antique Centre,
Cheltenham Road,
Burford Roundabout,
Burford OX18 4JA
Tel: 01993 823678

Deddington Antique Centre,
Laurel House, Bull Ring,
Market Square,
Deddington OX15 0SE

Friday Street Antique Centre,
2 & 4 Friday Street,
Henley-on-Thames
RG9 1AH
Tel: 01491 574104

Goring Antique Centre,
16 High Street,
Goring-on-Thames,
RG8 9AR
Tel: 01491 873300

Henley Antique Centre,
Rotherfield Arcade,
2-4 Reading Road,
Henley-on-Thames
RG9 1AG
Tel: 01491 411468

Lamb Arcade,
High Street,
Wallingford OX10 0BS
Tel: 01491 835166

Oxford Antiques Centre,
The Jam Factory,
27 Park End Street,
Oxford OX1 1HU
Tel: 01865 251075

Oxford Antiques Market,
Gloucester Green,
Oxford OX1 2DF
Tel: 01865 242216

Shropshire

Cleobury Mortimer
Antique Centre,
Childe Road,
Cleobury Mortimer,
Nr Kidderminster
DY14 8PA
Tel: 01299 270513

Ironbridge Antique
Centre,
Dale End, Ironbridge,
Telford TF8 7DW
Tel: 01952 433784

Pepper Lane Antique
Centre,
Pepper Lane,
Ludlow SY8 1PX
Tel: 01584 876494

Shrewsbury Antique
Centre,
15 Princess House,
The Square,
Shrewsbury SY1 1JZ
Tel: 01743 247704

Shrewsbury Antique
Market,
Frankwell Quay
Warehouse,
Shrewsbury SY3 8LG
Tel: 01743 350916

St Leonard's Antiques
Centre,
Corve Street,
Ludlow SY8 1DL
Tel: 01584 875573

Stretton Antiques Market,
36 Sandford Avenue,
Church Stretton SY6 6BH
Tel: 01694 723718

Telford Antique Centre,
High Street, Wellington,
Telford TF1 1JW
Tel: 01952 256450

Welsh Bridge Antiques
Centre,
135 Frankwell,
Shrewsbury SY3 8JX
Tel: 01743 248822

Somerset

County Antiques Centre,
21/23 West Street,
Ilminster TA19 9AA
Tel: 01460 54151

Dulverton Antique
Centre,
Lower Town Hall,
10 Fore Street,
Dulverton TA22 9EX
Tel: 01398 23522

Guildhall Antique
Market,
The Guildhall,
Fore Street,
Chard TA20 1PP

Taunton Silver Street
Antiques Centre,
27/29 Silver Street,
Taunton TA1 3DH

Staffordshire

Antique Centre,
128 High Street,
Kinver DY7 6HQ
Tel: 01384 877441

Barclay House Antiques,
Barclay House,
14-16 Howard Place,
Shelton,
Stoke-on-Trent ST1 4NQ
Tel: 01782 274747

Rugeley Antique Centre,
161-3 Main Road,
Brereton,
Nr Rugeley WS15 1DX
Tel: 01889 577166

Stoke-on-Trent Antique &
Collectors Centre,
The Potteries Centre,
Winton Square,
Station Road,
Stoke on Trent ST4 2A

Tudor of Lichfield Antique
Centre,
Lichfield House,
Bore Street,
Lichfield WS13 6LL
Tel: 01543 263951

Tutbury Mill Antiques,
6 Lower High Street,
Tutbury,
Burton-on-Trent
DE13 9LU
Tel: 01283 815999

Suffolk

Debenham Antique Centre,
The Forresters Hall,
High Street,
Debenham IP14 6QH
Tel: 01728 860777

Old Town Hall Antiques
Centre,
High Street,
Needham Market
IP6 8AL
Tel: 01449 720773

Risby Barn Antique
Centre,
Risby,
Bury St Edmunds
IP28 6QU
Tel: 01284 811126

Snape Antiques and
Collectors' Centre,
Snape Maltings,
Snape IP17 1SR
Tel: 01728 688038

Waveney Antiques
Centre,
Peddars Lane,
Beccles NR34 9UE
Tel: 01502 716147

Surrey

Antiquarius Antique
Centre,
56 West Street,
Dorking RH4 1BS
Tel: 01306 743398

Antiques Arcade,
22 Richmond Hill,
Richmond TW10 6QX
Tel: 0181 940 2035

Antiques Arcade,
77 Bridge Road,
East Molesey
KT8 9HH
Tel: 0181 979 7954

Antiques Centre,
22 Haydon Place,
Corner of Martyr Road,
Guildford GU1 4LL
Tel: 01483 67817

Antiques & Interiors,
64 Station Road East,
Oxted RH8 0PG
Tel: 01883 712806

Cambridge Parade
Antiques,
229-231 Carshalton Road,
Carshalton SM5 3PZ
Tel: 0181 643 0014

Dorking Antiques Centre,
17/18 West Street,
Dorking RH4 1DD
Tel: 01306 740915

Duke's Yard Antique
Market,
1a Duke Street,
Richmond TW9 1HP
Tel: 0181 332 1051

Farnham Antique Centre,
27 South Street,
Farnham GU9 7QU
Tel: 01252 724475

Fern Cottage Antique
Centre,
28/30 High Street,
Thames Ditton
KT7 0RY
Tel: 0181 398 2281

Maltings Monthly Market,
Bridge Square,
Farnham GU9 7QR
Tel: 01252 726234

Old Smithy Antique
Centre,
7 High Street,
Merstham RH1 3BA
Tel: 01737 642306

Reigate Antiques Arcade,
57 High Street,
Reigate RH2 9AE
Tel: 01737 222654

Surrey Antiques Centre,
10 Windsor Street,
Chertsey KT16 8AS
Tel: 01932 563313

Victoria & Edward
Antiques Centre,
61 West Street,
Dorking RH4 1BS
Tel: 01306 889645

Wood's Wharf Antiques
Bazaar,
56 High Street,
Haslemere
GU27 2LA
Tel: 01428 642125

Sussex

Antique Market,
Leaf Hall, Seaside,
Eastbourne
BN22 7NH
Tel: 01323 27530

Antiques & Collectors
Market,
Old Orchard Building,
Old House, Adversane,
Nr Billingshurst
RH14 9JJ
Tel: 01403 783594

Bexhill Antiques Centre,
Old Town,
Bexhill TN40 2HA

Chateaubriand Antiques
Centre,
High Street,
Burwash TN19 7ES
Tel: 01435 882535

Cliffe Antiques Centre,
47 Cliffe High Street,
Lewes BN7 2AN
Tel: 01273 473266

Cliffe Gallery Antique
Centre,
39 Cliffe High Street,
Lewes BN7 2AN
Tel: 01273 471877

Collectors Market,
The Enterprise Centre,
Station Parade,
Eastbourne
BN21 1BE
Tel: 01323 32690

Copthorne Group
Antiques,
Copthorne Bank,
Crawley RH10 3QX
Tel: 01342 712802

Courtyard Antiques
Market,
13, 15 & 17 High Street,
Seaford
BN25 1PE
Tel: 01323 892091

Eagle House Antiques
Market,
Market Square,
Midhurst GU29 9NJ
Tel: 01730 812718

Foundry Lane Antiques
Centre,
15 Cliffe High Street,
Lewes BN7 2AH
Tel: 01273 475361

George Street Antiques
Centre,
47 George Street,
Old Town,
Hastings
TN34 3EA
Tel: 01424 429339

Hastings Antique Centre,
59-61 Norman Road,
St Leonards-on-Sea,
TN38 0EG
Tel: 01424 428561

Horsebridge Antiques
Centre,
1 North Street,
Horsebridge,
Nr Hailsham BN27 1DQ
Tel: 01323 844414

Kollect-O-Mania,
25 Trafalgar Street,
Brighton BN1 4EQ
Tel: 01273 694229

Lewes Antique Centre,
20 Cliffe High Street,
Lewes BN7 2AH
Tel: 01273 476148

Mamies Antiques Centre,
5 River Road,
Arundel BN18 9DH
Tel: 01903 882012

Midhurst Antiques
Market,
Knockhundred Row,
Midhurst GU29 9DQ
Tel: 01730 814231

Mint Arcade,
71 The Mint,
Rye TN31 7EW
Tel: 01797 225952

Newhaven Flea Market,
28 South Way,
Newhaven BN9 9LA
Tel: 01273 517207/516065

Nineveh House Antiques,
Tarrant Street,
Arundel BN18 9DG
Tel: 01903 884307

Old Town Hall Antique
Centre,
52 Ocklynge Road,
Eastbourne BN21 1PR
Tel: 01323 416016

Petworth Antique Market,
East Street,
Petworth GU28 0AB
Tel: 01798 342073

Pharoahs Antiques
Centre,
28 South Street,
Eastbourne BN21 4XB
Tel: 01323 38655

Seaford's Barn Collectors
Market & Studio Book
Shop,
The Barn, Church Lane,
Seaford BN25 1HL
Tel: 01323 890010

Shirley,
Mostyns Antique Centre,
64 Brighton Road,
Lancing BN15 8ET
Tel: 01903 752961

Treasure House Antiques
& Collectors Market,
31b High Street,
Arundel BN18 9AG
Tel: 01903 883101

Upstairs Downstairs
Antique Centre,
29 Tarrant Street,
Arundel BN18 9DG
Tel: 01903 883749

Tyne & Wear

Blaydon Antique Centre,
Bridge House,
Bridge Street, Blaydon,
Newcastle-upon-Tyne
NE13 6EN

Vine Lane Antique
Centre,
17 Vine Lane,
Newcastle-upon-Tyne
NE1 7PW
Tel: 0191 232 9832

Warwickshire

Antiques Centre,
High Street,
Bidford-on-Avon,
Alcester B50 4AA
Tel: 01789 773680

Antiques Etc,
22 Railway Terrace,
Rugby CV21 3LJ

Dunchurch Antique
Centre,
16/16a Daventry Road,
Dunchurch,
Nr Rugby CV22 6NS
Tel: 01788 817147

Ely Street Antiques
Centre,
Stratford-upon-Avon
CV37 6LN
Tel: 01789 204182

Leamington Pine &
Antiques Centre,
20 Regent Street,
Leamington Spa
CV32 5EH
Tel: 01926 429679

Meer Street Antiques
Centre,
Meer Street,
Stratford upon Avon
CV37 6QB
Tel: 01789 297249

Old Cornmarket Antiques
Centre,
70 Market Place,
Warwick CV34 4SD
Tel: 01926 419119

Old Curiosity Shop,
30 Henley Street,
Stratford-upon-Avon
CV37 6QW

Smith Street Antique
Centre, 7 Smith Street,
Warwick CV34 4JA
Tel: 01926 497864/400554

Spa Antiques Market,
4 Windsor Street,
Leamington Spa
CV32 5EB
Tel: 01926 22927

Stratford Antiques
Centre,
59-60 Ely Street,
Stratford-upon-Avon
CV37 6LN
Tel: 01789 204180

Vintage Antique Centre,
36 Market Place,
Warwick
CV34 4SH
Tel: 01926 491527

Warwick Antique Centre,
20-22 High Street,
Warwick
CV34 4AX
Tel: 01926 495704

West Midlands

Birmingham Antique
Centre,
141 Bromsgrove Street,
Birmingham B5 6RG
Tel: 0121 692 1414/
622 2145

City of Birmingham
Antique Market,
St Martins Market,
Edgbaston Street,
Birmingham B5 4QL
Tel: 0121 267 4636

Wiltshire

Antique & Collectors
Market,
37 Catherine Street,
Salisbury SP1 2DH

Avon Bridge Antiques &
Collectors Market,
United Reform Church
Hall, Fisherton Street,
Salisbury SP2 7RG

Marlborough Parade
Antiques Centre,
The Parade,
Marlborough
SN8 1NE
Tel: 01672 515331

Micawber's,
53 Fisherton Street,
Salisbury
SP2 7SU
Tel: 01722 337822

Yorkshire

Ginnel Antique Centre,
off Parliament Street,
Harrogate HG1 2RB
Tel: 01423 508857

Grove Collectors Centre,
Grove Road,
Harrogate HG1 5EP
Tel: 01423 561680

Halifax Antiques Centre,
Queens Road,
Halifax HX1 4LR
Tel: 01422 366657

Malton Antique Market,
2 Old Maltongate,
Malton YO17 0EG
Tel: 01653 692732

Memory Lane,
69 Wakefield Road,
Sowerby Bridge
HX5 5EN
Tel: 01422 833223

Micklegate Antiques
Market,
73 Micklegate,
York YO1 1LJ
Tel: 01904 644438

Montpelier Mews Antique
Market,
Montpelier Street,
Harrogate
HG1 2TG
Tel: 01423 530484

West Park Antiques
Pavilion,
20 West Park,
Harrogate HG1 1BJ
Tel: 01423 563658

York Antique Centre,
2 Lendal,
York YO1 2AA
Tel: 01904 641445

Scotland

Bath Street Antique
Galleries,
203 Bath Street,
Glasgow G2 4HG
Tel: 0141 248 4220

Corner House Antiques,
217 St Vincent Street,
Glasgow G2 5QY
Tel: 0141 248 2560

King's Court Antiques
Centre & Market,
King Street,
Glasgow G1 5RB
Tel: 0141 552 7854/7856

Victorian Village,
53 & 57 West Regent St,
Glasgow G2 2AE
Tel: 0141 332 0808

Wales

Cardiff Antique Centre,
69-71 St Mary Street,
Cardiff
CF1 1FA
Tel: 01222 30970

Jacobs Antique Centre,
West Canal Wharf,
Cardiff
CF1 5DB
Tel: 01222 390939

Offa's Dyke Antique
Centre,
4 High Street,
Knighton,
Powys
LD7 1AT
Tel: 01547 528635/528940

Pembroke Antique
Centre,
The Hall,
Hamilton Terrace,
Pembroke SA71 4DE
Tel: 01646 687017

Swansea Antique Centre,
21 Oxford Street,
Swansea SA1 3AQ
Tel: 01792 466854

If you would like
your name and
address to feature
in our Directory of
Markets & Centres,
please telephone us
on 01580 766411

DIRECTORY OF COLLECTORS' CLUBS

If you wish to be included in next year's directory or if you have a change of address or telephone number, please inform us by October 31st 1996. Entries will be repeated in subsequent editions unless we are requested otherwise.

Antiquarian Horological Society
New House, High Street, Ticehurst,
E Sussex TN5 7AL
Tel: 01580 200155

Antique Collectors' Club
5 Church Street, Woodbridge, Suffolk IP12 1DS

Arms and Armour Society
Field House, Upper Dicker, Hailsham,
Sussex BN27 3PY
Tel: 01323 844278

Association of Bottled Beer Collectors
Thurwood, 5 Springfield Close, Woodsetts,
Worksop, Nottinghamshire S81 8QD
Tel: 01909 562603

Association of Comic Enthusiasts
17 Hill Street, Colne, Lancashire BB8 0DH

Avon Magpies Club
13 Coleridge Road, Paulsgrove,
Portsmouth, Hampshire PO6 4PB
Tel: 01705 642393

Badge Collectors' Circle
3 Ellis Close, Quorn, Nr Loughborough,
Leics LE12 8SH
Tel: 01509 412094

British Art Medal Society
c/o Dept of Coins and Medals,
The British Museum, London WC1B 3DG
Tel: 0171 323 8170 extn 8227

British Association of Sound Collections
National Sound Archive,
29 Exhibition Road, London SW7 2AS
Tel: 0171 589 6603

British Beermat Collectors' Society
30 Carters Orchard, Quedgeley, Glos GL2 6WB
Tel: 01452 721643

British Button Society
33 Haglane Copse, Pennington,
Lymington, Hampshire SO41 8DR
Tel: 01590 674044

British Compact Collectors' Society
c/o Mrs J Edwards, 5 Holly Ridge,
Fenns Lane, West End, Surrey GU24 9QE

British Iron Collectors
87 Wellsway, Bath, Avon BA2 4RU
Tel: 01225 428068

British Matchbox, Label and Booklet Society
3 Langton Close, Norwich, Norfolk NR5 8RU

British Model Soldier Society
22 Lynwood Road, Ealing, London W5 1JJ

British Numismatic Society
The Royal Mint, Llantrisant, Pontyclun,
Mid Glamorgan, Wales CF7 8YT

British Stickmakers' Guild
44a Eccles Road, Chapel-en-le-Frith,
Derbys SK12 6RG
Tel: 01298 815291

British Teddy Bear Association
PO Box 290, Brighton, Sussex BN2 1DR

British Telecom Heritage Group
Tamarisk, 2 Gig Lane, Heathand Reach,
Leyton Buzzard, Bedfordshire LU7 0BQ
Tel: 01525 237676

British Telecom Phonecard Collectors' Club
Camelford House, 87 Albert Embankment,
London SE1 7TS

British Watch & Clock Collectors Association
5 Cathedral Lane, Truro, Cornwall TR1 2QS
Tel: 01872 41953

Button Collectors Society
33 Haglane Copse, Pennington,
Nr Lymington, Hampshire SO41 8DR
Tel: 01590 674044

Buttonhook Society
2 Romney Place, Maidstone, Kent ME15 6LE

Calculators Collectors' Club
77 Welland Road,
Tonbridge, Kent TN10 3TA

Cambridge Paperweight Circle
34 Huxley Road, Welling, Kent DA16 2EW
Tel: 0181 303 4663

Cartophilic Society of Great Britain
116 Hillview Road, Ensury Park,
Bournemouth, Dorset BH10 5BJ

Charlotte Rhead (Newsletter)
c/o 49 Honeybourne Road, Halesowen,
West Midlands B63 3ET

Chintz Club of America
The Chintz Collector, PO Box 6126,
Folsom, CA 95763, USA
Tel: 001 (916) 985 6762 (& fax)

Cigarette Packet Collectors' Club of Gt Britain
Nathan's Pipe Shop, 60 Hill Rise,
Richmond, Surrey TW10 6UA
Tel: 0181 940 2404

**City of London Photograph &
Gramophone Society**
63 Vicarage Way, Colnbrook, Bucks S13 0JY

Clarice Cliff Collectors' Club
Fantasque House, Tennis Drive, The Park,
Nottingham, Nottinghamshire NG7 1AE

Comic Enthusiasts' Society
80 Silverdale, Sydenham, London SE26 4SJ

Comics Journal
17 Hill Street, Colne, Lancashire BB8 0DH
Tel: 01282 865468

Commemorative Collectors' Society
25 Farndale Close, Long Eaton, Nottingham NG10 3PA
Tel: 0115 902 727666

Corgi Collector Club
PO Box 323, Swansea, Wales SA1 1BJ
Tel: 01792 476902

Costume Society
c/o State Apartments, Kensington Palace,
London W8 4PX
Tel: 0171 937 9561

Crested Circle
42 Douglas Road, Tolworth, Surrey KT6 7SA

Cricket Memorabilia Society
29 Highclere Road, Higher Crumpsall,
Greater Manchester M8 6WS
Tel: 0161 740 3714

**Crunch Club
(Breakfast Cereal Collectables)**
15 Hermitage Road, Parkstone, Poole,
Dorset BH14 0QG
Tel: 01202 715854

Disneyana Magical Moments & Memories
31 Rowan Ray, Exwick, Exeter, Devon EX4 2DT
Tel & Fax: 01392 431653

Doll Club of Great Britain
Unity Cottage, Pishill Bank, Henley-on-Thames,
Oxfordshire RG9 6HJ

Embroiderers' Guild
Apartment 41, Hampton Court Palace,
East Molesey, Surrey KT8 9AU
Tel: 0181 943 1229

English Playing Card Society
11 Pierrepont Street, Bath, Avon BA1 1LA
Tel: 01225 465218

Ephemera Society
Rickards, 12 Fitzroy Square, London W1P 5HQ

Fan Circle International
Sec: Mrs Joan Milligan, Cronk-y-Voddy,
Rectory Road, Coltishall, Norwich NR12 7HF

Flag Institute
10 Vicarage Road, Chester, Cheshire CH2 3HZ
Tel: 01244 351335

Friends of Blue
10 Sea View Road, Herne Bay, Kent CT6 6JQ

Friends of Broadfield House Glass Museum
Compton Drive, Kingswinford, W Midlands DY6 9NS
Tel: 01384 273011

Furniture History Society
The Furniture & Woodwork Collection,
The Victoria & Albert Museum, London SW7 2RL
Tel: 01444 413845

Goss Collectors' Club
25 Sycamore Road, Awsworth, Nottingham NG16 2SQ

Goss & Crested China Club
62 Murray Road, Horndean, Waterlooville,
Hampshire PO8 9JL

Hat Pin Society of Great Britain
PO Box No 74, Bozeat, Northants, NN29 7JH

Historical Model Railway Society
59 Woodberry Way, London E4 7DY

Hornby Railway Collectors' Association
2 Ravensmore Road, Sherwood,
Nottingham NG5 2AH

Hurdy-Gurdy Society
The Old Mill, Duntish, Dorchester,
Dorset DT2 7DR

International Bank Note Society
43 Templars Crescent, London N3 3QR

International Bond and Share Society
Hobsley House, Frodesley, Shrewsbury,
Shropshire SY5 7HD

International Collectors' of Time Association
173 Coleherne Court, Redcliffe Gardens,
London SW5 0DX

**International Correspondence of
Corkscrew Addicts**
Ambrose House, 29 Old Church Green,
Kirk Hammerton, Yorkshire YO5 8DL
Tel: 01423 330745

International Dolls' House News
PO Box 79, Southampton, Hampshire SO9 7EZ
Tel: 01703 771995

King George VI Collectors' Society
24 Stourwood Road, Southbourne,
Bournemouth BH6 3QP

Lace Guild
The Hollies, 53 Audnam, Stourbridge,
West Midlands DY8 4AE

Magic Lantern Society
Prospect, High Street, Nutley,
Sussex TN22 3NH

Matchbox International Collectors' Association
Toy Museum, 13a Lower Bridge St,
Chester CH1 1RS
Tel: 01244 345297

Mauchline Ware Collectors' Club
Unit 37 Romsey Industrial Estate,
Greatbridge Road, Romsey, Hampshire SO51 0HR

**Memories UK Mabel Lucie Attwell
Collectors' Club**
63 Great Whyte, Ramsey, Nr Huntingdon,
Cambridgeshire PE17 1HL
Tel: 01487 814753

Merrythought International Collectors Club
Ironbridge, Telford, Shropshire TF8 7NJ
Tel: 01952 433116

Model Railway Club
Keen House, 4 Calshot Street, London N1 9DA

Mug Collectors' Association
Whitecroft, Chandler Road, Stoke Holy Cross,
Norwich, Norfolk NR14 8RG

Musical Box Society of Great Britain
PO Box 299, Waterbeach, Cambridgeshire CB4 4PJ

National Horse Brass Society,
12 Severndale, Droitwich Spa,
Hereford & Worcester WR9 8PD

New Baxter Society
c/o Museum of Reading, Blagrave Street,
Reading, Berkshire RG1 1QH

Old Bottle Club of Great Britain
2 Strafford Avenue, Elsecar, Nr Barnsley,
South Yorkshire S74 8AA
Tel: 01226 745156

**Ophthalmic Antiques International
Collectors' Club**
3 Moor Park Road, Northwood,
Middlesex HA6 2DL

Orders and Medals Research Society
123 Turnpike Link, Croydon, Surrey CR0 5NU

Oriental Ceramic Society
31b Torrington Square, London WC1E 7JL
Tel: 0171 636 7985

Passenger Ship Enthusiast Association
PO Box 358, Coulsdon, Surrey CR5 1AW

Perfume Bottles Collectors Club
Great Western Antiques Centre,
Bartlett Street, Bath BA1 2QZ
Tel: 01225 837932/310388

Pewter Society
Hunters Lodge, Paddock Close,
St Mary's Platt, Sevenoaks, Kent TN15 8NN
Tel: 01732 883314

Photographic Society
5 Station Industrial Estate, Low Prudhoe,
Northumberland NE42 6NP

Postcard Club of Great Britain
34 Harper House, St James's Crescent,
London SW9 7LW
Tel: 0171 733 0720

Pot Lid Circle
Buckinghamshire
Tel: 01753 886751

Quimper Association
Odin, Benbow Way, Cowley, Uxbridge,
Middx UB8 2HD

Railwayana Collectors Journal
7 Ascot Road, Moseley, Birmingham,
W Midlands B13 9EN

Royal Doulton International Collectors' Society
Minton House, London Road,
Stoke-on-Trent, Staffordshire ST4 7QD

Royal Numismatic Society
c/o Department of Coins and Medals,
The British Museum,
London WC1B 3DG
Tel: 0171 636 1555 extn 404

Royal Winton International Collectors Club
Dancers End, Northall, Bedfordshire LU6 2EU
Tel: 01525 220272

Scientific Instrument Society
Dawes, PO Box 15, Pershore,
Hereford & Worcester WR10 2RD
Tel: 01705 812104

Shelley Group
12 Lilleshall Road, Clayton, Newcastle-under-Lyme,
Staffordshire ST5 3BX

Silhouette Collectors' Club
Flat 5, 13 Brunswick Square, Hove,
Sussex BN3 1EH
Tel: 01273 735760

Silver Spoon Club
Glenleigh Park, Sticker, St Austell,
Cornwall PL26 7JB
Tel: 01726 652269

Silver Study Group
The Secretary, London
Tel: 0181 202 0269

Susie Cooper Collectors Group
PO Box 7436, London N12 7QF

SylvaC Collectors Circle
174 Portsmouth Road, Horndean,
Hants PO8 9HP
Tel: 01705 591725

Thimble Society of London
Stand 134, Grays Antique Market,
58 Davies Street,
London W1Y 1LB
Tel: 0171 493 0560

Tool and Trades History Society
60 Swanley Lane, Swanley,
Kent BR8 7JG
Tel: 01322 662271

Torquay Pottery Collectors' Society
Torre Abbey, Avenue Road, Torquay,
Devon TQ2 5JX

Train Collectors' Society
Lock Cottage, Station Foot Path, Kings Langley,
Hertfordshire WD4 8DZ

Transport Ticket Society
4 Gladridge Close, Earley, Reading,
Berkshire RG6 2DL
Tel: 01734 579373

Trix Twin Railway Collector's Association
6 Ribble Avenue, Oadby,
Leicester LE2 4NZ

UK Perfume Collectors Club
PO Box 1936, Bath, Avon BA1 3SD
Tel & Fax: 01225 837932

Victorian Military Society
Moore-Morris, 3 Franks Road, Guildford,
Surrey GU2 6NT
Tel: 01483 60931

Vintage Model Yacht Group
8 Sherard Road, London SE9 6EP
Tel: 0181 850 6805

Wade Collectors Club
14 Windsor Road, Selston,
Nottinghamshire NG16 6JJ
Tel: 01773 860933/0374 209963

Wedgwood Society of Great Britain
89 Andrewes House, The Barbican,
London EC2Y 8AY

**Wireless Preservation Society & CEM National
Wireless Museum**
52 West Hill Road, Ryde, Isle of Wight PO33 1LN
Tel: 01983 567665

Writing Equipment Society
4 Greystones Grange Crescent, Sheffield,
Yorks S11 7JL
Tel: 0114 266 7140

INDEX TO ADVERTISERS

INDEX

Key to Front Cover Illustrations

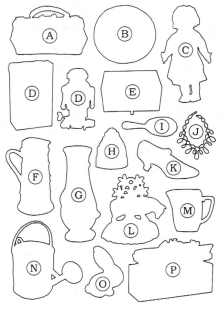

A. A late Victorian leather bag, 13in (33cm) wide. **£30–50** *Ech*

B. A Clarice Cliff plate, decorated in Oranges pattern, 6in (15cm) diam. **£150–250** *PC*

C. A Lenci felt doll, with painted features. **£90–100** *P(B)*

D. A Japanese tinplate mechanical robot, early 1960s. **£50–60** *CSK*

E. A Tunbridge ware tea caddy, 1830–50, 9¼in (23.5cm) wide. **£400–500** *MRW*

F. A Doulton Lambeth lemonade set, designed by George Tynmouth, with silver mounts, c1876, jug 10¾in (27.5cm) high. **£550–650** *YY*

G. An Art glass vase, c1950s. **£35–40** *COL*

H. A kitchen copper mould, c1860. **£120–150** *WeA*

I. A silver-backed hair brush, Birmingham 1898, 10in (25.5cm) long. **£30–35** *WN*

J. A gold and ceramic necklace, 1970s, 19¾in (50cm) long. **£50–85** *GLT*

K. A pair of brocade shoes, 1920s. **£50–100** *Ech*

L. A pair of Staffordshire figures, depicting a cow and a bull, by Obadiah Sherratt, c1830, 8in (20cm) high. **£1,800–2,200** *JO*

M. A Wade water jug, c1960, 5½in (14cm) high. **£15–18** *COL*

N. A galvanised 2 gallon watering can, with brass rose, 15½in (39.5cm) high. **£25–35** *WAC*

O. A Bourne Denby rabbit, c1930, 8¼in (21cm) high. **£100–120** *WN*

P. A battery-operated toy Batmobile, by Cien-GE, Taiwan, mid-1970s. **£80–100** *CSK*